Conspiracy in Mendoza

DOLORES LUNA-GUINOT

Order this book online at www.trafford.com
or email orders@trafford.com

Most Trafford titles are also available at major online book retailers.

Note for Librarians: A cataloguing record for this book is available from Library
and Archives Canada at www.collectionscanada.ca/amicus/index-e.html

Printed in Victoria, BC, Canada.

ISBN: 978-1-4269-2185-8

Library of Congress Control Number: 2009912304

*Our mission is to efficiently provide the world's finest, most comprehensive
book publishing service, enabling every author to experience success.
To find out how to publish your book, your way, and have it available
worldwide, visit us online at www.trafford.com*

Trafford rev. 11/12/09

www.trafford.com

North America & international
toll-free: 1 888 232 4444 (USA & Canada)
phone: 250 383 6864 ♦ fax: 812 355 4082

FOREWORD

History has given us a lifestyle and culture in the past and in present times. All in life has a historical root, that's why we live under the sign of history.

Chile's history should be widely known, although it is shown in a simple way, without a lot of data considered, so that it may be understood everywhere, while trying to study and understand great processes of the past. In this way, we will be able to follow Chilean people path and their historical development since the arrival of the first men to America, following from pre-hispanic Chile, Conquest, Colonial times, Independence and the Republic.

> *"Chile, rich province, and mentioned*
> *in the famous Antarctic region,*
> *Respected by remote nations*
> *As being strong, main and mighty,*
> *People that produces is the best,*
> *So haughty, brave and warlike,*
> *That no king has ever ruled over them,*
> *It has not ever been subjected to foreign rule".*

Alonso de Ercilla y Zuñiga

CHAPTER 1

PREHISTORY

There are great gaps as to how and when Homo sapiens settled in America and the date of the first population in Chile cannot be exactly specified.

This task is even more difficult when one goes back more in time. It seems to be that the first settlement in America is located in the very Chilean Patagonia's pampa. It can be traced south of Santiago de Chile in Monte Verde site. It is discovered that Behringia pass or Behringia Strait was a land bridge which connected America and Asia, it happened that emigrants traveled quickly toward south through the pacific corridor 16000 years ago; therefore, first Americans came from Alaska to Chile directly to Monte Verde Coast where they fed themselves with seaweeds from the site.

In Chile, according to archaeological testimonies, man lived in Antofagasta region around 1000 BC; in San Vicente de Tagua-Tagua around 9000 BC and in Tierra del Fuego between 9000 and 8000 BC.

Economic base was changing: hunting, fishing to the first agricultural experiments. Hunters could not ultimately settle in any place so they became nomads, they traveled in small groups of families. Sometimes, two or more families united in order to make bands.

There were no social differences and the leader was the oldest relative. Society developed and they grew up from a band into a super-band and set up permanent settlements in which garbage accumulation gave rise to shell formation. Later, they became a tribe and a chief assumed the leadership of the group giving rise to the leader and the led ones. The head lived in contact with the community and he was only different by the use of certain symbols of prestige as jewels, feathers; apart from this, he was like the rest of the society with respect to other things.

1

There are several hypotheses about the origin of Chile's name; although, it can be stated that this name was initially given to the central part of the country.

The most fundamental word "Tchili" comes from the old Quechua language, meaning cold or snow, name given by the Indians to the river and the Aconcagua valley.

It is also believed that the word Chile would come from the Aymara word "Chilli", where the land ends, i.e., where the sea begins.

Peruvian Indians called it: Chile or chili because of the river watering the Arequipa region, the place where they came from.

Chile, with its long and narrow territory, is perhaps the country having the widest variety of ecological systems in America; that's why there were multiple economic activities, whereby fishermen, gatherer or farmers coexisted together.

The diversity of ecological systems allows us to lay down comparison with respect to cultures' development. That's why a Chilean pre-history should begin with the identification of the ecological areas. The following ecological areas can be established according to the climatic characteristics from which depend flora and fauna:

Northern area: from Arica to the Aconcagua river.

Central area: from the Aconcagua river to the Biobío river.

Southern area: from the Biobío River until the Chiloe island.

The southernmost area: from Chiloe island to Cape Horn.

Economic base was changing: hunting which was a male activity so the fishing was, they tamed the llama and tranformed it in a useful loading animal.

The seafood culture, agriculture and recolection were women's tasks which belonged them: tillage, sowing and harvesting, that's why religion incorporated the cult of fertility reflected in female small figures.

The agriculture in the north was settled by the Atacama people in the region between Loa and Copiapó rivers, adapting themselves to its poor conditions and it was involving a labor of more hands and the sown fields should be constantly protected both from animals and men who built in some places pucaras or areas protected by walls. There are demonstrations that they worked the Chuquicamata copper.

Perhaps, a change of climate turned even more inhospitable the Atacama Desert causing the emigration to Arica and Tacna.

South of the Atacama people, between the valleys of Copiapó and Chiapa rivers during the kingdom of Tupac Yupanqui took place the conquest of the cross valleys of northern Chile by the Diaguitas, contemporary to the Atacama people, they were farmers who were cultivating corn and potato by practicing irrigation. They knew how to melt copper and raise llamas and guanacos. Both the diaguitas and the Atacama people had a higher cultural level than that of the indians from the central part of Chile.

Diaguitas also stretched out from Salta to La Rioja, Argentina, on the other side of the Andes Range.

People practicing agriculture lived from Chiapa River to Reloncavi Gulf, in the longitudinal valley in the center, they were "picunches", that is to say "northern people" in mapudugun language, it referred to pre-hispanic Chilean people, the northern branch of Mapuche River.

The picunches were living between Choapa and Itata rivers growing specially corn, beans, and potatoes in the valleys of this region, for which they were building irrigation channels. They raised the guanaco which provided them wool and meat. They dwelt in thatched huts plastered with totora reeds and their roofs were also covered with totora reed.

The huilliches, men or southern people, inhabited the south of the longitudinal valley from Tolten River to Reloncavi's gulf. Their culture was similar to that of the Picunches.

The Mapuche or Araucanians, whom we will talk about later, were living between Itata and Tolten rivers, though it would be better to fix them as north limit the Biobio. The Mapuche, picunches and huilliches were speaking the same language, mapudungun; although, this language stopped being spoken in the picunche zone after the Spanish conquest.

The cuncos were living in the coasts between Bueno River and Chacao canal. They later left the continent and settled themselves in the northern half of Chiloe Island.

Firstly, villages appeared and then the cities ensued. They evolved from the tribes to the headship, and these gave rise to the states or civilizations.

The intellectual activity also prospered, every person was able to provide himself what he needed and devoted himself to other tasks. This way, merchants, craftsmen, warriors, nobles, artists, etc. appeared. Mathematical and astronomical sciences developed and were closely related to sowing and crop activities.

The cultural enrichment was also reflected in certain religious conceptions, as the belief in life after death which the deceased faced with his body specially preserved, transforming it into a mummy by means of a simple preparation: his body was tied wrapping it with a mat; or by means of a more complicated preparation: corpse's internal organs were extracted and it was filled with diverse elements once the interior cavity was dried, face was covered with layers of mud and decorated with hairpieces.

While these people were living as growers in the longitudinal valley, diverse nomadic people were crossing the regions of both sides of the mountain ranges devoted to the guanaco's hunt and the picking of forest's fruits. These men, the pehuenches or men from the pehuen, inhabited the Andes region between Chillan and Valdivia, and they were continuously going from one to another side of the mountain range. They were very skilful at throwing the "boleadoras" (leather thongs tipped with leather-covered stones) that were made of three ropes having a wooden ball tied to its ends, they were used in the pursuit of fugitives to tangle them in their limbs and make them fall down. It appears that they were descendants of the tribes from the Argentine's pampa.

The puelches, "eastern people", were located south of the pehuenches in the valleys of the Valdivia mountain range; they were not as taller as the mapuche. Finally, the tehuelches, called Patagonians by Magellan, were in the Patagonian plateau and the Patagonian Andes. They were very tall, devoted to the guanaco's hunt and were coming in their incursions up to the Strait of Magellan and the Atlantic coast.

The ona, also called "fueguinos" were the most austral people of "Tierra del Fuego". They were subdivided in three groups: the ona in the Grand Island, they lived on hunting and fishing, they wore furs from guanaco and fox which they hunted; the alcalufes, fishing Indians and the yagans, who as the former spent their lives in the canoes sailing through the canals.

In the southern islands, they were fishing people which we know the following from: the chonos who were fishermen, they mingled with the cuncos who were farmers from the island.

The chonos sailed in vessels formed by three boards sewn with vegetables fibres, they had a wide scooped oar and the anchor was made of wood and stone. These marine elements used by the Indians could be Polynesians, since there were navigators from Polynesia who reached the Chilean coasts, above all the Chiloe archipelago. They settled south until the present day Chonos and Guaitecas archipelagos.

The alcalufes, perhaps relatives to the chonos, lived in the islands and canals south of them, until the Tierra del Fuego, they sailed in canoes and boats wherein the families took with them the fire, the harpoon, the shelled-knife and the axe, besides other utensils for fishing and hunting.

The yagans or yamanas were the most austral population in the continent; they lived in the southern part of Tierra del Fuego and in the islands south of Beagle Channel.

The onas, alcalufes and yagans were named as fueguinos.

While these people lived in Chile, the Quichua developed a much more advanced civilization in Peru making a mighty empire which had Cuzco as its capital, home of the Incas or emperors. The inca empire was the most famous civilization which occupied an immense territory in South America, which comprised: To the north until Pasto in Colombia, to the south until Constitucion in Chile with Maule River, part of Peru, Ecuador, High Peru now Bolivia, Argentina and in the south of Colombia (?).

It is believed that it began to establish in the XI century of our age, it was the stage in which the Inca civilization reached its highest level of organization and it was consolidated as the pre-hispanic state having the biggest extension in America.

The Incas as rulers were the first statesmen in America, since the government of all of them was for the benefit of the subjects of the empire, people was the raison d'être of the Inca state by mandate of the god Inti.

Because of archaeological and anthropological information, it is being studied the true process of occupation of Cuzco. Due to the collapse of the tayquipala kingdom, this caused the migration of its people in a group of roughly 500 men who slowly settled in the foundation of Cuzco.

Manco Capac established the Inca Empire nearly in 1200 A.D., he was its first ruler. Manco Capac unified the huallas, poques and lares, and he settled with them in the low part of the city. In this way, it was started the Urin Cuzco dynasty. Later on, he ordered the building of the first Inca residence, Inticancha or Sun temple. Mama Ocllo was his sister and wife.

The imperial model began with Pachacutec, it then continued with Amaru Inca Yupanqui, Tupac Inca Yupanqui and Huayna Capac.

Tawantinsuyo, original name of the empire, means in Quechua: the four regions and it comes from the division in "suyus" that the empire had: Chinchaysuyo, Collasuyo, Antisuyo and Contisuyo.

It was a political and social formation that reached imperial characteristics and achieved the unification of one of the most immense territories in the Andean area. The Incas were its ethnic leading group.

The empire began with the victory of Pachacutec over the confederacy of the Chancas' state in 1438. The Inca chieftaincy was reorganized after the victory by Pachacutec in the Tawantinsuyo. Since then, the Inca Empire began a new stage of great expansion in the hands of the ninth Inca, Pachacutec, and his brother Capac Yupanqui. Later, the tenth Inca, Tupac Yupanqui extended the empire's borders to the south, reaching up to Maule River in Chile, and finally Huayna Capac would consolidate the territories and the highest development of his culture. After this peaking period, the empire would enter in its decline because of several problems, being the main one the fight for the throne between Huayna Capac's two sons, Huascar and Atahualpa. Huascar was born of his legitimate wife and Atahualpa was born of his concubine, a princess from Quito, this latter was his father's preferred son, bequeathing him before he died the northern part of the Empire with Quito as its capital and to Huascar the rest of this, with the old city of Cuzco. This grave mistake caused that the empire fell down in a bloody civil war. Atahualpa envious for not having Cuzco, declared war on Huascar, and defeated him with a big army and took him prisoner.

When he and his army were celebrating their triumph, the Spaniards arrived.

Mythical period, also called Sacred Time. Its origins are lost in the legend of Manco Capac, founding hero and model of Urin Cusco dynasty. Quechuas were civilized by two personages who came from Southern Peru, Manco Capac and Mama Occllo, child of the sun, who emerged from the depths of the Titicaca Lake by orders of the Sun, with the commission of heading toward north in search of the place where they could establish a great empire.

Manco Capac was the first Inca. His descendants were conquering countries until they formed a great empire which extended from the south of Colombia to Maule River. It included Ecuador (Quito), Peru, the Bolivian plateau, Argentina and Chile until the aforementioned river.

The conquest of Chile was in the years 1443 to 1445. The Inca Tupac yupanqui, knowing that there was a much peopled region, sent general Sinchirunca to inspect and dominate it until the Coquimbo valley, subduing Atacameños and diaguitas in the year 1460.

Later, Huayna Capac, hi son and successor, sent new armies that crossed Maule River, but they could not advance more to the south of Biobío River, where mapuches' tough resistance compelled them to set up as border of their conquests the Maule River, which served as the empire's southern border. This happened in 1485.

Atacameños, diaguitas and pichunches were easily subjected to the Peruvian inkas' authorities since they were not in conditions to militarily face them.

In fact, Inca's domination respected as it may be possible customs and beliefs of the subjected people; its influence was above all in the political order.

Huayna Capac organized his country's administration; he appointed chieftains or rulers and imposed on inhabitants an annual tax in gold. Gold-panning sites were made in Marga-Marga and Tiltil where it was melted the gold into disks, but it was also taken to Cuzco in powder and nuggets. In order for them to move, as there were no loading animals nor the wheel was known, Empire's famous roads, which really were paths, were extended through Chile alongside the Atacama Desert and the small north, until the limit of the Mapocho valley.

CHAPTER II

VASCO NUÑEZ DE BALBOA
AND
FERDINAND MAGELLAN

The XV and XVI centuries were very fruitful for Spain in relation to political creations, great discoveries and conquests in American lands.

The first authorities appointed by the kings in America were the governors who started the conquest. This system has been already exercised in Spain during the war for the expulsion of the Arabs. It consisted in entrusting this enterprise to nobles or plebeians who were in charge of the expenses in exchange of the title of governor and the property of the new delivered lands. They should advance the reconquest.

This system was extended to America, where governors were defraying their conquering expeditions and were given the government of the countries they conquered, becoming masters and lords. They had the advantage of not causing expenditure to the royal treasury and promote individual initiatives.

The later creation of viceroyalties and governorships under the kingdom of Charles V ended with the system of governors

The "House of Hiring" was established in Seville on January 10th, 1503, it had jurisdiction over dealings, commerce and navigation to the Indies. These functions were ratified by royal order issued on August 10th, 1539.

Ferdinand Magellan, Portuguese sailor, was associated with cosmographer Rui de Falero, and both of them offered their services to the Spanish Crown.

8

The capitulation by which Magellan was appointed Captain-General of the fleet and governor of all the lands he may find was signed in Valladolid on March 22nd, 1518.

The famous cosmographer Rui Falero could not go aboard since he had an attack of madness before sailing.

Magellan guided by the house of hiring had sailed from Seville on August 10th, 1519 with an expedition made up of five vessels bound for the west with the intention of reaching the Moluccas, in the conviction that those islands were located within the area of Spanish domain fixed by the Tordesillas Treaty. Searching for a pass that would allow going around the Indian continent, Magellan discovered on October 21st, 1520 the strait that took his name. After overcoming terrible difficulties, four out of the five vessels of the fleet crossed the Strait, whose discovery of this pass between the two oceans had to necessarily lead to the southern part of Chile. He followed the plotted route stopping to reconnoitre the surrounding lands.

Magellan told the expeditionaries that they should disembark:
- Take advantage of reconnoitre these lands so cold and look if there is any human being alive.-
- Master, there are some big footprints over here, indeed, we can see over there Indians having very bit feet wrapped with furs, they are big-footed and besides they are very tall, they are "Patagonians".-

They later knew that these were Tehuelche Indians.

Magellan said:
- From now on, we will call these lands the Patagonia. Let's go back to the ship and we will sail south of the Strait.-

When they were sailing for a while, they reached an island where they disembarked.

By night, one of the sailors, who were on guard duty, very surprised screamed:
- Look, Master, there are great many kindled bonfires, although no man can be seen, surely the torrid midday sun burn the dry grass.-

Magellan, with his men facing the bonfires, knelt on his knees, he said raising his sword:
- In the name of God, Spain and our King, we will call this region as Land of fire.-

Tomorrow very early, we will go aboard to leave this Strait, we will have terrible storms, which perhaps may cause us to founder, since I know that Balboa's southern sea is very heavy throughout the year.

The stormy sea, due to Providence, was calm that day and this made that Magellan did not find the terrible storms when sailing the Strait, on the contrary everything was in calm, that's why he baptized the southern sea discovered seven years earlier by Vasco Nuñez de Balboa, with the name of Pacific Ocean, as it is now known.

To discover this Ocean had cost a lot of sacrifice to Nuñez de Balboa; he was guided by Indians and climbed these rough mountains along with some Spaniards, dodging risks and sufferings until they reached the Panama Isthmus where he sighted the immense and unknown sea, when he was getting ready to sail it, Governor Pedro Arias Davila, sent by the king, arrived and accused him of his having rebelled against him and had him executed by beheading in 1519.

After leaving the Strait, Magellan headed for Asia, toward the Moluccas since that was the purpose of his expedition.

On April 27th 1521, Ferdinand Magellan could not end his voyage because he was killed in combat against Indians in the Philippine Islands.

The last survivors and exhausted partners of Magellan's expedition continued their painful three years voyage under the command of Juan Sebastian Elcano; they crossed the Indian sea with the vessel Sancti Spíritus, turned the south of Africa and finally arrived in Spain, they completed the first journey around the world on September 8th 1522.

This event moved Emperor Charles V to organize another expedition under the command of Friar García Jofré de Loaysa who penetrated into the Strait of Magellan without reconnoitring its shores on April 8th 1526.

One of its vessels, "San Lesmes" was dragged by the storm, having reached up to the 55 degree and it went back with news of having reached where the lands ended, they had found Cape Horn.

The participation of Magellan and Loaysa in the discovery of Chile was accidental; its true discoverer was Diego de Almagro.

CHAPTER III
DIEGO DE ALMAGRO AND FRANCISCO PIZARRO
THE CONQUEST OF PERU

D iego de Almagro was born in the Almagro village, in La Mancha region, he was Elvira Gutierrez's and Juan de Montenegro's illegitimate son.

Diego was reared completely abandoned, he did not even learn how to read and write.

As a boy in 1514, he went on board Pedro Arias de Avila's expedition, so-called Pedrarias Davila, who replaced Diego de Nicuesa in the governorship of "Castilla de Oro" the Isthmus of Panama. He was accompanied by famous conquerors such as: Hernando de Soto, Diego de Almagro and Sebastian Benalcazar, with a fleet of 17 vessels and an army of 1300 soldiers, who did expeditions from Santa María del Darien in several directions.

Francisco Pizarro was born in Trujillo, Extremadura town. He was the illegitimate son of Captain Gonzalo Pizarro. He lacked any studies since he spent his childhood taking care of hogs. He had come to America with Alonso de Ojeda in 1509 when he was a boy, and he also accompanied Vasco Nuñez de Balboa in several expeditions departed from Venezuela and Urabá, and the discovery of southern sea in 1513, he was then at the orders of Gaspar Morales, reaching the Pearls Island, where in addition to subdue the tribal chief, he contacted the chieftain called "Buru", after whom it was named the Inca Empire. Pizarro later went along with Pedrarias Davila to Panama.

Two years after Pedrarias ordered the beheading of Balboa, he founded the city of Panama, which became at one time the centre wherein the expeditions intended for the exploration and conquest of the Andean countries would depart.

Governor Pedrarias entrusted that naval mission to Pascual de Andagoya in 1522, who only reached up to San Juan River where he was very ill and had to return to Panama after having failed in his expedition.

Pedrarias, very soon after Andagoya's failure, thought that among the Spanish soldiers of fortune around him two captains were distinguished: Francisco Pizarro and Diego de Almagro, and when he was aware of the intentions of the two captains to explore the south with the help of Gaspar de Espinosa and the priest Fernando Luque, who besides was to contribute with the money to buy the right of conquest to Pascual de Andagoya; at once, Pedrarias thought of joining them and form a new society, which after a few meetings and dialogues was decided to be called the same as a former one, "Empresa de Levante".

One night captains Pizarro and Almagro got together to drink in a small tavern and, while drinking, they started talking about their future conquests:

- Francisco, I have heard that in the expedition of Captain Nuñez de Balboa, he was speaking that there was in the shores of the southern or pacific sea, as they are calling it, a powerful and opulent empire called Inca. Verily, I tell you that it would be very important that we should undertake the discovery of that rich empire, since we count on the support and enough money from the priest Hernando de Luque for this undertaking, though I have even heard from the Indians that there is an Inca considered to be divine son of the Sun, worshiped by his people as a god, and he commands armies of conquering warriors in a civil war.-

- My good friend and partner Diego, you know that such Indian you are talking about is named Atahualpa, who is known as the bastard, I have been told that he is son of Huayna Capac and a "mitimae" called Tupac Pallacoca. Atahualpa has taken prisoner his brother Huascar, son of a cuzcoan mama-Cusi-Raymi, legitimate wife of Huayna Capac.

In my expedition to Pearls Island, we contacted with a chieftain called "Buru" who spoke to us about the great Inca Empire which we the Castilians started calling Buru or Peru in memory of that island chieftain.-

- Oh, Francisco! Desires of adventures and being able to get fame and fortune for the benefit of my son Diego are invading me, born of a beautiful Panamanian Indian called after being baptized as Ana, my great love. Although I may be far away, my thoughts are always with them. Some day, I will go back and I will take them with me for living in those new lands.-

Francisco Pizarro was also very eager with the journey and made a comment:

- Tomorrow, we'll start preparations; I'll be in charge of searching people, among who have joined us is the conqueror Lucas Martinez Vegaso, precisely from my town Trujillo, we would take Bartolome Ruiz de la Estrada as co-pilot, we'll collect vessels, arms and money for buying victuals, etc. We'll do everything in our own, that is to say, without counting upon the governor. You'll be in charge of collecting the money from priest Luque, who as promised would contribute with 20.000 pesos, and also to prepare the contract for the signing of the undertaking.-

- Don't worry, I'll sign tomorrow the contract and will get rid of Pedrarias who is in Nicaragua as Governor and he will not be aware of his exclusion from the undertaking.-

- I think, my friend Diego, that upon excluding Pedrarias from the contract, we're doing good because he was a traitor to the great Vasco Nuñez de Balboa who finished one the best feats of the Spanish conquest in these lands by discovering the southern sea and founding Nuestra Señora de la Antigua Darien and San Sebastian de Uraba. Perhaps for envy, though they were son-in-law and father-in-law, but that king Charles V may grant him the appointment of "Adelantado" of the southern sea and governor of Panama and Coiba, which made Pedrarias jealous, he was about to be dismissed from the governorship, and Vasco was aware of this when he received a letter asking him to come urgently to Acla, he did not hesitate to go in his help, and Pedrarias ordered me to go to his encounter and capture him and his four companions, who were also mine. Believe me my good friend that I am sorry to have performed that order because there was no justification for his behaviour.-

- I knew that you captured Nuñez de Balboa, but I never knew why was he accused of being a traitor to the Crown?-.

- That was a stratagem of Pedrarias who accused him of usurpation of power against him and trying to create a government apart in the southern sea, which was territory to the Crown.

All these accusations were denied by Nuñez de Balboa. He also accused his friends Fernando de Argüello, Hernán Nuñez and Andrés Balderrábano as accomplices. All of them were sentenced to death. Pedrarias watched the execution hidden as a coward behind a platform.-

- After the beheadings and exposing the heads, what did you do with the corpse of Nuñez de Balboa?-.

- I never knew it; perhaps they threw it into the sea.-

- Then, it is not to be surprised that he may do the same to us, accusing us of being usurpers and traitors to the Crown.-

- I don't think so, because when he may want to be informed about; we'll be owners of the Inca Empire, although we will have to go to Spain to ask the King permission.

It took them one week for the shipping preparations. Pizarro, Almagro and Bartolome Ruiz de la Estrada, as pilot of one of their vessels, adventurously sailed from Panama one morning very early in the year 1526, arriving at the entrance of San Juan River. After exploring by sea the coasts of Colombia and Ecuador, Bartolome Ruiz de Estrada sailed bound for South and discovered the equatorial coast, Esmeraldas and Manabí. He discovered the Punta de Passaos, the Isla del Gallo and the Coaque lands.

Almagro, Pizarro and Ruiz sailed toward Barbacoas up to Atacames. They decided that Almagro should come back to Panama in search of reinforcements, staying Pizarro and his men in the Isla del Gallo, whereto they had been moving to avoid the attacks of the natives and get rid of the harshness of the climate, waiting for the longed for reinforcements.

In Panama Governor Pedro de los Rios was opposed to send what Pizarro wanted and he sent two vessels under the command of Pedro de Tafur requesting Pizarro and their men to come back.

But the pride and energy of Pizarro overcame above everything; he drew a line on the sand of the beach with his sword and looking toward South, told his people:

- By this way, you go to Peru to be rich - and then pointing toward north he added: - By this way, you go to Panama to be poor.-

Only thirteen soldiers crossed the line, and they are since then known as "the thirteen of the fame", Pedro Alcón, Alonso Briseño, Pedro de

Candía, Antonio Carrión, Francisco de Cuellar, García de Jarén, Alonso de Molina, Martín de Paz, Cristobal de Peralta, Nicolás de Ribera, Domingo de Soraluce, Juan de la Torre, and Francisco Villafuerte, the rest of them went on board with Tafur on their way back to Panama.

Pizarro with the thirteen brave adventurers decided the conquest of Peru, that's why Bartolome Ruiz de Estrada was sent to Panama in search of reinforcements.

He decided their moving to Goegona Island, where Ruiz de la Estrada joined them after seven months with a small vessel and some men. Pizarro headed for Tumbez with them but did not put on shore, Alonso de Molina and the Greek Pedro de Candia did it, where the natives gave them an austere reception sending some rafts to harass them, although without attacking. They captured three rafters, and saw among them a 15 years old little Indian, very rebel with the conqueror, this one captured him and offered him to Pizarro, whom was very fond of him and had him baptized with the name of Felipe, "Felipillo" for everybody.

He explored the southern coasts up to Santa; there he got more precise information about the Incas. Pizarro was sailing southward Chan-Chan but did not put on shore.

Returning then to Panama in 1528, where he found great hostilities on the side of Governor Rios. Partners decided that Pizarro should go to Spain in order to get from the Crown the authorization to fulfil the conquest of the Inca Empire.

Empress Isabel, Charles V's wife, in 1539 signed in Toledo an agreement with Francisco Pizarro, in which he was authorized to discover and people Peru up to 200 leagues from North to South beginning from Santiago River, and was granted the titles of Governor, Captain-General and "Adelantado" of the future conquered lands.

Diego de Almagro was granted the title of Governor of the fortress which would be founded in Tumbes, the title of Pilot of the southern seas to Ruiz de la Estrada, and the bishopric of Tumbes to Hernando de Luque.

On the other side, Empress authorized Simon de Alcazaba another 200 leagues south of aforementioned Santiago River as limit.

Pizarro returned from Spain along with his loyal Felipillo with the necessary credentials, resuming the preparations and talking with Almagro on the first stage of colonization.

- At once, I will ask my interpreter Felipillo who is completely reliable and good for any work, he is trustworthy and I have even given him a horse, as I tell you my good friend Diego, I will ask him to search people, we count upon my half brothers by my father's side Hernando, Gonzalo and Juan; also, my half brother by my mother's side Martin de Alcantara and the conqueror Sebastian de Belalcalzar who was mayor of the city of Leon in Nicaragua, you have to know him from the voyage to Darien with Pedrarias Davila in 1514.-

Almagro disappointed with the distribution of prizes noted:
- You know my good friend Francisco that I completely disagree with the gifts granted by my Lady and Majesty Isabel. I think that I deserve more titles.-
And Pizarro replied:
- I don't want you to be angry at any time; my desire is to be in good relation with you and the rest of the companions. In order to show you a sign of good will, I grant you my title of "Adelantado".-

The expedition departed from Panama on January 1531 without waiting for Almagro, with five ships, 183 soldiers and 27 horses, under the command of Pizarro, which would increase later with the people that Almagro could recruit. After too many months, Pizarro landed at the port of San Mateo, in present day Ecuador, from which he advanced toward south to the Island of Puna, receiving reinforcements sent by Sebastian Belalcazar and Hernando de Soto. He conquered the zone of Guayaquil and departed 5° degrees latitude south. He founded in the coast San Miguel, the first Spanish centre in Peru, and penetrating into southeast daringly up to Puna and Tumbes, where they heard of Atahualpa's presence, who was recovering from his wounds in his Cajamarca residence after having fought in the outskirts of Quito, where he was proclaimed the only Inca of the Tawantinsuyo, having defeated Chieftain Chapera from Cañari kingdom, he who had joined Huascar by sending troops from Cuzco under the command of Atoco to occupy Tomebamba, Atoco and Chapera tried to invade Quito, impending this Atahualpa who defeated the enemy, who was executed in Quito, and upon heading for Cuzco, he fought the rebellious punas and was hurt in combat. Atahualpa ordered to kill all of the cañari, even their wives and sons who fought against him.

Pizarro, without waiting for Almagro's reinforcements, headed for Cajamarca with a small force of 120 soldiers and 70 horses.

Upon knowing the landing of some foreigners, Atahualpa sent spies to know how many they were and whether they were mortals; upon hearing that they were not over 200 men, he decided to send emissaries to give them a good reception by inviting them to a friendly interview, in that way, by enticing them into the interior of the country and have them exterminated by his troops.

Pizarro had the same idea, and commissioned his brother Hernando, who along with Hernando de Soto and the Indian Felipillo acting as interpreter, should go to look for the Inca in Cajamarca and convey his greetings. Felipillo found there a very beautiful Indian girl who was one of the many wives of the Inca. Upon seeing her, Felipillo fell completely in love with her.

Atahualpa entered without arms into the square with his entourage. During the interview that both chiefs held in the Cajamarca square in presence of their armies, and in the course of this, Pizarro was not sure about the good intentions of the chieftain, and sent the dominican priest Vicente Valverde, accompanied by Felipillo, and with the bible in his hand should try to get a conversion from Atahualpa, and should try to convince him that he lived in sin, therefore his soul was condemned.

The Inca, who did not understand why there were so many words, snatched the book from the priest and threw it away. The dominican cried angered and Pizarro, understanding the risks that they were in, at the shout of "Santiago" 160 Spaniards came, some of them on horse back, Pizarro resorted to his boldness ordering the trumpets be played to frighten the Indians who were running out terrified because of that sound unknown to them, the latter and the violence of the horses made them to surrender. Immediately after, Pizarro knocked down Atahualpa from his litter taking him prisoner.

Atahualpa sought to buy his ransom offering Pizarro to make the room that he dwells fill with gold and silver objects, and he complied staying apparently liberated.

Felipillo saw Atahualpa again after his capture and liberation and became one of his worst enemies. He alienated Spaniards giving them alarming news about supposed warlike preparations, when he really wanted the Inca to be killed so that he may have the Indian girl he was in love with.

As Huascar, Atahualpa's brother, remained as a prisoner of his in the Jauja fortress, offered the Castilians a higher amount of riches if they help him to recover his throne but his brother ordered general Cha cuchima to drown him in the river.

Once the fabulous ransom booty was delivered, notary Pero Sanchez de Hoz certified the amounts being delivered to everyone, and after setting aside the royal fifth for the Crown of Castilla, this as proprietress and usufructuary of the American soil and subsoil according to the dictum of Pope Alexander VI's bull, amongst other taxes, established a tribute of one fifth, that is to say, twenty percent over every precious metal extracted from rivers, mounts and mines. Each soldier received more than 20.000 pesos. The chiefs' portions were fabulous.

Almagro and the treasurer Alonso Riquelme arrived at Cajamarca and were astonished at seeing the treasure received.

Once the treasure was distributed, Pizarro and Almagro denied Atahualpa his promised deliverance; they accused him of trying an uprising and executed him by strangling on the hands of the hangman on November 16th 1533.

Lucas Martinez de Vegaso left written document on the last will of the Inca; he said that he commended his sons to Governor Francisco Pizarro, serving as witness the friar Vicente de Valverde.

The Inca's death caused the subduing of the entire country.

Once the Inca was executed, Felipillo claimed his share of the inheritance, which was to have the Colla, thus he lied in the royal bed with woollen bedspreads, until he departed for Cuzco, forgetting the beautiful Indian girl.

In Quito, Rumiñahui defeated Cozopanqui, Atahualpa's uncle and declared himself as chief of Quito.

On marching toward Cuzco, Pizarro stopped in Jauja, and then entered in the Inca capital on November 23rd 1533, they settled in the chosen places and devoted to search the Inca's treasures. Conqueror Juan Ruiz de Arce at last found them in the Sun's temple in the important capital of the Inca Empire, Cuzco.

The conquest of Peru could be accomplished with this.

Pizarro established in Cuzco a town council, similar to colonial-style of those times, he founded the church of Santo Domingo, allotted lands and Indians among the conquerors. Thus he founded the Christian Cuzco.

Upon knowing the conquest of Peru, Charles V started doing territory concessions in the southern part of America, even so the scarce knowledge that he received from those lands.

According to the agreement or capitulation between the Sovereign and Francisco Pizarro, it was granted to him for the conquest of Peru the lands located between the first grade southern latitude and grade eleven around altitude Chincha, with a wide of 200 leagues from east to west.

Almagro received from the Spanish Crown the agreements that allowed him conquer 200 leagues south of the territories of Pizarro.

Later on, on request of the German bankers Függer, the Emperor granted them the lands located south of those given to Pizarro, up to the Strait of Magellan, with a wide of 200 leagues from east to west.

The Függers were at that time the moneylenders of the Hispanic-German state, also the kings of England and the German princes.

Charles the V, with the huge concession, that stretched the south of Peru, almost all the Upper Peru, that is to say the present Bolivia, the entire of Chile and great part of Argentina, it can be seen the high grade of indebtedness which have attained the Emperor from the mighty bankers. The Függer after that concession that made them almost owners of South America resigned perhaps pressed by the king of Portugal, or that they thought that it was more suitable to be owners of the riches of America in Spain by means of collecting the interests on the loans.

Freed the Crown from the compromise of it bankers, the Sovereign proceeded to a new partition of lands because new aspirants to conquerors appeared.

Disagreements between Pizarro and Almagro began due to the partition of the government of lands between them.

- Captain Pizarro, the governorship of the New Toledo which is being granted to me, south of that governed by you, does not clarify that Cuzco is in your governorship, it rather seems to be mine.-

- You know, my Captain Almagro that it has been agreed between the Sovereign and me with the Capitulations of Toledo that Peru would belong to me with a width of 200 leagues from east to west, being understood that Cuzco would be part of it.-

- I'm sorry for you Pizarro, but by not agreeing, and the lack of a clear delimitation, it will be the most coherent to reach an agreement; the sovereign will be informed about our dissatisfaction so that he may again delimit the conquered lands.

Upon knowing the difficulties arisen between Pizarro and Almagro, and freed from the compromise of the bankers, the Sovereign could proceed to a new partition of the lands. Charles V as a result of the capitulations of 1534, partitioned the territories at issue in four fringes located the ones south of the others:

To Francisco Pizarro the New Castilla, from the first to the fourteenth degrees, approximately up to Pisco. As all these concessions would extend all over the width of territories belonging to the Crown of Castilla, as per the Treaty of Tordesillas the New Castilla would be integrated by: Quito (Ecuador), north and center of Peru and the north of upper Peru.

To "Adelantado" Almagro the New Toledo, from the fourteenth to the twenty-fifth degrees, that is to say, up to a little south of Tatal. It comprised: southern Peru, the rest of Upper Peru and part of northern Chile; but the city of Cuzco, polemic divergence between Pizarro and Almagro, remained without being mentioned.

The issue stayed unresolved then.

Relationships between Pizarro and Almagro had worsened, Peruvian Indians decided to take Almagro away from rebelling against Pizarro, considering an over-stated fame of rich, where gold, silver and great mines of other metals abounded, thus causing that Almagro might be interested in that land.

Continuing with the partition done by the Sovereign, hereby it was granted to Pedro de Mendoza: the New Andalucía, from the 25th to 36th degrees in the Santa Maria Island, at the coast of Arauco, stretching from the Pacific to the Portuguese domains and the Atlantic coast. Pedro de Mendoza conquered the Plata region and then departed to the Pacific; he founded there the first Buenos Aires in 1536. His lieutenant Ayolas started the conquest of Paraguay, where Salazar de Espinosa founded the city of Asuncion in 1537 after the depopulation of Buenos Aires; it became the nucleus of the colonizing of the eastern sector of the New Andalucía.

To Simon de Alcazaba: the New Leon, between the 36th and 48th degress, the Island of La Campana, the Atlantic and the Pacific. Alcabaza was killed by his own people in an expedition to the Patagonia, being transferred by the Crown the concession to Francisco de Camargo and Pero Sánchez de Hoz, stretching it to the south up to the Strait of Magellan, so that the future Chilean territory was divided in four governorships in 1536.

In fact, Alonso de Camargo was the first one, who sailed the coasts of Chile from south to north, from the expedition of Francisco de la Rivera, successor to Francisco de Camargo in the concession granted to the latter by the Emperor.

In this partition done by Charles V over the desk and without almost having knowledge of geography, it was omitted the Andes range. Chile was divided in four transverse fringes.

Before trying the conquest of Chile, Almagro went to the north in 1534, asked Pizarro permission so that Felipillo might accompany him. The voyage consisted of getting together with Sebastian de Benalcazar, lieutenand of San Miguel of Piura, that by using funds obtained from former campaigns, and without authorization from his chief Pizarro, they may rise up with the conquest of Quito, the most northern city of the Inca Empire until that moment, and in those lands where he thought about founding the present Quito. At the same, the "Adelantado" Pedro de Alvarado was coming from Guatemala to the coast of Manabi with five ships, 500 soldiers, some Indians from Guatemala and many dogs.

He seized two other ships in Nicaragua and landed in the bay of Caraquez to conquer these very same lands of Quito.

When the "Adelantado" Benalcazar started advancing toward the future Quito, the Inca chief Rumiñahui hastened to take out the gold from the city, send it to the Andes and burn the city.

Upon coming Benalcazar and seeing what it happened, the town burned and the virgins with their throats cut as punishment for their fraternizing with the Spaniards and that the town's riches were a tale, he was annoyed and went toward Cayambé; in Quinche, he started torturing the Indians so that they may tell him where the gold was hidden, so asking reached he to Riobamba, where he found Almagro who joined him to jointly face Pedro de Alvarado, who disputed them the booty. Felipillo passed to Alvarado's side thinking that he would win and even suggested him Almagro's death. Alvarado sold the remaining of his expedition at seeing that these lands were poor, and decided to come back to Guatemala, pleading in favour of Felipillo so that Almagro may pardon him.

On August 23rd 1534, Almagro founded near Cicalpa the city of Santiago de Quito.

Sebastian de Benalcazar and Almagro sought in what place they may found the city of Quito. Almagro founded it in Colta to accentuate juridical and royal rights of Quito, over the burned ruins of the ancient Inca town, calling it San Francisco de Quito in honour of Franciscan missionaries, thus was founded the Spanish city of Quito in present day Ecuador.

By Pizarro's order, he sent a royal writ stating that Captain Sebastian de Benalcázar should deliver to Marquis (without a marquisate) Francisco Pizarro all that had been conquered in the province of Quito, by order of that marquis, and designated Lorenzo de Aldama as Quito's Governor, who could not fulfill the order of seizing Benalcázar and take him to Cuzco for executing him.

Gonzalo Pizarro was designated Quito's Governor by his brother Francisco in 1539; he took possession of his new office on December 1st, 1540. He had his triumph be celebrated as a result of the general satisfaction by the winners. It was that way how Sebastian Benalcázar's, Hernando Girón's and Captain Montemayor's lives were pardoned.

The Indies Council granted Benalcázar the governorship of Popayán.

Father Jedoco Rike advised Gonzalo that he had himself crowned king of Peru and offered to go to Rome to obtain the Pope's consent, with that purpose it was designated Sebastian de los Rios to be part of the commissioners, and also the hearer Cepeda who was representative to the King of Spain, insisted on the same, but Gonzalo, although being flattened by the idea, ended refusing the idea and assure again his loyalty to the King.

If Gonzalo had had a premonition about his tragic fate, he would surely have accepted the crown, and Peru may have been since then an independent kingdom, changing the routes of History.

Gonzalo Pizarro in his condition of Captain General of Peru, arriving at the city of San Miguel knew that there were so many fighting indians in his territory, arranged that one of his captains Alonso de Mercadillo with 130 men may found a city in a zone where gold had been found, who peopled the city that is called today Loja in memory of his birthplace in Spain.

CHAPTER IV
DIEGO DE ALMAGRO DISCOVERS CHILE.
1535-1536

Almagro for the conquest of Peru and confining to the government of the New Toledo, decided to obtain his own governorship, starting new adventures and marching to the conquest of Chile, which has been greatly exaggerated by the Indians, without minding to surpass the limits assigned to his jurisdiction. In 1534, he got the Monarch to authorize the conquest of the New Toledo and began immediately his journey to Chile.

At the same time, Gonzalo Calvo Barrientos was preparing his journey; this personage had been Pizarro's soldier, who had his ears cut as a punishment for some thefts. He fled from Peru because of the shame and humiliation he felt on the part of his countrymen. He moved out to get into the unknown Collasuyo, the southern region of the Inca Empire. He was the first Spaniard crossing this territory. He greatly befriended Michamalongo, who believed to see in this white man a creature come from the sky and the indians obeyed him completely. He settled in the Aconcagua valley.

Before his departure, Almagro commissioned Captain Ruy Diaz that he may organize in Peru a small fleet with which he would follow the coast toward South, in a parallel voyage that should meet at the end with the two branches of the expedition in some determined latitude in which Almagro en Diaz would stop their advance and would try to come into contact.

Almagro entrusted Ruy Díaz:
- Captain Díaz, before your departure toward South, I beg you to sail one of your ships close to Panama in order to pick up my son and once you are on board, follow the route that I have pointed

out until you join with my son and the 110 soldiers to the main
body of my expedition.-

Almagro spent great portion of his fortune to equip a splendid army,
paying magnificently to his soldiers.

He departed from Cuzco at the beginning of July 1535, with more
than 500 infantrymen among which there were many hidalgos, member
of the military orders, jurists and priests and 200 Spanish cavalrymen,
accompanied by a large Lumber of Peruvian Indians, who were loading
provisions, munitions and some quantity of llamas for transport.

The Inca pauyo was in command of these indians and a prestigious
priest, the Villac Umu and also travelled, after asking permission to his
master Pizarro, the indian Felipillo as interpreter. They took the route of
the Bolivian plateau, he went over the high Plateau of the Collao, went
along the lake Titicaca and continued by the bank of the Desaguadero
river, which takes the waters of that lake to the Poopó and after crossing
the deserted highlands of Chica, camped in Tupiza where he got together
with prince Paullo Túpac who had prepared him the way.

In January 1536, he continued his march through the lands of the
diaguitas up to Chicoana to the west of the present Argentinian city of
Salta, where he stopped waiting for melting of the snow from the Andes.
The overflow of the rivers took place with the summer torrential rains,
which was a new difficulty, since fording one of them, the provisions and
many llamas were lost dragged by the currents. They already crossed the
desert called Campo del Arenal in seven days with very little food.

At once, the expedition turned bound for southwest in search of the
range, and at the same time the calchaquíes indians chased them, having
to hurry up the march.

The passing of the range was already made in the last days of March
1536 by the San Francisco pass in front of Copiapó. The sufferings were
extreme over there since the great altitude of more than 4.000 meters
caused during the day a terrible hot and in the night a deadly cold which
most of the indians could not endure, dying next to the beasts that went
along with them. Flocks of vultures and condors follow the expeditionaries
to devour the corpses that were remaining in the journey.

The expedition seemed lost without remedy. One night, at 4.500
meters, seventy horses perished by cold, a soldier Jerónimo de Costilla,
his toes were separated from her feet when he took off his boots because
they were completely frozen.

The army was exhausted, it could not keep walking and retreating was
impossible, Almagro making extraordinary efforts, decided to advance

with a group of his best men, and after three days without eating, they came down to the Copiapó valley following the Paipote ravine where they picked up some provisions which were supplied by the Atacama indians, this way they could mitigate a little the terrible famine of his exhausted companions. In total of the great expedition that departed from Cuzco, They arrived at the Copiapó valley 240 Spaniards, 1.500 indians, 150 negroes and 112 horses.

The first thing that Almagro and his men did after having been comforted was to celebrate the first mass in the valley, which would reassure the spiritual character and would encourage to continue the conquest.

Almagro thanked the Atacameños from the Copiapó valley his great help and his friendship, they may not have been able to continue the way without it.

Almagro did not find those good relations in the next valleys of Huesco and Coquimbo like those of Copiapó. The new settlers were hostile and aggressive. Shortly after, upon having news about the killing of three Spaniards who had been gone ahead in Tupiza, they captured several indians, who should be bloodily punished. One night, Villac Umo, Felipillo and thousands of mitimaes, who were accompanying them, abandoned them, they disappeared without a trace. Almagro sent armed groups of cavalry in persecution of the fugitives, and they only captured Felipillo, but no high priest. Almagro ordered that he may be tortured so that he should talk whatever he knew and the indian disclosed that Manco Inca had rebelled against the Spaniards in Cuzco, he also confessed that he had incited the Chilean chieftains to rebellion.

Almagro, who had pardoned Felipillo's treason in another occasion when he went over to Pedro de Alvarado's army in the kingdom of Quito, pardoned him again, since he showed to be very regretful for his wrongdoing.

When they reached more southward, found that the indians of the fertile and farmed valley of Aconcagua received them under submission, these indians led by inca chieftain or governor, were well advised by the spaniard Gonzalo Calvo de Barrientos who fled from Peru to Chile to hide his shame because of Pizarro's punishment, and also really for seeking fortune in Chile.

Friendship with the aborigines lasted very few, since traitor Felipillo convinced the inca chieftain that Almagro wanted to seize all their lands. Once the intrigue was detected, the chieftain was killed by beheading.

In May 1536, Almagro got together with other spaniard Anton Cerrada on the banks of the Conchali River, who was also seeking fortune in front of the southern limit of Coquimbo. There, Almagro heard about one of Captain Ruy Diaz's ships that had just anchored in the cove of Los Vilos. It is about the San Pedro vessel, small-sized, piloted by Alonso Quintero and loaded with arms, provisions, clothes and other materials greatly needed. They unloaded all the belongings with the help of inflated leathered-rafts that the chango indians from the coast wore.

- Captain; I introduce myself Alonso Quintero, I joined the small fleet of Captain Diaz which I am espying in the sea a few miles from here, I presume he will soon arrive these coasts.-

- Don Alonso Quintero, you are welcomed in these places, your news and your loading have been very helpful to us.-

- My Sir and friend Almagro, my intentions are to continue exploring the bay, although I will tell you that it will be difficult to sail it, since at the first time that this voyage from Peru to Chile is done by this unknown coast, which appears in the maps in blank or by a straight line mentioned as extreme unknown land...-

Quintero, such skilful pilot sailed two days later, explored the bay which was later named Bay of Quintero in honour of that great navigator. Almagro did not know anything else about him. As Quintero had earlier said about pilot Ruy Diaz, this latter joined with the main body of Almagro's expedition. He was coming with 120 soldiers and the conqueror's son, Diego nicknamed "El Mozo" (The Young), who was actually called Diego de Montenegro Gutiérrez, born in Santa María de Darién-La Antigua, in 1522.

The expeditionary force was reorganized; at first, Almagro occupied the valley of Aconcagua and started exploring the country from there. His disappointment was increasing the more he moved ahead, he understood that such territory was very poor and only inhabited by farming indians who lived in grouped dwellings (rucas) with straw or totora roofs located in the river valleys full of thickets and a quincha or fence of branches surrounded the ruca.

More southward the inhabitants were fighting tribes which had defeated Inca's armies.

Meanwhile Almagro went through south, the ship Santiaguillo arrived by sea, a exploring company under the command of captain Juan de Saavedra sent from Peru with provisions for the expeditionaries. He advanced toward the coast and Saavedra wanted to stop in a beautiful bay inhabited by changos, it captivated him so much that he called it Valparaiso, it was September 1536.

Almagro, in order to know better those southern tribes, had sent a numerous expedition at the height of winter in the year 1536, under the command of Gomez Alvarado, who reached up to the confluence of Nuble with Itata, where a numerous force of well organized warriors was facing him. They were the mapuche or auracans, name given by the spanish conquerors, they were armed with stone hatches, arrows, long pikes and clubs or mallets in which they sticked boned points, shells and sharpened obsidian stones. They generally made war by surprise, where they were fiercely shouting (chibateo) and they were going to fight for the first time with the Spaniards.

The indians attacked by deploying in line of battle in the open field.

Gómez de Alvarado, after great combat and a lot of difficulty, finally got the indians go back confused by the horses, the soldiers' armors and the steel arms. The spaniard achieved to defeat them in the combat f Reinohuelen, but almost all the horses and great part of the soldiers were badly hurt by the arrows and mallets. In fact, it was a "pyrrhic" victory. Gomez de Alvarado intimidated by the warlike force of the araucans, and badly impressed by the territory and the great hardships of an expedition undertaken in the height of the winter, came back and told Almagro the difficulties he had for winning the battle with some brave indians and in a terrain so adverse.

The country had Almagro's son caused the wretched impression, the resistance of the southern indians, the poverty, the lack of means of civilization, the lack of gold and silver, persuaded his father that he may come back to Peru.

- My father, I think that you don't have much to do now, it would be better to go back to Peru where there are organized cities, great roads and abundant riches in gold and silver, and thus you will occupy on your interests in the Cuzco issue. –

- Diego, my son, you are right, today September 10th 1536, we will leave the beautiful lands of Chile, we have not found the richness in gold that I hoped, but I found an unequalled beauty paradise. We will undertake –added he – the return by the Atacama Desert following the ancient Inca's road, in order to be free of the sufferings of a new journey through the range. I will commission Ruy Díaz that he may open us the route, we will go organized in small groups. I estimate that the first days of November, we will start to depart from Copiapo, we will provision of llamas and above all a lot of kind of containers for taking water since we will cross and rest in Atacama and will continue by Antofagasta and Tarapaca deserts until we reach Arequipa, if everything is all right and we have few losses, we will reach more or less in February 1537.-

They returned to Peru such as Almagro hoped that it may be without great losses, especially men, although some of them got sick on the way and this caused them some delay.

At his arrival, the country was having an indian uprising after Felipillo alienated them about the Spaniards. They were under the command of Inca Manco Capac II whom Pizarro had granted a whit of authority appointing him puppet king after the execution of Atahualpa. The inca rebellion started brewing, helped by Mama Asarpay, Wayna Qhapaq's daughter and sister of Francisco Pizarron's woman, meanwhile he entertained in the bank of Rimac river trying to found the city of Lima. Mama had access to the palace and spied the Spaniard's defense plans, at once she inform these to the army of Kisu Yupanqui, and on May 6th 1536, Manco Capac's armies attacked and burned Cuzco.

Upon concluding her mission, Mama Asarpay returned to Cajamarca where she was taken prisoner and taken to Cuzco, where later Francisco Pizarro had her killed.

Two hundred thousand indians had besieged conqueror's brothers, Hernando and Gonzalo Pizarro with 200 more Spaniards in the city.

Almagro went into Cuzco, attacked the peruvian indians and forced them to raise the siege, saving the Pizarro brothers from sure death. It can be said that with this victory is completed the conquest of the Inca Empire.

Almagro decided to incorporate Cuzco into his governorship, occupied by force the disputed city, on April 19th 1537, taking prisoners to Hernando y Gonzalo Pizarro.

Francisco Pizarro sent Alonso de Alvarado in defense of Cuzco.

Almagro's lieutenant Rodrigo de Ordoñez consolidated the capture of Pizarro brothers, defeating Alonso de Alvarado and the Pizarro's army that went in aid of the captured on July 12th 1537 in the so-called battle of Abancay. This action of Almagro supposed disrespect to the Crown's power and offense to Francisco both parties decided to entrust the solution to a moderator, the provincial of the mercedary Francisco de Bobadilla.

While this was being solved, Almagro went on with his troops and hostages to Chincha, founding the Almagro village.

Francisco de Bobadilla settled quickly that the city of Cuzco belonged to the governorship of New Castilla on November 1537; therefore it was in favour of Pizarro's partisans.

Francisco Pizarro, wanting to have a capital nearer to the sea and Panama, since Cuzco was in the interior and very southernmost, he settled in the bank of the Rimac River and near to the coast founded the city of Lima of the Kings, in honour of the Queen Juana de Castilla and her son the King Charles V.

Pizarro was in the city of Lima, which he had just founded; before this situation, he started negotiations with the purpose of gaining time, in these it was agreed that Almagro may continue in possession of Cuzco, while the King decided to whom the city belonged, Hernando and Gonzalo Pizarro would be freed on condition that they abandoned Peru.

Pizarro brothers did not fulfilled their word, and Pedro Peranzules, one of confidants more close to Francisco, accompanying Hernando Pizarro, moved toward Cuzco to rescue the city.

They were in front of a great force and marched against Almagro, already very sick who could not even ride a horse, the command had to be trusted to one of his lieutenants Rodrigo Orgoñez, commanding 700 Almagro's partisans, being defeated two miles from Cuzco in the batttle of Las Salinas by Hernando Pizarro who took as quartermaster to the future conqueror of Chile, Pedro de Valdivia, commanding 1000 Pizarro's partisans.

Victory after two hours of combat smiled on the forces in whose fronts the imperial flags waved, one of them the most hardened was waved in the hands of captain Peranzules, escorted by Gaspar Rodriguez de Camporredondo.

Almagro, old and sick, was captured in his hiding place of the Inca fortress of Sacsahuaman, was jailed in the prison of Cuzco, where he was judged by treason and usurpation, being condemned by Hernando

Pizarro to death penalty without having been sentenced, he was strangled in his own cell on July 8th 1538. The corpse was taken to the square where they exhibited his head in a pike. He was buried in Cuzco and later on in the convent of La Merced.

Hernando Pizarro, who had been exiled from Peru by this action, was captured in Spain by the Council of Indies and sentenced to 18 years of prison in Medina del Campo, wherefrom he administered the family inheritance, married to his niece and was released in 1561.

The defeaters went into the city of Cuzco, totally subjecting it to looting.

All Peru was subjected to Francisco Pizarro.

The event of Almagro's death left the conquerors deeply divided in two bands: pizarristas (Pizarro's partisans) and almagristas (Almagro's partisans), these ones under the control of Almagro's son, the Young, who would lead Peru to a spiteful and bloody civil war which lasted for more than seven years.

While these facts happened, Pedro de Valdivia planned a journey to Chile.

CHAPTER V.
PEDRO DE VALDIVIA.

The illustrious conqueror of Chile, don Pedro de Valdivia was born in the year 1502 in Villanueva de la Serena (Badajoz) Extremadura province.

He belonged to a wealthy family of gentlemen. He followed the career of arms, participating in the campaigns of Flanders and in the wars of Italy fighting in the battle of Pavia.

He left the ranks to marry in his native city of Villanueva de la Serena, with Marina Ortiz de Gaete, having no offspring with her.

Because of his adventurous spirit of that time, he went on board for America later in 1535, leaving his wife in Spain, with the hope of coming back for her soon.

He enrolled in the expedition of Jeronimo de Ortal, undertaking a journey to America and reached the island of Cubagua in 1535, where after being distinguished by taking part in the conquest of Venezuela with his friend Juan Fernandez de Alderete, they stayed some months in Coro in 1536 and he knew Francisco Martinez Vegaso in the expedition of Ambrosio Alfinger, when such territory and the northwestern region of present Colombia had been granted to the Welser, german bankers who sent several expeditions to explore and conquer this region. After this feat Valdivia went to Peru a year later, serving under the orders of Hernando Pizarro as quartermaster, aiding to defeat Almagro in the battle of Las Salinas in 1538.

He obtained, in reward for his services, a rich silver mine in Porco and an indian's encomienda in the valley of Canela, a rich and fertile land.

Valdivia, knowing that Emperor Charles V had authorized to "adelantado" Pizarro for exploring the New Toledo, requested from Him the respective authorization to conquer and settle the province of Chile, in order to get the glory he mostly sought.

His companions were trying to dissuade him about his determination.
- Perhaps, haven't you heard Almagro's partisans talking bad things about these so inhospitable lands?

Valdivia annoyingly replied.
- I'm able enough if I want to conquer Chile, even though I have to sell all my possessions for covering the expenditures of the expedition, my resolution is steady.-

- Alas, my good friend, I think that you don't know what you do; perhaps it may be that you have lost your judgment, since I don't think that with the bad reputations that those lands have, so they say, they are not able to feed 100 Castilians, I don't think you may find someone so dumb who wants to go with you.

Valdivia overcame all those unfavourable news, and tried whatever it may be to get permission from Pizarro in 1538 for going to this southern country. At last, he succeeded in getting the authorization in 1539, being appointed his lieutenant governor, acting on behalf of Pizarro. He was also authorized to take Felipillo in the expedition as interpreter.

In the first preparations, he spent all his money, which he presumed it was not enough to buy horses, weapons, llamas, seeds, etc.

When he already believed that his dream might not come true, he attained to convince the merchant Lucas Martinez Vegaso, brother of his friend Francisco, to finance the expedition. It was granted to Lucas, as distinguished Pizarro's soldier of "the thirteen of the fame", some extents of crops comprising Moquegua, Tacna and Tarapacá; therefore he was a very wealthy man.
- Captain Valdivia, I will fund part of the expedition, but in exchange my brother Francisco Martinez is to supply you a considerable amount of goods, which you will buy him at a low price, making him partner of half of the benefits which may produce the conquest of Chile.

Once solved this difficulty, another one graver was presented, since no one wanted to travel to Chile. Valdivia was not intimidated by that and talking with the merchant, he commented.
- Don Lucas, I don't want to lose fame and prestige that this journey may bring me, I am willing to depart even though it may be with a dozen men only.

Even a third difficulty was presented to him in the person of Pedro Sanchez de Hoz, former secretary to Pizarro that had just arrived from Spain, whom Emperor Charles V had granted him the previous year in 1539 the appointment of Governor of Tierra Australis, whose territory stretched since the Strait of Magellan to the South Pole, giving him authorization to discover and govern all these lands and the neighbouring islands that he may discover, though in the provision, it appears, that he was excluded with regard to Chile.

As Pizarro knew of the good relationship that Sanchez de la Hoz had with the court and that he could get the pardon for the killing of Almagro with his influence, he was persuaded to become associated with Valdivia and Martinez to carry out together the conquest of Chile.

Pizarro got together with both of them to end the preparations.

- Gentlemen Valdivia and de Hoz, the most convenient to undertake a good expedition is: that you Sanchez de Hoz, as contribution to the society recently established and you are known for not having any capital, you should stay in Lima to get 50 horses, weapons and munitions, which you will send by sea in two vessels in a four months deadline.

CHAPTER VI

PEDRO DE VALDIVIA'S JOURNEY AND THE BEGINNING OF THE CONQUEST.

Due to the so big discredit of Chile, Valdivia did not get any moneylender that may advance him enough money, had to form a partnership in addition with merchant Francico Martinez Vegaso to whom were joined Juan de Encino, Captain Alonso de Monroy, a woman, widow Ines de Sanchez as domestic servant, after the opposition of the usurer Francisco Martinez that did not accept her, although after discussion and having convinced him, contributed with other 10.000 Castilian pesos in goods that were bought to him. In addition to his participation as partner, he should receive the half of all that the company may produce.

They also took 11 Spaniards more and one thousand auxiliary Indians to carry the equipment.

Valdivia had known Ines de Suarez when he had just come back from the battle of the Salinas in 1538 where he fought together with her husband captain Juan Malaga killed in battle. Ines came to Peru in search of him, of whom she could know that had died.

In recompense for being widow of a Spaniard soldier, she received a small extent of land in Cuzco, where she settled, in the same way an encomienda of natives.

Captain was a medium height man, happy faced, very good-natured, candid and liberal souled, eating and drinking anything, dressed to kill and very seductive of women. One day in Cuzco, when dismounting in the main square, he noticed a 30 years lady, well dressed, having a nice face, she was buying in a flowers stand when her purse fell down, running to pick it up he asked her very kindly.

- Where are you from, Lady? , I have never had the pleasure of seeing you, my name is Pedro de Valdivia captain from the Spanish royal armies.-

Madam Ines, a little bit upset replied him.

- I live in a small ranch in the outskirts of Cuzco, I came from Spain not long ago in of my husband that died fighting in the battle of Las Salinas, maybe you as a soldier have known him, and his name was Juan de Malaga.-

- I think I knew him, I knew that he was extremeño like me, he was from Plasencia in the province of Caceres and I am from Villanueva de la Serena of Badajoz.-

- What a coincidence, I am also extremeña, Caceres, my name is Ines de Suarez and my native home is in Plasencia very near to the Cathedral. My sister Asuncion and I were seamstresses, and my grand-father was artisan cabinetmaker and worked for the catholic priests of the brotherhood of La Veracruz.-

A close friendship was shaped between them which led them to be lovers.

They departed from Cuzco on the first days of January 1540. The expedition took the way of the deserts by the Arequipa valley, passing through Moquegua and Tacna; it reached Copiapo, where it began the territory belonging to his jurisdiction continuing until it reached Tarapacá.

New difficulties presented to Valdivia, his quartermaster Alvar Gomez died because of the difficult way, and his partner Francisco Martinez should have been transferred to Arequipa badly injured because a horseback falling down.

On the way, several groups of soldiers of fortune were joining them, which at first increased to twenty the number of expeditionaries, but another group formed by Rodrigo de Araya joined them later on, with 16 men coming from Tarija, shortly after some other 80 came, Francisco de Villagra succeeded in persuading several Diego de Rojas' men who had joined in Tarapacá, they totalled 110 that were seeking a place to form a partnership. Francisco de Aguirre joined them in San Pedro de Atacama that was going to be their best support, with 15 riders, 10 harquebusiers and crossbowmen, besides they have achieved to gather a great quantity of corn and forage for the horses, Rodrigo de Quiroga and Lopez de

Ulloa, Alonso de Monroy, Juan de Bohon, Juan de Abalos Jufre, Jeronimo de Alderete, Juan Fernandez de Alderete, Gonzalo de los Rios, Alonso de Chinchilla, Gaspar de Vergara and the chaplain and chronicler Rodrigo Gonzalez de Marmolejo, thus was formed a great army of 150 braves added in Tarapacá. These men played a remarkable part in the formation of the Chilean nationality.

Sanchez de Hoz had stayed in Lima gathering supplies and store for the expedition, lacking in resources, could not fulfil what has been agreed to with Valdivia, being chased by his creditors due to the huge debt contracted with them, they imprisoned him once he was found. They later allowed him to be released on parole so that he may gather the money and pay his obligations. As soon as he was free, got together with some accomplices Pedro Sanchez, Antonio de Ulloa and Juan de Guzman, so that they may help to look for the expedition and join them. His intention was to murder Valdivia and being on command.

They found the expedition near the town of Atacama La Chica in the middle of the desert and Sanchez de Hoz and his accomplices penetrated in the camp at midnight, reached until the tent where Valdivia was supposed to be sleeping and stabbed him to death to usurp the leadership of the army. But this was not there because he had gone to inspect some lands, traitors found instead Ines de Suarez sleeping that upon hearing a noise, she shouted, being awakened the other soldiers, that at once Luis Gomez y Pedro de Toledo who was in command in absence of Valdivia came and the latter captured them, but upon seeing that he was a haughty personage, he did not take any measure against them; but he sent a messenger to Valdivia telling him what had happened. Valdivia came back three days after his absence and put into jail the conspirators. For a moment, he thought about hanging Sanchez de Hoz but he pardoned him and exiled his accomplices.

Shortly after, on August 12th, 1540, it was signed the settlement in the town of Atacama by public deed which dissolved the partnership made between Pero Sanchez de Hoz and Valdivia and he resigned the concessions that Charles V granted him in 1539 in favour of the latter. Therefore, Valdivia became Governor of the Antarctic lands before being governor of the conquered lands in Chile.

Following his march toward the Aconcagua valley, the same route that the governor Almagro had taken before, in the middle of the attacks by the Indians sent by the chieftain promaucahue Michimalonco who stole them and destroyed the foods trying to cut them off the pass. Valdivia arrived in the Copiapo's, very wide and fertile valley flanked by the Andes range, beginning with the region he had to conquer.

In Copiapo he discovered another conspiracy leb by Juan Ruiz and manipulated by Sanchez de Hoz, but this time Valdivia did not feel pity and hung Ruiz as a lesson.

Finally, on December 1540, after eleven months of march, the expedition penetrated in the valley of the bank of the Mapocho river that was divided opposite to a hill called Tupahue, to which the Spaniards called San Cristobal, leaving a long island in the middle that was containing a small hill that the picunche called Huelen, where they camped surrounding the west side. In this valley, he decided to found a city, and very excited because the environment, talked to his expedition:

The nature of this soil, sound fertile and surrounded by irrigation ditches network derived from the Mapocho, those of Apoquindo, Tobalaba and Nuñoa that the picunches have well built, I will found here a city that with the proximity of the Mapocho River and the bushes that exist in its bank, we will have insured the water and the fuelwood, the Huelen Hill, which will be called from today Santa Lucia, for his vision that will give us in case of an assault of the aborigines, on February 12th in the year of our Lord of 1541 I will found the city of Santiago del Nuevo Extremo, in recollection of apostle Santiago, Patron of Spain, my country, and of the region of Extremadura, my land.-

Foundation of Santiago

According to the royal ordinances on the foundation of cities, Valdivia commissioned the builder Pedro de Gamboa to build the new city. The terrain was divided in squared blocks by 138 varas and about 12 varas for the street, nine streets were traced from east to west and 16 from north to south. Each block was divided in four huge lots closed by pieces of wood. Inside they were built wooden ranch plastered with mud and the roofs were covered by reeds. The middle block was intended for the main square wherein the most outstanding people of that time lived; Pedro de Valdivia, Diego Garcia Caceres, Pedro Gomez, Pedro de Miranda, Francisco de Aguirre, Jeronimo de Alderete, Antonio de Pastrana and Alonso de Escobar, this was the new core of the town and in the same square was built the tree of justice, the "picota". In case of emergency the neighbours should join in the main square, closed area with trunk of trees planted and fastened among them, the same way they were built in Spain. The north side was set aside for the Governor's house and the prison, and the west side for the Cathedral.

It was appointed a town council or city council made up of two mayors and six councillors.

Valdivia met with each of his men to decide offices which were to be appointed.

- I congratulate myself so much to be with you captain Aguirre and be able to talk about our past times when we fought in our dear Spain with the imperial troops of his Majesty Charles V, I heard of you that you also took part in the Battle of Pavia.

- Certainly General, I took part in that battle and in the assault of Rome in 1527 under the orders of don Gonzalo Fernandez de Cordoba.-

- Gentleman Aguirre, once that the Town Council is established, I will appoint you as the first ordinary mayor of the "encomenderos".-

- Sir, it will be a great honour for me to perform the position of mayor, in which I will put the best of my knowledge and labor to your service.-

- As the first ordinary mayor of dwellers, I will appoint Juan de Abalos Jufré and councillors Juan Fernández de Alderete, Francisco de Villagra, Martín de Solier and as councillor and treasurer Jeronimo de Alderete, being procurator Antonio de Pastrana. –

The council summoned all the neighbours to a broader meeting, open council. In this assembly Valdivia was appointed Governor due to the distance of Peru and above all because of the civil war between the followers of Almagro and Pizarro, and Captain General on behalf of his majesty and by the will of the people. Valdivia accepted the title on June 11th 1541. Next to it, he signed in a sealed envelope the name of this successor in case of death.

Already as Governor and Captain General, he appointed Alonso de Molina as Lieutenant General to the recently established city of Santiago on July 20th 1541; he should judge and sentence in such a position the entire lawsuits that may be presented. Besides, he should preside over the council during its deliberations.

Next day, Valdivia rewarded in gratitude to his companions, allotting them lands and Indians in encomiendas.

He also took notice of the need of be provided with gold and a ship for being in contact by sea with Peru in order to bring men and the necessary elements. He started looking in the coast for a suitable port where there may be forests, and in that place he found it in the broad beach of Cocon. The building of a ship was started over there in which worked 20 spaniards that had come from Santiago with a few "chaconas" and among them was coming the first negroe stepping on Chilean territory, he was called Juan Valiente.

In order to get the necessary gold to finance the conquest, he put to work the yanaconas in the gold panning sites of Marga Marga, with a scort of 12 riders under the order of Gonzalo de los Rios, one of the faithfull servants of the leading conqueror, assigned to keep the Indians under obedience. These gold panning sites were exploited by the Indians long before commanded by chief Michimalonco chieftain of the Aconcagua valley.

One night the Governor being in Cocon received a startling letter from his lieutenant Monroy who was asking him to urgently go to Santiago since a conspiracy was plotted by some Spaniards.

Immediately he rode his horse and started going to Santiago, he left an eight man garrison in charge of keeping the works of the shore.

He was aware that the chief of the conspiracy was Martin de Solier, noble gentleman from Cordoba and one of the councillors from Santiago who, two months before, had had the determination of raising Valvidia for Governor. His main accomplices were Antonio de Pastrana who had been the city's procurator, who had written the request so that Valdivia may accept the post of Governor, Pastrana' son in law called Alonso de Chinchilla, Sanchez de Hoz, Martin Ortuño, Bartolome Marquez and some other three lesser important persons. The plan consisted in killing Valdivia, seizing the ship being built and going to Peru. This conspiracy was spread by the discouragement of having to always live with weapons at hand in addition to the conviction that they would lose their lives in the conquest of a country whose poverty was similar to the information they had received in Peru, and also surely for the sake of envy due to the last appointments in Monroy and in some of his captains for the most trusted positions in the Colony, causing all this parties and rivalries.

Valdivia spread all his annoyance and energy that the circumstances deserved, immediately ordered that the six characters were captured and shut them in different rooms under the custody of the High Constable of the city and he started proceeding the open process, by this he put into prison the syndics procurator Martin de Solier, Sanchez de Hoz was kept in prison. Solier was beheaded as hidalgo's privilege, while the rest of them, without considering Sanchez de Hoz that was pardoned, were publicly hung.

After that, he wrote Charles V and Hernando Pizarro emphasizing that the conspirator were Almagro's followers and were coming from Peru with the agreement to murder him.

As soon as he left Cocon, the neighbouring chieftains allied to Michimalonco, Tangalongo and Chigaimanga rushed at the works killing almost all the Spaniards and yanaconas, only Gonzalo de los Rios and the colored soldier Juan Valiente could run away by galloping.

- Alas Governor, we have been attacked by the chieftains Michimalonco, Tangalonco and Chigaimanga being unable to defend ourselves from the sudden attack that took us by surprise, as soon as we could, soldier Juan Valiente and me, we got out running to get your help.-

By chance, Captain Gonzalo, I hope that all of them aren't dead, and tell me, how didn't you realize that they wanted to attack you?-
No, I didn't. Because once we arrived in Quillota valley, the main chieftain Tangalonco was distracting me with some coarse grains of gold so that I couldn't see all of his people ambushed next to us, while I was looking at the gold grain, the Indian started to shout and they suddenly

appeared everywhere, and were impetuously throwing arrows against all of us, although we desperately fought they killed nearly all of us and set fire on the brig, only Juan Valiente and me could escape alive thanks to our horses being saddled when we saw the Indians coming out from their hideout.-

Governor very annoyed said:

- In retaliation, I will have seven chieftains seized and put them in a cage so that they may not escape.-

The natives near Cachapoal were showing obvious signs of preparing a rebellion. Valdivia suspected an attack to the newly founded city. One yanacona girl gave him the news that the surrounding forests were filled with hostile natives. He sallied on September the 9th to scatter the native gatherings, leaving 50 soldiers and 500 yanaconas under the command of Alonso de Monroy.

Upon knowing this situation, chief Michimalonco fell on Santiago in the dawn of September 11th 1541 in charge of 8.000 and then 20.000 natives completely destroying the city and burning houses by means of firing arrows.

After eleven hours of fight, plight was so desperate that priest Rodrigo Gonzalez Marmolejo stated that the battle was like Judgment Day. Priest Lobos, as army chaplain said as he was killing with his sword that he was sending the assailing natives to hell.

Ines de Suarez

Ines de Suarez distinguished in the defense besides taking water and food for the fighters and encouraging them in their hopelessness, took the sublime decision of going to the house where the leading chieftains were under the protection of Francisco Rubio and Hernando de La Torre, ordering them to behead the seven encaged chieftains.

She then, armed with a sword, went to the battlefield, encouraging soldiers and fighting like one of them.

In order to scare the assailants, they were shown the decapited blood-stained heads sticked to pikes, causing this that the natives went in retreat. Four Spaniards died and the others were injured, but aided by abnegate Ines, who also assisted as a nurse for the soldiers, healing their injuries.

Three years later in 1544, Pedro de Valdivia recompensed Ines de Suarez with a medal for her action in this battle.

On his returning, Governor only found the city's smoking rubble and ordered his people:

- What a disaster! We all have to rebuild the city of Santiago right away; we'll rebuild it surrounded by fire-resistant adobe walls. We shall also build in this very same place a chapel, which we shall call "Our Lady of Rescue", in gratitude to the help that she has given us. We will share Santiago's outskirts in small farms in which we shall grow cereals and vegetable watered by the Mapocho, I shall myself dig, sow and till like everyone. We will be always armed and our horses saddled in daylight, half of you will be on guard by night and change your turns. To you Madam Ines, I assign you the care of the few livestock you could save, how many could they be?-

- Lord, I could only save from the fire two fowls, three pigs and a small portion of wheat.-

On January 1542, Valdivia sent by land Alonso de Monroy in search of supplies and reinforcements to Peru provided with the best horses and five soldiers. He took stirrups and other tools made with the scarce gold that they had obtained from the gold panning sites with the intention of impressing the Spaniards from Peru so that they may decide to come to conquest Chile.

Upon passing through Northern Chile, Monroy was surprised and taken prisoner by the natives of Copiapo, but achieved to escape and reached Lima to consolidate the entrusted goal. Alonso de Monroy delayed one year and a half to convince them, being able to send to Chile the rescuing ship "Santiaguillo" with supplies, under the command of

Diego de Villalon, arriving Santiago in 1543 when famine and misery spread among its settlers.

Monroy was personally bringing 70 cavalrymen reinforcement by land, a lot of horses that were mingling with other races, wherefore he was one of the makers of the chilean horse race.

Merchant Francisco Martinez, partner to Valdivia, came among the 190 men that went on board, with the intention of collecting his earnings, but the Governor had not accumulated any, he only had great debts. He proposed the dissolution of the society, agreeing to the 5.000 pesos in gold that he was offered.

At once, wheat seed was distributed among the native chieftains; these soon grew cereal and barley on a large scale.

Knowing about the dangers that Monroy had gone through on his journey by land from Santiago to Lima, which it lasted three months, the Governor wanted to have a city in the middle of these two and settle in it "encomenderos" that may defend it. He ordered Captain Juan Bohon to found the city of La Serena in 1544, called this way in memory of the Extremadura valley. Duration of the journey between Santiago and Lima theoretically lasted ten days.

CHAPTER VII
MURDER OF FRANCISCO PIZARRO

Rumours about the death of Francisco Pizarro, at the hands of Diego de Almagro, the Young, were curiously spreading by the mouths of the natives in Santiago in 154, this fact had not taken place.

Four months before the foundation of the city of Santiago, there were conflicts with the almagristas in Peru.

On Sunday, June 26th 1541 the almagristas appeared in Lima's Main Square. Pizarro was calmly inside his palace, when suddenly a group of 18 almagristas or Chileans as they were also called, commanded by Juan de Rada, entered the palace frightening the guard of honour with white arms, and at the shout of "long live the King!" , "death to the tyrant!", he was hit in the throat with a pike and then struck in the head with a vase, causing him the death.

Once they were masters of the situation in Lima, the almagristas named Diego de Almagro, "the Young", as Governor.

Charles V, knower of the grave events in Peru, sent Don Cristobal Vaca de Castro as Commissioned Judge and Governor of Peru, who defeated the almagristas in the battle of the Chupas, nearby Huamanga on September 16th, 1542.

Diego Almagro "The Young "pretended to take shelter with the rebel incas from Vilcabamba, but he was captured and beheaded in Cuzco's Square.

King Charles I of Spain and the V of the Holy Roman Germanic Empire of the House of Habsburg (1516-1555) created the Viceroyship of Peru, by means of a royal writ signed in Barcelona on November 20th 1542. This viceroyship had a huge extension. From the Isthmus of Panama, in the north, to "Tierra del Fuego in the south.

The future Captainship General of Chile would be one of the most austral colonies of the Spanish Empire, due to its remote position from the great centres and commercial routes and the conflict with the mapuches. Its economics was only intended to sustain the Viceroyship with raw materials such as grease, leathers, wheat and the few spaniards who lived in the ground. Chile was the poorest province appertaining to the rich Viceroyship of Peru.

The first Viceroy, Blasco Nuñez de Vela, came to Peru in 1542. His task was not easy because of the immense territory. He had a heavy load since he was responsible for each one of the "audiencias" established in South America comprising: Panamá, Nueva Granada, Quito, Lima, Charcas, Santiago and Buenos Aires.

In his post as Captain General and Governor, he should protect the Viceroyalty against the attacks of corsairs and pirates, and the internal attacks product of revolts and popular uprisings. Viceroy was equally the main responsible for spreading the catholic faith and evangelizing the natives.

Viceroys in Peru showed different titles: Lieutenant, Governor and Captain General of the Kingdoms of Peru, Mainland and Chile, President of the Royal Audience, President of the Higher Board of Royal Income, President of the Tribunal and Royal Audience of the Accounts, Superintendent of Police Court, Captain General of Districts and Governor of Provinces, Inspector of Castles and Fortresses, Ecclesiastic vice-patron, General of the Navy of the Southern Seas.

In the beginning the viceroys' mandate should not exceed three years, but due to so long and exhausting voyage which entailed reaching to America, the Council of Indies extended his staying to five years. Peru's Viceroy lived in the city of Lima, in a sumptuous palace destined for them, surrounded by a brilliant court, in the middle of great luxury and riches and guarded by guard of honour.

Blasco Núñez de Vela, sailed from Sanlúcar de Barrameda, on November 3rd, accompanied by the "oidores" of the new Audience, and some other illustrious gentlemen. He arrived at "Nombre de Dios" on January 10th 1544, and passed from there to Panama where he showed signs of his violent character. Leaving the Audience in Panama, he went on board to Peru and reached Tumbes on March 14th , from there he passed to Piura and then to Trujillo, where he was solemnly received.

From Trujillo he made his way for La Barranca, where he could read what was written on a wall, a warning of his future fate "To whom is coming to take away my estate, take his life" and he finally reached Lima on May 17ᵗʰ 1544, where he was received with pomp and great splendour.

The new Viceroy, suspicious of his predecessor Vaca de Castro being the author of the pasquinade which was threatening him, imprisoned him in his palace; he was put him on board a ship bound for Spain. He tried to hang Antonio del Solar at his home, La Barranca's "encomendero" where it had been written the pasquinade, finally, in a burst of anger he stabbed collector Juan Suarez de Carbajal to death suspecting him accomplice of the escape of some gentlemen who were forced to leave Lima because of his violent behavior. They sought refuge in the fields of Gonzalo Pizarro.

The violent new Viceroy had the difficult mission to deprive the conquerors from their encomiendas and "repartimientos", to all whom had been actively involved in the disputes between pizarristas and almagristas. This caused a great uprising of the struck ones, commanded by Gonzalo Pizarro.

The encomenderos from Peru rose against the Crown. The Hearers of the Audience of Lima captured the Viceroy and expelled him to Spain. Hearer Juan Alvarez who was taking him, landed in Tumbes and released the Viceroy for him to go to Quito, wherein he appointed Rodrigo de Ocampo Governor of that place. The Viceroy advised by the new Governor, told him that they may leave together toward San Miguel de Piura, with the intention of handing him over to Gonzalo Pizarro who was there. The Viceroy dreadful of being captured by Pizarro returned to Quito. On his way, he had Rodrigo Campo beheaded as traitor. He went out of Quito to Popayan being chased by Pizarro, reached Pasto trying to continue his way to Lima, but he came back to Popayan where the viceroy and his few men faced Benalcazar. Gonzalo Pizarro, under pretext of being hurt his interests and those of the other conquerors; they were warlike marching toward Lima, taking Sebastian de Benalcazar as general of the pizarrista armies, 600 Spaniards, 200 harquebusiers, and 140 cavalrymen.

Among the slave that had been brought by Spaniards to Peru, there were a great quantity of Moorish and Berbers, they were famous by their cruelty and were always willing to serve their masters by accompanying them in the battles and in the execution of the worst crimes.

The viceroy desperately fought with the spear in his hand, showing bravery and strength in spite of being old, until finally his spear was broken, he fell down because of a mace blow by Hernando de Torres, neighbour from Arequipa. He was captured when he fell down from his horse.

Benito, brother to collector Juan Suárez de Carbajal who had been stabbed by the Viceroy in Lima, found him dying lying in the field, being helped by priest Francisco Herrera, and after saying him the worst insults that the old viceroy endured with dignity and certainty, in the act of taking revenge for his brother's death, he ordered one of his moorish slaves to cut his head, dragging it by the ground up to Quito wherein it was nailed in the pike, and Juan de Torres, called the madrileño to be distinguished from his namesake- one of the thirteen of the fame, made a tuft out of his white beards that put in his cap and shew off like a symbol in the streets of Quito and Lima; the naked corpse of the unfortunate was picked up from the battlefield by Vasco Suarez who buried him over there, and captain Juan de Olea withdrew his head from the pike and gathered it with his body. It was built a chapel called by some Royal and by others La Veracruz in the place he was buried.

Benalcázar was hurt and captured but he achieved to escape. The balance of the battle was: 50 casualties in the Viceroy's side and 20 for the pizarristas , 70 prisoners were shot by the pizarristas and the royalists hurt were killed by the natives and negroes for robbing them.

Some encomenderos wanted to get rid of Spain and believing that it was possible to defeat the Viceroy and then rise up against Pizarro, they wrote to the Pope Paulus III so that he may invest Gonzalo Pizarro as king of Peru, which the Pope didn't reply at all.

After the "Santiaguillo" loaded with munitions, another ship arrived, the "San Pedro" under the command of the Genoese Juan Baustista Pastene who came to explore the austral region. He informed Valdivia about the grave events happened in Peru, the death of Pizarro, the battle of Añaquito with the death of the Viceroy and the beheading of Diego de Almagro, "The Young".

Valdivia took him into his service appointing him Lieutenant Governor of the seas; he at the same time established a maritime base in Valparaiso and was charged of exploring the southern coast.

Pastene set sail from Valparaiso with the ships San Pedro and Santiaguillo. The voyage gave the Genoese as result the knowledge of the Chilean coasts up to the 41 degree south latitude, that is to say up to the San Pedro bay.

On his return, he had not accomplished to explore the austral lands, but he discovered several ports taking possession of the lands. His major discovery was that of the town of Aynil at the mouth of Aynileno River that was named as Valdivia, also discovered the mouth of the Biobio River. Because of these informations, Valdivia was determined to start a new expedition toward South which should take him up to the Biobio. Alonso de Monroy departed from La Serena to Peru on September 4th 1545 in order to ask new help to increase the conquests of Chile. Upon reaching Callao on the 28th of that month, Peru was in a calamitous situation due to the internal wars organized by Gonzalo Pizarro that had rebelled against the authority sent by the king Charles V. Alonso de Monroy's mission was to rescue men, but he could not comply with that mission because he died in Lima in 1545.

Valdivia, impatient with his new conquests, did not wait for Monroy's reinforcements, finding on the way with a fierce native resistance, which culminated in the battle of Quilicura, he was convinced of his forces' weakness once he was failed.

With this defeat, he was encouraged to go on to Peru in order to serve the Monarch's cause by means of helping to its pacification and thus gain the official title of governor and obtain the necessary help for the ending of the conquest of Chile.

He left Francisco de Villagra in charge of the government of Chile during his journey.

Sanchez de Hoz took advantage of Valdivia's going to Peru; he really deceived some colonists who shipped all the gold they had because they thought that they were going back to Peru, when the ship was loaded with this gold, Valdivia went on board leaving the distressed colonists. Sanchez de Hoz took this opportunity to conspire again. This time, he did it under the shadow and the one who appeared as the leader was Hernan Rodriguez de Monroy.

The conspiracy was discovered by Francisco de Villagra, in charge of command because of Valdivia' absence, and Sanchez de Hoz was beheaded without any previous trial, his head was walked in the main square proclaiming his crime of betrayal to the King's service.

After the death of the Viceroy Blasco Nuñez Vela in the battle of Añaquito, Gonzalo Pizarro became the absolute leader of the Viceroyalty of Peru, without observing the laws of the Crown and those of the Royal writ.

The emperor had had to leave toward Holland to attend to problems, leaving his son Felipe in charge of the government of Spain, the Crown decided to send Don Pedro de Lagasca to restore the royal authority in the Peruvian territory after several consultations, which was informed on May 16th 1545 and the mission of subduing Gonzalo Pizarro.

Lagasca sailed from the port of San Lucas de Barrameda on May 26th, three months after the battle of Añaquito had ocurred.

The dreadful smallpox epidemic broke out in the very same year of 1545; the natives did not have biological defences against it. On this occasion the epidemic killed two thirds of the natives from the present department of Piura, which was left entirely depopulated. It was still remembered that a smallpox epidemic killed Inca Huayna Capac in Quito.

Since Panama was the arrival point to access the Pacific, before the Crown may decide about the peruvian issue, Gonzalo Pizarro had sent a fleet under the command of Hernando de Bachicao to seize Panama with the purpose of preventing the royal forces may obstruct his plans. But Bachicao exceedingly surpassed his commission and seized the cities of Panama and Nombre de Dios, which were whimsically governed during four months, doing all kind of abuses until he was summoned by Gonzalo, who replaced him with Pedro de Hinojosa whom was sent with 22 ships, He had a more humane behaviour toward the panamanians, winning for himself the affection of the people immediately.

Priest Pedro de Lagasca was arriving Panama on July 25th 1546 bearing a letter from the Spanish monarch addressed to Gonzalo Pizarro, in which he was ordered to be at the orders of the Pacifier and in a way he was excused of his rebelliousness. The firs thing that Lagasca did was to arrest Hinojosa that upon disagreeing Gonzalo's attitudes surrendered the fleet and went over to the royal forces with the troops he had brought from Peru. This fact meant the decline of Gonzalo Pizarro.

Lagasca appointed Hinojosa Captain General and at the end of November 1546, the troops were leaving toward Tumbes, going to Cajamarca afterward and reaching Jauja finally, where Hinojosa established his general headquarters.

In 1547, Valdivia reached to Peru together with Jeronimo de Alderete in search of help and support as Governor in the presence of the representative to the Crown in Peru. He arrived in the meanwhiles don Pedro de Lagasca was preparing to subdue the rebels. He interviewed Valdivia and this in order to be in Lagasca's good grace and prove his loyalty entered the army for fighting in the battle which appeared it would be bloody because of the deployment of troops by both factions. Hinojosa joined Lagasca's armies days later, in which Valdivia also took part and both of them fought the battle of Jaquijahuana, near Cuzco, on April 9th 1548, where the pizarrista forces were defeated and executed Gonzalo Pizarro and his lieutenant Francisco de Carbajal, called as "The Demon of the Andes" together with other insurrectionists were beheaded the day after.

Lagasca, with utmost diplomacy, was pacifying Peru.

Hinojosa took part in the board that condemned the guilties, and ordered their execution. Because of this fact, he was not feeling so sure about his decision, arising now the dilemma of joining the insurrectionists.

Later on, the Crown was informed about Hinojosa's doubts which were not well received in the ranks, and for attracting him to the royalist cause, the new Viceroy of Peru Antonio de Mendoza, upon his arrival at Lima in 1551, appointed him Governor of the province of Charcas.

Afterwards, Hinojosa took possession of his charge and settled in Potosi, where the insurrectionists' rebellion was still latent. He achieved that some rebel captains may join him, but there was one of them, Sebastian de Castilla whom could not be convinced to desist from his seditious intentions, and joined to two of his followers Melchor Verdugo and Lope de Aguirre the tyrant that played the Amazon River's tragedy, these two individuals assailed Hinojosa's home and killed him on May 5th 1553.

The good doing for the sovereign's cause by Pedro de Valdivia earned him to be confirmed by Lagasca in the governorship of Chile in the name of his majesty Charles V, pointing out the limits north of New Extremadura in the parallel 27th in the mouth of the Copiapo river, and in the south in the 41th's, near the lake Llanquihue, that is to say, between the Caldera and San Pedro bays, with a width of 100 leagues from the Pacific coast up to the interior of the continent. Being consequently located, within them, besides the indicated part of present Chile, the Tucuman and Cuyo provinces, which had formed part of the governorship granted to Pedro Mendoza in 1534. And also the Patagonia. This new delimitation by Lagasca was confirmed after by Charles V. The arrival of Valdivia's hostile neighbours from Chile to Peru because they did not go on board in Valparaiso and were dispossessed of their gold, caused a "residence judgment" for Valdivia whom have just gone to the south, he had to come back from Arequipa to face charges against him, among them, the illegitimate union with Ines de Suarez.

The Viceroy, after hearing the allegations against Valdivia, exonerated him from all the charges, except the one relating to Ines Suarez.

Lagasca invited him to an interview in which emphatically communicated him:

- Sir Governor of the Kingdom of Chile; I imperatively order you to end your 10-year-relation with madam Inez de Suarez, my condition as priest does not allow a public and notorious extramarital relation, therefore I order you that you have her married with a neighbour that you name and I recommend you to follow the directives from the Holy Church regarding your legitimate marriage with madam Marina Ortiz de Gaete.-

- Excellency, I promise under my gentleman's word to completely execute your sentence and bring my wife to the American continent.-

Defeating the love that he was feeling for madam Ines, he obeyed what was agreed by don Pedro Lagasca in the sentence, and joined madam Ines in marriage with one of his best captains, don Rodrigo de Quiroga, whom was later Governor of the Kingdom of Chile and madam Ines legitimate governess, leading a quiet and religious life, providing in the building of the temple of La Merced and the Montserrat hermitage in Santiago.

At the same time, he ordered Jeronimo de Alderete to travel to Spain and bring his legitimate wife madam Marina to Peru and that she may live with her brother captain Diego Ortiz de Gaete whom had gotten on board for the Americas in 1535, fighting next to him in the battle of Jaquijuana in 1549. Valdivia would never see Madam Marina again.

Once Peru was pacified, Lagasca delivered the government to the Royal Audience meanwhile the second viceroy, whom was already named, arrived. He got on board in the port of Callao with 17 huge boxes containing silver bars, which mostly came from the Potosi mines that were starting to produce and would soon reach worldwide fame.

After helping to restore the royal power in Peru and with desired title of Governor, Valdivia came back to Chile with 200 men, taking the oath before the town council on July 20th 1549, with a great honour by his men.

During his absence, the natives destroyed the city of La Serena.

Francisco de Aguirre named Lieutenant Governor of the zone between Choapa River and Atacama, was charged with the reconstruction of La Serena destroyed by the natives in the North, since he had shown inflexibility in the war against the natives and in their punishment.

Aguirre founded the city again on August 26th 1549, building a fort to defend it from the attacks and keep the communications with Peru. Northern Chile was free from risks since then, but it was also very much depopulated and with less manpower since many natives had gone away leaving without hands the gold panning sites and the farming tasks. Aguirre was named Lieutenant General of La Serena.

CHAPTER VIII.

PEDRO DE VALDIVIA CONQUERS SOUTHERN CHILE. THE INDIAN LAUTARO.

Upon his return from Peru Valdivia decided to undertake the conquest of Southern Chile; his intention was to exceed the delimitation of parallel 41 marked by Lagasca and extend his governorship up to Magellan Strait.

Valdivia went out of Santiago in command of 200 Spaniards and a great corps of auxiliary natives commanded by Michimalonco who had become his loyal ally, reaching up to the Biobio region which enters there into the sea where there is infinite number of fishes. They camped in that place taking advantage of the sea to be able to be helped by the galley and a small galleon commanded by captain Juan Bautista de Pastene who would go in their search in that place. They started building, by the force of the arms, the fort of Penco on February 23rd which could be apparently defended from a powerful army and for the rest of the conquerors during the guards of vigilance and to be able to go fighting whenever they want. At the beginning of April, they knew that the entire population was gathering to attack them. One day in the afternoon, 40.000 natives showed up before the small fort, captain Jeronimo de Alderete faced them with 50 cavalrymen, the riders attacked them in such a way that they succeeded in frightening the natives, being the first combat with the mapuches.

Pastene reached with help to the fort of Penco on time. Such was the battle of Andalien, where the natives had to withdraw after a fierce night fight with great casualties.

At the end of this battle with the defeat of the mapuche in Penco, Villagra and Pastene convinced Valdivia that the entire region was

53

completely pacified, and Valdivia founded the city of Concepcion of the
New Extreme on October 5th 1550, in the neighbouring coast of Penco.

After the defeat the main "toquis", Colo-Colo was found among
them, agreed in making the peace with the Spaniards, regaling them
with llamas and maids as it was their custom. Captain Pedro de Villagra
received the small Indian girl Guakolda to his service.

The year that Lautaro was born between the coasts of the Pacific
Ocean and Nahuelbuta in the region of Ragco, which would be called
Arauco by the conquerors, is the same year that Valdivia reached America
in 1535.

Nicknamed by his people the "heroe" and known as Alonso Lautaro
by the Spaniards.

He was captured one day while marauding by the surroundings of
the newly founded Concepcion. He was a strong boy about 15 years,
warlike, rebel, warrior and impulsive.

Valdivia kept Lautaro near him during his captivity, having a special
consideration toward the boy, whom he wanted to inculcate the catholic
faith and incorporate him as his servant, orderly and page. He had him
baptized with the name of Alonso.

Alonso Lautaro, already very integrated with the spaniards,
accompanied his master in his incursions in the Arauco lands and they
even travelled to Santiago, and they entered later in the full Araucania in
the valley of Cautin, founding in the confluence of this river with that of
Las Damas the city of La Imperial. The boy led the replacement horses
of his boss, taking care of the feeding and tiding of them. When Lautaro
did not travel felt prisoner in the small city of Concepcion surrounded
by some adobe walls, a place so different, completely different to his own
place where their homes were built at the open spaces in the forest, living
completely free.

He thinks that in this small and closed city nothing belongs to their
inhabitants that have to buy their food, fuelwood for heating, the clothes,
the materials for building their rucas, which the Castilians call houses.

Lautaro goes one morning to the main square where it is located the
market for the selling of corn, beans, potatoes, gourds, etc.

Upon alighting from the horse he saw some grouped maids, laughing
and almost playing who were going to buy some fruit, there were among
them one whom he watched attentively, she was very beautiful, his entire
attention centered in her, her hair was brown very long, rosy complexion
and big slit black eyes having a very sweet look, the boy fell in love with
her, his mind went blank, he did not remember what he had to buy

and closing to one of the stands, he took the first thing he found. Upon returning to the house, Valdivia asked him:
- Did you bring me the grease I asked you? -
- Sir, they didn't have it, they will receive it tomorrow, but I brought some rich fruits which you will like.-

Next day, he went quickly to the square to see whether he may find the Indian young girl. She was there buying beans, after taking courage he approached her:
- Also, I am going to buy beans, they look good, and my master will like them. It is quite strange that in a small city like this, we haven't seen each other before, have we?, my name is Alonso Lautaro and yours?-

The young girl replied him very anxioulsy:
- My name is Teresa Guakolda.-

Lautaro:
- I live with my master, the Governor, whom has sent me to buy some things-.

Guacolda:
- I am serving in captain don Pedro de Villagras's house and I help in the kitchen and other housekeeping tasks. I would be happy if I lived with my mother and sister, but I think that being separated from them is a consequence of a huekufu's curse, the evil's spirit, who is responsible for all the calamities which ocurr.-
- Both of us feel subject to humiliations, I, son of a lonko Kuriñanku, must take care of horses and you obliged to serve in a Spaniard's home. They have even changed our names, they call you Teresa and to me a very strange name Alonso, but it is very important that we may continue seeing each other. I only ask not be separated from you because I should be obliged to fight against by own people. -
- That god may not allow it and if it were so, I am fourteen years and will wait for many more years, forever. -
- I have two loves, you are one of them my dear Guakolda and the other is the feeling I have for freedom.-

Three days before going out of Concepcion, Lautaro and Guakolda learned about their respective journeys, his destination was Santiago and that of hers, to follow her masters.

By the morning, he went to say goodbey to Guakolda.
- Goodbye Guakolda, we'll see each other the next moon. -
- Goodbye Lautaro, will you remember me? -

He left Concepcion three days before than the girl did; he marched turning his head while he was moving away. He thought that advancing more to the north of the Maule River was to enter with evil's spirits. At last, they arrived at Santiago del Nuevo Extremo, or the Indian Flanders, as it was also called, the boy found a gloomy city, there were neither children nor women, there are no homes, they are made of mud and straw, some of them are two-story houses which are hidden among fruit trees brought from Spain. It has elapsed three years and the boy is 18-year-old tall and stout young, who was always accompanying a lonely, aged and sad Valdivia who maybe saw in the boy those years of his youth passed in Spain.

After the Governor gave several orders to rule the city, at once he left toward the south, always accompanied by his groom. They reached to La Imperial, followed toward south and crossed Tolten River, entering into the domains of the huilliches, natives who were less warlike than the mapuches but more advanced. They succeeded in subduing them and the Governor founded the city of Valdivia in a beautiful valley near the port and river, which discovered the loyal admiral Pastene in his voyage by the south coasts. It was named temporary Captain of the new city don Lorenzo Bernal del Mercado and one encomienda in the region.

Valdivia was very hopeful by the prevailing apparent stillness, at once he entrusted Captain Jeronimo de Alderete a city near the lake Mallayquen. As the natives spoke about a region rich by the gold and silver mines, it was named Villarica, although it was the poorest city in the kingdom of Chile.

The signs of restlessness were soon visible with parcial uprisings which ended with that of the island of Pucureo, between Villarica and La Imperial cities.

The governor crossed the Bueno and Maullin rivers, reaching the Reloncavi gulf while he was exploring the southern lands in charge of his detachment.

He founded the forts in Arauco, in the seashore, and Tucapel and Puren in the western and Eastern slopes of the Nahuelbuta range on his return to the north entering the full Araucania.

Gomez de Almagro was named as chief of the port of Puren. Later on, he founded the city of Los Confines at the confluence of the Malleco and Huequen Rivers. It was given that name because it was located in the confines of the Concepcion and La Imperial jurisdictions.

The young Lautaro, loyal companion to the Governor, was watching with great interest the possession takings and that Valdivia, in the foundations of the cities, allotted the lands among its neighbours and gave them indian encomiendas. Each city was assigned its council.

- I shall be toqui (he thought) some day and with which I have learned from the Spaniards, I shall found beautiful cities, where the houses have windows and the doors are always opened, Guakolda will be there in one of them, we will marry and have a lot of little indians. Perhaps it will be true very soon all this, that I may join with people of mine and end with these oppressors killing them all.

Valdivia, anxious of taking possession of the transandean region of La Nueva Extremadura, sent Francisco de Aguirre to Tucuman, whom at being in La Serena it was easier for him to cross the range and he so did it. Aguirre disputed with Nuñez de Prado, whom did not recognize Valdivia' authority, for this zone while in Tucuman. He founded the city of Santiago del Estero on the banks of the Dulce River two years later in 1553. All these city and fort foundations in the very extensive southern territory had weakened his security forces because of the distances between them; the Governor thought that the mapuches were subdued. However, war continued as a result of Valdivia being establishing cities and forts in Araucanian territory with the purpose of subduing them.

Petrehuelen Ulmen one of the most important men of the entire zone of Arauco, presented himself when the Governor was worried about fortifying the mines by establishing a garrison in Quilacoya and besides he had reinforced the Arauco fort.

Lautaro stayed next to his master when Petrehuelen presented himself to talk with Valdivia.

Lautaro wanted to hear talking about conflict, but Petrehuelen was only talking about peace. Rage invaded his body, he would want to attack those present there, and only an instinct of survival prevented him from doing it.

Meanwhile Petrehuelen and Valdivia were interchanging smiles, false flatteries and promises of peace.

Lautaro felt discouraged when his chief told him to get ready the horses for going to Concepcion.

At the same time the Governor was organizing the colonies, the araucanian chieftains were gathering summoned by the old Colo-Colo for the election of a toqui who should lead the war against the Castilian invaders. Everyone was disputing the command without reaching an agreement; a heavy trunk was brought to the meeting, deciding that he who may bear it more time on his shoulders would be chosen toqui.

Paicaví was the first: he bore it six hours. Elicura stood nine hours. Puren, half a day. Ongolmo, a day and a half. Tucapel, 14 hours. Lincoyan stood twenty hours.

When everybody thought to consider Lincoyan as victorious, Caupolican presented himself, whom walked one day and one night with the trunk on his shoulders. An amazed Colo-Colo proclaimed:

- With this marvelous effort, Caupolican is the winner, he is the first leader from the Arauco hosts, and he is raised to rank of "toqui"!-.

Lautaro escaped to the region of Nahuelbuta, the same night that he had to get ready the horses, wherein the auracanian tribes had just chosen Caupolican as toqui and joined him. Lautaro encouraged his countrymen suggesting them how to defeat the Spaniards and their dreadful horses.

As soon as Caupolicán received his hierarchy and authority, he gathered his men to attack the Arauco square, which was very well defended and had artillery units, rapidly going to the Tucapel fort.

The araucanians presumed their action plan preliminary to the attack to be brilliant because its simplicity. Everything was centered in the Tucapel and Puren forts. The first one should be destroyed. Thus Valdivia would be attracted to that place, which the board of war had pointed out as the most appropriate to fight the battle.

One hundred indians assailed the garrison brandishing heavy maces to pull the horses down. Castilians repel them but they feel unable to reject another attack, they decide to abandon the fort and take refuge in Puren. Tucapel was burned and destroyed.

A Group of huincas from Puren marched to Concepcion to ask help to Valdivia who upon knowing about the native uprising but not believing that the araucanian rebellion was of grave important, went with only 50 cavalrymen and a force of 200 auxiliary picunches, going quickly to Quilacoya in aid of the Tucapel garrison.

A few days before the great confrontation, the Puren fort is attacked by a mapuche army divided in five corps.

Juan Gomez de Almagro, chief of the fort, ordered a charge of cavalry and infantry, the araucanians resisted them taking out squadrons with pikes, cudgels and clubs to pull them down.

Lautaro was training them telling that the Castilians were men who also got tired like them. They should not be even allowed to rest a minute in order to defeat them.

CHAPTER IX.

THE BATTLE OF TUCAPEL.

After the first mapuche attack to the Puren fort, Gómez de Almagro was enclosed with his garrison in the fort. By the afternoon he charged again but the mapuche handed over the field and withdrew without offering too much resistance.

Gómez de Almagro, sure of having defeated the mapuche, sent a messenger to inform his triumph to Valdivia who was on his way, to encourage them to continue their march.

The mapuche did not intercept the message since they wanted it to be read and thus attract him toward Tucapel.

In Quilacoya, Valdivia received the news of Juan Gomez de Almagro's victory in Puren fort and replied summoning him for December 25th in Tucapel.

But Lautaro intercepted the message and sent part of his warriors to Puren so that his adversaries may think they were about to be attacked, while he waited with the main body of his army for Valdivia in Tucapel

Gómez tried to leave with 14 cavalrymen on the night of the 24th to gather with the governor the next morning, but the night patrol captured an armed native marauding by the outskirts of the fort. When he was questioned, he confessed that a great army was in the environs ready to attack again, in view of that Gomez decided to stay that night in Puren, but when reconnoitering the outskirts of the fort the day after, he took notice of the trick plotted by the mapuche by means of distracting his forces, he left immediately in the help of Tucapel with the 14 cavalrymen that he thought to take the day before and some auxiliary natives. Several squadrons of mapuche attacked them without giving them time to dismount, an unequal combat for the few Spaniards that were fighting the whole day, they succeeded in breaking the siege by night and they went to La Imperial.

This epic of the 14 braves sent from Puren who bravely fought and many of whom died in combat, only a few managed to reach Concepcion and they have entered the History with the honourable title of "**The fourteen of the fame**".

Valdivia left toward Arauco, got to the fort two days after, stayed there forty eight hours, leaving that place with 35 men bound for Tucapel without finding on the way any sign of rebellion through the very wooded and uneven places they were crossing, because the yanaconas that portered the baggage and the auxiliary natives could not continue due to the awkward road, they decided to walk, the march was too slow, they rested in Labalebu by the night. The continued their march after hearing the Holy Mass the morning after. Valdivia sent forward six explorers to reconnoitre the way and inform him any novelty.

the hours passed, the night fell and the explorers were not coming back, the Governor was worried, but as it was December 24th he hoped to receive Gomez de Almagro with reinforcements from Puren, he decided to camp without taking notice of the enemy.

Spaniards spied in the far the smoking debris of the Tucapel fort at the daybreak of the 25th, but as they were getting close they neither saw any man nor heard the least noise.

Valdivia was suddenly attacked by platoon of natives emerging from the forests, without hesitation he divided his troops in three squads, ordering the first one to charge against the enemy, starting a tough combat which proved useless the impetus and the skill of the Spaniards before that wild crowd which was continuously renewing.

The Castilian offensive was resisted by a wall of spears firmly fastened in the ground; at last they achieved to advance scattering the field with death and desolation. After a fierce combat the mapuches retreated, they did not do it in disorder, but they were sliding through the gorges in search of refuge. But they returned to the charge with another squadron so numerous as that of the first one.

A second Spanish squad also replaced the former one that retreated with its horses and injured riders. The native archers that accompanied the Spanish hosts were scattering the sky with arrows which were stopped by the mapuche with their hardened leathered-shields. The mapuche were relieving, the second squadron for the third, for the fourth, for the fifth and so on.

The Valdivia's squads were only three, heat is exhausting, many Spaniards were badly injured, and they were insufficient to complete the three squads. The horses lost their spirits, the cavalrymen got tired, but they were hopeful about the Puren reinforcements.

Valdivia understood that they didn't have enough men left to resist, but in a great bravery impulse he decided to risk all in a last desperate attempt and ordered his men, he shouted with him on command:

- To the charge my soldiers! - Viva Spain! - Victory!-

They ghastly observed how the Caupolican's hosts fled in complete disorder.

Lautaro was waiting, heard the sound of the kulkul or trumpet three times, it was the signal to enter in combat.

-At last my hour has come!-

He approached haughtily to the mapuche ranks, advanced lightly until he reached a place between the two armies, and commanded a squadron formed by 200 mapuche anxious to fight, brandishing a pike they were imperturbably marching against the Spaniards.

Valdivia already had only nine soldiers with their arms tired and a priest, the horses battered and the rest of the Castilians were dead.

Those brave conquerors, discoverers of worlds, great strategists, should escape from that hell, the few Spaniards who followed Valdivia in the retreat were dying as they advanced, he was only accompanied by the priest Del Pozo, and they badly achieved to reach the town of Pilmaiquen, where the great toqui Caupolican was the master.

With the horse badly injured, he bogged down in a marsh, and a tired Valdivia since he was 55 years old, was captured by the mapuches.

He was taken to the presence of Lautaro and Caupolican, Valdivia face to face with Lautaro, spoke to him:

-Hello Alonso.-
-Hello Master.-

- I see that in the time you were with me you learned many of the tactics of war; indeed, you have known how to fight the battle as I have done it myself.-

- I had a good master in you, sir.-

- I beg you to allow me keeping my life and I swear you by my honour that we shall move away forever from these Arauco lands.-

Lautaro, Caupolicán and the rest of the toqui were listening to them but the old Leocato, warned them that they should not believe in their promises, that as soon as they let him go he would come back with many Castilians killing all the mapuches. Without finishing talking, he picked up a shell from the ground and started ripping up his flesh and offered it to the toquis for them to eat, while he was ripping him, the priest Bartolome del Pozo who was accompanying him, was confessing him and when his body was completely torn, Leocato shot his huge mace on the Governor's head following Caupolican's orders, thus they ended with the life of the Spanish warrior. Later on, they took out his heart and breaking it in pieces, the toquis ate it all, the head was stuck and walked in a pike, and then they emptied the skull and used it to drink chicha.

So it was the end of the troubled life of the first Governor of Chile, after having founded a very modest colony then, but it was destined to be a strong and haughty nation that remembers him with respect and veneration.

The news of Valdivia's death caused great consternation in the entire colony.

After the defeat of the Tucapel battle, the council of the city of Valdivia, its chief magistrate Lorenzo Bernal del Mercado who was deeply concerned by Pedro Valdivia's death, went ahead to take the first steps to name Francisco de Villagra, the late conqueror's trustworthy man, having him temporary Governor of Chile and putting Bernal del Mercado under his orders after he left his encomienda and the chief magistrate of the city of La Imperial was only naming him Captain General and Supreme Magistrate of his governorship. The news of Valdivia's death reached Santiago with a messenger asking help for Concepcion, and the council immediately named Captain General and Supreme Magistrate of the Nuevo Extremo to Rodrigo de Quiroga instead of opening his last will, starting this way a long period of arbitrariness. In order to find a solution, they decided to divide the governorship in two zones to the north and to the south of the Maule River. Rodrigo de Quiroga would be Governor in the north and his wife madam Ines de Suarez, Governess; Francisco de Villagra, in the south. The council of Santiago decided to open the sealed sheet containing the will of Pedro de Valdivia in which he appointed as his successor in case of death, firstly Jeronimo de Alderete, and as second successor in case of death of the first one to Francisco de Aguirre, but neither Francisco de Villagra nor Rodrigo de Quiroga figured as successors.

Jeronimo de Alderete was not recognized by the Royal Audience of Peru as heir to the Governorship of Chile, that's why he had to travel to Spain so that the Court may make his rights valid.

The King named him Governor of Chile and Captain General on October 17th 1554, stretching the limits of the Nueva Extremadura up to the Magellan Strait, entrusting him besides the reconnoitering of "the lands and populations that may be in the other part of said Strait" and the taking and possession "of the lands and provinces that fall into the demarcation of the Crown of Castilla, that is to say, up to the South Pole.

On his voyage of return, it took one year to reach Chile from Madrid to Santiago, when he came to take possession of his charge, Alderete one of the most worthy conquerors fell very ill, making a call in Panama, in the island of Tobago. Harmed by the yellow fever, he died without achieving to take the position which the King had granted him.

In the will that named Jeronimo de Alderete, he was absent in Spain, not knowing yet about his death, and the second heir Francisco de Aguirre whom was in Tucuman, it was agreed by the south to name Francisco de Villagra as his legitimate heir. Francisco de Aguirre, in Tucumán, was informed about these facts by his friends of La Serena; he immediately went to that city, which received him as Captain General and Supreme Magistrate. He communicated this election to Santiago, stating that the troops under his command were willing to support him in this charge, which otherwise belonged to him by right in virtue of Valdivia's testament.

The Council of Santiago did not agree with the threat, that's why Aguirre sent his son Hernando with part of his troops, which were disarmed in Santiago. In order to settle this situation, the council of Santiago submitted it to an arbitrable verdict by two lawyers who lived in Santiago, the advisers don Alonso de las Peñas and Julian Gutierrez de Altamirano. Villagra accepted to be subject to the arbitrable verdict by the advisers but Aguirre rejected it, distrusting the decisions that Santiago may take. Finally, the conflict was solved when a petition was sent to La Audiencia de Lima, which determined that the councils should take the command for six months, until the Viceroy may appoint a new Governor, and if the deadline expired, Villagra would be the Governor, staying meanwhile in charge of the southern army. Aguirre ignored the verdict, but he knew that his forces were not enough to defeat Villagra if there were a confrontation, that's why he unwillingly accepted it.

After Villagra knew his appointment as Captain General and Supreme Magistrate by the councils of the three cities that he was visiting, the only fortified towns which had not been abandoned by the Spaniards. Villagra marched toward the city of Valdivia, continued with 80 soldiers until La Imperial and from there to Concepcion, wherein the mapuches razed the fields, took the livestock and plundered the houses.

The panic in the south by the defeat of Tucapel and the afraid of being attacked by the araucanians were followed by the decision of Villagra to depopulate Concepcion, starting the flight of its inhabitants to Santiago, leaving their belongings in complete disorder and anarchy, causing disputes with the administration in the capital .

Lautaro anxious to expel the Spaniards from entire Chile prepared his troops to march on Concepcion, asking himself:

- Will Guakolda be there, will she remember me yet? Although, in this moment the most important thing for me is that before beginning the attack to the city, send an emissary to find her and that he may bring her to me safe and sound. -

Upon his return, the emissary talked to Lautaro:

- Great toqui, there are no humans beings there in the city, it is empty. -

- Good, I will be able to burn it without fear of Guakolda's being there, even though I will continue his search wherever she is and, at last I will find her. -

Lautaro, in charge of a legion of araucanians, then passed to the Biobio river as an exterminator on the way to Concepcion where they looted and burnt its houses, firing the entire city, Lautaro on the top of hill was watching the destruction, yelling with contentment and speaking in mapudugun his language, he said he was he who would finish with Spaniards, throwing them away from the entire Araucania.

Villagra knew the facts and went in campaign in charge of a detachment with three arms, since it incorporated six small canons or culebrinas, the first ones which were used in the country. Lautaro whose plan consisted in making the spaniard to leave to open field, he let them advance until the Chibilonco valley where the road which continues to the south, they climbed it by the serrania of Marigüeñu that interrupts the region stretching until Concepcion, between the coast and the sea ranges. Villagra suspicious, before starting the climbing, sent a patrol of 30 men in charge of Alonso de Reinoso, but many a group of natives attacked the outpost, which had to stand back fighting very hard until it joined with the main body of the troops.

Lieutenant Reinoso could verify that the natives drew back, informing about it to his captain:

- Sir, the Indians are withdrawing toward the summit of the hill of Marigüñu.-

Villagra got up with his army chasing the numerous groups which had faced that of Reinoso. At the summit, he deployed his soldiers so that they could resist the charge of the mapuches, placing there his artillery.

In that place, the battle of Marigüenu took place on February 26th 1554, that in the presence of the proximity of the forces, Villagra had to accept the combat in a plain closed to the east by an impenetrable forest and cut on the other side by the sea.

Lautaro had strategically chosen this site to locate their men ambushed in the woods, so that to the extent that Villagra climbed the mountain, the mapuches closed them in the rearguard. Just like in Tucapel they attacked them again and they were replaced by others in order that they rest and may be able to attack again.

Villagra at the head of his army was always fighting in the first rank, when the mapuches took notice of him centered all of his efforts to attack him, until they could spear him and throw him away from his horse, but one of the soldiers managed to rescue him, being able to return to his fighting post, bleeding and badly injured. At the end of eight hours of ceaseless combat, the spaniards due to heat, thirst, dust and weariness have just got weak, taking advantage of the appropriate moment, the leader Lautaro rushed at the spaniards with all his reserves whole, Villagra saw the great danger and played retreat toward Concepcion and, upon seeing it destroyed, they continued to Santiago. The tragic balance of the battle was the death of two thirds of the Spanish army.

Villagra come to Santiago to settle his situation, compelled Rodrigo de Quiroga to leave his command. At the same time, Francisco de Aguirre was returning to Chile from Tucuman, encouraged by his son:

- Father you should claim what is yours by right, go to Santiago and demand your second place in don Francisco de Valdivia's testament and, as we know that don Jeronimo de Alderete is negotiating in Spain without knowing whether he will return, you would be the first in the order. -

- You are right my dear Hernando, even though there are rumours that don Jeronimo de Alderete is dead, it is not very sure but if it were so, I will myself snatch from usurper Villagra what does not belong to him. -.

After going into great competence they entered into a fight between the two rivals, but since Aguirre did not have any support, Villagra was victorious.

In the extreme south there were no news about the destruction of Concepcion nor the defeat of Marigüeño.

In the city of La Imperial the Governor's cousin, Pedro de Villagra had stayed and he had had Guakolda come here from Concepcion, before the disaster. Don Pedro fortified the city and seized the initiative of organizing several reconnoitering expeditions in the south to be able to assault and destroy several mapuche forts from the surroundings.

The city of Valdivia was still, since the huilliches lived in perfect harmony with the Spaniards.

Pedro de Villagra decided to travel to Angol, rebuilt by the spaniards, Guakolda accompanies him together with his other servants. A year later she was sent to Concepcion, which the Spaniards were trying to rebuild by orders coming from Peru.

Villagra had sent part of his servants to Concepcion, because he had in mind to settle there when it may be entirely rebuilt.

Meanwhile, the problem of the command still provoked upheavals and disagreements in Santiago. Aguirre kept reiterating to menacingly put into effect by force Valvidivia's testament that the town council was waiting for the resolution from Peru, which at last came on February 13th 1555. The Audiencia had decided to cancel any naming of successors made by Pedro de Valdivia and decided that the authority would pass to the councils. Aguirre in disagreement was opposing, but at last he unwillingly delivered the command, unlike Villagra that delivered it with responsibility and by his own will.

The agreement of the Audiencia de Lima was complemented by the order of discharging two thirds of the Spanish forces in Chile; this caused disputes, which were immediately noticed by the mapuches. Although later the Audiencia aware of the dissensions caused by the wrong agreement, rectified its error by naming Francisco de Villagra Corregidor (Chief Magistrate) and Justicia Mayor (High Judge) of Chile, though this was made in a very serious moment since Lautaro had accomplished to gather a great many army of mapuche and promoacaes.

Lautaro thought that his fight for the freedom of his people would be in vain if they allowed the Spaniards to occupy their lands again. He would have to expel the invaders from the mouth of the Biobio River. Taking advantage of the anarchy that had caused the Lima's resolution among the Spaniards, Caupolican was moving toward the south against La Imperial and Valdivia cities. Lautaro was preparing two campaigns against Santiago with the hope of stirring up a revolt among the picunches and seize the capital with their help, even though he had to firstly detroy other cities such as Los Confines (Angol) in the Araucania, at the foot of the range of Nahuelbuta, he defeated again the Spaniards wherein its inhabitants fled all together.

Lautaro advanced toward Concepcion that had been populated again a month ago. Its inhabitants saw one morning in great horror that stockades of mapuche lancers and archers were raising in front of the walls of their city threateningly. Spanish soldiers were desperately attacking them, but the mapuches kept advancing with their fierce shouts of war willing to defeat or die.

Panic seized the Spaniards, their captains ordered to play retreat, fleeing by sea and land, abandoning everything.

Those who fled by sea in the only ship anchored in the bay achieved to escape, Guakolda was among them, those who did it by land had worst luck, that they were destroyed by Lautaro's warriors to cut their fleeing. Only a small group of soldiers accomplished to break the siege and continue toward the north.

A Messenger told Lautaro that he had seen Guakolda among the ship's passengers.

- Guakolda is safe and sound! I can now destroy this damned city that must disappear. -

Meanwhile Caupolican kept advancing with his hosts by the south, Lautaro was crossing the Maule and was marching on Santiago, with the hope of raising the picunche and free the country with their help.

When it was known in Santiago that Lautaro kept advancing into the capital, Spaniards' panic was indescribable, they thought about a retreat to La Serena or a return to Peru as well.

In order to stop the advance of the araucanian hosts, Governor upon being sick, sent his son Pedro de Villagra the "Young".

Lautaro's great army was being decimated by a typhus epidemic which caused the death of almost the entire ill population; neither had they achieved to have the adhesion of the picunches, who almost all of them were voluntarily subject to the Spaniards. His great army of 400.000 warriors was reduced to only 800 men with whom he advanced toward Santiago.

The confrontation took place on the Banks of Malaquito River and at the beginning it was favourable to Lautaro, but the inclemency of the winter compelled them to suspend the campaign until the springtime that would undertake it again with new energies.

Lautaro accomplished to gather new forces with which he directly marched to the capital. He camped again by the Malaquito river, but upon seeing him surrounded by the Spaniards, began the march and established the camp in Peteroa, chosen place to concentrate his forces which were defended by the front and the flanks.

The Corregidor knew where the camp was by means of some allied natives, they had to climb a mountain at the height of the highland guided by picunche indians, night fell and they took refuge between the underbrush and at the daybreak of April 1st 1557 they attacked the mapuches, Francisco de Villagra already recovered from his illness, and his cousin Pedro de Villagra with a few auxiliaries marched guided by an Indian traitor to the ruca where Lautaro was sleeping, who upon seeing him surprised defended himself bravely, but at last he was killed after a 5 hour fight until the Spaniards succeeded in defeating the mapuches. His sectioned head was exposed many days in a pike in the main Squire of Santiago where Guakolda wept for him bitterly for a very long time, the mapuche hero who was to simbolize one day the patriotic feeling of the new people.

The spaniards thought that with his death at last finished the mapuche resistance, but the fight would have to last for more than three centuries.

CHAPTER X.
GARCÍA HURTADO DE MENDOZA.

Francisco Villagra did not enjoy so much time his success in Peteroa since the viceroy Andres Hurtado de Mendoza, marquis of Cañete, named as new Governor his son don Garcia Hurtado de Mendoza y Manrique, a 22 year-old haughty young, who signed "Don Garcia de Mendoza" that belonged by birth to the haughty castilian nobility. He had an education which used to be given to very religious noblemen with an absolute loyalty to the king, very indifferent to money matters, but at the same time he was violent, reckless and abusive.

With his 22 years old, he showed a brilliant background, fought for the emperor Charles V in Italy and in the Low Countries, acquiring great militay experience.

The new Gobernor set down near La Serena, accompanied by a brilliant entourage of ladies and gentlemen. Among these came poet Alonso de Ercilla and the german noble Pedro Lisperguer or Peter Leisperberger descendant to the ancient Saxon-Wittenberg house and former page of emperor Charles V, and the jew-polish Bartholomaüs Blümlein from plebeian origins, both of them translated into spanish their names like: Pedro Lisperguer and Bartolome Flores who married the daughter of inca Tala Canta, madam Elvira de Talagante.

Besides, he brought a great arsenal of arms which supplied the conquerors' armies for a very long time, came accompanied by 500 men that formed the greatest military core that had stepped on in Chile. He brought some cannons and harquebuses, these latter needed, because of their weight, to be supported in a forked post or in a tree, which immobilized the harquebusier, it was needed to burn the wick which was attached to the cannon's ear.

So far, the spanish soldier's offensive arms were the pikes having almost three meters long, made of ash tree wood finished in an iron point that the rider sharpened with straps to the horse's chest and to the saddletree to give it more strength and the soldier used it as the modern bayonet, though the usage of the sword was the arm most widely used by the cavalry. They also used axes for the battle and clubs.

His father the viceroy had charged him with the pacifying of Chile.

Francisco de Aguirre had come from his conquest of Tucuman and he made them proclaiming him as Governor in the city of La Serena, disobeying Villagra's authority. The young Governor as his first political measure to end the discord, on his way through Coquimbo, ordered that Villagra who was in Santiago and Aguirre in La Serena and continued disputing the power, were imprisoned and sent to Lima in one his ships wherein the Real Audience will judge them. Villagra was accused of having assumed the command by force and having withdrawn gold from the treasury to undertake the defence of the South. At last, he was absolved at the beginning of March 1559.

By Hurtado de Mendoza's mandate that had more resources than Valdivia had had, pilot Juan de Ladrillero and Francisco Cortes Ojea set sails with two small ships disposed to a new reconnoitering of the Strait. Thrown (blown) by Northern winds, they sighted the Chiloe and Guaitecas archipelagos; but due to a dreadful storm in the gulf of Penas, the ships separated. Cortes' ship disappeared between the islands and channels of the western coast of the, reaching parallel 52° 50' he came back to North without finding the mouth of the Strait.

Meanwhile, Ladrillero's ship was exploring the channels reaching at last the Strait, sailing it until near the eastern mouth, taking possession of the Strait of Magellan in 1557, in the name of the King and the Governor of Chile.

Ladrillero showed the possibility of sailing the Strait of Magellan in both directions with this voyage.

The Crown kept the explorations of the intrepid Ladrillero top secret in order to avoid that pirates hostile to Spain may use this route to attack the Pacific's possessions.

Also by orders of Don Garcia, the ultra cordillera region of Cuyo was explored by captain Pedro del Castillo, whom crossing the Andes by Uspallata without any resistance from the indians, founded the city of Mendoza and San Juan in 1561.

The new Governor faced an unsolved problema. Soldiers brought from Peru were coming with the sure hope of receiving lands and indians to work them, and when not being available any of them, thought of leaving the old encomiendas of Concepcion vacant, which caused the protests of the encomenderos, therefore the city was populated again for the third time by the new encomenderos coming from Peru.

Don García directly proceeded toward Concepcion and started a campaign against the mapuche in the Araucania, going by sea landed in the island of Quiriquina with wretched climate and supply conditions. He had sent by land the cavalry under the command of don Luis de Toledo. García made the mistake of omiting in his expedition the veteran captains who accompanied Pedro de Valdivia, great connoisseurs of the land and the indians'attacks. He had them built the Fort of San Luis, where the spaniards had to work alone with great efforts since they had refrained from taking the auxiliary natives. Without having finished the fort, they were surprised by three great squadrons of mapuches led by toqui Caupolican who was massively attacking them with excessive rage, bearing spears, shields and swords that they had picked up from the defeat of the Spaniards, with which the struggle was almost levelled. The advantage of these was the cannons, the harquebusiers and the wall stone throwers.

The battle in the fort of San Luis threatened to be a second Tucapel. The few men that had stayed in the ships came in their help, but they were still being very few, the Governor inexperienced to fight the indians immediately realized the kind of enemies he was facing up to. At last, the reinforcements came by land gathering in Arauco; 600 Spaniards, 4.000 auxiliary natives and 1.000 horses, the greatest army that had so far been operated in Chile.

The araucanians withdrew and don Garcia decided to cross the Biobío and continue to the South, thinking that he can pacify the region. However, he had to face again the Caupolican's mapuche armies, who came into clash, starting the battle of Lagunillas, where Rodrigo de Quiroga showed his bravery to save many soldiers. The combat ended without vanquishers or defeated but Galvarino was made prisoner, example of araucanians' matchless courage. The Governor ordered that they should cut off both of his hands that Galvarino, with great fortitude, placed his left han on the trunk in which it should be cut it off, when it was cut without showing signs of pains he put his right hand, thinking that he also had to put his neck, he knelt down in a cutting position.

The Governor said to him that he may go, his life was pardoned and he moved away swearing take revenge.

Rared the araucanians before Galvarino's punishment, they started to battle again in the region named Millarapue, a very propitious valley for making easier the ambushes. The fight lasted from the dawn until the two hours in the afternoon with the entire defeat of the mapuche. Don Garcia finished off the battle making thirty chieftains hanged whom have been taken prisoners, among them was Galvarino who fought in the first rank although not having hands. He was condemned as the other chieftains to be hanged from a tree, but the poet don Alonso de Ercilla was sorry for him and tried to save him alleging that he had seen him to pass to the spaniards' side, Galvarino said to him with arrogance:

-I don't want the Spaniards to spare my life -.

Alonso de Ercilla immortalized in his famous book "Araucana" the cruel sacrifice and the haughty and exemplary behaviour of Galvarino.

The Spaniards hurried to hang him because he had such a degree of pride.

After the atrocities done by don Garcia with the mapuches, the mystic Gil Gonzalez de San Nicolas was in charge to let the Council of Indies to know about.

After these confrontations, Hutado de Mendoza founded the fortress of Cañete and continued toward the unexplored lands of the south, reaching until Reloncavi's gulf where he discovered the Chiloe archipelago.

While the spaniards were exploring the south, as soon as Caupolican saw that Hurtado de Mendoza had divided his forces among the Tucapel fort, the once again populated Concepcion and the recently founded city of Cañete de la Frontera, projected an attack to the fort of Cañete, but betrayed by an indian named Andresillo whom warned the chief of the Squire, thus being the attack a failure since that upon warning the spanish soldiers about the imminent attack they make them flee from the fortress.

At once the same Andresillo took the spaniards to toqui Caupolican' ruca where he was taken prisoner and led to Cañete.

The great toqui wanted to parley, but the spaniards did not trust his promises and captain Alonso de Reinoso, chief of Cañete' Squire, condemned him to die impaled. This cruel punishment consisted of seating the victim over a stake finished in point, attached to a scaffold, Caupolican was raised in chains to it, when the executioner that was a negroe slave closed to him, Caupolican kicked him to the ground badly injured. The Spaniards succeeded in seating him over the sharpened stake and without showing any sign of pain he endured the ghastly agony during many hours until the stake crossed him from top to bottom, while one of his wives Fresia was crying before the toqui.

Caupolican's punishment in which don Garcia did not take part, horrified many contemporaries like don Alonso de Ercilla who exalted him in his famous book "La Araucana".

This way the brave Araucanian toqui died in 1558, symbol of an indomitable race with great strength and daring in defence of his land the Auracania from the Spanish conquest.

After Caupolican' death, Garcia Hurtado believed that at last he had subdued the mapuche people by terror, but in fact Caupolican's death gave them more impetus to organize guerrilla warfare whereby there wasn't any day that some yanacona or encomendero would die in the hands of the mapuches.

When the number of dead yanaconas was already 400 in addition to a score of disappeared or dead Spaniards, the Governor was convinced that he was absolutely wrong, at once ordered to abandon the Tucapel fort and transfer it to Cañete. While in Quiapo, the mapuche decided to continue the Lautaro's tactics, building an admirable fort which constantly challenged Hurtado de Mendoza's armies who attacked the fort in 1558, whose existence obstructed the communications among his troops, with an army of 300 Spaniards, several auxiliary indians and two small cannons or culverin that were useless. Later on, he would achieve to surprise the mapuche rearguard obtaining this way a hard victory and sending to hang more than 100 mapuches as punishment.

Starting Garcia Hurtado to order the government of the colony, the Spanish domination was definitively settled to the north of Biobío and in the Cuyo region. The Spanish population increased and the family life started to regularize with the arrival of Spanish women. The indigence of the first times changed into a bearable poverty. While being busy with all of these duties, he knew that Francisco de Villagra was designated Governor of Chile by the King of Spain Philip II on December 20th 1558, assuming the charge in 1561.

The cause of this attitude taken by the King could be found in the viceroy's and his son don Garcia's authoritarian behaviour, attitude which led them to enmity with many conquerors, whose complaints constantly reached to Spain. Also on the other side, the King had seen the designation of don Garcia for the government of Chile as an act of favouritism by the side of the Viceroy of Peru.

García Hurtado without waiting the arrival of Villagra, got on board to Peru wherein the residence judgment was awaiting for him, it was an ancient practice of Castille's legislation that every Spanish official, viceroy, governor, corregidor, etc., at the end of his mandate should be responsible for his conduct and the complaints against him because of the management of the King's funds and of the branches of the administration.

The sovereign, bearing in mind his services, approved his conduct and a few years later, he granted him the honourable and high charge of Viceroy of Peru.

It can be said that with the government of Garcia Hurtado de Mendoza terminated the Conquest, although the truth is that the lands of the Arauco were never subjugated by the Spaniards.

On beginning his new mandate, Francisco de Villagra reorganized the regulations on the labour in the mines and canceled the encomiendas that Garcia had granted in Concepcion to his friends and companions.

When he was going to Cañete in order to renew the military actions, the Governor got sick. He was only 50 years, but afflicted by the gout, disease affecting the joints, was unable to walk, assumed his duties and was being carried in stretcher to La Imperial and then to Angol where he arrived at on March 1565. Once in Concepcion being laid down in his bed, he organized the troops that under the command of his son Pedro "The Young" would be facing the mapuches. The military campaigns proved to be negative for the Spaniards, whom were defeated in Catirai and forced to depopulate Cañete. His last years were characterized by the continuous defeats of Arauco.

He organized a new expedition, but his exhausted body got sick. Besides, he suffered in this war the death of his son Pedro "The Young", which got worse his mental and physical condition. He appointed his cousin Pedro de Villagra for the continuing of the campaign, granting him later the title of Governor-Interim thanks to a power granted by the Viceroy.

The six cities of the South willingly received Pedro de Villagra as Governor-Interim, whereas Rodrigo de Quiroga's followers in Santiago refused to accept him, which turned into evident hostilities when Villagra decided to regulate the labour of the indians protecting them, which arose general discontent among the encomenderos.

The attempts of political agitation were alarming and Villagra could not prevent them since in Santiago nothing was done to help him, there were signs of general rebellion in La Imperial and in Valdivia, which Villagra knew how to dominate at last. All these reflected the fight of interests between Villagra's policy and the encomenderos.

The death of the Viceroy Conde de Nieva worsened even more Villagra's situation since he was the Viceroy's protégé. The disturbances in the cities precipitated his fall with the triumph of Rodrigo de Quiroga, whom was illegally proclaimed Governor.

Pedro de Villagra died in Lima, bequeathing the indians of his Parinacocha encomienda.

The fight with the mapuches continued, they built a fort which intercepted the communications between the cities South of Angol and Concepcion. The skirmishes were now directed by the chieftain Loble and attacked and caused casualties among the Spaniards that every time were reducing the defences of Concepcion and Angol defended by Bernal del Mercado in charge of only 80 men, it was defined as one of the greatest Spanish victories in Arauco's land. The mapuches lost more than 1.000 warriors besides his toqui Illangulien. But they continued attacking and harassing the Spaniards, they never submitted nor accepted to follow the fate of the Northern Indians compelled to servitude by the Spanish encomenderos.

The posesión of Chile costed Spain in soldiers and money more than the rest of America.

At the end of the XVI Century, the first religious communities were established in Chile, founding houses or monasteries in all the cities.

The "mercedarians" were the first to come to the country, serving as chaplains at the beginning of the conquest and only later they founded convents.

The dominicans and the franciscans were the first to found convents and had some illustrious monks, it may be mentioned among them the franciscan Diego de Medellin, who ruled the Santiago's diocese at the end of the Century mentioned above.

The dominicans founded a school-university which would later become Pontifical University.

The jesuits, like the augustinians, arrived in 1593 and founded schools and colleges. The arrival of the Augustinians caused heavy incidents with the other religious orders, which even flooded and burned his convent.

In addition to teaching, they devoted to preach and evangelize the indians in their own language. One of them, the famous father Luis de

Valdivia, the rector of the Company of Jesus, composed a grammar and a dictionary of the language of the country, also the fathers Ovalle and Rosales distinguished as historians.

The order attained to own rich estates, houses, warehouses, and a great deal of slaves, they had all these because of many bequests and donations.

All these so rapid outcomes were due to the cultural superiority over the rest of the clergy, its harsh organization and discipline, its missionary activities preaching and confessing, its colleges and schools and its great capacity of progressive and active administrators. Its main school in Santiago was that of San Miguel and its most remarkable church, that of La Compañía.

As far as nuns are concerned, the first nuns to settle were the "clarisas" and the Augustinians.

The successors pertaining to the first conquerors were: Rodrigo de Quiroga who subdued Chiloé and founded the city of Castro; Lorenzo Bernal del Mercado who had some triumphs over the mapuches; Martín Ruiz de Gamboa , Rodrigo de Quiroga's son-in-law, who easily subdued the grand island of the Chiloe archipelago, founded the city of Chillan.

They were following; Melchor Bravo de Saravia, Alonso de Sotomayor who estimated that the pacification could not be made whilst there were not a numerous line army instead of the neighbours' and colonists' contingents helped by auxiliary indians, but he did not get anything from the Spanish State, in fact. One part of the clergy thought it possible to pacify the Indians by means of the preaching but it did not work out in the araucanians, it thus was considered in Peru that Chile was a "grave for Spaniards".

Martín García Oñez de Loyola successor to Sotomayor founded the city of Santa Cruz near the confluence of the Bibío. Upon being Oñez de Loyola in La Imperial with his forces gathered on December 21st 1598, he received news that the Longotoro fortalice in Puren had been attacked and exterminated the contingents. He undertook a journey through the Araucania accompanied by three religious, 60 military men, 300 yanaconas and some servants; they camped by night near Angol in the Curalaba place.

He had been warned about the danger by the evident signs of rebellion and that the chieftains Anganamon and Pelantaru were in charge of the huilliche natives.

He decided to camp in Curalaba on the banks of Lumaco river in two days' journey, disregarding any measure of precaution for the advance in enemy territory, he did not post guards nor reconnoitered the surroundings and allowed his people to sleep calmly. That same night, three native squadrons led by Anganamon, Pelantaru and Gauiquimilla secretly came near the spanish camp and hope for the dawn to come. When the reveille was played, the natives in charge of chieftain Pelantaru fell upon the camp, turning it in a wild massacre. Onez de Loyola was beheaded along with his captains and 48 soldiers, dying the whole of the auxiliary yaconas. This event marked the end of the Spanish warlike superiority, taking in the future new strategies for the pacification of the Araucania.

As a consequence of the so called Curalaba Disaster, almost all cities and forts to the South of Bibio River ended being abandoned by the conquerors, except for that of Castro.

The period of the Colony of Chile would begin after these events.

CHAPTER XI.

THE COLONY.

At the beginning of the colonial period, Chile's territory was extended from Copiapo to the North, as South frontier the Biobío River until the Strait of Magellan and, in line one hundred leagues parallel to the coast took the Tucuman and Cuyo transandean provinces and almost the entire Patagonia. These provinces were only forming part of Chile until 1563 that they were annexed to the Viceroyalty of Mar del Plata.

During the first years of the conquest, Chile was a Governorship until 1554 that the emperor Charles V gave it the denomination of Kingdom of Chile with the purpose of proclaiming king of this distant country to his son Prince Philip in order to ease his marriage to Mary Tudor heiress to the throne of England.

The end of the XVI Century and the beginning of XVII was a time of disasters for Chile, the years between 1560 and 1600 were a sucession of disasters for the conquerors: the Arauco war, its bad governors, its scandals of all kind, epidemics, earthquakes, and attacks of english and dutch privateers.

The reigns of Charles V and that of Philip II during the XVI century marked the period of Spanish preponderance, almost a century during which the Spanish empire was the first western power so much by his European dominions as by those she had in America, it was said: "When Spain is moving, the world is trembling" and "The sun is not rising in the dominions of the King of Spain".

On the other hand, its numerous dominions only gave it a more seeming power than a real one, because they did not form only one surface but they were scattered in Europe, Asia and America, separated among them by the distances, the variety of races, culture and economic development. In Spain itself nearly one million Moorish were anti-catholic by beliefs and by heart. The religious reformation had left a similar problem in the Low Countries. Because of this, it was notorious the lack of moral and religious unity.

Charles V and Philip II kept the Spanish preponderance but they weakened Spain dragging it into wars that only called forth losses of lives and wealth, in such a way that both monarchs lived begging money to the courts, mortgaging the future remittances from America, delivering to foreign capitalists the mines of Spain, or running into debt with the german bankers, the Függer and the Welser.

At the end of the reign of Philip II, it begins to be felt the decline: the english burned with impunity the port of Cadiz in 1596 and the State was terribly indebted, it was only kept the army and its external prestige.

The decline of the XVII century took place under the reigns of the last sovereigns of the House of Austria, Philip IV, Charles II and Philip III, who expelled the moorish for religious and internal security motives, depriving the kingdom of half a million farmers who cultivated the lands of the southern high nobility.

One of the factors of the Spanish decline is the mental illness of some sovereigns and the mental weakness of others.

The illness started with the grandfather and the father of Isabella the Catholic. The defect had remained hidden in her but it did not delay to be violently shown in her sons madam Juana la Loca and prince don Juan.

Emperor Charles V fought against the protestants and the advances of the Turkish Empire, he ended by abdicating leaving the Empire to his brother Fernando, and Spain, the Low Countries and the Spanish America to his son Philip II, who did not know to take advantage of the great generals that he had, such as don Juan de Austria, the duke of Alba, Alejandro Farnesio and others, and statesmen such as Antonio Perez, Granvella, his sister Margarita, he distrusted everybody and badly paid their services. As far as descent is concerned, his son prince Charles became crazy and he had to be confined, dying soon after. His other son, Philip III succeeded to the throne but he was unable to rule. Charles II the bewitched was epileptic and idiot and died without descent. The House of Austria in Spain ended with him.

These centuries were also of decline for Chile.

A great earthquake destroyed the city of Concepcion on February 8th ,1570. People walking in the streets did not know what to do, they believed that the world was ending because they saw black water flowing from the gaps of the land and the odour similar to bad sulphur which seemed something coming from the hell, then the sea waves came followed by a big tsunami which flooded most of the city, leaving a great deal of dead fishes.

In those times, travelling between Callao and Valparaiso took at least three months, more or less the double of time that it was taken in the journey between Valparaiso and Callao. This delay was due to the fact that sailors skirted the coasts, so that when coming from Peru they should yield the resistance of the southern winds and of the stream which is called today Humboldt current.

Sailor Juan Fernandez set sail for Chile in 1574 following his friend pilot Hernando Lamero's advice that had already travelled on occasions to the Solomon Islands, gaining great experience in relation to winds and currents. Fernandez left the route so far followed, headed for the west and then for the south by high sea with which he achieved to arrive his destination in only thirty days taking advantage of the Humboldt current. On his way, he discovered an archipelago in front of Valparaiso, which was called after his name, Juan Fernandez.

One morning, he went aground on an unknown island and was amazed by exotic vegetation of ferns and autochthonous plants, he then realizad that they were three islands which he called: Santa Clara, Más a Tierra y Más Afuera.

The island of Más a Tierra became famous because of the character that inhabited it. In Robinson Crusoe's gifted work is told the abandonment of the Scottish sailor Alexander Selkirk by a privateer called Stradling.

At present, the islands "Más a Tierra" and "Más Afuera" are respectively called with the names of Robinson Crusoe and Alexander Selkirk.

With this new route, the sailor Juan Fernandez greatly contributed to the progress of the navigation and the commerce in the Pacific coasts.

Years later, Fernandez came back to the islands named after him and left there some goats which were breeding, which would serve for the privateers and pirates to feast.

Chile, due to the strategic situation of the Strait of Magellan and to the great extension of its coasts, was exposed to suffer raids and attacks of the privateers and pirates from the powers hostile to Spain, such as: England and Holland.

The plundering to which they were devoted made them fear to be stripped of their booty so that they were often hiding under the ground their treasures with the hope of coming back for them some day.

It was called privateer to the sailor carrying out his adventures authorized by his government, and pirate the one who did it on his own will.

The English privateer Francis Drake, whose purpose was to sell negroes, kill Spaniards and ransack the ships loading gold, in charge of five ships penetrated the Strait of Magellan, losing four of his ships, continued with the only one he had "The Pelican" by the Chilean coast until Valparaiso, continued toward La Serena and on being repelled, he went on to Peru. After ransacking Arica, he got through Callao taking hold of a ship ready to sail with a shipment of hides and more than one million and a half gold ducats, which he ransacked and burned, went to the Northern coasts where he seized valuable spoils, reached beyond the bayo f San Francisco of California, from there he was bound for the Moluccas and Java, in order to cross the Indian ocean and turn the Cape of Good Hope, reaching England at last in 1580 after having had a voyage of three years of navigation and having gone on the second journey around the world. The riches that the privateer requisitioned yielded for the enterprise a considerable profit estimated in fifteen times the invested capital.

Queen Elizabeth of England rewarded him by bestowing him Sir and the people saw Drake as a national hero.

The English pirate Bartolome paid a devastating visit to Chile in the Coquimbo bay, wherein its inhabitants fled from La Serena upon seeing him, the corregidor only stayed to deal with him, whom demanded a payment of 100.000 pesos as ransom for the city. As the neighbours did not have where to get the money from and the delivering was delaying, Sharp thought he was being cheated so that they may attack him by surprise, he decided to withdraw after previously ransack the city, taking whatever of worth he found and he then burned the city. Coquimbo's inhabitants terrorized by Sharp, to whom they called "charqui", give rise to the saying: "charqui came to Coquimbo" meaning an unexpected and not so pleasant visit.

Later on, Sharp headed for the Juan Fernandez Islands and after passed to the Atlantic through the Strait of Magellan.

The unfortunate city of La Serena was again attacked by the pirate Davis who after several rains through the Pacific coasts, with two ships and 80 sailors between English and French, were presented in the Coquimbo bay.

Neighbors went out to stop the landing but they were defeated, which allowed the invaders to reach until La Serena, wherein the inhabitants encircled them, having to trench themselves for more than thirty hours in the church and convent of San Francisco. At last, they undertook the retreat of the Pacific by the route of Cape Horn.

The viceroy of Peru Francisco de Toledo gathered with Pedro de Sarmiento de Gamboa:

- Due to the raids of the privateer Drake, I have determined captain Sarmiento to send from Callao an expedition with the purpose of closing that road to the privateers, and once we study the adjacent regions to found towns.-

- Your Highness, you are right with your determinations. On my side, I would be delighted to be able to be the chief of the squadron, even though some dishonest people have blamed me of being always chased by misfortune, which some call "mal fario" (bad luck), questioning my capacity and boldness.-

- Don't talk about it any more, prepare the ships and go to the channels region and, sailing the Strait, try with your misfortune, stumble upon the privateers to face them without being defeated by them.-

Pedro de Sarmiento de Gamboa's misfortune proved not to be a groundless rumour since the five ships were separated forever by the tempests. That of Sarmiento's achieved to cross the Strait and was headed for Spain at once, where Philip II entrusted the Viceroy a new expedition to fortify the Strait, but upon returning to Chile the quarrels between the crew and the tempests turned the navigation a torture. One of the ships bearing implements and foods was displaced by the currents outsider the Strait, by which Sarmiento arranged that one of the expedition went by land skirting the coast until they reached it. 100 soldiers departed in charge of Sarmiento himself that went through more than 80 leagues, standing the attacks of the Indians. The company's fatigue was such that Sarmiento had to go alone until find help for his men. In spite of all the setbacks, two cities could be founded, one on the Northern bank of the western mouth; and the other, in the Brunswick peninsula. They were called "Nombre de Jesus" and "Rey don Felipe". These two cities founded by Sarmiento, separated between them and without natural resources of any kind had an unfortunate end because their inhabitants died by hunger and by cold, excepting one who was rescued from the island Nombre de Jesus that the privateer Tomas Cavendish after having entered in the Strait sighted some bonfires lighted by the 15 men and the three women who were still alive. Taking advantage of the favourable wind, the privateer only set on board one of them named Tome Hernandez, leaving the rest of them to perish.

The sinister Nombre de Jesus was called Port of Hunger.

When Sarmiento was on board his ship, he was getting ready to visit the unfortunate cities to take them resources, a great tempest arose which threw his ship to the Atlantic. He came back to Rio de Janeiro to organize again the succours of the abandoned. When he achieved to provision his ship, a storm threw her against the coast near Bahia, saving herself miraculously.

He continued in his endeavour and achieved to equip a new ship, in which he had to face a mutiny of his sailors after saving them from another violent tempest.

Following with the misfortune of Sarmiento; he was taken prisoner by the English privateers of Sir Walter Raleigh and taken to England where he gained the sympathy of Sir Walter and that of the Queen Isabella, who kept a conversation in Latin with him for more than an hour and a half, which allowed him a gift of one thousands ducats and a safe-conduct for going back to Chile. Later on, he passed to France where he was captured by the Huguenots who kept him in captivity for years. At last, he was rescued by Philip II.

Governor Rodrigo de Quiroga had to face another great earthquake. On December 16th 1575, five cities were half destroyed: La Imperial, followed by the earthquake with a big tsunami, in which 100 Indians were drowned; Villarica, Osorno, Castro and Valdivia, and the tsunami caused that two ships were foundered with their crew.

Philip II, due to the spoliation by the English pirates, thought of the need of fortifying Chile's defences sending to this colony a dynamic and energetic man. Because of it, he sent the young captain of the thirds of the Flanders don Alonso Sotomayor, appointing him Governor on March 19th 1591.

This new Governor had to face the incursions of the english pirate Tomas Cavendish, who anchored in the port of Quintero, where they failed, having a loss of the death and prison of ten english; but they could even spur the dispatch of reinforcements of the viceroy Garcia de Mendoza from Peru with 200 men.

Sotomayor shocked with the eternal lack of resources, but thus and all his passing for Chile was recognized as having an intelligence and character higher than that of his predecessors and which the colonial administration was not going to see again until the arrival of the Governor Alonso de Ribera.

Richard Hawkins crossed the Strait, seized valuable spoils in Valparaiso in 1593, finding the fleet of the energetic viceroy Garcia Hurtado de Mendoza and after a bloody combatHawkins surrendered on condition that he may be treated according to the laws of the war, that is to say, under the guarantee for him and for his own people. Don Garcia restricted to send him to Spain where he suffered a very long prison.

The Dutch privateers were sent by the capitalists that were organizing commercial enterprises with the purpose of practising the privateering, extending the commerce through America and taking hold of Peru.

The Brothers Simon and Baltasar de Cordes were the first privateers having come to Chile. Their expedition was shipwrecked by the torments when they were crossing the Strait, so that one of their ships surrendered to the Spaniards and others were forced to continue until Asia. It only stayed in Chilean waters the ship commanded by Baltasar de Cordes that landed in Chiloe Island in 1600 and proclaimed himself with great ostentation the Archipelago's King, who after obtaining provisions of the Indians from Carelmapu, headed for the city of Castro which was delivered to him without resistance, expelled the neighbours and seized their women. The settlers that had fled taking their arms achieve to organize. They were present in place well prepared, and at the same time a Spanish detachment that upon getting across the Chacao channel in canoe, after bitter combats could expel the dreadful false king, thanks to the heroical action of one of the women prisoners, madam Ines de Bazan called the "Castro Heroine", who on being prisoner to the Dutch, damped the cannons' and harquebuses' wicks, preventing them from to fire, Baltasar de Cordes at first wanted to hang her, but he was sorry for her and made her whip and expelled her. On not being able to fire their arms, thanks to Ines that recovered Castro, the privateer had to abandon the coast of Chile bound for the Moluccas after a heavy fight.

Philip III named Governor of Chile to Alonso de Ribera in 1601, reputed captain of the thirds of Flanders. His military politics was to abandon the zone south of Biobío, reinforce the army, and fortify the new frontier by founding the forts of San Pedro de la Paz, Nacimiento, Santa Margarita de Austria and Paicavi.

At the beginning of XVII century, 1615, the privateer expeditions of the Dutch Spilberg, Schouten and Le Maire came to America. A squadron in charge of Jorge Spilberg, a very experienced sailor, crossed the Strait of Magellan, reaching the depopulated Valparaiso, landing some force in Papudo to be supplied with foods and recognize the region. After defeating the Viceroy's ships, he continued through the Peruvian and Mexican coasts, seizing valuable spoils.

Cornelio Schouten and Jacobo Le Maire following the extensión of the Eastern coast of Tierra del Fuego, discovered the Strait that was called Le Maire, the island of the Estados and rediscovered the Cape Horn, which they called Horm in memory of the Dutch city bearing that name.

The practical result of his voyage was the discovering of a new road to pass the Pacific by the route of the Cape Horn which would be the most used until the steamships were introduced.

It was so far thought that Tierra del Fuego was part of a great austral continent stretching up to the Pole, such continent exists more to the South and it is the Antarctic.

When the Council of Indies knew that the Dutch had found a new pass, organized a new squadron in charge of the Nadal brothers, these after being provided with Schouten's and Le Maire's voyage dairies as their respective maps and courses, they set sail with two caravels toward the extremity of Tierra del Fuego, discovering on passing beyond Cape Horn some islands they called Diego Ramirez in honour of the cosmographer of the expedition. Those islands are part of the meridional extremity of the South American continent.

Holland as maritime power organized two powerful expeditions destined to respectively attack Brasil and Peru.

The one destined to Peru, entrusted to Jacobo L'Hermite, was formed by eleven ships and a crew of two thousand men.

After ransacking the archipelagos of the South, they called in the island of Juan Fernandez and then went on to Peru, blocking Callao and the Peruvian coasts for five months. They failed in the attack to Callao, in which L'Hermite was killed, continuing the blockade his second mate

Hugo Shepenham on July 2nd 1624. But being the crew devastated by diseases and combat casualties, they decided to get back to Holland by the Asia's route.

Brouwer reached the western coast of Chiloe in May 1643 and soon after he Landed in Carelmapu. They had decided to settle in Valdivia. On the death of Brouwer, Herckmans was in charge of the expedition that proposed an alliance to the mapuches to help them in their fight against the Spaniards. A curious parley was held on the fourth months of his arrival in September. The mapuches authorized the Dutch to Guild a fort and they were committed to provide them supplies in exchange of arms, Herckmans thought of taking hold of Chile and provoke an uprising in Peru, but so much insistence on knowing where the gold mines were, and that they had fortified in Valdivia, made the Indians suspect, denying them any help. The Dutch were convinced that they had nothing to do there, and weighed anchors bound for Pernambuco.

The governor-interim, field-master Francisco de Alaba y Nureña in the eight months of his tenure, he was especially devoted to the vigilance of the coast in order to prevent Dutch landings.

The Dutch enterprises perturbed the Spanish commerce on the one hand and contributed to the progress of the geography on the other since their chiefs drew up valuable hydrographical charts of Tierra del Fuego, and of the archipelagos and neighbouring channels.

The calamities produced by the great earthquakes were added to the wars and the privateers. In 1570, Concepcion suffered a great earthquake followed by the outflow of the sea by a great tsunami, flooding most of the city. Five years later, similar calamity would lash the austral cities of Valdivia, La Imperial, Villarica and Castro. In La Serena, a great earthquake on June 17th 1604. In Arica, a big tsunami on November 24th 1604, it was again lashed by the earthquake with big tsunami on December 16th. An earthquake happened in Coquimbo in 1639, another earthquake, in Santiago on September 6th 1643. The most frightful was that of the night of May 13th 1647 that at 10:30 in the night when many settlers were sleeping, a dreadful noise startled the "santiaguinos", and it began at once a very strong earthquake which caused that the city of Santiago was left in a lot of ruins.

The towers of the churches, temples and houses fell squashing the people running in the darkness of the night, screaming and crying without knowing where to go. According to survivors, the seism lasted the praying of three creeds' time.

Earthquake in Santiago.

Bishop Gaspar de Villaroel was rescued badly injured from the debris of the convent, went to the church where he gathered some priest and friars, who were badly injured like him, did not prevent them from giving spiritual assistance to the dying people and to the terrified settlers who had survived the earthquake. Out of the six hundred houses, just a few were hardly standing. More than one thousand people died.

An earthquake occurred in Arica in 1650; in Concepcion, an earthquake on March 15th 1657; in Arica, a big tsunami on March 10th 1681; in Santiago, earthquake on July 1690.

The importance that the colony gradually acquired made it possible that Philip II established, in Chile, a tribunal for the administration of justice in representation of the Crown with the name of "Real Audiencia", whose members had the title of "Oidores".

It was established in the city of Concepcion in 1567, being their first president don Melchor Bravo de Saravia. This tribunal only lasted seven years, at the end of which it was closed.

Later in 1607, king Philip III established it again but it was in Santiago this time, being presided by the Governor, a regent, a dean, three "oidores" and a prosecutor, minor judges were the Council's mayors and its resolutions could be appealed in the Audiencia.

Spain also established Laws for the Indians, which regulated the lesser acts of the life of its vassals, even the hour in which they should go to bed: at nine hours in the afternoon during winter and at eight hours in the afternoon during summer. There were curfew and punishments for those who walked after those hours. It forbade the governors and "oidores" of the Audiencia to obtain properties, negotiate, make close friendship, be godparents and marry in the country wherein they work.

The penal laws allowed the torment or torture in the square with the so called tree of justice or roll where Indian or Negro delinquents were tied in a thick post to be whipped. This base instrument, like the gallows, could not lack in the squares of the capitals.

The Audience's lawyers were useless to pacify the araucanians. The Jesuits believed in a more effective plan. Father Luis de Valdivia put into practice what was called "defensive war" by which the Spanish troops should not pass the Biobío and the missionaries were entrusted the conversion of the Indians by means of the preaching.

Father Valdivia, after travelling to Spain to expound his ideas to the King, came back to Chile authorized to put them into practice in agreement with the governor Alonso de Ribera. The araucanians did allow that the missionaries entered in their territory, but an unexpected setback ended the plan.

It happened that some of chieftain Aucanamun's many women, running away from him, sought shelter with the Spaniards, as they did not want to turn them back, Aucanamun ordered to kill jesuitic missionaries, fathers Horacio Vechi, Martin Aranda and the assistant brother Diego de Montalban, on the banks of the lake Lanalhue, after having undressed them, put the three missionaries in the open field, where they could be well speared, the corpses stayed lay in the field, being food for the animals. All these events caused a general uprising among the Indians that, like unbeatable hordes, destroyed the seven cities south of Bibio: Villarica, Arauco, Cañete, Angol, La Imperial, Valdivia and Osorno.

Governor Ribera then attacked the Araucania by fire and sword, with applauses from the military and encomenderos who had argued father Valdivia's plan.

Alonso de Ribera's close friendship with Juan Rodulfo Lisperguer became even more attracting due to the concern he felt toward his two determined sisters Catalina and Maria.

In consequence, conflicts between the Governor and the highest ecclesiastical authority became real battles between Ribera and bishop Juan Perez de Espinosa, who unwillingly saw the Governor because of his having a fame of worldly, by being in concubinage with two beautiful "santiagueñas" Maria Lisperguer and also her sister Catalina, both of them married and aunts to Catalina de los Rios y Lisperguer, called "La Quintrala".

Bishop Perez de Espinosa tried, by all means and by means of a meeting of discontented neighbours, to inform the Inquisition in Peru about the Governor's liberal behavior.

The rupture with the Lisperguer arose from an incident with a married woman that don Alonso had, it caused that Juan Rudolfo was sent to prison, which he could escape from, but the exasperated and jealous sisters poisoned the water from the jar in which the Governor was drinking and to avoid leaving any trace about this, they killed the Indian that followed her orders.

Ribera, on suspecting about the indian who was marauding his yard and verifying the actions that almost poisoned him, ordered to capture both women, but they had already taken refuge in the convent.

Because of his good government and having established a permanent and proffesional army to wage with some success the

war of Arauco, king Philip III tried not to pay attention to the love-affairs of the handsome don Alonso, named him Governor of Tucuman and abandoned Chile.

The defensive war was restablished for some time; but convinced that it did not have favourable results, the general opposition against father Valdivia grew. Franciscan Pedro de Sosa and Colonel Pedro Cortes went to Spain to ask the abolishing of the defensive war, King Philip IV order to restablish the offensive.

War, encomiendas and the smallpox eliminated the Indians, as the Spanish population was increasing because Spain was sending an uninterrupted current of military reinforcements, with which the percentage of white blood increased, mingling with the native blood and forming with this one only race. It was never attained that the mapuches were part of the mingling of blood; they were also decimated by suffering the great smallpox and typhus epidemic.

The Chilean people showed later on military conditions coming from this kind of Spaniards that arrived to Chile, whom had more military capacity due to the Arauco war than the others who were in the rest of the American countries, which did not come from the native race since the picunches and the huilliches were not good at war and opposed little resistance to the mapuche and inka invasions and to the very same conquerors.

Spain acknowledged the mapuche nation's independence on January 6th, 1641 by the Treaty of Killin, setting as frontier between the two nations the Biobío River. After 100 years of a sterile colonialist war, it capitulated before its own impotence and resigned to its designs of conquering the territories beyond the established frontier imposed by the mapuches and ratified by Spain in the Treaty.

The Mapuche nation or Mapuche federal state was formed by the meli-wixan Mapu and they were four autonomous regions known as: Puelmapu, Willimapu, Pikunmapu and Lafkenmapu.

Its independence was first acknowledged by the Inca Empire, then by Spain and later on by the republics of Chile and Argentina. It was the first independent nation of the Americas acknowledged by a European power. Independence that was extended during the Spanish Empire colonial period and was prolonged during the first seventy years of the independence of Chile and Argentina, concluding it only after the defeat of the mapuches in the Patagonia in 1885.

At the end of the XVII century, Chile was still an extremely backward country. The first governors had generally been distinguished military, but little wise in government. Santiago seemed to be a village, its houses with one ground floor and many of them made of straw; the temples, convents and monasteries were protruding. Idleness and monotony were part of the colonial life. The morning religious services and the afternoon naps took up most of the day. The curfew bells rang at the ninth hour in the evening in winter and at the tenth hour in summer and the doors were closed and all the streets remained empty and dark. Journeys were very troublesome and slightly common. Foreign news arrived from time to time, for the lack of mail, upon having no big business, nor banks, nor newspapers, nor politics, the subject of discussions were only about domestic issues, gentlemen drank chocolate, and all, yerba mate from Paraguay, tea and coffee, like wines and liquors were considered drugstore remedies.

The scarcity and the high price of books caused Chile to be kept in general ignorance since there was no printing press during the colony and the few books that came from Spain were about the lives of Saints or other devout works, which were the things that the unyielding Ecclesiastical

Tribunal of the Inquisition allowed to read; aside from some philosophy, sacred sciences and law books for priests and lawyers.

Inquisition

In this time the Church in America was already a powerful organization and apart from evangelizing the Indians, it was observed that of dominating the creole society and the state itself.

This urge for dominating was seen in the fights between Franciscan and Dominicans, and between Dominicans and jesuits in the colonial universities; between friars and secular clergy in the bishoprics, and between the church and the civil power for questions of jurisdiction.

The history of the communities in this Century was stormy.

In Chile, the clergy never reached excessive richness therefore such disputes were of minor intensity. For the same reason, in its temples was not observed the great baroque ornament that characterized the Hispanic Creole architecture of the XVII century.

In this century, the college of the dominicans and the college of the jesuits of San Miguel were transformed in Pontifical Universities where the doctor's degree in theology was awarded, being the major honor to which it was possible to aspire.

But it didn't take long for a long rivalry to arise between the Dominicans and the jesuits since they were disputing for the pupils and fighting for the monopoly of the university education.

Concerning law studies, which could not be followed in Santiago's Universities, Chileans should follow them in the University of San Marcos, in Lima.

Chile was the poorest of the Spanish American colonies since there were not rich mines like those of Peru and Mexico. During the colony some copper mines were worked, but they did not were the main industry. They had to slowly make their scarce fortunes, becoming the main national industries: agriculture, livestock and commerce.

Chile could only live by the special and direct support from Spain in relation to manufactured goods and from Lima.

A disastrous monopoly system ruled the commerce; it could be only practiced by the port of Seville, whose privilege passed to Cadiz later on. An office named the Casa de Contratación (House of Contracting) completely intervened, ruling the quantity, the mode and time in which the goods should be dispatched for America.

Once in a while, a fleet of galleons sailed from Cadiz with Spanish goods, which could only head for three or four ports in the Atlantic, to which the merchants of the colonies could go. These exchanged their goods there in a great fair, sold and bought to the price that the merchants from Cadiz wanted to impose them.

Galleons came back to Spain loaded with goods and gold from America, and they were many times plundered by the English and Dutch privateers, that the spaniards had some times to suspend the departure of the fleet, and they other times had to be escorted by other galleons.

All these events and the prohibition to foreigners of the practice of commerce in America were causing the smuggling on large scale.

The merchants from Chile had to go the far-off fair of Portobello, on the other side of Panama, to be provided when the galleon did not arrive from Spain or buy second hand from the Peruvians.

The Potosi or Lima royal treasuries had to help the government of Chile with an annual subsidy called "real situado".

Inquisitor secretly proceeded by applying torture to get statements from the so-called sorcerers or wizards that supposedly had pact with the demon, as well as those accused by heretical words or readings. The accused was generally condemned to the loss of his possessions and to a long and heavy prison, but they were sometimes condemned to be burned in the blazes in the middle of a solemn ceremony called "Auto de Fe".

There was no Tribunal in Chile. But there were indeed "comisarios"(commissioners) of the Holy Office in Lima, in charge of sending to that city the Chileans accused, who were really a few.

Spaniards set the frontier in Biobío and spread their forces or thirds (infantry regiment) in distinct forts. One day, the mapuches fell upon the infantry regiment of Yumbel killing 100 men in the neighboring stream of Las Cangrejeras, in such circumstances don Francisco Lasso de la Vega, famous military from the infantry regiments of Flanders, came as Governor. He was named by Philip IV, landed in Concepcion with the commission of concluding the Arauco war in two or three years.

Lasso de la Vega organized an army of 800 soldiers with new troops recruited in Santiago, avenged the defeat of the Cangrejeras, smashing the mapuches in the battle of La Albarrada near Lebu in 1631.

He promulgated a new ordinance of rates which modified some dispositions of Esquilache's, which ordered the payment of the rate and suppress the personal service.

The new ordinance allowed the Indian to pay the rate in specie or in work, left to his volition to live in "reducciones" or "encomiendas" and fixed the value of the wage. The defeat of chieftain Naucopillan in Angostura left the region between Bibio and Angol free of enemies that is why Lasso de la Vega decided to advance the frontier until Angol and people again this city.

Ended the period of eight years of government by Lasso de la Vega, his government can be considered the most remarkable during the XVII century despite the lack of resources and soldiers. The King named Francisco Lopez de Zuñiga, marquis of Baides, as his replacement, who sent Philip IV information in which he pointed out the weakness of the Spanish power.

A curious character of the colonial times was a woman who enlisted in the Spanish troops and served as second lieutenant in the war against the araucanians. She had a not so nice physical appearance and rude manners. Her name was Catalina Erauso, more known as the "Monja Alférez" (nun second lieutenant) who at the age of four years entered along with her three sisters (Maria Juana, Isabel and Jacinta) into the dominican convent of San Sebastian el Antiguo in the village of the same name in Guipuzcoa, her native town, escaping dressed as a page on the night of March 18th 1600, on being still novice. In the following months, she was in the populations of Vitoria, Valladolid, Bilbao and Estella, where she came back from to San Sebastian just thirteen years after her

flight; she did manly occupations for all that time, under the names of
Pedro de Orive, Francisco de Loyola, Alonso Diaz, Ramon de Guzman
or Antonio de Erauso. After, she went to Sanlucar de Barrameda wherein
she enlisted as cabin boy in a ship that sailed toward America of which
Esteban Eguiño was captain, an uncle, first cousin of Catalina's mother.

She went on board on Easter Monday 1603 bound for Venezuela
whence she went to Cartagenas de Indias, wherefrom she passed to
Nombre de Dios in Panama. When the ship was already loaded with
the silver to come back to the Peninsula, Catalina stole the captain 500
pesos and she got off, walking around some months while she spent the
money, she was employed by a merchant who took her to Trujillo, in
Peru; she became swordswoman, killing a man in a duel, therefore she
was forced to escape to Lima; months after, she enlisted as soldier in a
company which went to Concepcion in Chile, where she joined with his
brother that was fighting in Arauco, to whom she introduced as one of
his youngest brother who did not see him fifteen years ago. She fought
with the Indians in the attack of the Valdivia village, for which she
was awarded the rank of second lieutenant. She acquired fame as great
swordswoman but having killed three rivals, whom were wearing big
wide-brimmed hat which make it difficult their recognition. It happened
that one of them was but his own brother Miguel. She had to flee to
Tucuman, Potosi, La Plata, Charcas, Cochabamba, La Paz, Cuzco, Lima,
Callao in Peru, while being hurt in a new encounter, she disclosed her sex
to the bishop of Guamanga don Agustin de Carvajal that got the most
complete confession of her secrets, settling her in the convent of Santa
Clara of Guamanga with the appropriate habit, calling her the "Monja
Alferez". Shortly after, the bishop died and Catalina kept wearing the
nun habits in the convent.

Being known all of these events in Lima, the archbishop of the
city don Bartolome Lobo Guerrero ordered the transfer of the Monja
Alferez there, where she was received and also entertained by the viceroy
Francisco de Borja; she lived in the convent of La Santisima Trinidad in
the peruvian capital for three years, until a prohibition came from Spain
to continue living in the convent because she was not a professed nun.

Catalina escaped and in her wandering she used the names of Pedro
de Orive y Alonso Diaz Ramirez and after several altercations with the
justice and committing some crimes, she was sent to Spain in civilian
clothes in the silver galleon San Jose, whose captain was Andres de Onton
in the fleet of general Tomas de Larraspuru, during the voyage she took
part in another event of stabbing by game disputes. Upon reaching Cadiz
on November 1st 1624 to be judged and being condemned to death,

pardoning her upon knowing her sex and by the multiple war services rendered to the King, who granted her a 500 peso pension to be paid by the Royal Treasury of Manila, Peru or Mexico. She moved to this last place, settling as muleteer and died in Cuitlaxtla, village near Puebla on July 20th 1650, practising this occupation.

It is also known in the colonial history a land owning woman, from the chilean aristocracy, who lived in the middle of the XVII century called Catalina de los Rios Lisperguer, nicknamed "La Quintrala".

She was born in Santiago in 1604, was daughter of Catalina Lisperguer Flores and Gonzalo de los Rios y Encio, son of the spanish conqueror Gonzalo de los Rios, contemporary with Pedro de Valdivia.

The clan which was to be famous by its masochistic sensuality and its women's bloody spirit came from the concubinage between a german Carpenter, Bartolome Blumen or Flores and madam Elvira, chieftain of Tagalante, they had a daughter, Agueda Flores that married Pedro Lisperguer the wealthiest man in Chile.

They had eight children among whom Catalina and Maria caused so much pain to the governor Alonso de Ribera.

The nickname "La Quintrala" of her niece Catalina came from her habit of whipping her slaves with branches of quintral, an autochtonous bush having red fruits.

Catalina was raised in the bosom of a family of wealthy landowners, being the Rios y Lisperguer renowned in Santiago's society in the XVII century. However, she did not receive enough education since she was half illiterate until her death. She was sadly famous by the many murders and sacrileges that she did, without having been ever prosecuted by the justice.

Catalina was too much beautiful, very tall, a long and redheaded hair and vivid green eyes. Elements so strange as spanish, indian-american and german blood met in her, that's why she was sexually attractive to men.

One of her aunts induced her to the heathen practices of bewitchment with her grandmother Agueda Flores, illegitimate daughter of the german conqueror Bartolome Blumen or Flores and madam Elvira, chieftain of Talagante.

When the Quintrala was still too young, it began to show in her a bloody sensuality.

Her first victim was her own father, corregidor Gonzalo de los Rios. This happened when she was barely 18 years old while her father was ill lying in the bed, she killed him by means of a poison she put in the chicken of the supper prepared by her:

- Father, I bring you a very Light supper so that it shall be easy for you to eat, first take this chicken broth, and then I have prepared from the breast a stew which you will like very much -.

At midnight, her father began screaming, writhing in pain, dying almost at once.

In spite of having been reported the crime to the authorities, she was not prosecuted due to family influences.

She fell in love with a religious called Pedro Figueroa, to whom she pursued to weariness, without obtaining results.

Her grandmother Agueda Flores, who was her guardian since her parents' death, decided to marry her by which she offered a huge dowry, after this the Spanish soldier Alonso de Campofrío y Carvajal, son of an illustrious conqueror having the same name, came to marry her by his own convenience. Marriage did not completely calm down Catalina who sent one of her slaves to kill the priest of La Ligua estate, whom married her to Pedro de Figueroa, since Catalina had never forgiven him that he had rejected her, the attempted murder failed since the slave was afraid and warned the priest.

The husband was aware of his wife's merciless customs, he was benign with her and it is said that he even loved her, that's why he became her accomplice.

They had a child who died young.

Catalina began having lovers, among them, a man called Enrique de Guzman knight of the Order of Malta, a young merchant that won her love. Soon, she found out that he thought to marry a beautiful limeña. On considering that he had trifled with her feelings, in despair, she made him killed in a tavern and accussed of the murder to her negro slave that followed her orders, being executed in Santiago's Main Square.

Catalina kept in her house the Christ of La Agonia, a big wooden carving placed in a little altar in her bedroom, wherein she used to pray for her crimes. One day after having whipped with a bush o quintral one of her servants until his body was completely bloodstained, she at once went to ask the pardon to the Christ.

- Alas! Why are you looking at me with pitiful eyes? And you keep looking at me while I'm moving, don't look at me anymore

As it seemed that the Christ kept staring at her everywhere, very angry and with her satanic impulse, she opened the window and threw the Christ to the street.

- Go to the hell with the demon, get out, get out, I don't stand men who don't receive me well, get out of my house -.

The Augustinian fathers picked up the Christ and took it to their Church of San Agustin, placing it in an altar.

Having inherited from her uncle don Gonzalo de los Rios, large lands in the coastal valley of Longotoma and the estate of La Liega, acquiring after others in Cuyo and Petorea, established her residence in the estate El Ingenio where there is still the vine of quintral, with its branches she whipped the servants. In this estate, it began happening dreadfull events, so much during the life of her husband as after his death in strange circumstances.

Wealthy cattle-dealer and landowner, she managed herself the activities of her properties. She rode through the valleys and often got closed to Pichidangui "Cave of the Quintrala", it was there where she killed her servants. A negro slave who suspected about so many disappearances of his colored companions, called Natucon-Jeton, was grimly murdered since Catalina kept him without being buried for two weeks, hanged by the feet with a bush of quintral in his mouth and paper stating "a callar" (be quiet).

Her cruelty was so extreme, that in that same year, her servants rebelled against her, escaping from the estate toward the mounts and neighboring regions. She made them come back by force by means of a writ of the Real Audiencia. Her steward Ascencio Erazo captured them and took them to the estate where Catalina presided over the punishment with her nephew Jeronimo de Altamirano.

One morning, clergy Luis Vasquez paid a visit to her:

- Lady widow of Campofrio, with all my respects I should condemn your behaviour so much in your way of wanting to sexually attract men, as well what we know about your cruelty with your servants, whom are distinct every time without knowing anything from the former ones -.
- Father, don't believe anything that the gossipmongers tell you, I don't pretend to seduce men, I'm not to be blamed of being so beautiful and sexually attract them, on the other side if my servants disappear because I send them to other of my many estates for working, therefore I beg you that you don't meddle where you are not required.-

- It's my duty as an ecclesiastical authority to inform so that it may be proceeded with an inquiry -.

That same night while being in his library, father Vasquez heard the creak of the rear door and upon getting close to see, a hooded person fell upon him, stabbing him in the back near the shoulder and in his side, upon screaming the father, the hooded man escaped. The vicar succeeded in saving his life, but suspecting that Catalina was the one who attacked him.

The Real Audiencia started a secret official investigation, based under the Bishop Francisco Luis Salcedo's accusation, relative to the clergy that was attacked, don Luis Vasquez. It commissioned the "oidor" receptor de camara don Francisco de Millan to perform an investigation.

He ordered Catalina, her steward and his nephew to be kept away from the estate, so that their victims could be more comfortable telling the crimes committed by their boss, which were known to be more over forty. The commissioner of the Audiencia, horrified, found accusations enough and these submitted to the capital.

In Santiago, it was commissioned the oidor Juan de la Peña Salazar, who in the capacity of bailiff moved to the estate and took the murderer to Santiago to be subjected to a criminal suit because of slow and cruel slaughter of her servants

Upon entering captured Catalina in Santiago on May 13th 1647, it was felt a heavy crash continued by an earthquake of great intensity; Catalina escaped in the confusion of the moment, taking refuge in the Church of the Augustinians wherein the Christ of La Agonia which she rejected was. Se was coming close to the wall where the little altar was in and asking him in prayers that if she were not condemned to death, in gratitude she would put candles in its altar for life and would donate all her fortune to the poor, when she witnessed that the Christ's thorn crown fell upon the throat as if meaning that it hurt him such a severe punishment to the city. The only wall that did not fall down in the destroyed church was the one supporting the Christ which saved the persons who were close to him, among them Catalina.

The criminal prosecution was so long and bothersome that La Quintrala died before it was ended in 1665 at the age of 61, alone and despised. She left paid 20.000 masses and 20.000 pesos for the salvation of her soul, and that a procession of the image in the day of the earthquake's anniversary should be for ever costed with her incomes, called since then The Lord of May. She was buried in the Church of San Agustin, in Santiago.

War of Succession in Spain. XVIII Century.

The American treasures mainly serve the Spanish Kings for waging long religious wars against the english, german and dutch protestants. Considering themselves wealthy with the gold from America, Spaniards neglected the work and the great cost of the wars waged against Europe, which at last impoverished them, since the factories disappeared and their gold went to enrich the foreign industry, which supplied them with goods.

It was the year 1708; taking advantage of the war of succession in Spain, the last privateers visited the coast of Chile. The expedition commanded by the English captain Wooder Roger and accompanied by the noted buccaneer Guillermo Dampier. They stopped in the island of Mas a Tierra in the Juan Fernandez archipelago wherein the privateers were used to call to take a rest. They saw, over there, with great surprise, a man dressed with goats fur and having a completely wild appearance that was making signs and at the same time shouted at them when they were approaching him:

- Dont't run away, my name is Alexandre Selkirk and am Scottish, from the county of Five -.
- What do you do here completely alone? How have you come to this place?-
- I was sailor from the ship "Cinq Ports", after an irreconcilable fight with the "contramaestre", I was abandoned in the island as punishment by the privateer Stradling, alone with a trunk of tools, a little of tobacco and a Bible. It has been four years and four months that I woke up here, with no other company that the wild goats which have helped me to survive, living me food and company in my horrified loneliness, the first days were of despair and repentance for having been a cruel man without any conscience, becoming a mystic helped by the Holy Bible.-

Captain Wooder Roger put him on board in his ship, returning him to England.

End of the House of Austria.

As the last of the Kings of the House of Austria, Charles II the Bewitched died in 1700 without leaving succession, an archduke of Austria and a French Prince were disputing the vacant throne.

The accession of French Prince to the throne of Spain alerted the European Powers which meant for them the Alliance franco-spanish y the rupture of the so long European balance, which caused a long and general European war called The War of Succession of Spain (1701-1714).

The struggle ended with the Treaties of Utrecht and that of Rastadt, in which it was established that Philip V, of the House of Bourbon, which is the dinasty coming from the french region of Bourbonese, grandson of the powerful Louis XIV king of France whom achieved to put him on the throne in 1700 and stayed as king of Spain and America, renouncing all his rights over the throne of France. By the same Treaties, Spain granted Gibraltar to England, and the spanish Low Countries and almost all of its italian dominions to Austria.

The Bourbons were more absolutists and authoritarians than the Austria. These ideas were contrary to regionalism and the jurisdictional spirit of the Spanish people.

Philip V improved the public administration and increased the wealth which was better managed than in the XVII century and being not so religious. He also improved the fleet and the army, it was activated the mining, and contributed to the unity upon trusting the old kingdoms to officials appointed by the monarch, except that of Navarra, which continued in charge of its viceroy, and increased the influence of France over Spain. In order to prevent the ships from the difficulties of the navigation by the Guadalquivir, whose riverbed has scarce depth, it was transferred the monopoly of Seville to the port of Cadiz in 1717, becoming the headquarters of the Casa of Contratacion.

Philip V was succeeded by his son Fernando VI. The Spanish government started to grant authorization to commerce with the colonies to some Spanish companies, which could send registered ships; these were private merchant ships which arrived into the Americas with the King's permit. All these important reforms moved the collapse of Spain and of its American colonies with the development of the commerce which increased the Spanish immigration, going many Basques to settle in Chile, mainly from Vizcaya, town of sailors and merchants, they were no soldiers destined for the Arauco war any Langer, but merchants and officials.

The Basque and the Navarre like: Zañartu , Urrutia , Balmaceda , Eyzaguirre , Sanfuentes , Vial , Urrejola , Urmeneta , Errázuriz , Larraín , Aldunate , Vicuña , Echenique , Lecaroa...etc, were people having great intuition for the business. The castilians from Castilla La Vieja, were mostly coming from the mountainous province of Santander: Bulnes, Tagle, Ruíz Tagle, Tocornal, Alcalde, etc.

Once they had enriched, they brought their relatives from Spain, since the geographical conditions of the center of Chile were very similar to those of their lands, therefore it was easy for them to settle in the country.

By means of the Law of the Indians, no foreigner could go to America without having a licence from the king or the House of Contratacion under pain of suffer terrible punishments, even though these dispositions like many others of the spanish legislation were not strictly fulfilled.

Philip III authorized the permanence of foreigners under payment of taxes, later on it was granted letters of naturalization to foreigners who wanted to settle in Chile, being the case of the portuguese that with the union of Spain and Portugal since 1580 until 1640, allowed the entering to the country of a great deal of soldiers and merchants: the Pereíra, Barbosa, Almeida, Rivadeneira, etc.

The arrival of the Bourbons to Spain made easy the Entrance of the Franch, merchants, sailors and smugglers: Subercaseaux, Pradel, Letelier, Morandé, Dublé, etc.

The Italians also came in large numbers as soldiers, sailors, merchants: Pastene, Gallo, Croce, etc.

The enmity between Spain and England hindered the arrival to Chile of the English, although however there was someone that stayed when the pirates' incursions, and reached to established a family on marrying women from the country, as it was the case of the English physician Jorge Edwards at the end of the colonial time. However, the Irish, on being catholic, were very numerous those that served as military and engineers: O'Higgins, Mackenna, etc.

Also, those from the countries of Northern Europe left descendants in Chile like the polish Borcosque or Borcowsky; the swede Peter Campaniu who adopted the surname Bari, and the baron swede-german-polish Timoteo de Nordenflych, his daughter had descendants with Diego Portales.

In short, the Bourbon accomplished to stop Spain on the brink of the abyss from which the Austria had left it.

The phenomenon of change also came to The Enlightenment moving to America through Spain, and it was in the American continent where it reached its maximum meaning. The American authors, under the influence of the Old World, saw their history with other eyes, almost everybody were Spaniards or direct descendants of Spaniards, living rise to the appearance of two typical notes from these times: the indigenism and the "criollismo".

We are attending to the formation of the colonialist conscience in front of the Spanish state fiscal policy at the same time that the Creole society takes the protagonism. This is the origin of the American Enlightenment of the friar Benito Jerónimo Feijoo.

The scheme of the feijonian rationalism penetrated in the American cultural environment since the middle of the XVII century, based above all by reason of the ideas of renewal and liberty, secularization and criticism, as diffusing vehicle of these ideas, the press played a very important paper acquiring a great influence over the American society. The literary societies existed since the XVIII century, but it is in this moment when many of these cultural centres are officialised and take importance.

With authorization of Philip V, it was established in Santiago a royal university in 1747 that in his honour was called San Felipe and of which don Tomas de Azua was the first rector, from where soon began to go out of their classrooms the bachelors, licensed, masters and doctors. Philip V was succeeded by Fernando VI and this was succeeded by his brother Charles III who was the most reformists of the Bourbons. He gathered great ministers such as: Aranda, Campomaes and Floridablanca who showed great concern for the economic reforms giving more commercial freedom, which meant to end the privilege of the House of Trade (Casa de Contratación) of Cadiz, in 1765 authorizing other eight ports in Spain for the commerce with Cuba.

During the XVIII century Chile was visited by the most notable navigators and explorers of that time which moved as much the French as the English and Spanish governments to send maritime expeditions destined for acquiring more knowledge of the world.

The English John Byron left from England to explore the Atlantic between the Cape of Good Hope and the Strait of Magellan with the purpose of discovering islands and lands in that zone, because they continued believing in a great austral continent. His observations after exploring the channel of the Strait served then to draw a new chart, more safe than the former ones (1764-1766).

Shortly after, the famous French navigator Bougainville undertook a scientific voyage around the world. He crossed the Strait of Magellan, continued by the Pacific, although without coming near the western coasts of America. His chart of the Strait was inferior to Byron's (1771).

The english James Cook made two voyages around the world, exploring Tierra del Fuego, drawing a valuable chart of this land.

Charles III, on observing that these navigators' opinions about the Strait were contradictories, wanted to have it explored sending the Spanish sailor Antonio de Cordoba in two occasions, studying the hydrography and the climatology of the region, drawing maps and plans. But the tempests of the Strait's seas, made them decide that the way of the Cape of Good Hope was safer for the navigation until the invention of the steamships.

The next year, Charles III sent a new expedition in charge of the italian Alejandro Malaspina to follow the route of the Cape of Good Hope and study the western coasts.

Charles III decreed the return of the post service to the Crown, which had so far been in the hands of the Carvajal family, since Charles V had granted them the exploitation of the american posts with the title and the incomes of the Higher Post of the Indies.

This family did not give the due development to so important service; therefore in 1768 the last post master was the Chilean Fermin Francisco de Carvajal y Vargas that upon being ceased he was indemnified with the title of duke of San Carlos.

After this reform, a ship left from La Coruña twice a month bringing the correspondence to Montevideo and from this port it was sent to Chile via Uspallata, this last journey lasted one month.

It also appears in this time the Economic Societies of Friends of the Country, based on the idea of the personal enlightenment through the municipal schools, which were added to the parochial ones and to those founded by diverse religious orders. These Economic Societies welcomed the liberal and conservative groups, all these Academies multiplied beginning with the Royal Academy of the Spanish Language. With the encouragement of these centers, it increased the presence of geographers, voyagers and European scholars in America: Humboldt, Malaspina, Jorge Juan, Antonio de Ulloa, etc., the New World entered into a great scientific activity.

As far as Chile is concerned, the admnistration undewent some important changes.

From the Kingdom of Charles III to the governors, called now captain-generals, they started to appoint persons who had done the administrative career and knew the needs of these countries. In Chile there are the cases of Guill and Gonzaga, Jauregui, Benavides, O'Higgins, Aviles, del Pino and Muñoz de Guzman, many of them in reward for their valuable services received the charges of viceroys of Peru, New Granada and later on that of Buenos Aires. The governors became civilian officials instead of military ones because of their residence in Santiago and the end of the Arauco war.

It was up to the Governor don Antonio Guill y Gonzaga to expel the Jesuits from Chile and to confiscate their properties which were sold by the treasury. Out of is product, it was ordered to provide every exiled an alimentary pension of four real per day, and the rest of it, to the foundation of public institutions of charity and instruction.

The Governor, was very religious, had a particular affection for the Jesuits, and was very sorry to fulfil the order of expulsion.

The illustrious bishop Alday contributed to fulfil the Royal order. All of this was made with the mayor secrecy, according to the instructions from the minister and adviser of Charles III, Pedro Pablo Abarca de Bolea, and count of Aranda. In a same night, all of the houses of The Company in Chile were occupied and their members sent shortly after to Italy. In total, they were nearly four hundred, only a few of them managed to be hiding in time.

The immense power that the Jesuits exerted in America and the secret interference in politics and State issues which was attributed to them made the king Charles III, through his minister the count of Aranda signed the decree of expulsion from Spain, the Indies and the Philippines, of the Company of Jesus from his dominions on February 25th, 1767.

The expulsion arose: 1° in the usurpation of the tithes and the violation of them done in the churches; 2° in the burning of bishop Palafox's books in Mexico; 3° in the independent and despotic regime in the reducciones of Paraguay; 4° in the constant intromission in politics; 5° in the criticism made in the meetings against the royal and governmental authorities; 6° in the participation in the indigenous rebellions; 7° in the preaching against the government in Manila.

More than 2600 Jesuits were led to the shipping ports to be taken to Europe. The immense majority of them were Spaniards and creoles, their march caused an irreparable empty during many years.

Among the chilean jesuits expatriated were the father Manuel Lacunza, profound theologian, the father Miguel de Olivares, chronicler and the young abbé Juan Ignacio Molina, historian who later wrote his noted "Civil and Natural History of Chile" about The Colony.

In Chile, the possessions of the jesuits were immense, their estates were the most important and were over fifty, among them were those of La Compañía, Longaví, Ocoa, Chacabuco, Limache, Bucalemu, La Calera, Las Tablas, Viña del Mar, and thus until almost sixty.

Small farms and estates were under the direction of a jesuit who kept the accounts and the exploitation, being the best equipped with farming implements.

They exported wheat, tallow, wine, brandy and charqui, which were taken to the warehouses that The Company had in the ports, in order to take them later to Peru.

In addition to being great farmers, they were skilful industrialists which made them become the main economic power of Chile since they had great warehouses, mills, bakeries and drugstore, they grew hemp to manufacture ropes, built minor vessels in the shipyards of Quivolgo, furniture, bells, organs, woolen fabrics, etc.

When they arrived, disguised as brother coadjutors, brought skilful german artisans who settled in the estate of Calera de Tango, in the outskirts of Santiago, these artisans made in their workshops there true works of art of silver jewelry and watchmaking.

All this vast industry provided them large sums of money, which they lent as if they were a private bank, charging high interest rates.

The truth is that the expulsion of the order entailed a heavy blow for Chile's industrial progress.

The jesuits were the first to be expelled from Portugal by the minister marquis of Pombal in 1759, then from France in 1764, and immediately from Naples by the minister Tanucci, and in Spain by the minister count of Aranda in1767. Finally, the Catholic States pressed the Pope Clemente XIV in 1773 so that he may abolish The Company of Jesus in the whole Christian world. The exiled jesuit priests had to make use of all of their intellectual power and they became under the way of their exquisite historic, scientific and literary works, hidden way of a trend toward independence, because of resentment for having been thrown from their respective countries.

The Free Masonry also collaborated in the Americas, the lodges' secret changed into a street shout in favour of Liberty. Illustrious citizens and intellectuals attended as active members to the meetings of the compass and the square.

The printing also collaborated, although with the natural restrictions, with gazettes, newspapers and other means of written expression.

In general, the liberalism completed this panorama of restlessness with its libertarian movements established in secret societies.

During the mandate of this same governor, don Antonio Guill, it was started the building of the famous Lime and Pebble bridge over the Mapocho river in 1767, being Santiago's corregidor don Luis Manuel de Zañartu, utilizing in the works the inmates of the jail and those sentenced to hard labour. It took thirteen years to build it and one hundred thousand hen eggs were used, their whites blended with quicklime and reduced into a fine powder, provided an excellent cement to glue the big blocks of pebble, and its cost reached the large sum of 200.000 pesos in that time. It was the most marvellous colonial work which Santiago had for a little more than a century since the subduing advance of the progress finished with its existence, for giving way to the new canalization of the Mapocho River. The bridge was demolished during the president Balmaceda administration in 1888.

The Spanish South America had been comprised in only one viceroyalty, in that of Peru until 1739, date of the establishment of the viceroyalty of Nueva Granada.

Later on, as Portuguese and Spaniards were disputing the possession of "The Eastern Band" of the Rio de la Plata, on August 8th 1776, during the government of don Agustin de Jauregui took place, by royal writ of Charles III, the establishment of the viceroyalty of Rio de la Plata, fixing the capital in Buenos Aires and incorporating in its territory the former governorships of Rio de la Plata, with the provinces of Buenos Aires, Tucuman, Paraguay, Potosi, Santa Cruz de la Sierra, the province of Cuyo which included the cities of Mendoza, San Juan and San Luis, which belonged to Chile during two centuries, and the territories of Potosi and La Sierra from the Audiencia of Charcas, segregated from the viceroyalty of Peru, which was damaged when it lost the mining territory of Charcas, measure that seemed provisional, but soon it was definitive.

After the segregation of the province of Cuyo, the Eastern limit was stretching by the Cordillera de Los Andes and then continued by the Diamante and Quinto Rivers and the Atlantic coast until the end of the continent.

The official geographer of the Crown, don Juan de la Cruz Cano y Olmedilla published, in 1775, a map that was sent for his knowledge to the first viceroy of Buenos Aires, in which the captaincy general of Chile was formed by two sections:

"Ancient Chile", located between the Cordillera de Los Andes and the Pacific.

"Modern Chile", by all the vast region stretching between the Diamante and El Quinto Rivers, the Cordillera de los Andes, the Atlantic and Cape Horn, all of this formed the Patagonia or Magellanic Lands

Despite the establishment of the viceroyalties, the disproportionate extension of the colonies subsisted, with the great difficulty for the viceroys and captain-generals to attend the most remote regions of their jurisdiction. In order to avoid such inconvenience, Charles III established The Ordinance of Intendancies dividing the territories in "intendancies", in charge of an intendante, with military, administrative, judicial and fiscal attributions.

In 1778, by the ordinance of free commerce, Charles III advised by his ministers Galvez and Campomanes, authorized Buenos Aires, Chile, Peru, Nueva Granada and Guatemala to commerce directly with the spanish ports.

The ports of Chile prepared for this direct commerce were Valparaíso and Talcahuano.

The increase of the taxes and the expulsion of the jesuits caused in that time discontentment and excitement in the people, giving rise to the first revolutionary intention against Spain stirred up by three characters having the same name. Among the few foreigners that lived in Chile in that time were two French, Antonio Gramusset settled in Chile since 1764, trying to be ordained priest without achieving it, wanted to unsuccessfully seek fortune in the agriculture and he at last centered in the invention of a machine that should supposedly lift the water to a big height, the idea did not work out, and Antonio Berney, professor of Latin and mathematics, great reader of The Encyclopaedia, conceived the idea to emancipate Chile and establish a republic replacing the monarchical system. He communicated this project to Gramusset, who agreed and both of them began secretly the conspiration. The other conspirator was the landowner and illustrious Chilean "prócer" (leader of the independence movement) Jose Antonio de Rojas, he offered them moral support, whom wanting to take advantage of such discontentment, and they plotted a conspiracy in 1780, known as the "**Conspiracy of the three Antonios**" whose purpose was to establish an independent republic in Chile, by means of an uprising of the creoles. The government would reside in a collegial body under the motto "The sovereign senate of this very noble and very catholic chilean republic". It would be chosen by the people even the araucanians, it was abolished the slavery and the death penalty and the social hierarchies would disappear and the lands would be distributed among the chileans in equal parts. The future new chilean republic would fortify its ports, would create an army that would watch to impose the new projects: these were trusted to the Argentinean lawyer Mariano Perez de Saravia y Borante whom denounced them before the regent of the Real Audiencia don Tomas Alvarez de Acevedo, who had them prosecuted secretly and sent them to Peru wherein they suffered heavy prison in Lima. Later on, the French were sent to Spain. Berney died in a shipwreck in the coasts of Portugal during the voyage and Gramusset was to die in the prison of Cadiz three months later.

In order that those forerunning ideas about the independence were not known, the event was kept in secret, the Real Audiencia was not paying attention to the other accomplices of the conspiracy and that among them was the procer don Jose Antonio de Rojas, who had lived some time in France, whence he brought to Chile revolutionary ideas, many Voltaire's and Rousseau's books and some physical equipments with which he conducted experiments which gave him the fame of wizard before the Tribunal of the Holy Office, although he was not condemned when he demonstrated that they were chemical tests.

Another revolutionary uprising took place in Peru that same year. Jose Gabriel Condorcanqui, chieftain of Tungasuca, together with his followers captured the corregidor Antonio Arriaga in Tinta on November 4th, who left the King's birthday celebration banquet, and he was captured on the way to his home. The Corregidor was imprisoned in the town of Tungasuca where he was dressed with the habit of San Francisco, which was worn by the jesuits of the school where Condorcanqui studied. They hanged him under the accusation of having been a bad ruler. After the execution, Condorcanqui took the same name of Tupac Amaru I, nephew of Atahualpa, that was the last rebel Inca, He was condemned by the Viceroy Francisco de Toledo to death in Cuzco accused of the murders of the priests of Vilcabamba, he denied it.

This new Tupac Amaru II made a calling for the uprising against the bad government and achieved to form a huge army mostly formed by Indians, he went through most of High Peru and Low Peru.

The rebellion that began against the government was expanding, becoming a racial uprising in which the Indian's hate against the white man, who was dominating him during centuries, emerged. They defeated easily the militia of the corregidores from Quispicanchi, Lampa, Chucuito, Asangaro, Puno y Carabaya.

The Tupac Amaru II's hosts were cutting the throat to all the white without discrimination of age or sex. They were burying alive the white women in Tapacari and they were also cutting the throat to the mestizos.

Túpac Amaru II was amazed at the savage of the uprising that he had unleashed; he only pretended to end with the injustices of the bad government, with the "distributions" of the corregidores and with the taxes of the indians.

After being excommunicated by the bishop, he went to beg him to lift the punishment since he did not want to kill but only wanted to end with the government's abuses. As the bishop did not want to redeem him from the excommunication, advised by his wife Micaela Bastidas that was really the soul of the uprising, helping the Indians in their outrages, she made a mistake on December 28th 1780, which costed her life for sieging Cuzco, demanding its surrender, without achieving it. In Cuzco, Micaela was taken prisoner and condemned to death. They executed her by means of garrote before her husband was.

Condorcanqui hid in the mountains alone, having to retreat to Tungasuca, being chased by the Viceroy's troops, was defeated and killed in Tinta on April 5th 1781.

CHAPTER XII.
END OF THE COLONY AND THE OLD REPUBLIC

I t is called with the name of The Old Republic to the first period of the fight for the independence of Chile.

During the first years of the XVIII century in Chile, the misgovernment of the former period was still perceived that it had to be dismissed some governor by his brazen relations with the smugglers. It was the case of the Governor Juan Andres de Ustariz that, upon taking advantage of the arrival of the Bourbon to the throne of Spain, the French ships were authorized to call at the port of the colonies to be supplied, but no trading was allowed to them in any case. As far as Chile is concerned, the French started practicing the smuggling aided by the colonists and even by the government, as it happened with Ustariz, who was dismissed from his position in 1716.

After this period elapsed, it began an age of prosperity by the labor of its great governors and capable and efficient men, which has been called the Enlightened Despotism.

José Antonio Manso de Velasco, Brigadier and Knight to the Order of Santiago, founded several cities by getting from the landowners the lands as a donation. He was promoted to Viceroy of Peru because of his merits.

Domingo Ortiz de Rosas, Lieutenant General. During his government, the University of San Felipe was inaugurated, and the Mint started to operate.

He was succeeded by a noble catalan, Field Marshal Manuel de Amat y Junient, Knight of the Order of San Juan.

He was appointed Captain General, standing out by organizing an effective defensive force from the Urban Militias, he was appointed Viceroy of Peru based in his merits in 1761.

He started to embellish the city of Lima very much motivated by the love he felt for a mestizo artist from a theater in Lima, the dancer and singer with an outstanding voice Micaela Villegas Hurtado, known by many as "Miquita".

In a party that the viceroy made, Micaela appeared luxuriously dressed and jewelled, although she was not too beauty, she was very good looking and very charming, which delighted the sexagenarian Viceroy, who upon knowing her, talked to her:

- I'm very pleased that you have honoured me with your coming to my party for singing, I hope to have the pleasure of seeing you and listening to you more often from now on.-
- It's my pleasure Excellency, and I hope impatiently to attend more often to your parties.-
- Tomorrow, Shall you honour me coming with me to take a walk through the Alameda de los Descalzos? -.
- Delighted, Do you think it right at five in the afternoon? -.

The Viceroy rode her in his luxurious golden carriage, other days she rode a spirited horse following the carriage.

He made them adorn the Alameda de los Descalzos, whereby they usually walked, with marble statues of the greek mythology, he encircled it with a rail of toledo's wrought iron, he added plants making fairly large gardens full of trees.

Later on, he started calling her affectionately in catalan "Perricholi" that was how she was known.

He invited her to "La Quinta Presa", a country mansion of the middle of the XVIII century whereto she constantly went to parties and receptions accompanied by don Manuel.

One day, he declared her his love walking by La Alameda:

- My Perricholi, if you wanted you could have all the palaces, Jewels and riches of the world and you would do me the happiest man in the earth if you gave me your heart -.
- Your Excellency, I shall be your lover when you put the moon under my feet -.

The Viceroy wittily planned the building of the Paseo de Aguas, in front of a convent where his beloved lived in order that she may be promenading in her boredom moments, with some french-style arches and a very large fountain that could be used as a mirror and the heavens and the moon were reflected in its waters.

Once the work was finished, he patiently awaited a full moon night and, taking her by the hand until the side of the fountain, he whispered her:

- Today, I put the moon under your feet -.

He ordered that a small baroque-style palace be built outside of Lima for the dancer. As a fruit of this love affair, Manuel d'Amat Villegas was born, he who was one of the signers of Peru's Independence Act.

The love affair was over when the Viceroy returned to Spain in 1776, with a considerable wealth and retired from the public life, giving his lover the carriage with golden encrustations.

At his arrival to Spain, it was ordered to be built in Barcelona the Vicereine palace.

La Perricholi joined the convent, where she gave the golden carriage to the Carmelite nuns in Lima, wherein she died on May 16th , 1819.

The life of this character was made popular worlwide, it inspired Merimée to write and compose the operetta the carriage of the Holy Sacrament.

This nice romance served that the Viceroy, having a violent, haughty and authoritarian character, remarkably embellished the city of Lima in honour of his beloved Perricholi.

Amat's successor was the Brigadier Antonio de Guill y Gonzaga descendant of an illustrious italian family. We have talked about him because of his participation in the expulsion of the Jesuits. Although during his government he also founded new frontier towns such as: Rere, Yumbel and Tucapel el Nuevo.

He was succeeded by Field Marshal Agustin de Jauregui whom belonged to a noble family from Navarre.

He was gifted with conditions of administrator and ruler, applied Charles III's important reforms: the ordinance of free commerce and the segregation of the province of Cuyo that became part of the viceroyalty of Buenos Aires.

Upon understanding the impossibility of subduing the Mapuche by the arms, the Governor conceived the idea of assuring his tranquillity by giving them the right to have ambassadors before the kingdom's government as if the mapuche were part of an organized state. In fact, these ambassadors would be hostages in the hands of the authorities. The four vutamapus or ambassadors appointed some other representatives whom were respectfully and ceremonially lodged in the convent of San Pablo. These ambassadors that lived on the account of the royal treasury and under the protection of the authority did not know to honour their positions and visited the wealthiest neighbours asking them money for drinking.

The appointment of the four ambassadors was: Pascual Hueñumán (Cóndor de arriba), Francisco Marilevu (Diez ríos), Francisco Curilevu (Río Negro) y Santiago Picunmanque (Pluma de cóndor), these did not stand that peace and quietness of the convent and led by their habitual bellicosity devoted themselves to fight among them.

The ambassadors ended up going back to Araucania, pretending that Santiago's climate affected their health.

Jaúregui was promoted to the position of Viceroy of Peru due to his good services.

He was succeeded by Brigadier Ambrosio de Benavides, Knight of the Order of Charles III and experienced official in America's issues, although he was old and sickly when he took the position.

Early on his position, don Ambrosio delivered the government to the most capable officials.

He distinguished by the construction of buildings and public works such as: the town council and he had also the honour of applying the newly passed Ordinance of Intendants reorganizing the Captaincy General, dividing Chile in two intendances: Santiago and Concepcion.

He was one of the best ruler of the colonial times, leaving a great remembrance to the country.

He was properly succeeded by Ambrosio O'Higgins who had been intendant of Concepcion.

He was born in Ireland but lived in Cadiz practicing the commerce. He went to Chile where he definitely settled. He left the commerce and devoted to engineering works in Valdivia's fortifications, cooperating with the Irish engineer Juan Garland, later he entered the army, being promoted to War Commissioned and Captain of Dragoons. By that time of 1777, he met in Chillan a 18-year-old young lady, Isabel Riquelme, 34 years younger than Ambrosio. She was daughter of Simon Riquelme de la Barrera y Goycochea member of one of Chillan's noble families. A child, Bernardo, was born from his love affair on August 20th. Don Ambrosio kept his long career, being promoted to Lieutenant Colonel, General Field Master, Colonel, Brigadier General and Intendant.

When his son Bernardo was four years old and his mother got married, the child was taken out of his house by orders of Ambrosio and sent to the merchant Juan Albano Pereira's house in Talca, who was in charge of him for a time. Meanwhile, Ambrosio was appointed Governor of Chile from 1787 to 1796, Field Marshal, baron of Ballenary, Viceroy of Peru and marquis of Osorno.

Because of his labor, he deserved the widest approval of ministers Aranda and Floridablanca.

Among his works, we have: Foundation of towns like Vallenar, Combarbala, Santa Rosa de los Andes, Nueva Bilbao and the old Osorno which he rebuilt, the new dikes of Mapocho River, mining centres, agriculture centres, maritime centres and public works.

An expert in the indians due to his long performance in the frontiers, he accomplished with them the Negrete parley, the last one of the great parleys of the colonial times and thanks to it, an inalterable peace was kept for many years.

He abolished the encomiendas, with which he put an end to the mandatory work of the Indians.

His son Bernardo Riquelme, whom don Ambrosio never wanted to give his name, came back to the city of Chillan where he attended the school of the illegitimate children, he learned to speak mapudugun there since he had as school friends the most renowned chieftains' children. He then studied in the School of the Prince in Lima.

Don Ambrosio was promoted to the viceroyalty of Peru in 1796 where in spite of his being advanced in age, he also performed a brilliant labour of progress and good government.

After such a brilliant career, O'Higgins had a rowdy decline. Upon being informed the Spanish government about Francisco de Miranda's plans in favour of the independence of the Spanish colonies with the help of the English government, it took the measures to make them fail.

Being informed Charles IV that don Ambrosio's son, Bernardo Riquelme, was among the conspirators, who did not have his father's surname, although it was known whom he was son of, in fact, father and son never saw each other; The King decreed the dismissal of the Viceroy in 1800, dying one year after, leaving his son the inheritance that comprised: the estate of San Jose de las Canteras, having 16.689 hectares and more than 4.000 heads of livestock, located in the neighborhood of Los Angeles, in the South of Chile.

Previously to this event, Bernardo travelled to Europe. He lived first in Cadiz sometimes in his tutor's house don Nicolas de la Cruz, first count of Maule. He suffered from yellow fever in San Lucar de Barrameda and was about to die. The count of Maule was perhaps the only one that knew to receive him. After a few months, he was sent to England to the watchmakers' house Spencer and Perkins, improving his studies in a Richmond's Academy, near London. During his stay in that country, he knew his mentor Francisco de Miranda, independentist idealist of the emancipation of the Spanish America; he was giving him classes of mathematics and as he trusted him, told him about his plans. He returned in Cadiz in 1799, not achieving to enter the military career that he so much desired. He went on board in the frigate "Confianza" on April 3rd 1800 bound for Buenos Aires to get back to Chile, but a British warship captured the frigate, having to return to Cadiz.

His father was already dead in October 1801; he went on board to Chile and was almost shipwrecked in Tierra del Fuego, reaching Chile in 1802.

Ever since from now on, he called himself Bernardo O'Higgins Riquelme.

In 1806, he was Chillan's mayor and Sub-delegate to the island of Laja in 1810.

Late Ambrosio O'Higgin's successor was Gabriel de Aviles marquis of Aviles and Lieutenant General of the Spanish army.

He built the San Juan de Dios Hospital and improved the Orphan's asylum and the "Casa de Acogida"(settlement houses), works in which he had the cooperation of the creole philanthropist don Manuel de Salas that effortfully founded the so-called Academy of San Luis in 1797, naming it in honor of the queen Maria Luisa, Charles IV's wife. It was a school where it was taught arithmetics, geometry, drawing, latin, etc.

The Crown established the major controls for the leaving of books to South America, always fearing the spreading of libertarian ideas. Don Manuel de Salas travelled to Spain to be nourished in the fountains of the rebellious thought, complying with obtaining the ecclesiastical permit for the buying of every one of his books, but he was kept for a long time in Seville by the Tribunal of the Inquisition before he was able to go on board again bound for Chile.

In that time, the creole aristocracy showed his concern for the country by collaborating near the governors and with his own works of public goods, the so-called señor de Salas was an example of this.

Governor Marquis of Aviles was promoted to the position of viceroy of Buenos Aires. He passed from there to Peru with the same charge where he skilfully ruled until 1806.

He was succeeded by Luis Muñoz de Guzman that was the next to the last governors of the colonial time. He reached Chile accompanied by his wife madam Luisa de Esterripa and his daughter, who influenced in the change of customs in the so far coarse colonial society. A refined and good manners man, unsophisticated and affable that knew to attract the sympathies of the colonial society, turning the Government Palace into the center of the creole aristocracy that attended to his parties and soirées in a time in which the life of the halls had gotten great animation.

The hall was intended for receiving the visitors, it was the most important room in the wealthy houses. The visitors were served mistelle with yerba mate from Paraguay and candies, and the social gathering was enlivened with music when there was a piano or harp, which was played by the young ladies.

Young ladies' orchestra.

He built the custom house, the merchants guild, the Audiencia and the Royal Treasury and started the works of the Cathedral, the temples of

Santo Domingo and that of San Juan de Dios and the churches of Santa Ana and that of La Estampa.

Under his mandate, the smallpox vaccine was introduced in Chile.

The corvette "María Pita" set sail from La Coruña on November 30th 1803, with ten physicians and 25 children with their mothers, destined to keep the virus by means of successive inoculations during the voyage. Chile already had pustules that arrived from Buenos Aires sent by viceroy Sobremontes in 1805. Its main propagandists were the friar Pedro Manuel Chaparro, chilean, who was trying since long before the smallpox inoculation, and the student of medicine Manuel Julian Grajales.

The creole merchant don Nicolas Matorras was in charge of the difficult mission of vaccinating all Chile. He entirely devoted to it with altruistic spirit, achieving to vaccinate 7,600 persons.

Several causes were preparing the emancipation of the Spanish America's colonies.

Since the end of the XVIII century until the beginning of the XIX, the western world will watch a series of chain revolutions that at the same time affected western europe and America.

Revolution in France, independence in North America, Italy divided in small states since the Western Schism, Germany once finished the Holy Roman-Germanic Empire divided in several dukedoms, it is partially dominated by Napoleon, with the confederation of the Rhine, the United Kindgom is a great power master of the seas after the Trafalgar battle.

In 1764, it happened that the conflict between England and its thirteen American colonies, caused by the measures taken by the metropolis to recover expenses incurred during The Seven Years War with France. North American opposition to being taxed without their consent by The Crown culminated in the United States' Independence Declaration proclaimed by Thomas Jefferson and approved by the Philadelphia Continental Congress on July 4th 1776.

The English government considered such process as a humiliation and ordered its colonial army to counter attack. Benjamin Franklin's diplomatic activity obtained from France, which wanted to revenge his defeat in The War of the Seven Years, an Alliance with the insurrectionists in 1778.

Madrid tried to mediate in the conflict, but had to change its attitude because of the Family Pact between the French and the Spanish sovereigns since both of them were Bourbon.

France and Spain, although being absolute monarchies, were in favour of the rebels and against England with the purpose that Spain may recover La Florida, Menorca and Gibraltar.

Being in danger that the revolutionary spirit may be extended through the Spanish American territories, Spain sent a discreet help to the rebels, enough to weaken the English. The Venezuelan Francisco de Miranda y Rodriguez, called the "Precursor", took part in this Spanish division, since he was one of the first creoles that rose against the domination of the Spanish America.

France granted more than one million pounds to the colonists as support. She declared war against England and sent Rochembeau's fleets to America in 1780 and De Gras's in 1781, with these forces George Washington could put an end to the war on October 19th 1781. The Unites States Independence was acknowledged on September 3rd 1783 by the Treaty of Paris, also known as Versailles.

With the peace of Paris, Spain recovered part of La Florida, Gulf of Mexico coast and Menorca, except Gibraltar.

The 7.500 soldiers of Rochembeau's expedition, on their return to France, divulged the image of a new nation that had declared against the kings' absolutism and consecrated the democratic spirit of the calvinism and that of the english revolution of the XVII century.

Francisco de Miranda also talked about a nation freed from the absolutism when he returned from the expedition, beginning to spread these ideas through the secret societies having influence in libertarian principles and that of emancipation among the creoles that travelled to Spain to improve in the commerce or otherwise request public positions.

Francisco de Miranda founded The American Rationale in London, secret entity and alma mater in which were developed the most important meetings of South Americans seeking the revolution in America. This great American Rationale set up a few later, under the initiative of Miranda, a workshop in the fort of Cadiz –Spain- under the name of "Lautaro Society" or "Rationale Knights" and there were already affiliated in this Workshops in 1808 many great men of Spain and most of the South Americans staying in the Peninsula. It can be mentioned among the first, the count of "Fist in the face", pseudonym that he had taken because of the fists that he hit, he was Miranda's confidant, although it was never known his true identity, it is only known that he was a Spanish aristocrat.

The argentinian Jose Maria Zapiola was named as secretary to this lodge.

Bernardo Riquelme that did not yet used his father Ambrosio O'Higgins' surname, Viceroy of Peru in those times of 1788, Bernardo was directly related to Miranda, who gave him classes of mathematics, and a great friendship arose between them which inspired Miranda to trust him his plans. Bernardo met two south american priests in Cadiz in 1795, Jose Cortes Madariaga, chilean and Juan Pablo Fretes, these were his first collaborators in the organization of the lodge American Rationale formed in London by Miranda two years ago.

In the Cadiz's centers, they received the characteristic cross from Miranda's hands some men of the height of Simón Bolívar, José de San Martín, José Miguel Carrera, Carlos María de Alvear, Andrés Bello, José María Villamil, Mariano Moreno, Tomás Guido and the priest Juan Pablo Fretes, writer from paraguayan origin, he who greatly befriended Jose de San Martin during his stay in Spain.

This is the reason why it is intuited that the independence of America was being plotted before Napoleon's invasion to Spain, which is the reason that has been always given since then.

The North American merchant ships that reached the Atlantic and Pacific oceans to practice the smuggling under pretext of the hunting of whale and seawolf. The crew stimulated the creoles against the Spanish domination. Each of them was a potential ideological agent, in fact his main objective was that all America adopted the republican system and be separated from Europe, thus the young republic of the United States of North America hoped for its enlargement by taking hold of all the commerce and wealth of America.

The north American example seemed more attractive before the opinion of Voltaire's ideas against the despotism; those of Montesquieu about the division of powers; those of Rousseau in relation to rights and man's freedom; those of Diderot and D'Alambert, encyclopaedists that exalted the reason's priority and excellence so, when the General States gathered in France in 1789 summoned by Luis XVI to overcome the political and social crisis stimulated by the bankruptcy of the national treasury because of the war, the anxiety of freedom and equality overflowed.

The French Revolution that began as a transformation of the absolute monarchy into constitutional monarchy, ended taking France into a terrorist republic that, by the people reaction and alongside its successive stages, National Assembly, Legislative Assembly, Constituent Assembly with the Declaration of the Rights of men and the citizens, expression of liberalism's postulates, Convention and Directory that abolished the privileges, destroyed the royal power, the parliaments and the corporations and disabled the power of the Church, all of this propitiated Napoleon's coup d'état on November 9th and 10th 1799 which led the country to the military dictatorship, or Bonaparte's Consulate and then the Napoleonic Empire in 1804.

The death of Louis XVI in the guillotine by agreement of the Convention determined Charles IV to join England in a coalition against the revolutionary France, but after a disastrous war and under Manuel Godoy's influence broke with his ally and restored the relations, by signing the Peace of Basle the Spanish government signed a defensive and offensive Alliance with the Directory, only for the case of war against Great Britain and joined Napoleon, whom was supposed to become the master of Europe.

This new Spain's politics was going to bring dangerous consequences for the colonies in America.

As a new war against England was imminent, the King ordered the Governor of Chile on November 22nd 1804 to attend to the defense of the Kingdom with resources that he could find by himself without waiting assistance from Peru, and being independent in case of war, trying to reduce at the greatest extent the expenditures and the troop. This same order was repeated some days after on November 30th communicating this government the declaration of war against England and in this document was recommended how many decisions may be convenient for the defense and that he obtained from the vassals and other resources from the country which may be possible for this end.

The English fleet in charge of Admiral Nelson destroyed the french one commanded by the admiral Villeneuve and the Spanish one commanded by admiral Gravina in the battle of Trafalgar in 1805.

The loss of the Spanish navy in the battle was in the advantage of the revolution and the ancient rivalry between Spaniards and creoles, stirring constantly the spirit of revolt in the colonies.

Upon winning the war, England remained master of the seas, which allowed it to seize the Dutch colony of the Cape, in the extreme south of Africa and turned that point in the center of navy operations against the spanish america, falling upon Buenos Aires.

In compliance with the orders that the king had given of not receiving assistance of resources to Chile from Peru, this suspended the remittance of funds with which the troop from Valdivia's stronghold was paid in

1806, so that the government of Chile had to attend this expenditure with funds coming from the tobacco income of the kingdom. These innovations caused indifference among the Chileans since it was their general conviction that the kingdom would not be attacked by the English due to the great distance that England was and in such case there would be only attacks from privateers. This conviction of not being attacked disappeared when news arrived in 1806 that the English had invaded Buenos Aires in June of that year, it was at once thought that they would try to extend their dominions to the near regions and even to Chile that they prepared to reject the enemy before this eventuality, although without financial help from Peru nor veteran troops from Spain, they should defend by themselves with their scarce resources.

In order to prepare the defense, Governor Muñoz de Guzman gathered the colonels of the urban militia on September 1st 1806, informing them of the kingdom's military situation, the means of defense with which they counted on and the way of operating against the enemy in case that the so feared invasion occurred. At the end of the meeting, the Governor asked to be given by written the opinions expounded in the conference to be thoroughly studied. Out of the meeting with the most important personages of the city, they expressed in the document that the professional troops should be increased, even though, it would be necessary to increase taxes for sustaining them and even resort to the Church's properties. The Governor considered that this attitude was not right, and thought in the strictest economy for the defense without creating new taxes, asking the Colonel of Militia and Secretary of War don Judas Tadeo de Reyes to make a project of a defensive plan which consisted in war of ambushes and surprises, mapuche-styled, in order to attack the invaders at the time of landing and, in case that this failed he proposed to gather 4.000 or 5.000 agile , strong and brave men without home nor family that may stop them; resistant to bodily fatigue, cold, heat and rain; able in the handle of the knife, these men could form a voluntary corps of knifers, they should come from the mines and the small farms accompanied by their patrons whom would be named corporals, sergeants and captains to train them and command them. The commanders would be appointed among the landowners from the nobility. This plan was approved by the Governor.

The English had in fact landed in Rio de la Plata in 1806, in the place called Punta Quilmes. Buenos Aires was seized by British troops commanded by General Guillermo Beresford, whom also settled in the coast of the Eastern Band – Montevideo-.

Before so big an attack, a Spanish army of 2.000 men under the command of the officer Santiago Liniers and supported by the civil population defeated the British forces with the surrender of 1.200 English that delivered their arms before the capitulation of general Beresford, remaining prisoners of the Spaniards.

The news of the reconquest of Buenos Aires on August 12th 1806 disappeared the fears of the chileans to be invaded by the english, relaxing them from the tensions in which they have lived that year.

Shortly after, in 1807, there was a new British landing in which they seized the city of Reduccion and made the viceroy Sobremonte believe that their intention was to continue toward Montevideo. The British troops of General Samuel Auchmuty formed by 11.000 men seized the city of Montevideo at a price of important losses of human lives.

Before the news that the English had occupied Montevideo that same year, the Chileans' fears emerged again, returning to the warlike preparations. Under these circumstances, a Royal order reached Chile in which the Governor was informed that it could not be sent to him assistance from Spain because of the blockade of its ports and therefore they should make juntas in the towns and were agreed in them the best defensive plan. In order to raise the patriotic morale, the Governor sent an official communication to the council of Santiago in which it said among other things: *"The English coming to disturb this land is to go or die"* and it concluded *"I shall die in this land if necessary, surrounded by those that His Majesty has given me in custody"*.

The fear of an invasion increased in Valparaiso upon knowing the communiqué on the lack of naval and military assistance coming from the metropolis. They decided a good defensive plan by which they withdrew all the provisions that were stored for the exportation in case that the English were about to subdue the port. They chose by acclamation new councilors in Open Council, these were devoted without delay together with the Governor to put a defensive plan, undertook several public works that were financed by their own money because the city lacked enough incomes, without the need of imposing new obligations on the population.

In the attack to Montevideo, the Spaniards could not repel this English attack this time, since Buenos Aires did not have too many men in that time. The Spaniards were forced to capitulate and the viceroy had to take refuge in the city of Cordoba where he began searching supporters among the people discontented with the English presence. The confrontations under the command of Santiago Liniers took place in Buenos Aires with the defeat of the British forces that suffered during the confrontation more than 3.500 casualties and numerous injuries, capitulating their general.

The second attempt to seize Buenos Aires on the side of the English also failed. The Buenos Aires Mayor, Martin de Alzaga y Olivarria heroically contributed to save the city from the invasion, the admiral Home Popham suffered a loss of 3.000 men from his powerful army.

Being recovered Buenos Aires for the Spanish crown.

With these dreadful defeats, it was put an end to the British attempts to occupy the main Spanish towns in the Rio de La Plata, wherein once normality returned in 1807, Santiago Liniers was proclaimed Viceroy interim and ratified his viceroyalty, he received the title of count of Buenos Aires.

The commotion of these events reached to Chile, where they were fearful that the English now tried not only to invade the port of Valparaiso, but all the country. They quickly started the military preparations and the exercises and manoeuvres to stand an eventual British attack. The Unitarian conscience had its best symbol in the King as a common link of the dominions, his figure was respected and loved as a superhuman entity, and all this made the people of Chile to be protected in the case of a possible attack.

For these same reasons, when Francisco de Miranda organized in 1806 a flotilla from London, with which he went to the coast of Venezuela with intentions of proclaiming there a republic independent from Spain, its inhabitants did not want to hear him and the Enterprise failed, having to run away because they angrily expelled him.

The merchant Mateo Arnaldo Hoevel from Swedish ancestry reached Talcahuano, in Chile, at those times; he reached as purser of the "Grampur", with the purpose of practicing the smuggling, being discovered by the Spanish authorities that requisitioned the ship to be later auctioned: Hoevel, after a long process, managed to be given the money obtained by "Grampur"'s auction. Once obtained his purpose, this skilful merchant settled in the surroundings of Santiago and shortly after, when the first signs of independence started, he rushed to take part in the struggles, following closely the patriots' steps.

Meanwhile Napoleon, failing in the attempt to invade England, decided to ruin her by the Continental Blockade consisting in prohibiting the countries from the European continent any trade with England, but Portugal that lived on the English trade did not want to respect the blockade since had it meant the ruin and was placed under the protection of the English King George III in 1807.

Invaded Portugal by the French and Spaniards troops, the Portuguese royal family and the court took refuge in Brazil.

Unexpected events came to suddenly change the situation of the Spanish colonies.

Napoleon agreed with Charles IV and the minister Godoy between 1805 and 1806, this latter proposed him the invasion and going into a partition of Portugal. An Alliance with Spain guaranteed him the South front.

Napoleon prepared with Izquierdo, Godoy's secret agent, the Treaty of Fontainebleau on October 27th 1807, by which Portugal was divided in threee parts: that of the North, to compensate Etruria's dethroned kinds, that of the center, to change it for Gibraltar and other colonies snatched by the english, and that of the south, to Godoy as Prince of Los Algarves and, Charles IV to whom Napoleon guaranteed the posesión of this states in Europe, he would take the title of Emperor of the Americas.

Shortly before the ratification of the Treaty, french troops crossed the Pyrenees with Godoy's approval.

A series of disputes and intrigues divided the Royal family: on the one side the king Charles IV and his first ministry and on the other side the heir Prince Fernando, who was known because of his hatred for Godoy.

Don Ignacio Carrera y Cuevas, member of one of the wealthiest families of the Chilean aristocracy, descendant to Spanish nobles, sent to Spain his son Jose Miguel, haughty young, arrogant and stubborn to be submitted to Santiago's social considerations.

He studied in the "Carolino" school, where he had as schoolfriend he who would be a great guerrilla fighter Manuel Rodriguez Erdoiza, whose friendship they would always keep.

Don Ignacio sent him to Cadiz so that he may start in the learning of commerce, although Jose Miguel already had some military inclinations since he was lieutenant at the age of eighteen.

In 1807, with 22 years, Jose Miguel Carrera came from Chile to Cadiz. He brought a lot of letters to the friends of the mother country. On his arrival, he watched the number of officers in Cadiz with their beautiful uniforms and their distinctive of military ranks. José Miguel without worrying about learning commerce, he joined the regiment "Auxiliary Forces of Spain" stationed in Cadiz. He met in this militia the captain Jose de San Martin y Matorras and the lieutenant Carlos Maria de Alvear, both of them previously come from Argentina.

San Martín and Alvear introduced themselves to Jose Miguel Carrera:

- I'm captain Jose de San Martin, argentinian. My three Brothers have also followed the career of the arms: welcome to the regiment of Spain -.
- I'm lieutenant Carlos Maria de Alvear, also argentinian. So I say the same thing: welcome to the regiment -.
- Thanks, you're welcome, Jose Miguel Carrera, I'm Chilean, from Santiago, my father and my three Brothers are there. My father is Colonel of the Royal Militias and my two brothers also follow the career of the arms -.

Carrera very wondered, asked:

- San Martín Are you also argentinian? , but you do have andalusian accent -.
- I say! , yes , I'm argentinian, I was born in Yapeyu, a little town of the jesuit missions, frontier with Brasil. When I was four years old I came to the Mother Country with my parents, both of them are spaniards, from Castilla La Vieja, I was raised in Madrid where I attended with my three brothers to the Nobles Seminary of Madrid, where the seminarists could accede the career of the arms, exactly, the Guards of the Spanish Infantry, it is a corps of elite of the army, until I entered the Regiment of Murcia in 1789. My andalusian accent is because I live for many years in Andalucia, I have fought in Melilla against the moors, and also in Oran, besides combating the French in the Pyrenees in the campaigns of Rosellon, where I obtained the rank of second lieutenant, later I fought against the English in the battle of Trafalgar -.

Carlos María de Alvear commented:

- I was born in Santo Ángel Misiones Orientales, when I was 15 years old, all the family moved to the Mother Country. My father is the Mayor Diego de Alvear y Ponce de Leon, Commander of the fleet in which we travelled, who after fulfilled his mission of drawing the limits of Paraguay, we came in the "Medea", frigate that my father commanded, wherein I could travel because I went as cadet of the Regiment of Dragoons of Buenos Aires, and my mother and my seven younger Brothers with the goods and chattels went in the frigate "Mercedes". We had moved here from Montevideo in time of peace on August 9th 1804, but when we were in front of the coast of Cadiz, in the Cape of Santa Maria, in the Portuguese coast of Algarve, four English frigates approached by surprise under the command of the Commodore Graham Moore, the Brigadier Jose Bustamante y Sierra, Spaniard, trusting allowed them an approach, before the amazement of all that went in the ship, we knew that we remained as prisoners to her british majesty and taken to the port of Gosport. The Spaniards decided to send a delegation in a boat in order to parley and ask explanations, but as the English saw that our ships did not surrender, they sent a boat to parley with the frigate "Medea" that was carrying the flag, but my father said that this did not surrender, the English broke fire with incendiary cannonballs red hot, and in a moment of the scuffle they hit directly the frigate "Mercedes" that was destroyed when her magazine exploded, seeing how my mother and my seven younger brothers died. At the 12:30, the Commodore Bustamante surrendered the fleet, loosing 269 persons and having 80 injuries. They took us the few survivors kidnapped to Great Britain; we were there, my father and me, one year until 1805. The battle of Cape of Santa Maria was severely criticized by the British press, since the attack had been made in times of peace. Spain declared war on Great Britain on December 14th 1804, being the antechamber of what would be the battle of Trafalgar. Later, may father met Luisa Rebeca Ward who came with us to Spain and three years later they got married.

At the age of 18, I entered as second lieutenant in the corps of elite The Brigade of Royal Carabineers -.

José Miguel moved to Madrid, leaving among their companions a nice and unerasable remembrance; the same happened with the young cadiz girl, that the gracefulness of Jose Miguel's figure, the beauty of his countenance, the distinction of his manners, the ease and frankness of his manners, made him very popular and loved by them. Jose Miguel promised to write everybody, and he did it for a long time.

It was in Madrid where he was surprised to see in the streets Spanish and French officers without showing the utmost hostility.

Shortly after, he was aware that the king Charles IV had authorized the passing of the french troops through the Spanish territory bound for Lisbon in 1808 commanded by general Junot with 25.000 well equipped men.

All seemed to be developing in orderly form, until a straggling patrol of 50 French soldiers was attacked by some guerrilla patriots, thrusting the knife into french, who were sacked and abandoned in the outskirts.

A popular uprising, the famous Aranjuez revolt determined the fall of Godoy and Charles IV's abdication in favour of his son Fernando, Prince of Asturias, but he assured, on french General Joaquin Murat's advice, that the abdication had been forced.

Pretending that he wanted to settle the disputes between the Royal family, Napoleon knew to attract it to an interview in Bayonne, north of the Pyrenees. Charles IV came up to ask the Emperor protection.

On the other hand, the french Murat induced Fernando to be present before Napoleon in order to obtain his acknowledgement.

Father and son celebrated with Napoleon the famous interview, where Fernando returned the Crown to his father acknowledging him as king, all this concluded with Napoleon's idea of making father and son to renounce their rights to the crown of Spain and of the Indies. Charles IV abdicated in favour of his good friend Napoleon, who at once put in the throne of Spain to his eldest brother Jose Bonaparte, whom already was king of Naples. He installed in this latter charge his brother-in-law General Murat with the name of Joaquin I.

Fernando VII and his parents were retained in different places of France.

These detentions caused a general indignation against the French that were occupying Madrid. The Spaniards loyal to their king Fernando VII formed boards of government in the different provinces and a "Supreme Central" in Sevilla. Dispersed this latter by the advances of the French, it was replaced by a Council of Regency which was established in Cadiz, where the Courts or Chamber of Representatives were also gathered.

In 1807, the Spanish authorities of the port of Talcahuano detained the protestant physician Procopio Pollock, arrived to Chile in an American ship and, taking advantage of his stay in the country, he began to spread his democratic and republican ideas by means of conversations or distribution of documents that contained the Declaration of Independence and the Constitution of the United States. While his process was developing, he managed to befriend Juan Martinez de Rozas, Secretary to the Governor of Concepcion in that time, and Antonio Garcia Carrasco, the future Governor of the kingdom. Polack, supported by this friendship, could move to Santiago where he began spreading the independentist ideas through a written newspaper entitled "Gazette of Procopio". Pollock would continue as a combative figure during the process of the Independence, and even participating in the national politics.

At the beginning of 1808, it could not have been yet foreseen the emancipation movement in the Kingdom of Chile. The governor Muñoz de Guzman died and according to the disposition passed by Charles IV in 1806, the succession of the post should be assumed by the highest ranking military. However the Real Audiencia disregarded the order given by the King, and entrusted the government to its own regent don Juan Rodriguez Ballesteros whom took the oath at once.

Almost at the same time the doctor Juan Martinez de Rozas, former adviser to the Intendancy of Concepcion, whose capital was the head of the army command of La Frontera, induced the engineer's brigadier Francisco Antonio Garcia Carrasco to call a meeting for the highest ranking officers, that meeting agreed to acknowledged him as Governor by reason of Charles IV's royal order of 1806.

Before this armed forces' threatening attitude, the Real Audiencia had to rectify and acknowledge Garcia Carrasco as the best one entitled to the position six months later.

In fact, the effective intervention in the matter of the governmental succession was that of doctor Vicente Larrain, canon of the Santiago's Cathedral, the counsellor of the Real Audiencia was dealing with him the most important issues concerning his position, outside of the legal procedures. The communication between them in the matter of Garcia Carrasco was so evident; that La Real Audiencia believed that the judgments issued by its counsellor on the fulfilment of the royal order of October 24th 1806 about the governmental succession, in which Garcia Carrasco supported his pretensions to the charge of Governor-Interim had been written by the canon Larrain.

This event was the origin of a deep antagonism between the Government and the Audiencia, the two most powerful pillars in the colonial regime.

Garcia Carrasco, who had acceded to the government because of his seniority instead of merits, was a 65 years old military having neither administrative nor political experience, since he had spent the most part of his life in the Camps out of any social life or courtier manners.

Juan Martinez de Rozas, 49 years old and native of Mendoza, the Real Audiencia had granted him the title of lawyer in 1784 after completion of his law career in the University of San Felipe. In Concepcion, he was under the protection of Ambrosio O'Higgins, he married a wealthy heiress to the Urrutia family, he thus became the most influential man in the Spanish aristocracy or "pencona" as it was known, very refined, reader of the encyclopaedists, and he was introduced as a well educated person. With a domineering character and a great ambition of power, which made him an unscrupulous politician that aspired to satisfy his thirst of power and dominate Santiago aristocracy, besides, he felt a great resentment against the Spanish government for not having been appointed as adviser to the Captaincy General.

Carrasco, due to his administrative inefficacy and political incapacity, that's why he made Rozas his main adviser, because of both his gratitude for having been granted the post and for acknowledging him the capabilities that he did not have.

Due to the Real Audiencia's hostility and the Creole element, Rozas thought of attracting this latter, he induced the new Governor to made the decision of increasing the importance of the Council by the addition of twelve auxiliary councilors to this institution, all of them coming from the upper class such as: Manuel de Salas , José Antonio Rojas , Juan Manuel de la Cruz , Antonio Martínez de Matta , Ignacio de La Carrera Ureta , Francisco de Borja Larraín , José Pérez García , Tomás Ignacio Urmeneta , Joaquín López de Sotomayor , Juan Enrique Rosales , Antonio del Sol and Pedro Javier Echevers , all of them appointed by the Governor on July of 1808 without consulting the counsellor not the Real Audiencia. This measure seemed to be necessary before the estate of war with England; the Spanish instability demanded the strengthening of a powerful organization that served as a means of expression for the collective will.

He appointed the auxiliary councilors on July 12th for the time that the state of war and the grounded suspicions of invasion in the southern part of the continent may last.

On the July 14th, the already enlarged Council inaugurated its activities presided by the Governor, who ran into the dissatisfaction of the old officials by the modification of its structure and by the Council's pretension of intervening in matters of such an importance, they called this pretension excessive and illegal because of the enlargement granted. The opposition of the ordinary mayor Jose Teodoro Sanchez, was the representative of this attitude, ratifying his conviction, being absent from the meetings of the entity until the end of his mandate.

José Antonio Rojas was appointed doyen councilor. The new Governor Garcia Carrasco completely participate of the interpretation that the Council gave to the intervention he had in this issue, naming Bernardo Vera y Pintado on September 14th for the charge of Secretary of the Council.

Shortly after the integration of the Council, several mails coming from Buenos Aires were bringing startling news about the events recently occurred in Spain such as the revolt of Aranjuez and the abdication of Charles IV in favour of Fernando VII, conference of Bayonne, and uprising of the Spaniards against the french, acknowledgement of Jose Bonaparte as king of Spain, formation of the Junta of Sevilla, destined to direct the resistance against the Napoleonic invasion, etc.

These news caused in Chile great indignation, the creole and spanish reaction was unanimous in favor of Fernando VII and the integrity of the spanish Empire.

On December 1808, authorities and the people solemnly took the oath in favor of Fernando VII.

After the oath of the legitimate king, it took place an event that was to blur more Governor Garcia Carrasco's little prestige and at the same time discrediting the colonial administration and Martinez de Rozas' withdrawal.

The frigate "Escorpion" reached the Chilean coasts for the second time commanded by Tristan Bunker, who had established contacts with an American adventurer Henry Faulkner, the two smugglers agreed with the administrador of the estate Tocopalma, Jose Fuensalida to carry out their illicit business with plentiful smuggling of cloths from England.

The administrator wrote to the adventurer Faulkner informing him about the arrival of the ship, at the same time he let the delegate of the district of Colchagua Francisco Antonio de La Carrera know of the intentions of the ship's captain.

Gathered together Fuensalida, de La Carrera (not a relative of the Carrera family), and Faulkner, they agreed to seize the shipment and divide it among them: but as they lacked the forces to do it, they informed the Governor about their plans asking him to send them the necessary Dragoons. As to this, the Governor Garcia

Carrasco and his adviser Martinez de Rozas set a trap for the english smuggling frigate, deciding to hide this matter before the custom authorities.

In order to deceive more easily the privateer Bunker, they contrived the plan that by means of an alleged marquis de Larrain's steward, the one who would do the interchanging of English cloths by cooper.

Once the "Escorpion" moored in the dock on September 25th, Faulkner, De La Carrera's delegate and the alleged steward got on board, closing the deal. Meanwhile soldiers disguised as sailors were carrying the copper to the ship, and the dealers invited a banquet to the unlucky captain, they killed him and several other sailors at a given sign, they seized the frigate "Escorpion" and its merchandises without any difficulty. After this attack, they divided the merchandise among them, which caused a rejection of these before the honest people, prompting Rozas to withdraw to Concepcion and Garcia Carrasco, because of the absence of this latter, was discredited in his government due to the influence of councillors completely contrary to the Creole element which prevailed in the Council.

On the other hand, the supplantation of the presence of the marquis de Larrain's steward to attract them to the ambush and trap the merchants and kill them, outraged the marquis that wanted to clear his nonparticipation in this matter, presenting himself at the Real Audiencia on November 11th 1808, asking that he may be allowed to make a report to prove that he had no intervention in the capture and death of the English from the frigate "Escorpion" and that he had been supplanted by merchant from Santiago.

The tribunal accepted this petition. The Governor Garcia Carrasco intervened in favour of the impostor claiming the knowledge of the case; but the Real Audiencia refused, and the marquis could prove his innocence. To all this, it had to be added the annoying oppositions between the mandatary and the Real Audiencia, which did not forgive him the events occurred with his election in 1806. Many nobles were supporting the marquis, that's what was keeping the Governor away from the sympathies of the Spaniards who were the majority. So in this way, he did not count on the Creole or on the Spaniards.

Shortly after this event, it was known that the Spaniards that were up in arms against Napoleon had obtained a victory in the battle of Bailen, wherein Jose de San Martin fought getting the medal of the victors and the rank of Lieutenant Colonel under the orders of general Coupigny.

On September 15th 1808, Jose Miguel Carrera who had enlisted in the army was received by General Castaños the "victor" or to say it properly the "great absent" of the battle of Bailen, and was destined for the regiment Farnesio in formation, with the rank of Lieutenant. His entry represented for Jose Miguel being three years in the most important army in the world of that time.

The Council of Regency informed the government on September 18th 1808 the successful actions of the Spaniards against the Frenchmen with Jose Bonaparte's flight to the North and that of the French army of Aragon, the loss of the Frenchmen in Portugal that was turning into operational base of the army of General Wellington, to what news followed that the emperor had passed to Spain and recovered Madrid, which made them think that the war in the peninsula was very far from ending with a victory for Fernando VII.

The Central Junta sent emissaries to America so that they acknowledge Seville as the Central Junta. Some Chilean persons upheld that it was not indispensable to neither acknowledge and pledge obedience to Junta of Seville nor acknowledge Jose Bonaparte, and that it would be enough to pledge obedience to Fernando VII, and the kingdom could be governed by its present ruler and also by private juntas elected among themselves during the king's captivity without this changing their allegiance to the monarchy.

The defeatist look that the war against the Frenchmen was taking grouped the Chileans in two different factions: Goths or "Saracens" and Patriots.

The royalists or "Saracens" were the Spaniards and the creoles headed by the president of the Real Audiencia, high chiefs and officers, oidores, high officials and the Clergy in general, they demanded the allegiance to the Central Junta of Government established in Seville and regency of Cadiz. Out of the group of royalist creoles, Judas Tadeo Reyes, secretary of the Governorship, was among those having the highest moral exponent.

The patriots, whose number rapidly grew, were not still thinking of the independence; they adduced that it had to be established a National Junta of Government in Chile led by them, which may govern on behalf of Fernando VII, replacing Governor Garcia Carrasco. According to the Laws of Indies, they upheld that the Central Junta did not have the right to rule the American kingdoms, since they are integral part of Castile related to the King but not to the Spanish nation. This theory was supported by the most distinguished Chilean families that counted on the influence that their wealth of great lands peopled with tenants gave them. One of these families of the most important of the Castilian - Basque aristocracy, the Larrain was so numerous that it was called the Eight hundred or Ottomans with the reverend Joaquin Larrain on the top, and another of the most important in influence were the Carrera, descendants from the conquerors, also the Errazuriz, Eizaguirre, Prado, Ovalle, etc.

Among the group of patriots were also found the discontented with the regime, among who there were: the rebels by temperament such as don Antonio Rojas; ambitious like Martinez de Rozas; argentinians like don Bernardo Vera y Pintado, don Juan Pablo Fretes, Álvarez Jonte and

Manuel Dorrego, whom wanted to replace the Governor Garcia Carrasco with a Junta commanded by themselves.

The two parties were little by little provoking each other. The Spaniards began calling the creoles as rebels and insurrectionists; these called themselves patriots or patricians and called the contraries with the nicknames of Goths and Saracens.

The Governor favored the Council of Santiago which became the alma mater of the situation, taking the initiatives to prevent the dangers that were now threatening the Kingdom, taking the resolution of defense, agreeing a session to appoint and fill the positions of auxiliary councillors which had been declined by the former ones, agreed that Juan Martinez de Rozas, Manuel Perez Cotapos and Francisco Cisterna may occupy these positions and to name Bernardo Vera y Pintado and Joaquin Fernandez de Leiva as extraordinary secretaries, and the appointed persons were on duty that same month.

The Governor affirmed that:

- Don't think the Frenchmen of turning their ambitious looks to these dominions, believing us without help or means of defense, knowing the Council that the loyalty of the inhabitants of Chile does not degenerate at all from that of their fathers', who at the price of their heroic blood took out this country from the state of barbarity in which it was and joined it to the Spanish Empire, they civilised it, peopled it, and turned it religious. Being true that Chile is brave and has good horses and many resources of subsistence, it is also true that we are unarmed and short of basic need items to face the evils that may strike to us, however, we cannot stay inactive trusting in the distance and in our local situation, we will show the enemy, with the few resources we have but the arms in hand, that we only want to be Spaniards and the obedience to the domination of our incomparable King and Gentleman don Fernando VII-.

The Council was leaving witness that in the middle of its distresses, they wanted to have resources to help their brothers from the European Spain to be freed from the French yoke, cooperating for the good condition of Chile, in general, and that of the Mother Country.

These unequivocal manifestations of the Council of Santiago and of the whole kingdom for the national cause were not satisfactory for the aspirations of the European Spaniards that were skeptical about its sincerity.

In one of the social gatherings organized in don Antonio de Rojas' house, wherein many of the main creoles were gathering, the priest Joaquin Petinto was commenting before the gentleman Vera y Pintado and gentleman Rojas:

- Gentlemen here present: I think on my own and I believe that I am right that all these adhesions of the europeans to the city of Santiago, his Council and of the entire kingdom to the national cause, do not seem to me to be sincere since all the americans are traitors in their hearts and they don't rise because they lack forces to do it -.

Gentleman Vera y Pintado exclaimed:
- Reverend Petinto: I refute the difference that you do by calling them Europeans and Americans, I respectfully consider that call them that way is the characteristic of men without principles. We are Spaniards and Creoles, born or not in America, we are all faithful by due loyalty to the sovereign -.

In that time, the princess Carlota Joaquina de Bourbon, Fernando VII's eldest sister and the divorced wife of the regent Prince of Portugal Juan VI, exiled in Brazil, sent on September 1809 a messenger to the Governor Garcia Carrasco with the order of offering her services to Chile. She proposed that by being Charles IV's eldest daughter she had right to the throne when the King was absent, therefore she wanted that they accepted her as regent while the legitimate sovereign's captivity may last.

The president politely refused the offer.

The infanta had sent the count of Palmella to the Central Junta of Seville to claim her eventual rights to the throne of Spain and demand the abolition of the Salic Law, which she did not obtain.

In the environment of the patriots opposed to dona Carlota, among whom were counted José Antonio Rojas, Bernardo Vera y Pintado Juan Esteban Manzano and José Antonio Ovalle, upon knowing that Garcia Carrasco was in communications with the princess, he was accused of treason to king Fernando VII calling him and the few followers that he had as "carlotinos" which meant disloyal to the king and the Junta which may rule on his behalf.

In fact, Garcia Carrasco thought that dona Carlota pretended to create a throne at whatever cost in America.

This same Messenger had been sent to Buenos Aires by the princess, but her offering was not accepted, since they suspected that so much interest was perhaps to annex the throne to Brazil, and if it were so, they were delivering the country to Portugal, therefore it was as if it were to deliver it to England, although even so there were some carlotinos who thought of a crown for Argentina.

Information was sent to the government of Garcia Carrasco from Buenos Aires about the existence of seditious parties that were plotting against him, to which the Governor answered with a missive:

"I'm in need of auxiliaries and support for all my ideas: I do observe in these tribunals and municipalities so much popular contemplation and little adhesion to me".

A royal order issued in the Royal Palace of the Alcazar of Seville arrived on April 14th 1809, in which it was said:

"The King our Sire Don Fernando VII, and the Supreme Central Governmental Junta of the Kingdom, considering that the vast and precious dominions that Spain possesses in the Indies, they are not properly colonies or factories like those of the other nations, but an essential and integral part of the Spanish monarchy, and wishing to strengthen the sacred bonds indissolubly that unite both dominions, as also these heroical loyalty and patriotism that they have just so decisively proved to Spain in this most critical occasion that any nation has so far seen. Considering the judgement of the Council of the Indies of the last 21st of November, in which the dominions referred to, should have representation and being part of the Central Governmental Junta of the Kingdom by means of their respective deputies. In order that this royal decision may be effective, the viceroyalties of Nueva España, Peru, Nuevo Reino de Granada and Buenos Aires, and the independent Captaincies-General of the Island of Cuba, Puerto Rico, Guatemala, Chile, provinces of Venezuela and the Philippines have to name an individual each one representing its respective district".

The communiqué arrived Chile for designating deputies in the Courts of Cadiz in the capacity of being part of the monarchy and the patriotism that has been credited before Napoleon's attempt to dispose of the monarchy. Due to the tension between the Government and the Council of Santiago, it was indifferently received by both the creoles and the Governor, who refrained from communicating to the corporations the official letters in which he had been conveyed the news and stopped the decree. The Central Junta of Cadiz, upon not receiving news, decided to designate as representatives two creoles that lived in Cadiz: don Miguel Riesco and don Joaquin Fernandez de Leiva.

The popular concern on Spain's state of situation was intense. In a social gathering held in conspirator don Jose Antonio de Rojas's house on July 24th 1809, among whom there were some argentinian patriots that had contacts with those who were working in Buenos Aires for the formation of a Junta of Government: don Juan Antonio Ovalle, the Council's lawyer and the lawyer don Bernardo Vera y Pintado, don Juan Pablo Fretes and don Manuel Dorrego, the owner of the house was informing them:

- I have been very sorrowful because of what has happened in La Coruña with the death of English general Moor, the Frenchmen have seized Galicia, although, I really think that the Englishmen overstate the bad conditions of our things. I also inform you the news brought from Europe by an English frigate sailed from London in February and already reached Valdivia and they say that there is no hope that Austria and Russia declare to be in our favour and that England is embarking 70.000 men to Spain and that the army that had withdrawn from La Coruña has gone to Lisbon.–

Gentleman Dorrego suggested:
- We all know here that things in the mother country are getting worse and worse, that is why we should hasten the downfall of Garcia Carrasco and also that of the viceroy in Buenos Aires gentleman Hidalgo de Cisneros, forming ourselves a National Junta of Government. Indeed, my contacts have informed me that Garcia Carrasco and him are in constant communication each other-.

Quito on August 10th, 1809 gave the first shout in favour of the independence.

Don Juan de Dios Morales was the brain of the movement; in the night of August 9th, 1809 there was a great activity of the patriots and the people of Quito in general. The living room of dona Manuela Cañizares's residence in the house of the sacrarium alongside the Metropolitan Cathedral, which she was renting, was set up as assembly proceeding to elect a Sovereign Junta of Government, being elected president the marquis of Selva Negra don Juan Pio Montufar and vicepresident the bishop don Jose Cuero y Caicedo; secretary of state of the interior don Juan de Dios Morales; of Grace and Justice don Manuel Quiroga; of Treasury with Juan Larrea. The conspiracy burst out, the patriots got without difficulty the support of the local troops and captured the members of the government.

Don Antonio Ante was in charge of letting the count Ruiz de Castilla know his dismissal through a letter. On the 2nd of August 1810, it began the great massacre with the troops which had been sent by the viceroy from Peru, which were quartered in the city.

The First Shout of Independence.

Quito sowed the seed and America followed its example.

It was the first that gave the cry of independence; it followed Caracas on the 18th of April, Buenos Aires on the 25th of May, Bogota on the 20th of July, Mexico on the 16th of September and Santiago on the 18th of September.

It attained the imponderable title of "**Quito Light of America**".

Let's return to Chile. On 1810, a violent measure taken by the Governor Garcia Carrasco occurred, he was persuaded by the Viceroy of Buenos Aires' advices, Hidalgo de Cisneros, who advised him of being severe with those who were supposed to be conspirator.

One night, Governor Garcia Carrasco sent a troop to don Jose Antonio de Rojas's house, wherein the Council's lawyer don Juan Antonio Ovalle and the lawyer don Bernardo Vera y Pintado had been seen entering it. The three of them were captured and sent to Valparaiso to be embarked to Lima at Viceroy don Fernando de Abascal's disposal.

This severe measure, only based on suspicions, caused a violent reaction of the aristocracy, the Council, the Clergy and the Real

Audiencia, they menacingly demanded that the prisoners were released, which decided the Governor to revoke the order to send them to Lima; but this solution did not appease the patriots' exaltation that were already willing to change the government, and the exaltation was even greater when they knew that the prisoners Rojas and Ovalle had already been embarked to Callao on July 1810, Vera y Pintado was left in Valparaiso because of very high fevers which happened to him, it was even feared for his life.

Upon knowing all the city about the embarkment of these personalities, the aristocracy mobilized the neighborhood and the Council, and all together rushed in the building of the Audiencia wherein they obtained of the Governor the mandate of suspension of the sending of the prisoners to Callao and when they knew that the ship had already sailed, all of them demanded the Governor's resignation and to be replaced by a Governmental Junta.

The agitation grew with the news that the viceroy don Gabriel Hidalgo de Cisneros had been deposed in the course of an open Council with great popular participation on the 25th of May in Buenos Aires and the Creoles from Buenos Aires had established the first Revolutionary Junta. It was also decided the establishment of the National Junta of Government assuming the control of the viceroyalty. The two political trends were represented in it:

One monarchic and the other republican and liberal, respectively led by: Cornelio Saavedra and Mariano Moreno.

In Chile, the Real Audience intervened to avoid the establishment of the Junta, proposing the Council to get the Governor's resignation and be replaced by the highest ranking military, availing of the royal order of 1806. The tribunal demanded Garcia Carrasco that he may hand over the command to the militia brigadier, Mateo de Toro y Zambrano y Ureta, aged 83, count of the Conquest before an assembly of Council members, the highest ranking army and militia officers, this resignation was made on July 16th 1810.

The aspiration of establishing a Government Junta was heard outside the hall where Manuel Dorrego shouted several times:

We want a Junta!

He was silenced by those who were around him and taken away from there, Dorrego closed to the crowd presided by Juan Enrique Rosales and said that it had been lost the opportunity to establish a Govermnent Junta.

The new Governor descended from the old colonial families devoted to the commercial and agricultural business, this business that he continued with, achieving to amass a huge fortune, being owner of the La Compañía estate with 8.000 hectares near Rancagua, he was also owner of the so called Casa Colorada in Santiago and a store in the del Rey street. He was mayor and corregidor of Santiago, in this position he supported the building of the dikes, was superintendent of the House of Mint, in addition he gave in important military services for which he received the rank of Militia Brigadier and the title of count of the Conquest, the highest distinctions an American could receive from his king, in addition he was a monarchist intransigent to changes of the establishment. He accepted the position of President of the Government Junta on the condition that he would be in office while Fernando VII's imprisonment lasted.

His policy in the position was initially trying to please patriots and royalists, but he later had to incline to one or another faction, since in a moment in which the patriots seemed to be defeated, because the Governor followed the suggestions of the Real Audiencia that only acknowledged the Regency of Cadiz, which had been established on July 31st 1810 in replacement of the Central Junta of Seville. All these measures were supported by the oidores, the clergy, the merchants and the Spanish officials.

Both the royalists of the Audiencia and the juntistas of the Council wanted to handle the president to their whim, using of the fragile memory due to his advanced age and of his unsteady policy that was inclining to the opinions of the last one that was speaking to him.

The patriots were having the hope of not lossing since they knew that the Regency of Cadiz had named proprietary Governor to the Brigadier don Francisco Javier Elio, who during his government in Montevideo had shown his authoritarian spirit.

The attorney Juan Martinez de Rozas and his close friend, the young landowner Bernardo O'Higgins were supporting the agitation in the province of Concepcion, and it was supported in Santiago by the Larrain family.

The royalists had formed in palace diverse groups of relatives of the count, among who were his eldest son and the wife of this latter, the Spanish lady dona Josefa Dumont, who were in charge that nobody could approach the aged Governor to speak to him about changes of government.

At the same time the movement that asked for the Junta was activated from Buenos Aires, they were thinking that if they were not winning in Chile, the Argentinian patriots were going to be attacked by the royalists of Chile and by the forces of the Upper Peru whence the Argentinians were also attacked.

The count that at the beginning seemed to be inclined to the royalist party, he then took side for the patriots who at the beginning of September thought to resort to the force by weapons. The patriots were relying on powerful attorneys who were highly esteemed by the count of the Conquest, the attorney secretary of government don Jose Gregorio Argomedo and the adviser of this one, don Gaspar Marin, they managed that the command of the troop were delivered to chiefs of his confidence, at the same time they populated the city with the Melipilla and Rancagua militias, formed by the workers of their estates.

In spite of the requests and cryings of the daughter-in-law of the count dona Josefa Dumon in order that he did not give up, the patriots finally persuaded him and obtained from the count the authorization to summon a great Open Council or Junta of Notables which would be held on September 18th. In this way, the royalists and the Audiencia had been defeated.

The count summoned the Open Council assuring that he did it to provide peace and safety of the Kingdom in these dominions to don Fernando VII, although in order to say the truth, which the chilean patriots were claiming was the separation forever of the Spanish government.

This memorable September 18th, 1810 at the nine o'clock in the morning the assembly met in the great hall of the Tribunal of the Consulate, attending the Council, the highest civilian and military officers, the superiors of the religious orders and more than 400 neighbours, most of them were patriots who knew what they had to do.

The Governor count of the Conquest was standing up showing the emblem of power, resigning to the control he said:

- Here is the baton, have this and the command -.

The resignation of the Governor del Toro was accepted and the assembly resolved the establishment of a National Junta of Government that may rule the country during the captivity of Fernando VII.

After that, the attorney of the city don Jose Miguel Infante spoke on behalf of the Council and supported in the name of the neighborhood, whose representation he lawfully had, the convenience of establishing a Junta of Government as it was in Spain, the old legislation of the monarchy allowed the establishment of a Regency body in the absence of the sovereign and accordingly the forming of juntas. General Elio would not be accepted as governor named by the Council of Regency of Spain, since the Junta of Chile was enough to name its own governors. This aroused the protests of the spanish being present. When he ended his speech almost the whole assembly accepted Infante's proposition, shouting:

We want junta!, We want Junta!

And then it followed the naming of the seven members and two secretaries who would be part of that organization.

It was unanimously named as President Mateo de Toro Zambrano count of the Conquest, as Vice-president the elected bishop of Santiago Jose Antonio Martinez de Aldunate, Juan Martinez de Rozas, Fernando Marquez de La Plata, Ignacio de La Carrera, Juan Enrique Rosales and the Colonel Francisco Javier Reina as voting members, and two secretaries of the Junta, the lawyers Jose Gregorio Argomedo and Gaspar Marin.

For the time being, it had been accomplished the wish of exercising the command of the country.

At the end of the ceremony, all the party members gathered in the adjacent room congratulating each other.

Juan Enrique Rosales, voting member and former mayor of Santiago spoke:

- From now on, we have a lot of work left, as it is natural the suspicious Viceroy of Peru don Fernando Abascal will disapprove of the Junta, and it is possible that we suffer some unexpected attack-.

Colonel Francisco Javier Reina of the voting members replied:

- For the own stability of the Junta, we will need new troops, we will form an infantry battalion and with our excellent horses at least two cavalry squadrons and will enlarge the artillery corps, thus we will be ready for any aggression from the north. Now, for a moment changing of matters; Carrera, How is your son Jose Miguel?, I've heard that he has been injured in combat -.

- Yes, to say the truth, I'm frankly worried, since as you know, the news arrives with so much delay, I know that he fought among others, in the battle of Talavera de La Reina, wherein he was promoted to Captain of Hussars, then in the plains of La Mancha, in the battle of Ocaña, where he received a very grave sabre wound in the leg, they sent him to Cadiz for recovering, being promoted to Sergeant major of the Galicia Hussars with the right to wear the uniform and the medal. That is the last thing I know about him. I thank you very much for your interest in my son's health. Now, returning to the comments you have made about the formation of new troops, I think it would be suitable to carry out negotiations to obtain weapons in England and in Rio de La Plata-.

- Yes, I have also thought about it, but we have to proceed cautiously, in my case, for example, as a military of the line army I feel very much obliged to keep the necessary respect for the Viceroy of Lima, since the Captaincy General of Chile depends on the economic and on the military of the viceroyalty of Peru -.

Juan Enrique Rosales alluded:
- Another matter that worries us for the formation of the Junta of Government is to establish contact with the government of Buenos Aires to enlarge the Creole movement -.

Fernando Márquez de La Plata replied:
- This matter is solved, we have been informed that the Junta of Buenos Aires, before they knew about the formation of our Junta, sends us a lawyer before the Council of Santiago as its representative in Chile, as far as I'm concerned he is a pibe (a young man), he comes with the mission of obtaining help because of the dangers that are threatening it from the Upper Peru and Montevideo, centres of reaction of the royalist forces's authorities. We can receive this emissary don Antonio Alvarez Jonte, we will give him a reception as a diplomatic representative, arranging an official ceremony in the style of those that were carried out in Madrid, when it was free -.
- Gaspar Marín spoke :
- Peru is the consumer of our wheat and he is our supplier of sugar, we should prepare for a defense, since the Viceroy will strive to restore the old regime, and he knows that in the commercial and military sides we are losing -.

Months later, the Junta decided to help the government of Buenos Aires, arranging the sending of 400 men, a reduced quantity due to the scarce number of existing troops and the suspicions that aroused in Chile the possible preparation of an expedition in Peru.

Álvarez Jonte was informed that before the impossibility of detaching more forces, he was authorized to recruit people by his volition, task that the young Buenos Aires representative did with great activity, achieving to detach to Mendoza 500 men and a few of gunpowder. All these auxiliary forces detached by Chile were crossing the range to give their services in Rio de La Plata, where they stayed until their return to Chile in 1813 to fight against the viceregal army.

Juan Martinez de Rozas, Bernardo O'Higgins's close friend, was Los Angeles mayor in 1810 when they named him main leader of the Junta of Government, before he departed to Santiago, O'Higgins emphasized to him the need of establishing the freedom of commerce, and summon a National Congress, so that the people may get interested in a revolution.

Among the members of the National Junta of Government, Juan Martinez de Rozas was the most suitable to direct a revolution, since he was energetic, enlightened and intelligent.

The decease of the count of The Conquest occurred on February 1811, it favored Martinez de Rozas since he was given the powers that were in the hands of the late count.

The lawyer Martinez de Rozas organized corps of troops and bought weapons, decreed the freedom of commerce ordering that the ports of Valparaiso, Coquimbo, Talcahuano and Valdivia were open to the free commerce of the foreign powers allied to Spain and also of the neutral ones, and finished the preparations for the election of a National Congress that may replace the Junta. The purpose of summoning a Congress was to establish a true national representation following the new political ideas spread in Europe and in the United States, establishing a Constitution.

The Figueroa Mutiny.

In the meantime, the royalist party excluded from the Junta, dissatisfied with everything that this had done , they secretly plotted, and in the morning of February 1st, 1811, the day in which the elections of deputies in Santiago should be made, the Spanish Lieutenant Colonel don Tomas de Figueroa appeared in the main square with an army corps and relying on the support of the Spaniards, trying to put an end to the Creole movement, willing to stop the elections, demanding the dissolution of the Junta.

The patriots' resistance was rapidly organized with recruits under the charge of Colonel don Juan de Dios Vial. After a brief combat, the Figueroa mutiny was subdued that very same morning, and having suffered some bloodshed the mutineers were disbanding leaving fourteen dead and some injured in the square, meanwhile the leader Figueroa fled to be hidden in the convent of Santo Domingo, where Martinez Rozas took him out from and sentenced him to death, shooting him hours later in order to avoid clemency by the aristocracy.

Lieutenant Colonel don Tomas de Figueroa died as a gentleman without denouncing anybody, but the patriots blamed the Real Audiencia, being eliminated on June 1811.

With the Figueroa mutiny, it was put an abyss between Spaniards and patriots on shedding the first blood of the revolution and, later the Spaniards were reduced to whole powerlessness, observed and watched by the authorities and fearful of the strengthening of the Creole cause. They did not act again until the armed invasion may restore the old order.

During his convalescence in Cadiz, Jose Miguel Carrera received, on January 1811, the warm visit of his superior the marquis of Villapalma, bringing him news about Chile, telling him that on September 18th of the last year it had been established a Junta of Government in Santiago, in which his father was a voting member.

José Miguel hid his emotion and inside him he was deciding to return as soon as possible to his beloved Chile.

Carrera during his retreat in Cadiz was in contact with other young americans who had separatist ideals and he also embraced these ideas. After the visit of marquis of Villapalma, in which he told him about situation that Chile was going through, Jose Miguel wrote to his father who belonged to the moderate patriotic party:

"Father, I'm ready, the moment of the American independence has come: nobody can stop it with a good government, there are weapons, money and what is needed for the achievement of our freedom".

In a visit that Jose de San Martin paid to him, now with the rank of Lieutenant Colonel; both of them commented on the events in Chile and Argentina:

- As far as I can see you are almost wholly recovered, you even walk without the help of a cane -.

- Yes, it is so, Jose, so much that I'm thinking of asking my discharge of the army and returning to my country, which is going through a very difficult situation, the Governor has been dismissed and they have formed a Junta of Government in which my father is a voting member. I think that I can do there something important in favor of the patriots, my father and my brothers Juan Jose and Luis belong to this party -.

- They also formed a Junta in Buenos Aires, it may be that they enter in war against the Upper Peru and Montevideo, my thought is to ask my discharge and go to Argentina, since we will be in bad situation if the Frenchmen win, and in this state of anarchy in which Cadiz is found, the frequent emigrations to England and even more those to north America are the last proof of this bad situation in which it is found, but I can only resort to Lord Macduff, a Scottish nobleman I knew in the battle of La Albuera and he introduced me in the secret lodges, I can obtain a passport for England with his influence, the second lieutenant of carabineers Carlos Maria Alvear, who also wants to return to Argentina, will accompany me -.

The English frigate Jorge Caning coming from London arrived at the port of Buenos Aires on May 24th, 1812, after 50 days of navigation, it carried the Lieutenant Colonel of Cavalry don Jose de San Martin, the Captain of Infantry don Francisco Vera, the Ensign don Jose Zapiola, the Captain of Militia don Francisco Chilaver, the Second Lieutenant of Royal Carabineers don Carlos Maria de Alvear, the Second Lieutenant of Infantry don Antonio Arellano and the First Lieutenant of Walloon guards baron of Alembert. They arrived with the purpose of offering their services to the Government.

José Miguel asked permit for returning to Chile, but he was sent to prison because they thought that he pretended to join the seditious of the Junta of Chile.

He asked to be discharged from the service from his prison; he was free at the beginning of April.

The Congress of Regency authorized Carrera's return to his country. On April 17th, 1811, he managed to get on board the English warship "Standard" heading south by the Atlantic in search of the eastern mouth of the Strait of Magellan, seeing the Atlantic coast of Chile and more to the north the Santa Cruz Fort, Charles III had ordered the Governor

Agustin de Jauregui to build in 1778 this latter altogether with other ones in order to defend the Patagonia from the pirates' incursions.

The voyage through the Strait showed the desolation of the uninhabited coasts, the ruins of buildings in Puerto del Hambre, which made Jose Miguel think about those inhabitants who died of hunger because of the lack of supplies, all this in a climate of constant rain and wind which was propitious for feeling even more gloomy.

The sailingship turned to the North by the canals in search of the

Ports of the central zone, it arrived Valparaiso on July 25th, 1811 at the end of more than three months of voyage. Jose Miguel landed, and being impatient that same afternoon he bought a horse and restlessly rode to Santiago in order to see all his family and to be informed at his home about the latest events and the Junta's activities.

The meeting between father and son was very exciting; they fondly embraced each other for very long time:

- My dear son, how are your wounds?, although you look like very well. We are very proud that at the age of 26 you have the rank of Sergeant Major of the regiment of the Galicia Hussars, your brother Juan Jose is Major of Grenadiers and Luis, Captain of Artillery -.

- I'm completely recovered, wanting to hug mother and brothers, Is my sister Javiera still so pretty?, tell me, father, the political plans that my brothers and you have, and because I have come on the eve of a revolt, I'm ready so that the four of us together may fight for a noble and just cause -.

- The incident of the mutiny of the Spanish Lieutenant Colonel Figueroa demanding the dissolution of the Junta happened. Juan Martinez de Rozas's strong personality, on being dissatisfied with the subduing of the mutiny, he proposed some days after the dissolution of the Tribunal of the Real Audiencia, publicly asserting that this latter caused the instigation of the riot. The elections for deputies in all the country were held on the 4th of July and it took place the solemn opening of the First National Congress in the palace of the Audiencia.

- And who held the presidency? -.

- The whole Congress was made up of forty-two deputies, and the presidency was held by the oldest don Jose Antonio Ovalle and, secretary don Francisco Ruiz Tagle. The opening of the First National Congress was on July 4th, the friar Camilo Enriquez delivered a sermon and Juan Martinez de Rozas a speech and both of them expressed ideas on popular sovereignty and the need of introducing a constitutional system. The Congress was established under an oath of loyalty to the captive king don Fernando VII, and to say the truth, it had a great majority of deputies loyal to the monarch, as it is in general the Creole aristocracy that does not want great reforms. Only an elite group, to which the friar Camilo Enriquez belongs, passionate reader of Rousseau and of Raynal, admirer of the United States, this friar proclaims together with Bernardo O'Higgins the need of radical changes and even though they cannot publicly say their intimate feeling of independence, it is noticed that they want to fight to get their reforms as soon as possible, but the weight and the force of Camilo Enriquez's new political-social ideology that has broken with the tradition, and the revolutionaries deny their Spanish ancestors and they proclaim to be descendants of the mapuche aborigines of the Araucania, on disappearing the Junta of Government, its functions have been assumed by the National Assembly, with this it has disappeared the support that Rozas and the Larrain had so far had in the government.

The Congress was divided in: Moderates, they obtained with Eizaguirre 24 deputies; royalists, 4 deputies; extremists or radicals, 14 deputies. Among the elected that managed to head the extremist or radical party aspiring to the immediate independence of Chile are: don Manuel de Salas, don Bernardo O'Higgins and don Manuel Rodriguez Erdoiza, Martinez de Rozas has been excluded from the Congress.

The extremists opposite to the Moderate or Conservatist parties in majority who do not want to break with spain by force, next to these, are grouped the royalists that pretend the re-establishment of the old regime-

José Miguel exclaimed:

- Oh! My good friend Manuel Rodriguez Erdoiza is among the extremists in favor of the independence of Chile.-

Meanwhile don Ignacio was telling his son the latest events, Jose Miguel's youngest brother appeared in the hall:

- How are you brother? Welcome to your country -.

- I'm fine and you? my dear brother Luis Florentino Juan Manuel Silvestre de los Dolores, Are you well? –

Both brothers laughed and embraced each other. Shortly after, they were coming his eldest brother Juan Jose and his sister Javiera, her great beauty was known in the parties and soirees that she attended to, where she was aware of the country's situation. In fact, she was the first of the brothers, got married at the age of fifteen with Manuel de Lastra y Sotta, the son of a well-known merchant, and by an accident in the crossing of the Colorado River, which flows between Mendoza until the Patagonia, wading, he was dragged by an avalanche and fell to the water drowning himself, she was left widow with two children. Javiera was the patriotic motor of the family; she was the one who helped them by encouraging them and advising them in the political plans.

- My dear sister, Javiera, I have missed you so much, how are your kids?-
- Dear Jose Miguelito what desires I had to see you, the eldest child Manuel Jose has been asking all the day, when his uncle Jose Miguel is arriving. He is very studious, and the girl Dolores does not want to be back and she can read, add and count, the other boys are still very early. As soon as we are organized in all our immediate plans, we will often go to the parties and soirees where I will introduce you to some pretty young lady with whom you may think of formalizing a relationship -.
- You know sister that I'm always ready for those duties -.

Madam Javiera kept talking:

- I interviewed yesterday with the merchant Mateo Arnaldo Hoevel, from Swedish evangelical ancestors, whom have at the first signs of independence joined the patriots, he commented me that he considered that the United States should play an important role in the process of the chilean independence, for this reason he had written president James Madison, proposing him to carry out a treaty of commerce and navigation between both countries, and he might be American representative in Chile. He also commented me that, taking advantage of this support to the patriot party, he had asked the chilean citizenship, which has already been granted to him and, with that citizenship in his hands, he has been able to obtain commercial contract with the government for the importing of the first national printing, and some American typographers with it .-

José Miguel was very interested in the matter:

- But all this is wonderful! , I have to talk with Hoevel to ask him that they ship together with the proper printing implements a load of weapons and ammunitions to equip the patriot army in the forming.-

The first steps of the Congress were confused due to the lack of experience and the fight among the factions where the predominance of the moderates caused a true chaos. The more dauntless patriots were showing dissatisfied led by Larrain and Martinez de Rozas: some were inclined to reform the old institutions and were thinking of the idea of a coup d'état.

Santiago had elected twelve diputies, almost the whole provinces together, these deputies of the capital were generally conservative of the Congress, they were decreeing a government regulation and named an Executive Junta formed by three of its members, don Martin Calvo Encalada, don Juan Jose Aldunate and don Francisco Javier del Solar, but this latter did not assumed his charge being replaced by the Lieutenant Colonel don Juan Miguel Benavente, "rocista", therefore the new Junta was formed by three patriots in favor of the independence. Those of the South were extremists or radicals, the acknowledged Martinez de Rozas as their chief. Seeing that they were a minority, they decided to overthrow the majority of the Congress, alleging irregularities in the election, for this purpose it was set the date of the 27th of July for the plot, and it should be led by the Major of Grenadiers Juan Jose Carrera and his brother Luis Captain of Artillery, that he should at the hour agreed be present with his army, only 80 persons having bad appearance were present and the Carrera were not found, because at the moment his brother was informed of the plot they were going to organize, he persuaded them not to be present, meanwhile he would attempt to convince the most conservative faction to solve the problem in the most pacifying way, but his attempts failed since the majority of the Congress resisted the progress of the events. Jose Miguel decided that the only solution was that coup.

On the September 4th, 1811, it was visibly led by the Commander of Grenadiers Juan Jose Carrera, the Captain of Artillery Luis Carrera, and Jose Miguel Carrera, just arrived from Spain with the rank of Sergeant Major, filled with revolutionary projects and with the prestige of having taken part in the Napoleonic wars, revolted in Santiago a part of the garrisoned troops and a crowd of people previously trained, Javiera hid the soldiers in her home, she was charged with the receiving in the night and the dawn of the carts led by the gauchos filled with weapons to be distributed in the city.

All these people were present in the Congress building; Jose Miguel Carrera presented a paper with petitions, as it was said by the people. The demand for the Congress was destined to change its features by the removing of some deputies. Jose Miguel Carrera was carrying out his first military coup. He expelled seven conservative deputies from the Congress, and summoned the people for an Open Council so that they may elect a new Junta of Government with higher latitude of powers than the one existing in the Congress. The frightened deputies accepted the demands and in the following days the radical deputies for the provinces were designated.

Everything was done without bloodshed.

Martinez de Rozas was almost at the same time making a similar movement in Concepcion, establishing there a Provincial Junta independent from Santiago. Shortly after, the city of Valdivia followed Santiago's and Concepcion's examples.

Dominating now the Government and the Congress, Rozas and the radicals continued their work of reforms, abolishing the parochial rights in favor of the poor, he prohibited the slave trade in Chile and declared free the sons of these and those who may be born.

During this time, the Larrain or the eight hundred governed in Santiago and Martinez de Rozas did it in Concepcion with his own Junta of Government, but neither the ones nor the others would want to keep counting on the Carreras.

As the Carrera brothers saw that the results of the first mutiny did not completely satisfy the revolutionary aspirations, since the Radicals had entirely forgotten Jose Miguel Carrera, this made him conspire against them, as he had previously done it against the Conservatives. This time he utilized the Spaniards and obtained resources from them, making them believe that he was going to restore the colonial regime. This provoked rancour between Martinez de Rozas and Carrera.

Because the positions in the Government and almost every employment had been monopolized by the great influence of the Larrain family, Jose Miguel decided to provoke a second military coup, which he thought that would give him the presidency of a new Junta.

Carrera was giving three different motives for this second coup.

He made to circulate an anonymous pamphlet stating that this Congress suffered from the most imaginable nullity because in its formation it had not been consulted the citizen's free will and disregarded the general representation. He also added that the deputies' election would be invalid because it had been subject to the action of Kabbalahs and factions; such a situation is unacceptable for the people, whom did not have other choice than to resort to the arms.

On November 15th, at one o'clock in the afternoon and in the same year, the Carrera brothers, whom the Government had kept their commands without realizing the danger, made a second coup d'état. Francisca Javiera's action was so significant that between the revolutionaries it was used the phrase "Viva la Panchita" as countersign. That same morning, Colonel Juan Mackenna was informed that don Luis Carrera had revolted the quarter and controlled the artillery, he had sent two cannons to Los Huerfanos quarter, where his brother Juan Jose revolted the Grenadiers and at three o'clock in the afternoon the city was practically in the hands of the brothers, who formally kept the Congress. The room of the Government had received an official letter from Juan Jose, but it was established a triumvirate constituted by Jose Gaspar Marin for Coquimbo and Bernardo O'Higgins for Concepcion as substitute for Rozas who was absent, in fact he refused from Concepcion the position with which Carrera had tried to win him over, but headed by Jose Miguel Carrera for Santiago, thus starting the controversy over motivations and political interests that it all was a struggle for the power between the Larrain and the destruction of that family and the replacement for the Carrera.

The rocistas took in the Congress a hostile attitude and they managed to form a conspiracy headed by the captains Jose Antonio and Jose Domingo Huici whose objective was to murder the brothers and his sister madam Javiera. The Huicis, upon seeing them discovered, fled to Concepcion. Carrera, without Consulting the Junta, ordered reprisals against those involved in the unsuccessful conspiracy, among whom were also found, Carrera's representative in the Congress, Colonel don Juan Mackena, his dear friendo Juan de Dios Vial, Argomedo, Martin and Gabriel Larrain, etc. Carrera, upon discovering them, dissolved the Congress by force in Santiago placing several cannons in front of the room where the deputies were meeting and cordoned off the square with three battalions on December 2nd 1811, and from that time Miguel Carrera started an absolute predominance in the Government and established a dictatorship, in spite of the presence of the two voting members who were with him forming a Junta of Government.

José Gaspar Marín and Bernardo O'Higgins very soon resigned their duties of voting members, above all because of Jose Miguel's dissolving the Congress where the Larrains were dominating.

It thus started the power of the Carrera family over the Government of Chile.

On returning O'Higgins to his estate of Las Canteras where he lived as a farmer, accompanied by his mother and his sister on her mother's side Rosa Rodriguez, whom had taken the surname O'Higgins at the same time than Bernardo.

The Local Junta of Government established in Concepcion under the influence of Juan Martinez de Rosas did not recognize the changes made by Carrera, thus acquiring a great rivalry between both heads of state.

In this way Carrera was the owner of the province of Santiago, and Rozas allied with the Larrains, from Concepcion.

Both governments came to mobilize their forces: Carrera militarily occupied the line of Maule, whose troops were camping divided by the river, raising the town of Valdivia against his rival. The civil war was threatening and the Spaniards, taking advantage of these discords, prepared a reaction overthrowing the Revolutionary Junta formed by Carrera in Valdivia.

O'Higgins acted as mediator, arranging an interview between both leaders.

In view of the danger in common, both patriotic leaders agreed to the interview and concluded an agreement on the banks of the Maule River. Martinez de Rozas attended with 1.000 horsemen. They lunched together the two rival leaders, and agreed that a new congress would settle their controversies, after the hug of the Maule, Rozas returned to Concepcion and Carrera went to Santiago.

The peace remained apparently restored, but the country was divided: Valdivia and Chiloe occupied by the royalists who obeyed the Viceroy of Peru. Concepcion was governed by a Junta of patriots and Santiago by one of extremists.

Martinez de Rozas didn't delay to rise against Carrera in Concepcion.

The Government characterized the city of Concepcion as having an insulting arrogance due to its desires of independence from the city of Santiago. In front of the facts, the Junta published a Manifesto, in which it called Martinez de Rozas to order.

Carrera was weakening Rozas's power, he didn't send to Concepcion the necessary money for paying the garrison in the araucanian frontier, he sent secret emissaries that promoted diverse handlings and betrayals with the officers of that garrison in Concepcion, among whom were don Juan Manuel Benavente, that allowed him to make an end of the Local Junta on July 9th and later of the Junta of War established in the country.

As the troops loyal to the Junta of Santiago subdued the mutiny, which caused that the city had a three days party. In front of the events, they raised: the new Junta of Concepcion, the Junta of Government and the Bishop of Concepcion on July 30th 1812, leaving the leader Juan Manuel Benavente as chief of the province in the capacity of Governor-Intendant, all the rocista authorities were captured and replaced by authorities loyal to the Junta of Santiago on September 1812.

Martinez de Rozas , Carrera's prisoner , this latter had always shown some respect for the old man, however, on being pressed, he was sent to Santiago, he was deported from there to Mendoza, his native town, where he died four months later, on March 13th 1813.

Don José Miguel Carrera wielded the power during the whole year 1812, without any interest, always refusing to receive any pay and giving proofs of being so good ruler as so brave military, having the merit of having been the first ruler that drove the revolution into the way of independence.

His eldest brother Juan Jose was promoted to Colonel of Grenadiers, and the youngest Luis, Commander of Artillery, the three brothers were making use of the army.

The main reforms established by Jose Miguel were: the regulation of the Constitution of 1812, the first one that the country had and by which it was adopted the republican system. it comprised 27 articles and it established a government consisting of a Senate with seven members and a Superior Junta of Government with three voting members, it was seen by the patriots as a need for safeguarding the rights of the people, putting an end to the power that the kings of Spain had had. The Regulation acknowledged Fernando VII in an attempt to feign loyalty, the king must accept the Constitution, which meant to recognize Chile's sovereignty and the autonomy of its rulers and that no decree or order which came from any authority or courts outside of Chile's territory would have no effect. The rulers who may take steps against the will expressed in the constitution, the power would instantly pass to the hands of the people, whom would condemn such act as a crime of lese majesty. It clearly established that "the power resides in the people", articles 2,6 and 8.

The freedom of press was granted by the article 23rd, which would be subject to regulation in order to avoid the license.

Additionally, even though equality of Rights had been established by article 24th, Carrera abolished the nobility titles, and Bernardo O'Higgins accused him of being a Jacobin because of this.

It was established the election of the members of the Senate and of the Executive Junta every three years. But in practice, Carrera personally elected the first members of this Senate. And the regulation established that the present voting members of the Junta would be kept in their charges and would be replaced in the case of death or resign, article 4th.

This set of principles were an innovation with relation to the colony's juridical system, based on the monarchical absolutism inspired in the enlightenment as it was understood in Spain, most of the actions of his government seemed to be intended to create what it was called an enlightened public opinion, and this change supposed for the Chileans to be citizens instead of subjects and, even though the validity of the Constitution was brief and defective, like it was the code itself, it represented a great advance in the political ideas.

He created the first national flag made up of three horizontal fringes, blue for the sky, white for the snow of the mountain range and yellow for the cropping fields, and a "rosette" with the same colors which became mandatory to wear, it was shown by the military in their hats and then by the civilians and the clergymen. Carrera, influenced by Hoevel, inserted a Calvinist motto in the first coat of arms with two Latin sentences: **Post Tenebras Lux** (after darkness the light, coined in the Calvinist Switzerland of the XVI century) and **Aut Consilio Aut Ense** (For the reason or the force) that his sister Javiera embroidered. The new flag replaced the Spaniard one and it was in use until 1814.

It was established September 18th as a holiday, not only in recognition of the first step in the process of independence, but as a way of enhancing the nationalist spirit of the Chilean citizens.

In educational matters, Carrera issued a decree that forced the convents to maintain a children's school for male and later this measure became extensive to convents of nuns to give instruction to the poor girls.

He founded the National Institute and the National Library of Chile, and impelled the formation of a Economic Society of Friends of the Country, the night lighting of the streets and the repair of this, he founded the School of Grenadiers, the basis for the future Military School.

He took charge that the first complete printing that arrived from United States to Valparaiso may be set up in Santiago to create a newspaper. He named Friar Camilo Henríquez, whom had always showed him to be a decided patriot, in charge of the direction of the newspaper that was going to be published on February 13th 1812, a very important date, since that day the newspaper "Aurora de Chile" had just appeared with great rejoicing and enthusiasm.

The patriots listened its reading aloud in the streets, its pages served to spread the republican ideas sometimes furtively and openly other times. Henriquez expounded in his writings the ideas of the Social Contract of Rousseau, insisting continually in the principles of the popular sovereignty. The Spaniards listened with an expression of contempt and indignation.

Camilo Henríquez chose two letters of the newspaper "The Sun of Baltimore" to be published in the "Aurora de Chile":

"Through a resolution of the U.S., it is informed to the countries of America that as the nations begin to be autonomous and sovereign; the U.S. is willing to develop agreements and trade alliances".

The newspaper appeared weekly on Thursday, and its size was that of a legal size sheet of paper. Its collaborators were: Guatemala's writers don Antonio Jose de Irisarri; the Argentinian poet of the revolution don Bernardo Vera y Pintado; don Juan Egaña, Peruvian by birth, lawyer and writer, he prepared his constitution projects; don Manuel de Salas wrote about economy and, don Jose Miguel Infante and don Manuel Jose Gandarillas about charity. The "Aurora de Chile" was published until 1813.

During the period of the cause of the independence, relationships with the United States were established because President James Madison, upon knowing the events of the Spanish American colonies, sent to Rio de La Plata, Chile and Lima with character of confidential agent and with the title of consult to Mr. Joel Roberts Poinsett, aged ruler of the Presbyterian Church of Charleston in South Carolina. The Junta presided by Carrera received the Consul General of the United States before the Superior Government of Chile with a solemn ceremony, showing him great admiration for the Northern country, at the same time Poinsett expressed the desires of prosperity and happiness of his brothers of the South. Poinsett became great friend and consultant and adviser of Miguel Carrera whom he even accompanied in the beginning of the military campaigns of the old republic, becoming an active propagandist of the emancipating ideas from Spain, it was also Lockheed forward to obtain help and armament for the revolution by means of his intermediation, Poinsett finished up proposing him a constitutional project that was adaptation of the Constitution of his country, which was not accepted by the Commission in charge of its writing. Nevertheless, it was accepted the project after a discussion in Hoevel's house so that the term "roman" did not appear in the article that stated:

"The apostolic catholic religion is and will always be Chile's faith" that is why it was nationalized the chilean catholic church, with the intention of counteracting the strong feeling in favor of the Spanish monarchy, insinuating that in the future there could be an establishment of protestant churches in the chilean territory".

The celebration of the July 4th, anniversary of the Independence of the United States, carried out with a great official party in the building of the Tribunal of the Consulate where it was shown the new flag together with that of the Unites States. The candies, the mistelle, the toasts, the expressions and happiness of all the illustrious people that attended the soirée, among those that were wearing the showy full dress uniforms, don Jose Miguel Carrera that until in a given moment he dared to play the guitar, his father don Ignacio, his brothers don Luis, don Juan José that also made a small demonstration with the clarinet, and dona Javiera richly dressed with jewels and magnificent silk dress with embroideries in gold that made her stand out even more her beauty, having made cancel the minuet in the living room, imposing the country dance, the gavotte and tappings.

She was not accompanied by her husband don Pedro Diaz de Valdes Argüelles y Galan, Spaniard from Gijon, he was Councilor and Adviser of the General Captaincy, he continued loyal to the Spanish cause and he had renounced the Chilean nationality; knowing that in the party they would hoist the flag of Chile instead of the Spaniard one, he refused to go to the party.

That day July 4th 1812, it was hoisted the flag of Chile for the first time in the center of the living room next to the flag of the United States, what supposed to be a clear message of rejection to the Spanish Crown.

Hoevel was among the guests, whom Poinsett in virtue of the important services rendered by the merchant in favor of the patriotic cause named him Vice Consul so that he may act under his orders. Everywhere was inspired freedom, toasting with expressions of independence, but the ground was not still ready for it since most of them was of conservative spirit that were alarming before each impulse that was given in that sense, the patriots looked restless toward Peru.

Colonel Mackenna, coming closer to don Joel Roberts Poinsett, rebuked him:

- How are you, Mister Poinsett, coming from a free country, supporting the dictatorship of General Carrera? You should cooperate with the liberty of Chile and not be united for its slavery.-
- Mister Mackenna, with all my respects, I will tell you that if it were not for General Carrera, the kingdom of Chile would be nowadays subject to Lima.-

In 1813, the Spaniard Viceroy don Jose Fernando de Abascal, knowing that Carrera acted with absolute independence from Spain, he entrusted the submission of Chile since he had in Peru powerful elements: money, weapons, ships and enough soldiers. He had sent troop during three years against the revolutionaries of Quito and Upper Peru and, after having established his authority, the Viceroy conceived the possibility of subjecting the chilean and argentinian patriots by attacking them simultaneously; the army of Upper Peru would advance on Tucuman, while another army organized in the South of Chile would go against Santiago and, the first one that wins should help the other one by crossing the mountain range of the Andes.

This way indeed, the Viceroy entrusted the mission of Chile to the brigadier of navy don Antonio Pareja that went on board in Callao with a cadre of officials and with armament to organize an army in the royalist provinces of Chiloe with 1,400 recruited men and 700 in Valdivia, landing in San Vicente, in the bay of Talcahuano and, after occupying without resistance that stronghold on March 26th 1813, Pareja advanced towards the North and entered in Concepcion in front of 2.850 men, helped by high military chiefs and prestiged neighbors who remained loyal to the king, and in spite of that, the Governor don Juan Manuel Benavente had to resign, being replaced by the bishop Villodres, with what was profiling more and more the character of a civil war struggle.

Without appreciable resistances, Pareja's army that every time was recruiting more people during the march, advanced until Linares in the first days of May, a village 9 miles distant from Maule, with 2.000 fusiliers, 3.000 cavalry from the militia and where militiamen and loose parties were added, 200 artillerymen y more than 25 campaign pieces, he then entered Chillan, where they passed to his files, raising this way more than 5.000 combatants, stretching its lines until the Maule river.

Nothing less than receiving Carrera the official letter of Juan Manuel Benavente, in which he was informed about Pareja's landing in

Concepcion, he gathered the Junta, Congress and military authorities, reading shortly after the declaration of war to the Viceroy Abascal.

Juntas were set up to analyze the military organization. The imminent state of war and the fear to lose battles for lack of training and tactical expertise made that Carrera named "Junta" to what is known nowadays as "Commission", so that the Government may take note of it and may formulate the military education.

Dona Javiera at once mobilized groups of women to make bandage, store medicines and, she prepared them to take care of the wounded, she would take messages by herself and would transmit them.

The sudden invassion of Spanish field officer Pareja caused in Santiago a great alarm. The Senate understood that Concepcion was lost, the defense should be made in the Maule and Carrera should leave to Talca to organize it.

The Eight hundred of the Larrain family, thinking of the inefficacy of the patriots, offered donations and they ran to the arms, naming Colonel Juan Mackenna, relative to the Larrains by his wife's side, so that he went to join Carrera. As soon as they took the most urgent measures to combat the invaders, delivering the Senate the command of the army to Jose Miguel Carrera that, appointed General in chief with the mission to defend the Maule line, marched toward the South moving with his brothers to Talca to organize the resistance to stop Pareja's advance. Without stopping in difficulties neither preparations, he went in campaign accompanied by 14 Hussars, and conquering a march of 80 leagues, he put into movement all the militia available in four days, took away the suspicion men from the traffic places to prevent warning on the sad situation of his forces. He surprised the outpost of the invading army, and before this ended up occupying the southern bank of the Itata River, Carrera had already gathered 3.000 cavalry combatants, whom owed their salvation to the General's active dauntlessness.

The large Maule river flows from the mountain range with the speed of a torrent, it is divided in several very deep arms having endless number of slippy stones; this obstacle joined to the speed of the current prevents from crossing the fords by foot and by horse with great difficulty. These arms form endless islets covered with trees and bushes propitious for excellent ambushes.

Carrera soon realized the magnitude of Concepcion's disaster and sent urgent instructions to the local authorities so that they gathered all the militia, weapons and animals that they could. His main problem was to move away the militia of the intendancy from Concepcion to the North of the Mauler River.

Bernardo O'Higgins, on being informed about this, put all his horses to the service of the army, left his estate, becoming an improvised warrior with the rank of Colonel of the La Laja militia, leading them to Concepcion, city which was believed to be managed by the royalists. After receiving a message that ordered him to disperse his troops, O'Higgins hastened to be under the orders of Carrera, joining him in Talca, to whom he had not accompanied in his acts of government, he now gave him an effective and valiant help from the very first moment.

Carrera ordered him to go to Linares to intercept the step of the Spanish Commander Melchor Carvajal that went to Talca. The attack was combined and all was at the disposal of Consul Poinsett and Luis Carrera as General of the vanguard with 300 fusiliers in addition to 1.000 men among grenadiers and milita men and the cavalry militia for Maipu composed the attack division and don Luis with the remaining of the vanguard and three artillery pieces would follow it closely, everything was headed by O'Higgins and they were able to defeat the Dragoons of Carvajal in Linares, this action was one of the first chilean victories of the independence deserving O'Higgins the promotion to Colonel of the army granted by the Governmental Junta of Santiago, O'Higgins's figure due to this act was beginning to leave Carrera in the shade.

Jose Miguel Carrera attained to concentrate his troops in Talcahuano, the army managed to gather 4.500 men, most of them militiamen with scarce preparation, the commander was seconded by the Irish Colonel Juan Mackenna that graduated as military engineer in Spain, he fought several times against the Moors, the Englishmen and against Napoleon's French, he was a field officer with great capacity.

General Carrera dispatched Colonel Estanislao Portales to chase the royalist field officer Ildefonso Elorreaga with the purpose of surprising him, because he knew that the entire enemy army was in Yerbas Buenas. Nevertheless, the patriot detachment, under the command of Juan de Dios Puga, believed to see only Elorreaga's expeditionary forces in Yerbas Buenas, but in fact there were all General Pareja's forces.

The first encounter between the patriots and the royalist troops took place on April 27th 183 in the hillocks of Yerbas Buenas, where a corps of 500 patriots, most of them were from the Battalion of Grenadiers, among them was distinguishing the Second Lieutenant Santiago Bueras, action that deserved him to be promoted to Lieutenant Colonel; they crossed the river after shortly after midnight and rushed by surprise at

three o'clock in the morning, not only Elorreaga's party but the whole
Brigadier Antonio Pareja's army that had in that day advanced toward
that place and even they were not inflicted a defeat, confusion spread
in their lines disbanding and, Pareja didn't have anything to do but to
retreat to Linares to form winter quarters in Cauquenes or in Chillan. But
Carrera forced his march, and with four days of constant rains, crossing
large rivers and almost impassable estuaries, reached the enemy army
that occupied an advantageous position in the fields of San Carlos, being
in battle against them again, he ordered a battalion of Grenadiers to be
in the front and arranged that the cavalry flanked the enemy positions,
evading the 20 artillery pieces which defended the royalist cadre, which
began discharging on them and thus achieving to disorganize them,
the very same Colonel Juan Jose Carrera ran in disbandment until the
headquarter. At last, the Mackenna's division that came as refreshment
could not defeat the resistance of the royal fusiliers either, in a battle
which was not really decisive. The action was sustained with such an
effort and bravery that at last and taking advantage of the darkness of the
night, the Spanish troops secretly escaped and they were able to arrive to
Chillan to spend the winter there, it was on May 1813.

Leaving in the hands of the patriots more than 300 prisoners, five
cannons and 30 ammunition cars and supplies and stores.
Don Jose Miguel wrote in his war dispatch:
*"The vanguard under the command of Colonel Luis Carrera performed
prodigies of valour. The Chileans have never shown more worthy of
immortality, the soldiers of the country are owed the glory of this memorable
action. It is easy to conceive the deplorable state of our small army after so
bitter fight." Captain General of the Armies.- José Miguel Carrera.*

This deed allowed Carrera to occupy the region and the city of
Concepcion and Talcahuano, both places were taken on May 25th and
29th: Concepcion without resistance; Talcahuano after an action of more
than four hours of combat with the royalist infantry placed on the heights
that defended the entrance, and aided by the fire of the cannoneers that
mounted artillery of high calibre. But there was not anything that could
resist the enthusiasm of the patriotic soldiers.
Reduced the enemy, they were left in their hands 400 prisoners, four
ships, 1000 rifles, 1000 quintals of nitrates and some money abandoned
in his fearful flight, 120 patriotic soldiers had died in this combat. But
Carrera wasted a lot of time by not attacking Chillan at once, while
O'Higgins was reorganizing the army of the South, after a victorious

skirmish, defeated with 75 Dragoons a guerrilla of 200 men in San Javier and his column recovered the stronghold of Los Angeles and others of the Araucanian frontier.

By that time Chillan Viejo was an open city, located on a hillock, among the estuary of Paso Hondo by the north, the Maipo River by the west, and the Chillan River by the south.

When Carrera laid siege to Chillan, Poinsett and Mackenna had already drawn a sketch map of the emplacement of the artillery and fortifications. The siege lasted thirteen days, being the result deplorable since by maintaining it in the middle of the winter, lacking supplies and ammunitions, sheltered tents against the rains of extreme winter, it meant casualties since the soldiers died and deserted a lot of them, causing demoralization of the ranks of the patriots, though, they fought heroically, but in vain because the Spaniards had trenched during three months and had been supplied with provisions, set up trenches and good quarters waiting for reinforcements from Peru and they were aided by their guerrillas that crossed the nearby fields picking up the patriots' livestock, the Franciscan missionaries also rendered them valuable assistance.

Meanwhile, as they were organizing, General Pareja died in Chillan because of the depression of some Rights that did not arrive to definitive result and a pneumonia with high fever caused by the cold weather, taking the command of the stronghold the Captain don Juan Francisco Sanchez, Mackenna and O'Higgins pressed Carrera to force him to thoroughly launch an attack before the army is totally dissolved, pressure that was accepted, and in the night of August 2nd the army passed the Maipo placing its cannons on a small hillock. The attack was effective; the troops of Elorreaga and Carvallo were surrounded, beginning to retreat. General Spano and O'Higgins

General Spano and O'Higgins with a handful of soldiers penetrated into the royalist lines, a bullet hit in one of Mackenna's cannons and set on fire the adjoining magazine, which caused an infernal crash and an immense blaze spread to the nearby deposits, producing an unspeakable confusion, the officers that saved their life organized the defense against the attacks of the royalist column that advanced on the remains of the artillery. The slaughter and the night put an end to the bloody combat.

After 13 days of heroic but with many hardships Carrera had to lift the siege of Chillan and retire to Concepcion with big casualties and of the advantages they had so far obtained.

After the patriots had retreated from Chillan, Captain Juan Francisco Sanchez organized guerrillas, whose objective was to deprive the General

Carrera's army from resources, and interrupt its Communications to reestablish the royalist domain in the province.

Colonel Elorreaga seized Los Angeles and the untimely uprising of Arauco, in which the mapuche allied with the royalists to fight against the abuses of the commissioners, gave the army the absolute control of the territory locate south of the Biobio.

The patriot army was divided in two detachments that went through the fields between Chillan and Concepcion. O'Higgins sustained the combats of Guilquilemo, Gomero and Quilacoya.

Captain Sanchez's men left in pursuit of Carrera that had left a second division in charge of his brother Juan Jose and Mackenna in the confluence of the Nuble and the Itata Rivers, but they surprised the diminished division personally commanded by Carrera, being attacked the night of October 17th 1813 in the Paso del Roble where they were camped on the Banks of the Itata river, and in the middle of the darkness the confusion was unspeakable, they were cut by the enemy and Carrera was forced to seek his salvation by swimming, he plunged in the Itata river. O'Higgins deployed with his forces in help of Carrera reorganizing the disbanded patriot troops, confused in the darkness Colonel O'Higgins yelled to them:

> - To me boys! To live with honor or to die with Glory;
> he who is brave, follow me!

To the shout, the soldiers reacted and rejecting the attack, they successfully fought in three combats: El Tejar, Lajuelas and Maipon in the surroundings of Chillan. O'Higgins was riding on horse and in the middle of the fight he was hit in the leg being thrown from the horse with the saddle, in spite of this, he continued fighting until the situation forced him to retreat after three hours of bitter combat, what it seemed to be a defeat turned into victory on October 17th. Carrera himself, after the battle of Paso del Roble, called O'Higgins the first soldier of Chile writing in the battle dispatch:

"I cannot leave in silence the fair praise that so worthily deserves the above mentioned O'Higgins, whom should be considered, your Excellency, as the first soldier, capable by himself of bringing together and heroically unite the merits and glories of the Chilean State. Jose Miguel Carrera General in Chief. Official dispatch of the battle of El Roble, October 25th 1813".

After so big a combat, Carrera met O'Higgins and this told him with great grief:
- I have to tell you the great sorrow that invades me; as a sort of revenge for supporting the cause of the independence, the royalists have burned the house of my estate and cut down my fields, but that doesn't care me, the worst thing that oppresses me is that they have taken my holy mother and my sister as prisoners and, I don't know so far what may have happened to them -.

Carrera, first dismayed and then angered, replied:
- My dear Bernardo, I speak to you, firstly in my capacity as a friend and then as your superior: as the first, I'm deeply sorrowed and from my heart, as a superior, I cannot consent it and I will order that the wife of royalist Captain don Juan Sanchez be taken prisoner in reprisal and then, we will see how to exchange her by the two other ladies -.

Both military setting aside some differences that they had had, they shook their hands and O'Higgins enduring the tears said to him:

-I'm grateful, General -

While the war was sustained in the South, some important changes had taken place in Santiago. The Junta of Government is made up of don Agustin Eizaguirre, the secretary don Jose Ignacio Cienfuegos and don Jose Miguel Infante, this later was the alma mater of the government. In order to be nearer the field of war, The Junta moved to Talca. They proceeded to extinguish the newspaper "La Aurora de Chile" and ordered to be replaced by the "Monitor Araucano" appearing the first number on April 6ᵗʰ 1813, it should be published three times per week, and it would inform the reader about general events and the government providences and it would even publish weekly the revenues and expenses of the government. This document created in the style of questions and answers, tried to deliver definitions about those political matters being discussed in that time, such as freedom of expression, the monarchy by divine right and the equality of men before the law. Four months later, don Antonio Jose de Irisarri published a new newspaper the "Semanario Republicano", whose title indicated the editor's purposes: to spread all over the towns of the chilean state the liberal ideas, useful knowledge and the hate toward the tyranny, encouraging the ideas of independence and experiencing a great advance, that even the very same Junta of Government removed of its decrees the expression of being representative of Fernando VII's sovereignty.

As the situation in Spain stayed stationary, in such circumstances, the loyalty to the captive king was becoming in a simple mask for a greater group every time.

The country impoverished by the war, the South had become a critical problem and with the suspension of the trade with Peru, it began to feel the consequent evils of a prolonged campaign. The dissatisfaction became general showing in Santiago an adverse opinion to the way in which Carrera conducted the operations and many of them accused him of being the cause of those evils. The Junta of Government decided to separate Carrera and his brothers from every command of troops and name in replacement O'Higgins as Commanding General of the Army, measure that found some difficulties, not on the side of Carrera who surrendered the command without resistance:

- I don't have trouble to surrender the command to General O'Higgins: but I won't ever to any fellow from Buenos Aires, that as I've heard … they think to put in front of the army, someone from Buenos Aires.-

But indeed there were because of the adhesion with which Carrera counted on among the officers that were resisting the change of chief.

Don Juan Jose Carrera as Commander of Grenadiers was replaced by Colonel don Carlos Spano and Commander don Luis Carrera in the charge of artillery replaced by Captain Jose Domingo Valdes.

O'Higgins refused to accept the command during three months; only when Carrera resigned himself and withdrew to Concepcion he would accept to take the command, this was on January 28th 1814.

The good friendship until now between Carrera and O'Higgins was over when due to an imprudence of this last one during the proclamation addressed to the soldiers when being taken charge of the command, he remembered when the Viceroy Abascal had said that Chile was dominated by the whim of two youths whose arbitrariness and licenses were rejected by the very same country.

After handing in the command to his successor, the Junta was convinced that the presence of Carrera would hinder the command of O'Higgins, the Government offered him a commission of great importance in Buenos Aires in order to have him away but he didn't accept it.

One day Carrera, already with no escort, was going from Concepcion to Santiago accompanied by his brother Luis, crossing a land plagued by royalist guerrillas who took them prisoners and sent them to Chillan. One of the resentful because of the shooting perpetrated in Concepcion, Lieutenant Lorenzo Plaza de los Reyes, achieved to capture them in Penco and instead of mistakenly shooting Jose Miguel, as it was feared, in revenge for the death the captor's brother, they were taken to the already General Sanchez's headquarter.

At the same time that O'Higgins took charge of the army on January 1814, a reinforcement of 800 soldiers landed in the coast of Arauco, sent by the Viceroy of Peru, that knowing of the internal panorama of Chile, decided to send another pacifying expedition which may gather the forces of the country to direct them later against Buenos Aires. He sent together with a new chief of the royalist troops to the Spanish Brigadier don Gabino Gainza who set sails from Callao with scarce forces and they joined to those of Sanchez's army that in that moment arrived to the limits of misery for having endured without being discouraged the defeats and the total isolation in the open during more than eight months. Gainza with his forces brought from Peru and those of Sanchez, he joined some 3.000 men and in addition he had available the mapuches that kept their backs in the South and offered to go in his assistance as soon as they were demanded.

The mapuche people during the war of the patriots against the Spaniards developed a defense organization which was based on the ayllarehues or groups of nine rehues or chieftains and the butalmapus or big regions, which named a main chieftain as spokeman. A Parliament was gathered with General Sanchez in the square of Angol on January 3rd 1813.

The Junta had designated the Spanish Colonel in the service of the Chilean independence don Carlos Spano, the only one capable of taking the war with strategic knowledge on the defense of Talca.

Since the landing of the Spanish Brigadier don Gabino Gainza was known: Spano advised the immediate concentration of the forces of McKenna and O'Higgins to beat the royalist chief as soon as possible, they would had to retreat on the Maule River to avoid that the enemy may cut the communications with the capital.

On the first of March 1814, the Junta returned to Santiago, making the imprudence of taking most of the force that defended Talca, leaving Colonel Spano with the defense of the square only with 300 men, 230 of whom should leave the South. Having the royalist chief Elorreaga with

400 guerrilla men in a day's march. Spano warned the Junta about the difficult situation, he suggested an honourable capitulation, in the case that the royalist chief did not accept his conditions, Spano requested assistance to Bascuñan, since he only had 70 artillery men and 30 militiamen for the defense of Talca.

The royalist chief Elorreaga didn't doubt any minute to attack the square. The patriots managed to resist the siege from nine in the morning until noon when the royalists helped by a neighbour who

allowed the snipers to enter his home and placed them in the roof. From that moment the royalists were the owners of the situation, and they threw the Chilean flag that was hoisted in the center of the square, an officer suggested Spano:

-Gentleman, you can still survive through a free street.-

- I won't abandon, and I'll die for my homeland, the country that adopted me.-

These were their last words: a discharge threw him into the feet of the flag heroically defending Talca, having a small number of men. Colonel Spano's memory, while being Spaniard, he didn't doubt to offer his life for the liberty, lives in the conscience of the Chilean people as a symbol of disinterested heroism.

The fall of the city of Talca on March 1814 was a blow of great importance for the patriots, it was defended by the Spanish Colonel in the patriots' side don Carlos Spano, which darkened the military panorama, since it was lost the provisioning base of all the supplies for the aid of the forces of O'Higgins and Mackenna, which were divided each other, and sieged by the enemy, and the communications with Santiago interrupted. This fact alarmed Santiago's patriots that accused the Junta of Government from lowness and stupidity, it was held an Open Council in which don Antonio Jose de Irisarri expressed the urgency of creating a strong and vigorous government, replacing the Junta of Government for a Supreme Director of the State with the fullness of the public power, naming for that position the patriot Colonel Francisco de Lastra, Governor of Valparaiso, chilean who had served in the Spanish navy. In general, the alarm was because there was not news about the forces of O'Higgins and the road to the capital was free for the royalists; however

Gainza not daring to go to Santiago, he went directly to Chillan, leaving to his back the patriot army which was divided in two corps south of the Maule separated by some kilometres.

General Gainza left in the middle of March from Chillan to prevent that the two patriot forces may join, interposing between the O'Higgins's division which was advancing from Concepcion to join with the one camped near the Itata river under the orders of the Colonel Juan Mackenna.

On his retreating march from Concepcion to Santiago, O'Higgins espied royalist troops in the height of El Quilo. Without finding out of his quantity, he ordered the attack against the royalist troops that although being below in number, they were garrisoned by the closeness of Gainza: but as his assistance didn't arrive, they decided to abandon the siege.

O'Higgins instead of chasing them, he entrenched in El Quilo in a hill where he had prepared the artillery, espying the enemy from there.

General Gainza instead of attacking O'Higgins whom was very near, he decided to go against Mackenna, fortified in El Membrillar, this field was impassable due to its ravines in the Itata river. The royalist troops began the attack in complete disorder, surrounding all sides of the field of El Membrillar, being so within the patriots' gunshot. Already at nightfall with the rain and suffering many casualties, what it caused the dispersion of the royalists.

The following day, March 20th, field officer Urrejola that commanded the enemy division didn't dare to attack the one entrenched by Mackenna in El Membrillar.

O'Higgins entrenched in El Quilo was waiting that the time improved to produce the necessary union of his troops with those of Mackenna. Finally, both divisions met on March 23rd adding effectives consisting of 1.500 fusiliers and 200 artillery men with 18 cannons.

The patriots suffered nine days later a second setback in Talca. The Supreme Director don Francisco de La Lastra sent a division under the command of the 24-year-old youth, argentinian Colonel Manuel Blanco Encalada to recover Talca which was in the hands of the royalist field officer Elorreaga. He left from Santiago with 1.000 men to recover that city, whom were undisciplined outcasts, without having achieved to instill them in so little time the feeling of the homeland and the honour.

The march of the division of San Francisco was a continuous series of chaos, indiscipline, and disorders of all kind. They were defeated by the Elorreaga's royalist guerrilla in Cancha Rayada on March 29th 1814, leaving the road to the abandoned capital open.

Gainza rallied in Chillan and quickly advanced on Santiago, the united forces of O'Higgins and Mackenna ran in forced march to stop him, in a parallel march to that of the royalist, both armies crossed the Maule river almost at the same time; Gainza did it in rafts and protected by the royalists from Talca; O'Higgins by a ford toward the coast, by night and with the water until the chest of the horses and spied by the royalists. Once crossed the Maule, O'Higgins managed to entrench in the estate of Quechereguas near the Claro river, where he rejected twice on April 8th the attacks of Gainza that wanted to force the pace. Forcing the royalists to retreat that went back by the Maule to spend the winter in Talca almost in defeat on April 1814, wherein the inactivity of the troop caused the desertion of his army.

At those moments the future of the American Revolution was presented with bad omens. Everywhere the royalist armies obtained big victories by defeating all the colonies. The had just defeated the argentinians in the Upper Peru in the battles of Vilcapujio and Ayouma; the insurgents in Mexico and those of Venezuela ran the same luck and the Viceroy Abascal was free to send new troop reinforcements against Chile. Regarding Spain, they were joined to General Wellington's army and defeated the Frenchmen in Vitoria, forcing Jose I to pass by again the Pyrenees. Everything made suppose that a few later Fernando VII would be reestablished in his throne and would send great armies to reconquer the colonies of America.

But a suspension of the hostilities came to take them out of their afflictive situation.

During the year 1813, foreign ships entered the South Pacific, and for a time this new era seemed favorable to the Chilean patriots, since the United States was trying to help them against Spain. Commodore Bainbridge ordered Captain of Navy David Porter of the American frigate Essex to set sail to the Pacific in order to destroy the British whaling fleet.

He sailed by the Pacific nearly a year, until Porter comprehended that there were only one or two British whalers in that region. Many of the preys taken were sold together with its load in Chilean ports.

The Essex arrived at Valparaiso on March 13th 1813.

The Consul of the United States encouraged the hopes of the patriots that the ship was coming to help them in their fight.

The English Admiral Hillyar had arrived at the coasts of the Pacific with five British warships to chase the American frigate "Essex". Two of them, the Phoebe and the Cherub, under the command of the Captain of Navy Sir James Hillyar, arrived at Valparaiso five days after the Essex; a gust of wind broke her main "topmast", leaving her unable to go back to her roadstead.

The cannons of long reach of the British ships beat her and Captain of Navy Porter was forced to lower his flag.

This defeat of the Essex caused anguish to the patriots   that their commerce had enjoyed for a year Porter's protection. The British Commodore, settled his main mission, hastened to Lima to offer his services to the Viceroy of Peru as mediator in Chile between royalists and patriots.

Commodore Hillyar, after many meeting, arrived at Valparaiso with the permission of the proposal. To the government of the Supreme Director-Interim of Santiago don Francisco de La Lastra, these considerations made him admit the Commodore's pacific proposals, and he accepted these as a means of obtaining a truce in the fight.

On the 6th of February, Bernardo O'Higgins received a startling news in which it said to him; that two ships had left from Chiloe with a battalion of infantry to reinforce the royalist army in the South of Chile, and also that more reserves with a new Commander in Chief were arriving from Peru in the "Sebastiana" accompanied by el "Potrillo" and it joined to the merchant ships "Trinidad" and "Mercedes" in Arauco with reinforcements from Chiloe with a battalion of infantry.

O'Higgins was willing to take the offensive; but he received the order from the Director Colonel La Lastra to deal with Spanish General Gainza the proposal of a suspension of hostilities, which was received by the Spaniard with great enthusiasm because it meant to escape his imminent ruin in Talca.

Treaty of Lircay.

The treaty was concluded on the Banks of the Lircay river, therefore it was called the Treaty of Lircay, by which it was agreed that patriots acknowledged the King of Spain and the provisional authority of the Regency and The Courts of Cadiz, but they would preserve the right to rule by themselves, and the royalists would acknowledge the patriot government established in Chile while the Courts would solve the most convenient, would withdraw the troops from the territory in a deadline of two months, and on one and the other side, all the prisoners of war would be released, excluding the Carreras. To say the truth, it was that both parts acted so only to get time.

O'Higgins restricted by the kidnapping of this relatives whom he wanted to rescue, he acknowledged the "legitimacy of the colonial age".

O'Higgins and Mackenna, on behalf of the Government of Chile put their sign on the 3rd of May 1814 in that ill-fated Treaty which made the revolution coming back.

O'Higgins recovered his mother and sister, but he lost great part of this reputation because of this capitulation.

Gainza undertook his retreat to Chillan aided by O'Higgins; but instead of evacuating the country in the established deadline, he continued in that city waiting for reinforcements to renew the fight, he never really had the intention to fulfil that Treaty.

In July the Viceroy was informed that Gainza had not fulfilled the Treaty and stayed in Chile with a force of 2.000 men, the Viceroy thought of sending the regiment Talavera as reinforcement and some colonial militias in the ship "Asia".

On their side, the patriots didn't have the intention either to fulfil the Treaty after its signature, what they really proposed to do was to continue the emancipative movement, this is shown by a letter from the Director de La Lastra to the former chilean representative in Buenos Aires, don Francisco Antonio Pinto, which in its main part said:

"Indeed you should be sure that this State does not succumb; it is determined to be free at all cost, that the more they know their rights the more they hate the slavery; that they have absolutely forgotten the ancient system; that they want a liberal system, which supplies to this part of America, the most abandoned and beaten, the advantages that they have not until now known. These are the intimate and true feelings of Chile, and these are the liberal principles by which they have proposed to live".

In the ill-fated Treaty of Lircay was included a secret article in virtue of which Jose Miguel and Luis Carrera would be delivered to the Government that had the intention of taking them away from the country, in the ship in which Hillyar would return and deliver them to the Viceroy of Peru.

The Carrera Brothers, loaded with heavy chains were the object of derision and soldierly gibe in a prison in Chillan, it was for some months the cell of the victors of San Carlos, Yerbas Buenas, Talcahuano and Chillan, whom in their captivity, from the darkness of their prisons they aided more than 500 prisoners who were going out of the jails, leaving the corpses without their clothings so that they may cover their nakedness and became part of the Homeland's army, which was in the surroundings of Talca.

The brothers had made some friendships in Chillan, due to their good manners and sympathies they maintained relations with some prominent royalists.

The General Gainza made the baseness of grabbing the aid of 1500 pesos that Carrera's father and the meritorious Poinsett Consul General of the Unites States sent them by means of the Commodore Hillyar. The Government, General O'Higgins and his faction didn't hear the insinuating implorations of the People, the Officialdom, and the Army so that they may be helped, the Director cruelly refused and against the distressed Carrera family's requests to propose an exchange to General Gainza for the Spanish officers imprisoned in the last actions, and now they were strolling around Santiago between attentions and comforts.

When General Gainza was already preparing the escort that should lead the Carreras until Talcahuano to pass from there to the dungeons of Lima, with the complicity of Commander Urrejola they set them at large by opening them the door so that it may seem that Jose Miguel and Luis had escaped, so that they managed to get out of the prison with the deliberate purpose of overthrowing the Government and once they were in control they should break the Treaty of Lircay. With greatly exaggerated vicissitudes, and fearing more their patriot enemies than the royalist ones, they went to Talca and went home to get dressed because the Spanish general that captured them sold their luggage, as if he were a common thief.

The news of their freedom or flight caused bewilderment in the capital and de La Lastra overturned all his indignation against O'Higgins for not having captured them in Talca. It was given a prison order against both brothers, but in spite of this, Jose Miguel, disguised, entered in Santiago every day to prepare the takeover during two months which had been dated as the 18th of July, but it was postponed due to some circumstances of health reasons until the 23rd day, where the brothers gathered with the discontented that were seeking the fall of the Director de La Lastra under the accusation that the Treaty of Lircay was an affront for Chile. The movement was carried out with extreme care; some groups that were Jose

Miguel's supporters took hold of the quarters, they rebelled the Harrison, and gathered an Open Council handled by their friends and relatives that appointed a Junta of Government presided by Jose Miguel Carrera and integrated by the priest don Julian Uribe and don Manuel Muñoz Uzua that took hold of the artillery quarter, don Miguel Ureta received that of the Grenadiers and it was added to these that of the Dragoons. As his first measure Carrera ordered the prison of the Director de La Lastra and his collaborators, many members of the Larrain family, such as Irisarri and Mackenna, this last one was demoted from the position of Colonel; all of them were exiled to Mendoza, which favored to deepen even more the division of the patriots.

Carrera began moderately his Government supported by don Bernardo Vera y Pintado, whom was appointed his secretary. But this policy did not produce the expected effects since the presence in the Government of Vera y Pintado could not counteract the aristocracy's hostility toward Carrera, and specially the priest Uribe, whom had to be replaced by don Manuel Rodriguez former Carrera's school companion, having a great impulsive character, with the purpose of using him for his negotiations with O'Higgins and Gainza.

On the 29th day there were held in Talca an Open Council and other Junta of Government that agreed not to acknowledge the new Government and overthrow it by the force of the arms.

Carrera guided his purposes to distract O'Higgins with long negotiations, while he prepared his army to beat him.

Bernardo O'Higgins decided to march on the capital leaving 600 men in Talca to prevent a possible attack from the royalist General Gainza.

To the front of the most part of the forces and two cannons, O'Higgins started toward Santiago to reestablish the overthrown Government; but his troops were rejected by the "carrerinos" on the 26th of August, don Luis Carrera had chosen excellent defensive positions in the combat of "Las tres Acequias", and O'Higgins after an sterile shelling and an hour of fight, withdrew to the South, he sheltered in the estate of Paula Jaraquemada with the intention of continuing the actions, but shortly after, news were received that the Viceroy of Peru had not approved the Treaty of Lircay, supporting his attitude in a Junta of War that decided to send another expedition to definitely finish the war of Chile. He charged the Spanish officer Brigadier don Mariano Osorio for that difficult position, whom even though wasn't a gifted General, was a learned man and with quick intelligence, came with new reinforcements and money, he had landed in Talcahuano and went to Santiago with the charge of taking the command of the royalist forces in order to unconditionally subdue Chile.

The General went on board in Callao on July 19th, in charge of 5.000 well armed soldiers, among which it arrived the famous battalion of Talavera. Among the instructions that Abascal gave him in 24 articles: *"If the Government was submitted, it should fulfil and make fulfil, with the greatest scrupulosity, the forgiveness and forgetfulness of everything that has happened, without allowing in no way that, by word or by work, anyone may be mistreated, nor the least thing may be taken from his property; and if the Government refused the capitulation, it should force the capital to be surrendered, but taking care the Commander of saving the lives of its inhabitants and not allowing any kind of looting".*

The first Osorio's step, after receiving the command in Chillan was to send emissaries to parley with sealed letters for the patriot field officers. Once the main of them arrived to Santiago, Carrera and the priest Uribe imprisoned them, alleging that they didn't bring any credentials. At those moments the Junta was only having 800 men. Knowing Carrera of his weakness, he started an approach to O'Higgins, but without accepting conditions. Bernardo O'Higgins accepted the agreement with all of Carrera's demands despite the dissensions, and by resigning his charge of General in Chief, he didn't doubt to be under the orders of Carrera, whom he recognized as the President of the Junta and, agreeing to fight together for the Homeland.

In this complete ambience of confrontation, don Jose Migue took the time to marry his patient fiancée Mercedes Fontecilla Valdivieso, in the Cathedral of Santiago, on August 20th 1814.

CHAPTER XIII.
END OF THE OLD REPUBLIC.
THE DISASTER OF RANCAGUA.

Once his troops being gathered, and on being rejected the intimidation of the new royalist field officer, Carrera and O'Higgins were taking a walk arm in arm in the middle of the streets of Santiago.

The new campaign that was to be started was a severe danger for the patriots.

The patriot General Osorio advanced to the North and crossed without any inconvenience until Cachapoal River, while the patriots were ready to capture him, without having a well conceived plan.

Jose Miguel Carrera saw that it was most advantageous to occupy the Angostura of Paine, but O'Higgins thwarting him, decided that it was the best to face the royalist in Rancagua and he fortified the stronghold on September 25th 1814.

In front of the imminence of the royalist attack, the patriots with 1.700 soldiers inferior in armaments, under the command of O'Higgins with Colonel Juan Jose Carrera and Jose Maria Benavente were to be inside Rancagua, where they built adobe trenches in the four streets leading to the town square.

Don Jose Miguel, already being General in Chief, was located more to the North, in the rearguard.

On the 1st of October the royalists, with 4.500 men and 18 cannons, more than the double of the forces than that of their enemies, General Osorio appeared in the front of Rancagua.

O'Higgins ordered to post a watchman in the tower of the church of La Merced to watch the arrangements of the royalist for the assault. Each one of the four streets that were meeting in the Rancagua square went for the middle of the block, leaving the four corners closed, he built barricades and placed in each of the four streets two entrenched cannons, with the necessary fusiliers for the defense, he placed shooters in the towers of the churches La Matriz and La Merced, besides in the roofs of the neighboring houses. He ordered to hoist the flag of Chile with a black crape in the tower of the church of La Merced and in the trenches so as to show that there was no rendition.

The combats of day October 1st started with the march of the soldiers of the Talavera regiment without shooting a gunshot down the street of San Francisco which directly led to the southern trench, but on passing the small bridge that sheltered them, they received a grapeshot blast that paralized the advance and the Talaveras bewildered some seconds, they sheltered in the lateral street where they could open an effective fire, when they believed that the resistance was already beaten they launched again an attack down the Square, a new discharge of the patriots paralized them again, then General Osorio ordered to charge the Hussars of La Concordia that they rushed at the patriots and in three minutes the street was scattered with dead and wounded men, the fight lasted about an hour, until the royalists withdrew to be posted with their cannons at little distance from the patriot trenches, he placed his shooters in all the buildings that allowed to shoot, making the movements inside the houses and ordering to assault the four trenches at the same time, so it was until the darkness of the night ended with the day.

At the second day, Osorio ordered to cut the water and set fire to the houses. The patriots were thirsty to death, suffocated under the heat, the cannons didn't work for lack of water to cold them, anyway, they resisted after four assaults.

Osorio ordered the fifth attack, in the culminating moment of the battle, the watchman of the tower of La Merced uttered a scream with the countersign "Viva la Patria" announcing a third division sent to their aid by Jose Miguel Carrera, but the royalists in front of 400 artillery men attacked the militia men, whom fled without fighting.

At one in the afternoon the royalists launched the sixth attack, being rejected again, but O'Higgins only had no more than 800 men out of the former 1700 men, they were wearied, thirsty and exhausted. The fight was ending.

In the last attempt to save the survivors, O'Higgins ordered:

- Ride the one who can, we'll cross the royalist trench in order to leave the square. We'll be crossing through the enemy with the edge of our sabres.-

Colonel Ramon Freire said to him:

- Sir, General, be placed in the center of the troop so that this may project you -.

-No, my duty is to be where the worst danger is -.

In a moment they saddled the horses, forming a column of 500 men. They sent forward the mules with the baggages so as to confuse them; Captain Francisco Javier Molina was heading them, he ran over all the obstacles and resistance.

O'Higgins soon after nudged the spurs into his horse and with the sabre in his hand, broke the enemy lines at the head of a handful of braves, in his running he was reached by an enemy Dragoon that blew him with a sabre, avoiding the blow one of his assistants.

The platoon was dispersed when arriving to the glen, seeing that they had lost half of their troops. The defeated General arrived to Santiago with 200 survivors. Both patriots met for the last time, being evident the enmity between the two men, and both showed their anger to each other:

- O'Higgins, you are an obstinate stupid that didn't want to hear when I told you that the best defense was La Angostura de Paine -.

- And you, Carrera, are an ambitious coward, lacking of morals and patriotism, you decided to withdraw to Coquimbo in order to continue the resistance in the North, sending me a group of cowardly militia men to help us, that they fled before arriving to Rancagua -.

Paying no attention to the opinions of O'Higgins, Carrera continued with the preparations for the moving to La Serena where he decided with his family to flee to Mendoza, and on the 4th of October he was leaving Santiago, which he would not see any longer.

The disaster of Rancagua was the ruin of the revolution. The Santiago's patriots, wherein a dreadful confusion reigned, the people only thought of escaping in order to withdraw from the vengeance of the victors, some of them went to hide into their estate in the field, others like the Carrera brothers and O'Higgins with his mother and sister and the last hosts of the army, would emigrate to Mendoza by crossing the mountain range, but it was in that season of the year in which it was covered with snow, the patriots defeating the dangers that were haunting them, they decided to be on their way by climbing the Andes, without supplies, with no money and even with no clothes, the remnants of the army marched in his rearguard to favour the retreat.

Doctor don Juan Jose Paso, delegate of the Argentinian Junta, ordered the exodus, aided by don Gregorio de Las Heras, chief of the Auxiliaries of Buenos Aires, they together had the idea of sending ahead the animals to shovel snow off the path, and soon he began sending the first fugitives by groups. Most of the civilian refugees started descending the eastern slope of the Andes on the way to the refuge in Mendoza.

While the patriots with fatigue, cold and lodging in the open were crying their defeat and exile, the royalist advances were triumphantly entering in Santiago in the morning of October 5th 1814.

It still remained to be suffered by the wearied patriots the last battle fought before crossing the frontier with Argentina. In the old Villa Santa Rosa de los Andes, known today as Los Andes, wherein everybody who crossed the mountain range took a rest in an inn, in a place called the Papeles, in this place on the 11th of November 1814 in the hillside of the same name took place the Battle of the Papeles, in which a patriot soldier that on being chased by a great number of Spanish soldiers jumped with his horse on an enormous cliff under which the river flows. From that time on that wonderful place, with presence of imposing animals such as pumas and condors, is called the "Salto del Soldado". After that battle in which the managed that the Spaniards may withdraw, they continued their flight to Mendoza.

It was the afternoon of October 16th, the sun was setting among the abrupt mountains of the Andes, the Carreras in group by horse were ending in the first decline of the Pampa called the Divisorio, which follows from the pass of Villavicencio.

The Aconcagua, the highest Andean mountain, gave them refuge and protected them from the night. Toward the midday, it could be glimpsed the beautiful green valley filled with stock where it is located the city of Mendoza. The military entourage with their showy uniforms, the animation that was noticed among the first of the cortège, it made distinguish their high rank. They were the three Carrera brothers that were reaching to the gates of Mendoza, closing the rearguard to the emigration that had taken place after the disaster of Rancagua.

Together with them, two female figures of remarkable beauty, they were the wives of those two young military men, Mercedes Fontecilla that was pregnant, wife of Jose Miguel and Ana Maria Cotapos wife of Juan Jose, whom were following them at the slow pace of the mules. Another young woman more intrepid and more independent that was preceding them in their march, she was the eldest sister of the three military men, Javiera Carrera, a very remarkable woman because of her fighting spirit. Being threatened to death her and her seven children, she had to decide by saving her children and thus abandoning the country, leaving a written letter to her husband in which she recommended him to take care of the children well, specially the little Domitila that ate a few, she also said: *"I'm horrified by the behaviour of the Royal Army; to murder the suckling babies and their happy mothers. It is indeed an insult. However, you're telling me that women should not think, I have the right because of being a Carrera."*

She went accompanied by her small child Periquito of hardly three months old that was still breastfed and her loyal servant Lola.

The arrival of the Chileans in search of refuge was a motive of exceptional opportunity for San Martin's military plans They have come divided in two irreconcilable bands, Rausing serious problems in those moments in which the unity was imperious need.

On the one side O'Higgins, Alcazar and Freire with the majority of the civilians; on the other side, the Carrera Brothers, Uribe, Muñoz, Urzua, Benavente and half of the soldiers.

Once the night was already fallen, the walkers were arriving at the wide courtyard of a villa located in the first streets which serve as avenue to the city of Mendoza.

Carrera with all his men, they found an adverse reception on the side of San Martin and Mackenna, whom had an enmity against don Luis since the disaster of Rancagua for having argued don Luis the bad artillery positions and, in revenge, he influenced the Governor San Martin against the Carreras, accusing them mistakenly of treason and having stolen the national treasure, saying that they hid the public monies among the loads that they carried. At the customs of the cordillera, according to the land regulations of Cuyo, Carrera was notified that the cargo should be subject to inspection, and he answered that before consenting it he would deliver his baggage to the flames, because of his protest the custom guard allowed him to pass.

San Martin sent a note to Carrera; telling him that he would not leave unpunished such offence against the laws of the country and the authority of his government.

Once they had unloaded their baggages, and were preparing to rest, an officer was present asking for the chief of the Carrera family to deliver him a sealed letter from the Governor-Interim San Martin. That sealed letter meant the first word of a continuous threat which began with the first bolt that was unbolting in the prisons that were keeping them in that sinister place, which from that moment on it was going to be his dungeon, and in which it would be risen the scaffold of his immolation later.

San Martin had intended to receive the Carreras not as refugees but as hostile invaders, beginning his plan with a bitter complaint against them, because on the morning of that day of October 16th, they had refused to subject to inspection their baggages in the pass of the ravine of Villavicencio. But they were not going to be the only incidents of insults and scorns.

On the 14th of October in the morning, indeed, they had been in the pass of the path of Uspatalla the two generals Carrera and San Martin. A reciprocal discourtesy had touched the feelings of both leaders, San Martin for the plan he was thinking of doing, and Carrera because of the haughtiness, both of them crossed the road without greeting each other.

San Martin had shown bad manners, but significant in this first rebuff; his young rival was only imprudent. Few minutes after this encounter, Captain Juan Jose Benavente was threatened with the sabre of the irritated San Martin, because he had not raised his hat in San Martin's presence, and the officer Ureta was forced to dismount his mule and take in his shoulder the saddle.

General O'Higgins had withdrawn that morning with the Dragoons that protected the column of Carrera, and the same assistants of his received orders from San Martin to only obey O'Higgins. Upon seeing all these excesses in the country in which the emigrated general was searching exile, he wrote in his diary this phrase:

What a beginning!

That unpleasant scene, happened among the defiles of the mountain, foreshadowed the beginning of the humiliation and tears for the one and of glory and happiness for the other. The Chilean commander went down, defeated, humiliated and vilified by those summits that separated him of his homeland, where he could never return for ever because of the disaster of Rancagua. While O'Higgins was going up, for the first time the summits to build for him eternal fame and extraordinary triumphs.

Perhaps the main reason that San Martin had, among many others to sacrifice Carrera, was his conviction that he would never find in him a subordinate, but indeed always an equal or a superior. Although it was suspected, and in fact it was certain, that he acted by influence of the Lautaro Lodge.

The Carreras had some enemies that were constantly threatening them; Marcos Balcarce, chief of the Auxiliaries of Buenos Aires, Juan Jose Pasos deputy of those provinces, and later on the writer Irizarri and his cousin the already demoted Mackenna, both of them recently exiled by Carrera, they had been forming during some time the Governor of Mendoza San Martin's intimate circle; in fact, Mackenna had been intimate partner of weapons and life with the General Coupigny, on whose orders San Martin fought as assistant in the battle of Bailen, their intimate friendship came from that event. It was some time ago that San Martin had in mind to conquer Lima through the valleys of Chile, and thus obtain the independence of South America, but pretending firstly to annex Chile into Argentina.

During those four years called the Old Republic, however the numerous mistakes made by the several patriot governments between 1810 and 1814, an evolution had been operated in the political ideas that had served to open the first breach in the old institutions, showing that the possibility of reaching some day the most complete independence.

CHAPTER XIV.

THE SPANISH RECONQUEST (1814-1817)
GOVERNMENT OF OSORIO.

At the fall of Napoleon, Fernando VII returned to Spain and reestablished the absolutism: he dissolved the Courts of Cadiz, the Spanish liberals were chased, the king was surrounded by absolutists decided to end with the new revolutionary ideas, both in the peninsula and in America.

The reconquest was an absolutist period in which it was attempted to recover the colonies; therefore new military reinforcements were sent from Spain that contributed to subject with a violent repression the rebelled countries.

The Spanish reconquest in Chile was not characterized by acts of cruelty and bloodshed, most of the patriots were moderate in their acts by not giving rise to great on the part of the Government, and even those confined in the island of Juan Fernandez, the king exchanged their death sentence into prison.

Three days after the battle of Rancagua, the royalist forces under the command of General Osorio began entering Santiago at the sound of the bell tolling. The Spanish flag fluttered in the city and the aristocrats showed joy, applauding and shouting the victors when they were passing by the streets.

The low people, mostly illiterate, that had never understood exactly the object of the fight, were also applauding the royalist army and admired it as they had done it with the patriot one.

In the first months of the reconquest, don Mariano Osorio governed Chile, he was an even-tempered man, human and refined that wanted to avoid useless horrors, tried to promote the reconciliation between royalists and patriots by forgetting the past, but that initial benevolence soon exasperated the spirit of the exalted royalists and together with the pressure of the Viceroy Abascal forced him to feign a repressive attitude completing his mission of reestablishing the colonial regime. Pretending good desires of friendship, he made that many respectable patriots by their age and condition emerged from the retreat in their estates and returned confident to Santiago. Osorio agreed with the instructions received from the Viceroy Jose Fernando de Abascal y Sousa, was prepared to fall on those character that had had any participation in the revolutionary events, even though the main one had fled or stayed hidden. Long lists of those involved were made and other ones of those that were found to be involved by chance in the events supporting the patriotic cause without interest.

He ordered to create in Santiago as first measure some tribunals of vindication, so to say it of purification, where the suspects should purify there their behavior during the patriot governments, having to show that they had always been loyal to Spain. The tribunals worked during the whole period with great activity and sometimes acting with indulgence and others with extreme severity. It was established a Junta of Sequestration, whose purpose was the confiscation of the assets of the patriots and administer them by means of letting of the houses, small farms, estates, livestock and other assets of the creoles, they imposed excessive contributions, forced public loans, etc.

During three nights the soldiers of the Talavera battalion under the orders of Captain Vicente San Bruno were devoted to capture to the persons indicated in the lists that in the Lumber of 200 were imprisoned in the quarter of that unit and in the rest of the country the same orders were followed.

These arrests caused consternation in most of the Creole families because many of the detainees were confined in diverse places of the country; but a few of the most committed, approximately a group of forty was exiled to the island of Juan Fernandez in inhuman conditions and a new Council was designated.

The insolent and conceited soldiers of the Talavera corps, favourite of Osorio, were terrible because of their misdeeds, mainly their Captain Vicente San Bruno and the sergeant Villalobos.

In Santiago's jail a group of confined was victim of a brutal intrigue with the purpose of warning them and thus produce the terror in the population. They were set a trap giving those hopes of a subversive movement: but at the time signalled for the uprising a party of soldiers of the Talavera was present before the conspirators and murdered and injured some of them. That crime before the sight of the city was presented as an act of justice against the traitors to the King; however, the population understood the treason and the authorities themselves tried to hide the truth.

At the same time that the repression took so diverse shades, the Government was in charge of abolishing the reforms introduced by the patriots reestablishing the old institutions of the colonial regime. Regarding the trade, the oldest laws returned that tried to take away from the ports the foreign ships, although this measure could not completely be put into practice, because most of the ships were English and at that moment was in debt with England due to his help in the war of independence against the Frenchmen.

In the cultural aspects, the best two creations of Carrera's government: the National Institute and the National Library were dissolved together with the school founded in the convents.

The University of San Felipe, upon being dissolved the National Institute, returned to its former situation.

It was reestablished the authority of the bishop of Santiago don Jose Santiago Rodriguez Zorrilla, excluded by the patriots because of his contrary ideas, during the reconquest he was a powerful assistant of the Government. It was reestablished the Inquisition, ordering to continue sending to Lima the money with which Chile contributed to maintain it on the country.

The Viceroy Abascal enjoyed in the court of an immense prestige by the services that he rendered to the royalist cause, he distrusted of Osorio's total obedience, and he started to organize plans to request to Spain a new Governor that may replace him.

Jose Miguel Carrera that had most of the force continued in Mendoza commanding as chief of the chilean executive, calling himself "Supreme Government of the Kingdom of Chile"; however, he could take hold of the quarter of La Caridad in spite of his first difficulties, and settle with his 300 companions in that same cloister where his ashes would later rest. He attempted to rescue the royalist prisoners in Mendoza to attract them to his cause. The Chilean leader refused to acknowledge San Martin's authority, without resisting the verbal crashes and numerous incidents with him, this aided by O'Higgins, they took hold of most of the Chilean forces, reinforced with other detachments of Gregorio de Las Heras, they surrounded the quarter where Carrera had become strong, whom at last surrendered, and they made prisoners to him, his brother Juan Jose, don Diego Benavente and the priest Uribe.

Hardly two days had passed, when those in favor of Carrera, his two brothers, the two voting members of the Junta, Uribe and Muñoz Urzua, the Benavente brothers and others, received on October 19th an exile order to the village of San Luis de La Punta. All of them refused and supporting in the bayonets that they still had, established their rights. Uribe blinded by his impulsive spirit broke in insults, Muñoz Urzua moderately asked permission to pass to Coquimbo to live unnoticed, and Luis Carrera that was the most military, gave an answer of a haughty soldier:

- *"The hindrances of the military subordination that I have sworn take away from me the liberty of executing orders that don't come from the chief of the flags in which I'm enlisted and from the superior Government that is commanding us. For this reason, you will be pleased to excuse the lack of effect of your orders to leave for San Luis. They would surely turn against the authors of the fear that caused them in your expressing, although if it was considered the behaviour of my handling they should be decreed according to the merit, the justice and the reason from which I think I'm not separated Sr. Governor, and that I'm persuaded that you will always continue in your dispositions"* -.God be with you US forever.- Mendoza, October 20th, 1814.
Luis Carrera.

José Miguel on the other side was sustained with his own force; and he answered to the order of exile of Governor San Martin with a minute of his troops in which they swore to him eternal obedience.

San Martin was alarmed an instant and he changed tactics, and to the haughtiness of Carrera followed the shrewdness of the diplomat, intended for the moment to divide and spread the soldiers that supported Carrera. He gave passports to don Luis Carrera and Commander Jose Maria Benavente on October 23rd so that they may act as Carrera's emissaries in Buenos Aires. In fact, don Luis was to present his complaints before the Superior Director of the capital. Upon being informed San Martin about the intentions of his trip; in order to counteract the step, he sent Juan Mackenna and Antonio Jose de Irisarri to Buenos Aires, San Martin deceived Uribe by retaining him as member of the Junta; he entered into communications with Luis Carrera about the object of the service, and he even offered him aids in Buenos Aires. He had made that Balcarce gathered the veteran troop of the province, and in accordance with O'Higgins, he made that Alcazar, chief of the Dragoons, pronounced to be in rebellion against Jose Miguel Carrera, whom was indignant at the insubordination of his subordinate, he asked San Martin his soon punishment, since he was powerless to subdue him on his own, he sent him an official letter on October 29th:

"If for any reason you cannot accept my request; I assure you that I will leave the command of troops of Chile in the moment, command that degrades me when I cannot keep the dignity of my job, and when the disorder is consequent upon these actions. In such a case you can commission some person that takes charge of the Division until the Director's resolution arrives. I wish my tranquility and this situation drives me in despair."
José Miguel Carrera.- Mendoza October 29th, 1814.-

The emigrated general's confession revealed that San Martin's plan was already prepared. In the morning of October 30th, he executed it indeed, surrounding with his troop Carrera's quarter. Once they surrendered their arms, only two of them wanted to enlist in the flags of the Argentinian army and the rest of them were treated with rigor. Carrera said in his diary: *"I never, spirited of a generous indignation, despised more the Direction of Buenos Aires that when I saw the way they treated the constant troops of Chile".*

San Martin called them before his presence at one o'clock in the afternoon, and as a man who makes others obey him by means of conciliation, he asked them to be retained, confining them for this purpose to the sacristy of the church of San Agustin, place always favoured by the Governor San Martin for the punishments, because the chapel joined to the dungeon, there was left only a sad step for the executions...

General San Martin had a strange and singular habit in his race for power; that of visiting his enemies or rivals when they were in his hands after being already defeated.

This time San Martin's visit to the Carreras had something of that double spirit of vengeance and irony.

Upon entering the chapel, in the afternoon of that same day 30th, he gave Captain Servando Jordan a violent push whom left without greeting him; but he instantly composed and entered in the chapel courteously before the presence of the prisoners. his dialogue was brief and reserved but friendly, taking him his courtesy into offering a cigarette to those that surrounded him, except for Commander Diego Benavente whom was looking with an expression of despise that scene in a corner of the room, he refused him that so inappropriate military courtesy.

San Martin had hardly said his farewell, when the prisoners were confined in a narrow dungeon; the unlucky captives remained subject to a system of mortifications and privations. It already lasted two days this offensive insult when a part of those confined, having at hand a slip of paper, which has been kept among the papers of the Mendoza's files, they wrote San Martin this at the same time emphatic as rational protest.

"We are confined in this barrack forty eight hours as exposed to the public sight. A disgusting and reduced room kept by a sentry, it is the one destined to be our room in which we being upright and the beds are hardly contained in it. It is not allowed to close the door, and we sleep with a lighted candle to increase the heat that makes us sick; we don't have a right now to the most essential actions because an armed man is following us . What is it left to hurry our suffering and finish the existence of some men of honor that have just surrendered their valuable services to their homeland? Let us perish in the scaffold if we are criminal and on the contrary that the sacred and wise laws that rule this free country may come in our aid. If we are not granted asylum in this country, and we are at some aspect harmful for it, tell us to abandon it in the moment we are ordered to. We appeal to the generosity and offers from you but not the justice. May the Lord protect you forever... Mendoza, November 1st 1814. Jose Miguel Carrera –Julian Uribe – Diego Jose Benavente.-Mr. Colonel Don Jose de San Martin Governor Intendant of the Province of Cuyo

The numerous correspondences, that they sustained by that time, disclose the inequality of positions and it explains the course of the events.

While Carrera was consoling with sterile reproaches, San Martin was calmly making the preparations for the trip that should take away from his presence and his plans the refugees who were not necessary any longer because he had removed from them as much as it may be profitable, even the self-love and the haughtiness of those men, all of them but Luis had made a supplication or a complaint.

On the 3rd of November everything was ready; dona Javiera and her two brothers together with their wives got on a heavy stagecoach in which they were soon departing from Mendoza. The Commander Diego Benavente and voting member Uribe were galloping at the sideboard of the coach, and an escort of 30 Dragoons, commanded by the chilean Lieutenant Agustin Lopez surrounded the cortege.

Only a sad episode, although minimum, worsened that trip of Las Pampas, second emigration from Chile that the Carreras undertook by fleeing from Mendoza's dungeons to be confined in those of Buenos Aires. This incident was the robbery of three horses of O'Higgins's assistants that closely followed them in their march to Buenos Aires. On the 10th of November, he wrote San Martin from the posthouse of La Dormida a few kilometres away from Mendoza this sad suspicion about the loss of his horses. "*The cause of the flight of the three soldiers will be the bad example of the Carreras, whom were advising the soldiers that were not even corrupted that they may pass to the enemy before serving under the flags of Buenos Aires*".

Meanwhile, the stagecoach that served as prison for the émigrés had returned to San Luis on the 18th of November. Don Jose Carrera and his wife returned in it by orders of San Martin.

The love that he felt for Ana Maria and the seeming tranquillity of San Luis, Juan Jose talked to San Martin, and he didn't take side with his brothers and was not compromised in any of the Mendoza's turbulences.

His first care was to rent a house in Mendoza for his wife's resting.

But that apparent tranquillity was only a dream that would continue with an exhausting journey, because Juan Jose had San Martin as his implacable enemy.

Jose Miguel Carrera's painful journey had lasted 22 days since he left from Mendoza and only in Lujan he was withdrawn the guard that brought him prisoner by order of Director Posadas and whose services he had to pay on his own with 50 pesos which were an essential part of his resources.

While Jose Miguel Carrera arrived at Buenos Aires, a serious mischance was happening to his brother Luis that was going to cost him the jail.

Luis Carrera had arrived at Buenos Aires on November 6th, staying at a modest inn in one of the neighbouring streets to the river. Almost at the same time, the young writer Antonio Jose de Irisarri and his relative and companion Juan Mackenna arrived, sent by San Martin to watch over the steps of Luis Carrera, staying fatally at the house neighbouring to that of Luis and, upon being aware of the arrest of this brothers in Mendoza, he decided to revenge. Knowing that Mackenna was in the city living next to him, he sent him a note. One night, when returning to his lodging, Irisarri found on the table a challenging note that Luis Carrera had sent to his companion Mackenna:

"You have insulted the honor of my family and mine with your false and deceitful suppositions; you are to give me satisfaction by refuting publicly what you have said or with the arms that you want and in the place that you like. I await your reply with the bearer of this one."

The duel took place in Portachuelo on November 21th 1814, acting as godfathers the ship captain Taylor that had been innkeeper and was he who delivered the duel missive, and the doctor Hamhpord who accompanied him as surgeon, on the side of Mackenna acted as godfather Guillermo Brown.

Don Juan Mackenna O'Reilly was killed in the duel.

At dawn of day, Irisarri was informed, being very worried about his companion's fate, that under the porch of the Town Council was exposed to be recognized the corpse of a white man that had his neck crossed by a bullet.

Things were complicated for Luis, day after the police was at his home to capture him, blaming him for murder.

On being informed Jose Miguel about the event, he hurried to visit his friend since the days of Cadiz, Carlos Maria Alvear that exercised the position of Supreme Director of the United Provinces of Rio de La Plata, fierce enemy of San Martin.

The two procers met and "narrowed their friendship again":

- My dear good friend Jose Miguel! , It makes so happy to see you again after such a long time.-
- So do I, Carlos Maria, it is certain, it's been such a long time since Cadiz, although I must say that the motive of my visit is to beg a favor from you.-
- Whatever you wish and it may be in my hands to do it, you know that you may count on that.-

- My younger brother Luis has unfairly been accused of having murdered Juan Mackenna, when in fact, he fought a duel with him, and I suspect that it is San Martin's hand behind this because he wants to destroy us at whatever cost.-

- I'm sure it is so, he would also want to destroy me, and his hatred toward me is, even though I was his best man in his marriage, such that he plots to take me off of the mandate of Supreme Director to occupy it instead of me; even though I think that San Martin by himself is not capable of thinking, his mind and his hand are that of the Lautaro Lodge's, which has separated us between his partisans and mine. But since you and I belong to the same Lodge of the Rational Knights that I established in Cadiz, due to this connection and by its mediation, we'll release Luis from the jail, and besides, as punishment, I'm going to dismiss San Martin as Governor-Interim of the province of Cuyo, and I'll put the Colonel Gregorio Perdriel in his place, you will thus be able to see the humiliation of the man that has driven you into ruins. As you know when we reached Buenos Aires, from London, San Martin established the Lodge Lautaro of Buenos Aires in 1812; once he was designated Governor of the province of Cuyo, he set up the Lodge of Mendoza in 1814, and he has recently established together with O'Higgins the Lautarian Lodge dependent on the Lautaro one. In this lodge, secretly, they fraternize both the Chilean mandataries and the Argentinian ones, and both the military and the civilian, undertaking under oath to fight for the independence. If one of its members is elected for the Supreme Government, he cannot decide by himself anything without consulting the Lodge's opinion. In this one from Mendoza, O'Higgins is involved in an inexplicably hidden and mysterious power, that subordinates him to a strange and superior authority, in spite that the argentinians prevail, it is not strange that they pretend not only the expulsion of the Spaniards but also the annexing of Chile into Argentina; it is obvious, therefore, that there is no place for your nationalistic ideas in the project they are hatching, they have to eliminate the three of you in order to achieve it.-
- You are right indeed in what you say; they try to eliminate us the whole Carrera family, that's why, if we succeed in releasing my brother Luis from the jail, they will surely chase him until they finish with him.-
- In that sense, Jose Miguel, you don't have to worry, I'll tell my dear Carmen, my wife, that she hides him at home which is large and cosy, it was my grandmother's, it was known as Balbastro's house, he will be completely safe there, besides my Carmen as good Andalusian from Jerez knows how to cook very delicious stews.-

Jose Miguel was distressed:

- They don't forgive that I deserted the Lautaro Lodge as well.-

Alvear commented:

- It was in London when I knew him more closely in the secret meetings that we held in Park Road 23, Andres Bello's house, where Jose Matias Zapiola and Tomas Guido were also gathered; and then in the ship that brought us to Buenos Aires. I offered him to live in my house but he, after thanking me for it, told me that he would stay at the inn "Los Tres Reyes" in Santo Cristo Street, what he did frequent the gatherings that were held at home. Shortly after arriving, he married dona Remedios Escalada Quintana, marriage that didn't please her parents, they called him the "guarani" and they also said that the "yapezuceño" was marrying the little lady of Buenos Aires. She introduced him to the high society of Buenos Aires; she took him to the parties of the most distinguished families such as: the Mondevilles, the Sarrateas, Lucas, etc., and as I told you, he insisted on my being his best man, which I was very pleased to accept; that day everyone was running to and fro making preparations in the house in Florida Street, Colonel San Martin and that girl, Remedios, the most beautiful of the Escalada's daughters, were getting married. Although she was delaying a lot to appear, Bernardino Rivadavia said that it was time to enter, the ceremony was about to begin, the music was playing and the guests were wondering if they had seen the young girl Remedios, they answered that she would be getting ready, but what I could hear from her mother, the girl had been severely ill of her lungs, and that day she could hardly walk, they were about to cancel the marriage, but the doctor arrived and she was revived, I think she is still very ill. Afterward, our relationship got worse and lately we don't even talk if it were not for an official matter. Changing into another theme, And you, Jose Miguel, what are you doing now?-

- My sister Javiera is also in Buenos Aires, for the time being she is making her life by preparing Chilean and Creole food, sometimes he helps me to paint cards and we think to establish a small cigarette factory if everything goes well.-

Alvear commented:

- News have arrived at Buenos Aires that Napoleon has been defeated and confined to the Island of Elba, and that don Fernando VII has returned to Madrid after six years of captivity, and in his first act of government he has abolished the Constitution of Cadiz, he is sentencing to death to everyone who is opposing his sovereignty as the liberal are.-

Jose Miguel replied:

- It will be necessary to wait for events, since it has been known discouraging news about the approaching of an expedition of ten thousand Spaniards to Rio de La Plata; and Jose Miguel, I will tell you that as from today our salaries are reduced to the half, it has even been requested to the ladies that they cooperate in the task of collecting donations, I know that in Mendoza dona Remedios San Martin has donated all her jewels.-

Once the Alvear's order about the dismissal of San Martin as Governor arrived Mendoza, the population called for an open council, in which it was demanded the continuation of San Martin in the position, which it meant the total disregarding of the authority of the Supreme Director Alvear, appealing that the Director mentioned did not have power in that jurisdiction.

San Martin wrote in vengeance an official note to Juan Jose Carrera informing him the order:

"In the time of 24 hours after receiving this, you should depart for the capital, guarded by a corporal and four soldiers, being relieve from the Director, don Juan Jose Carrera, and warning yo for its precise fulfilment"-Mendoza-January 3rd 1815- Jose de San Martin- Governor of Mendoza.

Juan Jose in his official note informed San Martin:

"Mi situation is more wretched than it could be, you know that I am married to a lady that is not capable of separating from me without her life being in danger perhaps; that she is wearied of so many sufferings and is in a foreign country. I, trusting in what you have promised me, rented a house paying four months in advance, despite my shortage of money, since I have only 65 pesos now.

I request you to let me go to another estate, under arrest by my word, to work five or six days to have a comfortable trip, I await your kindness".

San Martin sent a message with Juan Jose' own assistant ordering him to pay 20 pesos that he had defrauded in an inn during his travel to Buenos Aires and that he should return the three horses which disappearance had been reported by O'Higgins.

In spite of his pleas of not departing without his beloved wife, Juan Jose was taken to Buenos Aires and was confined in the brigantine "25 de Mayo".

With the friendship and influence of Alvear, Jose Miguel Carrera thought that he might obtain a decisive support to achieve his intentions: to be recognized as legitimate government of Chile and to obtain resources to prepare an expedition for Coquimbo whence he was planning to continue the war for independence.

But this pleasure as the whole ones that an outlaw can reach far from his homeland was transitory.

Alvear proposed to use his army for an expedition to Chile, but the Council, led by San Martin' father-in-law, don Francisco Antonio de Escalada refused.

When Alvear had come to Buenos Aires in 1812, his uncle Gregorio Antonio Posadas resigned the charge of Supreme Director of the United Provinces of Rio de La Plata, and the Assembly appointed for that position Carlos Maria de Alvear, with only 25 years old. His mandate turned into a real dictatorship, supported only by the secret lodge which he belonged to and the officers loyal to the army. He organized a net of espionage and arrested his opponents without judgment. The severe press censorship, the persecution before a possible conspiracy, he executed without judgment a captain of the army who was hanged in the Plaza de Mayo. He was accompanied by a Mounted Grenadiers escort. All this caused unrest in the army that mutinied.

General Alvarez Thomas by orders of Alvear, went out with a squadron of the Battalion of Grenadiers to reinforce the garrison of Parana in order to contain the artiguist montoneras so called anarchists, they were General Artigas's federalists. But what Alvear overlooked in his foresights was that the same military man that he sent to punish his enemies would become the one who destroyed him, rebelling in Fontezuela, he intimidated the Supreme Director Alvear and forced him to leave the government and the country.

The city of Buenos Aires, so far a bastion of unity, joined the movement indirectly led by San Martin, and Alvear was overthrown on April 17th 1815 by General Ignacio Alvarez Thomas. It is here that Alvear had to give up his position only three months after having assumed it and take refuge in an English frigate. He went to Brazil while his supporters were captured including his uncle Posadas and the two Carrera brothers, who were arrested four days because of being involved in the guerrilla to help their friend Alvear.

The situation became adverse for the ideas of Carrera since the Council of Buenos Aires was made up of a group opposed to Alvear, who considered him as a dictator, to whom they removed from power and seized his properties, putting an end to Jose Miguel's hope of returning to Chile.

The replacement of his friend Carlos Maria de Alvear didn't completely dash Jose Miguel Carrerra's hopes. He was ingratiated himself with the new Director Alvarez and then requested the favors of that government in a petition submitted for consideration on the 8th of May:

"I only request weapons to equip a column of 500 Chilean émigrés that would come out into the valley of Coquimbo bearing 1000 reserve rifles. There is no more resource than to introduce at whatever cost it may be the spirit of popular opposition so much more attainable this day when the exasperation of Chile under the tyrant's yoke (he rightly said), it is for sure I won't receive the glory but Manuel Rodriguez will, the immortal guerrilla man of the first conflicts".

Marcos Balcarce, war minister, consulted San Martin the plan on the 11th of May, this step was not accepted; however, the director Alvarez Thomas replied to Carrera that patriotic zeal and his role in determining the destiny of South America filled him with satisfaction.

Nothing could keep Chile away from Jose Miguel's thought neither from his soul now that he was accused of having lost it.

Álvarez Thomas with unitarian tendency, did not want to recognize the autonomy of the provinces, and a final pact of union of the Oriental Band, Cordoba, Santa Fe y Corrientes neither they did the General Artigas with his demands of the delivery of rifles to Cordoba and Santa Fe.

The negotiations failed the same as the observation army that he sent with General Viamonte that invaded Santa Fe, causing abuses and outrages, infuriating the people that led by the leaders Mariano Vera and Estanislao Lopez took up arms, and after bloody combats General Viamonte was forced to capitulate.

This failure worsened the authority of Alvarez Thomas and he didn't have any choice but to resign his position.

O´Higgins after a brief stay in Mendoza moved to Buenos Aires, where the government of that city decided to incorporate him into the army being organized in Mendoza under the command of San Martin.

From that moment O'Higgins and the military men that followed him were closely cooperating with San Martin by preparing an expeditionary force that may liberate Chile.

One night after having dinner in San Martin's house, he was mentioning O'Higgins:
- How much I have been really sorry for the death by duel of that great military man, Mackenna!; no matter how much the Mendoza Lodge made that it may seem a murder, forcing the witnesses to remain silent and to disappear the duelling note; apparently, it must be that Alvear's Lodge has had in that moment more power. And what it annoys me more it is that Luis Carrera is on the loose. Now, changing to other issues. When General Belgrano retreated, having been defeated by the royalist General Pezuela from the Upper Peru, the Supreme Director of the United Provinces of the Rio de La Plata, don Juan Martín de Pueyrredón appointed me to replace him. He charged me with the formation of the Regiment of Mounted Grenadiers. At the time I stayed in front of my troops, I was convinced that the solution to the war could not be found in that region, since every time we penetrated in the plateau of Upper Peru, what we were really interested in was the adding of the Potosí mines to Argentina, but we were defeated because it was very difficult to fight in the 4.000 meters high land, and when these royalists were coming down the high plateau on their way to the valleys of the province of Salta, they were defeated; thus this fact was repeating during four years, while the Viceroy may renew the Spanish armies in the Upper Peru we will not be able to secure our independence; at last I made a decision to pretend that I was ill and requested the government of the province of Cuyo, I reached Mendoza a month later in September.-

- Then Jose, do you have any elaborate plan? -.

- Yes , firstly, to impose my projects to the leaders of Buenos Aires of organizing in Mendoza the bases of the Army of the Andes, building in El Plumerillo, a league far away from here, a training field, Sergeant Major Jose Antonio Alvarez Condarco will be in charge of this. It will be made up of mud wall barracks for the battalion of artillery, warehouses for the headquarters, the staff and the squadron of Mounted Grenadiers, a great square with a large wall of double thick mud wall, to exercise the troop in the target practice, and six squares destined to the regulation exercises, to collect money, weapons, and an arsenal where Friar Luis Beltran will be in charge of casting the cannons, ammunition, supplies, horses, etc., organize in Mendoza a medical service, Governor of San Luis don Vicente Dupuy is going to provide me with cavalry, I think most of them are gauchos, in short!, we will have to create everything and thus get a well formed and trained army , joining forces with the Government, later invade Chile and defeat the royalist, help the patriots of that country and by counting on them to increase our army, organize a fleet and afterward attack the Viceroy in his field, invade Peru by sea. We will have to establish a letter of marque between Argentina and Chile, although Director Pueyrredon has issued one with the captains he is sending throughout the world, Hipolito Bouchar and Guillermo Brown, on the side of chile, we will have priest Julian Uribe with the Chilean émigrés whom will also be part of this project; among whom we may find Nicolas Garcia, Ramon Freire and Pablo Vargas, all this will be extremely important to obtain our independence, with an unspeakable fleet we will weaken the enemy's economy based upon maritime transportation and by means of the privateers the Spanish ships will have scatter by diverse routes, while we will be free to focus and forcefully attack the chosen place. -

- But Jose, in order to so, we will have to hire at least 25 sailors having maritime experience but not a war one and once granted the letter of marquee, arm a vessel, even though a modest one. I also think that it would be a good idea that you send to Chile emissaries pretending to be repented, and spread feigned news to misinform the royalist authorities and be able to know the exact number and the situation of the King's troops. -

- Yes, Bernardo, it is a good idea, although as I have told you the schooner the "Contitución" is being prepared by Friar Uribe, and as to the matter of deceiving the royalists, we will have to think of some people from the chilean emigration whom may serve us as secret agents.-

- As to the emigration, I can tell you that we will be surely able to count on Pedro Aldunate, grandson of the count of the Conquest,

the lawyer Manuel Rodriguez Erdoiza and the muleteer Justo
Estay.-

- I completely agree, arrange me an interview with them soonest
possible. While we organize all the preparations, my first son will
be born; we await him, God willing, in the middle of August, and
thus I will be able to be close to Remedios during those difficult
moments for her, since as you know her health condition is not
so good, even though she seems to be healthy and excited about
having a baby girl. -

-José that's very pleasant news, congratulations! -

On December 19th, 1815, the frigate "Javiera" anchored in Valparaiso
bringing the new Governor of Chile on board, the field marshal Francisco
Casimiro Marcó del Pont, military man who had fought in the campaigns
against the French invasion and taken part in the defense of Zaragoza
with General Palafox.

He was a fainthearted and effeminate man, very inclined to luxury;
he had obtained the Government of Chile due to his family's influence,
the Encinas.

When he arrived at Chile, he was bringing numerous retinues of
retainers and servants, and more than eighty trunks and packing cases.
All his edicts and decrees were headed with all his titles and names: Don
Francisco Casimiro Marcó del Pont, Ángel Díaz y Menéndez, Knight
of the Order of Santiago, Meritorious of the Homeland in heroic and
eminent degree, etc.

Marcó del Pont showed a preference for the Spaniards, distrusting
the Chilean officers, which caused rivalries between them.

The new repressive policy began with judiciary character having the
purpose of preventing any intent of disturbing the public order, it even
figured in these measures that it would be applied the death penalty to
any attempt of opposition, it was forbidden that the people may move
from one place of the country to another without permission of the
authorities and bearing any kind of weapon, being forced to deliver them
in the artillery barrack in a three day deadline. He forbade the carnival
celebrations, the gambling houses, the tumultuous fanfares, causing with
these measures the popular displeasure because they were deeply used
to these old entertainments. The repressive policy began with the edict
intended for compelling the collect of the taxes. The gallows was set up

again in Santiago Square, ghost that had been withdrawn by the former Governor Osorio.

He held the presidency of the Military Tribunal of supervision and public security, which was comprised by him and three merchants.

The repeated clashes with the outposts in the mountain ranges, which led him to suppose that there was a powerful army in the other side of the Andes, made Marcó del Pont reinforce the frontier with General Elorreaga and his guerrilla in Aconcagua, and General Sanchez in Colchagua, while he maximized the policy of reprisals.

He also feared an attack by sea, and before the arrival of the warships, in order to be secured in the meantime he seized two smuggling ships and armed them for the defense of the coasts.

What most irritated the spirits of the Chileans was the total lack of fufillment of the Royal Decree that pardoned those confined in the island of Juan Fernandez, and disobeying the Viceroy's definitive orders, he only repatriated six out of the 48 convicts.

The neighbors ended up feeling such hatred for the soldiers of the Talavera battalion that none of the soldiers could go very far away from the barracks alone without being stoned, stabbed or thrown off the Mapocho river bridge. The people were crying out for vengeance and this was going to come from Mendoza.

The Lieutenant Colonel Santiago Bueras accepted San Martin's proposal, while being exiled in Mendoza, to secretly travel to Chile and organize a guerrilla in Aconcagua, but he was discovered and captured. The muleteers were of great help, exposing often their lives to take and bring secret correspondence.

The character who acquired more renown was the young lawyer don Manuel Rodriguez Erdoiza, that had acted as secretary of Jose Miguel Carrera, now in the exile, because of his great ability to mix with the people would be the one who would command the the famous guerrilla warfares that facilitated the Chilean-Argentine invasion, it was also among these secret agents don Pedro Aldunate y Tiero, grandson of the count of La Conquista and the muleteer Justo Estay, he who gave San Martin rigorous and exact reports on the number and the situation of the royalist troops.

San Martin, knowing that his army was lower, entrusted Manuel Rodriguez, in order to keep distracted and dispersed the army of the Governor Marcó del Pont between the Maipo and the Maule, to undertake in Chile a campaign of montoneras (horsemen guerrilla fighters), group of men having unlimited audacity, very skillful horsemen and even also real bandits.

These bands of montoneros (horsemen guerrilla fighters) were dispersing throughout the field from one side to the other by sporadically striking where they were less waited.

The spanish Governor Marcó del Pont set a price on the heads of the guerrilla fighters Rodriguez and Neira; but these men's prestige was such that nobody betrayed them, but these boldly made fun of all the persecutions. In one of his night forays, Rodriguez was very closely pursued by a squad of Talaveras and he had to take refuge in a church, after a while, the captain that was pursuing him knocked the door of the temple, a Franciscan friar opened and kindly invited him to enter:

- What brings you here, son?-

- Here, a fugitive has taken refuge from the law, to whom we were pursuing -.
- No son, I have not seen anything, but you can make sure by yourself, enter and look, I will light you with my candle and also I will help you to look for him all over the hiding places of this holy house-.

After searching unsuccessfully, the soldiers went away without suspecting that Manuel Rodriguez was not another that the own Franciscan that received them at the door.

Miguel Neíra was a famous highwayman, shepherd by occupation, he efficiently captained one of these bands during his youth, intercepting the royalists' mail and attacking small patrols of soldiers. Manuel Rodriguez and his montoneras (guerrilla horsemen) carried out two extremely bold attacks with his eighty reliable men and a crowd of peasants armed with stick, hoes, etc., they seized by surprise the city of Melipilla, dispersing the scarce forces of the garrison, meanwhile the montoneros were received with great cheers for the homeland. Rodriguez seized the money from the royal caja (colonial treasury office) and plundered the tobacco deposit that functioned for account of the Crown. At nightfall, they moved away with their montoneros (guerrilla horsemen) in order to avoid the pursuit that would be done from Santiago. Eight days later, Juan Pablo Ramirez organized a night attack and took hold of San Fernando, managing to put to flight the royalist chief together with eighty soldiers of the garrison. They did the third assault against Curicó, but they were rejected.

The guerrillas and the "montoneras" increased Marcó del Pont's repressive measures. It was prohibited to journey on horseback between the Maipó and the Maule and the death penalty was extensive to all guerrilla fighters, even to women patriots like dona Agueda Monasterio de Latapiat who was concealing the whereabouts of her sons and dona Paula Jaraquemada who put her estate of Paine into the service of the patriots. He sent against the montoneros, being dispersed in different places, numerous parties of soldiers that divided his army, and it was what San Martin pretended.

On the 24th of August 1816, Mercedes Tomasa de San Martin y Escalada was born in Mendoza.

San Martin wrote a letter to Tomas Godoy Cruz in 1816, deputy for Mendoza in the congress of Tucuman, telling him: *How long do we have to wait in order to declare our independence?* At the same time that he was sending delegates to the congress on behalf of the province of Cuyo with express orders of insisting on the declaration of independence from Spain of the southern provinces: the sessions began on March 24th 1816 with Alvarez Thomas as Supreme Director in the house of dona Francisca Bazan de Laguna in the Congreso street, in the center of San Miguel de Tucuman where it was proclaimed the independence on July 9th 1816, it was announced by a salvo of 21 gunshots; but soon Alvarez Thomas resigned and he was replaced by Gonzalo Balcarce on July 16, whom also resigned. On the 3rd of May, Juan Martin de Pueyrredon, from the porteño (people of the city of Buenos Aires) group, was elected Supreme Director with the purpose of pacifying and unite the whole territory, including the Upper Peru with the provinces of Charcas, Chichas, Cochabamba, Tupiz and Mizque, in the hands of the royalist at that time, they gathered in Tucuman with the provinces of Buenos Aires, Tucuman, Mendoza, San Juan, Catamarca, Salta, La Rioja and Cordoba, excluding Santa Fe, Corrientes, Entre Rios and the Oriental Band, because of political differences; among whom prevailed the antiporteño (against the people of the city of Buenos Aires) feeling to impose their centralist criteria. The main points to be dealt with were: Communicate with all the provinces to insist on the need of union and thus face the external enemy, elaborate a project of Constitution and declare the Independence.

On July 9th 1816, at the request of deputy Teodoro Sanchez de Bustamante, it was discussed the Project of Declaration of Independence.

After three months of meetings, the president of the Congress, don Francisco Narciso Laprida asked:
- Do the congressmen want to be free and independent from the Kings of Spain? -

-Yes, we do!-

It was proclaimed this day the existence of a new free nation and independent from Spain.

When the spirits calmed down, all the representatives began signing one by one the minutes and, they then sent it to the King of Spain to inform him of this decision, even though it was not completely resolved, because inside the Congress, it was recorded three main trends: the centralist or Unitarian system as Buenos Aires and Cuyo, the federalists of Cordoba that defended the provincial autonomies, and an intermediate group, those of the Upper Peru, that although they aspired to a centralist regime, they did not want Buenos Aires as head of the new state.

The Congress decided to elect a new national authority that may join the whole region, designating a Supreme Director, being elected don Juan Martin de Pueyrredon.

The Congress was transferred to Buenos Aires in 1817, before the possibility of a royalist attack on Tucuman.

Without more resources in Argentina, Jose Miguel Carrera decided to appeal to his acquaintances in the United States, mainly Poinsett, whom was a friend of his when he was ruling; with the purpose of gathering funds and supplies to liberate Chile from the royalist domain.

He went on board the "Expedition" without a penny in his pockets and being unable to speak English, which he managed to master in the three months that the voyage of the ship lasted.

On January 17th 1816, he arrived at the port of Annapolis, where he was received by a friend of his, the Commodore David Porter, whom would help him most during his stay of eleven months, because Robert Poinsett, in whom Jose Miguel trusted him so much, was avoiding him for such a long time.

From Philadelphia on February 7th, Jose Miguel wrote a letter to his wife:

"My beloved Mercedes. Which will be your situation? I feel sorry for you in these days and when you receive this, after delivery cares have already ceased, you will be entirely recovered. It has been two days ago that I arrived

at this beautiful town. I continue for New York and only today I know that a brigantine sets sail for Buenos Aires or Montevideo with 3.000 rifles; the owner of her offers me to deliver in your hands my letters by means of the steward. I hasten to take the pen and I can hardly write to you the very precise thing. That of Luis will inform you about my situation.

How is my Xaviera Roberta? Fill her with love on my behalf and kiss her (him), be patience with the second one.

On January 17th, I wrote to you in the brigantine in which Devereux was the steward, and I'm sure that the letter has been delivered to you and you will follow my recommendations. If you are in good health and well attended, I am glad and happy. Don't say that my letter is short because that of Luis is also for you. From New York where I will arrive on Saturday, I will write to you by means of somebody having my complete trust.

I'm in a hurry and I don't have time for anything.

I'm not absent-minded, I'm always the same and I eagerly wish to hug you. You should wait for me in the winter. Good-bye my dear Merceditas receive the tenderest regard from your persevering lover. José Miguel".

Luis Carrera wrote a letter to Joel Robert Poinsett:
"Mr. Joel Robert Poinsett.
Buenos Aires, February 8th, 1816.
My dearest friend; when I write to you this, I consider that Jose Miguel is with you and therefore you are informed about the events happened until his departure; hear now those which are presently happening. The present director Juan Martin Pueyrredon has actively taken part in the disagreements of the Chilean émigrés, protecting O'Higgins and his followers and oppressing in such way that it could be said as shocking. When O'Higgins left for Mendoza, he would be helped by order of this government with free relay, a coach for his family and 500 pesos for expenses, assigning him a salary at his destination. San Martin, as Governor of Mendoza, had to do with this; he has formally informed this government telling that O'Higgins was the most qualified and convenient for the kingdom of Chile. I assure you that San Martin and this government know the opposite and they know and even have confessed O'Higgins's incompetence.

I think of complaining to the Junta of Observation about this, and as I have said to you before that the scandal with which we are pursued may be known, and it can frankly be said that they have ambitious aims on Chile. San Martin is hated by this government and all those having the power, and if he were not supported by force, I would throw him from the command today. He think that it is risky to cross to Chile with less than 4.000 soldiers and it has even been said discreetly this, he doesn't dare to undertake it with

*such small force, because if he is defeated the government of Buenos Aires will
end up ruining him.*
*There is very little to inform you about, you will find out these by means
of the letter I'm writing to Jose Miguel.*
    Your ever friend in the distance.
    Luís Carrera".

Poinsett turned a deaf ear to the letter and to Jose Miguel, although
he later helped him by lending him 2.000 peso fuertes.

He managed to interview with the American president James
Madison, who apologized for not being able to do anything to aid the
liberation of South America, since at that time the United States was
negotiating the purchase of Florida from Spain and did not want to create
difficulties with the Spanish ambassador. However, Jose Miguel managed
to be related to several European military of importance, who advised
him how he should proceed, although in order to do this, he had to
enter the American Lodge Saint John of Jerusalem Nro. One, which was
good for him to achieve contacts that would be vital in his mission.

Many military were dazzled by his look, figure and the politeness
of his manners, which is why he turned out to be very convincing and
worthy of admiration. The best way was to directly go to the armament
makers contacting the firm Darcy and Didier

Meanwhile in Chile, his father was exiled to the island of Juan
Fernandez and the properties of the Carrera family were requisitioned
by the Spaniards.

After a year, Jose Miguel managed to gather an appreciable quantity
of weapons, ammunitions and supplies, two printing press, five ships, the
corvette "Clifton", the frigate "General Scott", the brigantine "Salvaje",
the schooner "Dakey" and the brigantine "Regente" where he hoisted the
flag of Chile, blue, white and yellow, with twenty five officers, sergeants,
physicians, etc., most of them Frenchmen and Americans.

He arrived in the port of Buenos Aires on February 9th, 1817 on
board the frigate "Clifton", with the purpose of continuing with his
ships toward the Pacific. At that time, the Army of the Andes, after more
than two years of preparations, on the 21st of January, San Martin and
O'Higgins had begun the crossing of the Andes from Mendoza with an
army of 4.000 soldiers, of which depended at that time the glory or the
ruin of Chile.

The Supreme Director of the United Provinces of Rio de La Plata don Juan Martin de Pueyrredon, renowned member of the Lautaro Lodge, invited Jose Miguel to have dinner in the palace of Government. Carrera, ignorant of the local political intrigues, made the mistake of accepting. Pueyrredón demanded him to put his flotilla brought from the United States under the command of San Martin, which Carrera emphatically refused to, adducing that by doing such a thing was equivalent to decide in advance the future government of Chile, and said:
- Then San Martin is not going to liberate the country but conquer it, he is not going to let the people choose their ruler but impose it.-

After Jose Miguel's attempt to set sails without authorization toward Chile, his fleet was requisitioned by Pueyrredon and Carrera imprisoned on the 29th of March on board the Brig. "Belen".

The grandson of the Supreme Director, don Manuel Alejandro Pueyrredon wrote about Carrera's return from the United States:

"General don Jose Miguel Carrera was a man of more than regular height, slim of body, white skin colour, tender and penetrating look, his head revealed a lot of intelligence, and indeed, that man was one of the talented ones in America. He had a superior intelligence, the gift of speech, the winning manners, and irresistible seduction; you could not talk four minutes with General Carrera without being his friend: even his voice was remarkable; he gave his words a metallic intonation which seemed a bell. With the time while I more treated that man, the more I admired him, I ended up feeling a brotherly affection for him, chiefly when he was wretched".

Jose Miguel managed to convince the Commander of the ship Manuel de Monteverde that an injustice against him was being made, on the 18th of April with the help of the commander and of the American officer William Kennedy, managed to escape, he reached Montevideo on board of a Portuguese brigantine where he received the protection of the Portuguese General Carlos Federico Lecor.

In Montevideo he managed to recover a printing press that he had brought from the United States, with it they were doing business as William P. Grinswold and John Sharpe and from here he sent documents to Chile and Buenos Aires. In it he also printed his "Manifesto to the peoples of America and their Countries", but it was not published until

1818. Since then, Carrera devoted to restore his honor which had been infamously offended and answered to every slander spread about him.

This asylum can be seen as dreadful for his political reputation and, possibly as an important element in the next shooting of his brothers.

However, at the beginning it all seemed to be good; a group of followers joined him, among whom may be found both Benavente brothers, Manuel Gandarilllas, Pedro Vidal, and Camilo Hernandez and besides, his old friend, the former Supreme Director Carlos Maria Alvear was in Montevideo:

- My good friend Jose Miguel, I'm happy to see you again! -
- So am I! It's a good thing that I managed to convince the Captain of the ship who helped me together with two American friends to come even here.-
- What the things are, Jose Miguel, who was to make me think that Lieutenant Colonel Alvarez Thomas was to betray me by making me leave the country, to whom I sent with a squadron in order to contain the federalist Artigas's montoneras. However, after so much pursuing the Artigas's montoneras, now I support the federalism.-

Even though one does not know which Carrera's concrete plans were, the numerous letter that he sent to his wife and some other documents allow glimpsing something. In the letter he informed Mercedes that he had been in contact with General Artigas, precursor of Federalism and that "from there to Chile" which is destined to be part of confederacy of South America.

Before start moving for his campaign, San Martin met the Supreme Governor Pueyrredon in Cordoba, asking regulations on his immediate civil and military policy. Don Jose de San Martin was appointed Captain General of the Army of the Andes in the operations of the campaign leading to the reconquest of Chile; likewise, on January 17, 1817, San Martin was authorized by strictly confidential instructions to appoint General don Bernardo O'Higgins as temporary president of Chile, after the city of Santiago was liberated from the enemy.

San Martin took as his priority, to order Sergeant Mayor Antonio Alvarez Condarco to travel to Santiago by the pass of Los Patos, the longest and most difficult one, in order to draw the map of the cordillera. He went on the pretext of taking to the Governor Marcó del Pont official news of the agreements of the Congress of Tucuman, which had declared the independence of the Provinces of La Plata. Once fulfilled his mission, Alvarez returned to Mendoza by Uspatalla, reconstructing in a paper the reliable data and with them San Martin minutely devised his plan of operations.

José de San Martín.

From the beginning of January 1817, with great precision, the liberator army began preparing the march. Everybody imagined that they were going to leave, but nobody either knew the day or the direction. The first one that began leaving was the Lieutenant Colonel Juan Manuel Cabot, on January 12th, he left from San Juan to join with a party of Chilean emigrants and continue to Coquimbo. On the 14th day of January, the Colonel Ramon Freire left from Mendoza to the South passing by the Planchon, he would join the guerrilla fighters of the central region, and on January 18th the Colonel Juan Gregorio de Las Heras, accompanied by Friar Luis Beltran, went to Uspatalla in front of a division of 900 men of the three arms. On the 19th and 20th, the first division mobilized, in front of the Chief of Staff, Argentinian, General Miguel Estanislao Soler, and on January 21th and 22nd the bulk of the army left, the second division under the command of General Bernardo O'Higgins, chilean, on the 22nd the Commander Ambrosio Cramer of the battalion number 8 left from Mendoza with direction toward Los Patos, and finally, on the 24th, the General Jose de San Martin, argentinian, who would join the rearguard of the divisions of Soler and O'Higgins that walked by the high Plateau toward the North until reaching Los Patos river in the place called El Leoncito. From there, they continued toward the South to reach the mountain top with great work and effort in the mounting that was done on mules, and finally, on February 2nd the army began the descent to Putaendo. Bernardo de Monteagudo Cáceres, lawyer and journalist from Rio de La Plata, was auditor of the Army of the Andes at the orders of General San Martin.

They had as principal aim to act in combination with the bulk of the army to attack the valley of Aconcagua.

Between Chileans and Argentinians, the Army of the Andes gathered 4.000 perfectly armed and disciplined men. Its ensign was the Argentine flag. Forming three divisions respectively headed by: O'Higgins and the Argentinians Soler and Las Heras.

They went out with two howitzers, seven field cannons, nine mountain cannons and two 10 ounce cannons. As the transportation of artillery presented great difficulties, the clergyman friar Luis de Beltran devised some narrow carriage having very low wheels with a pulley system to pass the cliffs with the cannons that the soldiers called the "vixens" and another of hanging bridge, both being transportable. Health care was in the hands of the English surgeon James Paroissien.

Provisions were accumulated for twenty days, cattle with pasture for the valleys they had to cross, everything was prepared with the maximum precautions in order not have any mishap due to the steep mountaintops of the mountain range.

The most contingent of the army, under the command of O'Higgins and the Argentinian Brigadier Miguel Estanislao Soler, would cross the mountain range taking the way of the pass of Los Patos o Valle Hermoso, to descend in Putaendo, at the same time a division under the command of the Argentinian Colonel Juan Gregorio Las Heras was crossing the mountain range by Uspatalla, San Martin crossed the mountain top between the 3rd and 5th, and both groups should meet the same day in San Felipe and in the village of Los Andes, former Santa Rosa de los Andes, separated in several divisions, by the passes of Planchon, Piuquenes and Uspatalla, in front of the province of Aconcagua and at the beginning of February all the division were seeing the Chilean territory.

The Army of the Andes had managed to cross one of the highest mountain ranges in the world, parading its soldiers at the edge of the cliffs having to do it one by one because of the rough of the terrain, and without having lost either any cannon nor loads of ammunition, even though San Martin never wanted to inform the number of soldier he lost in the passing of the mountain range.

The Governor Marcó del Pont was trembling in his palace on having known that the defeated patriots had crossed the Andes. Immediately, he ordered General don Rafael Maroto to be at the head of the royalist army and going out to the meeting of the patriots.

On the 4th at dusk, the outposts of the Colonel Las Heras fell on the royalist guard of The Andes by surprise. The General Soler fell on the garrison of the Achupallas. The royalist went in disorder toward San Felipe where the royalist Colonel Atero immediately understood that the army of General San Martin had crossed the mountain range. At once he sent an emissary to Santiago asking for reinforcements, bringing together a total of 700 men and forming a Junta of War, he decided that same night to withdraw to Chacabuco.

Marcó del Pont, began to organize the army to oppose the threat of the Andes. With great discipline, he gathered the officers Atero, Olaguer, Feliú, Cacho, Morgado, etc., well-trained officers in the fights against Napoleon, taking the army to a higher level.

On January 1817, the royalist army was made up of 4.317 men without counting the detachments from Coquimbo and Valparaiso and the ships of war. They were all well accredited, well dressed and disciplined men.

The Colonel Atero knew the night of February 6th that the forefront of the patriots was encamped with a total 600 men in Las Coimas, while the bulk remained in Putaendo. Atero decided to attack immediately. El Coronel Atero supo la noche del 6 de febrero que la vanguardia de los patriotas estaba acampada con un total de 600 hombres en Las Coimas, mientras el grueso permanecía en Putaendo. The combat of Las Coimas on February 7th liberating Putaendo, was brief because of the superiority of the patriot cavalry who managed to displace Atero, having to withdraw to save the remains of his defeated forces to San Felipe el Real.

On the 8th, Las Heras and Soler were entering the village of the Andes, and O'Higgins in San Felipe el Real, liberating them. The concentration took place the following day South of Curimón, in front of the mouth of the Aconcagua valley that goes to the way of Santiago and descends to the Chacabuco slope.

Only 1600 men between Chileans and Spaniards managed to get together under the command of the Spanish General Rafael Maroto.

San Martin, not knowing that the royalist army was disperse, not wanting to give them time to concentrate all their forces, and upon knowing that those of Maroto were separated from him only by the Chacabuco slope, ordered that the divisions of O'Higgins and Soler climb the hills and fall on the royalist.

On February 12th in the morning, in the Chacabuco slop the General Maroto accompanied by Quintanilla, Elorreaga, Marquelli and Calvo did reconnaissance of the mountain top. O'Higgins for his part undertook the march through the old slope, this path was more short but more sloping and rough, losing in the climbing his two cannons that hurled down themselves. Soler took the second way, that of Montenegro softer but longer.

Battle of Chacabuco.

O'Higgins started the combat, it was 11.45 in the morning and it was hot, and he had to face alone the whole of the royalist forces. The rifle gunfire was extending for more than one hour, and the royalist cannons, very well aimed at, were annihilating the cavalry and the infantry; O'Higgins's position was even more difficult since he lacked cannons and Soler did not appear with his forces, the Commander Cramer proposed him to charge the fixed bayonets, organizing two columns of assault that were thrown on the right royalist wing. The Mounted Grenadiers could not pass in assault formation due to the deep riverbed of Las Margaritas River, having to withdraw in disorder but without suffering many casualties. O'Higgins and Cramer launched an assault again, directing now the cavalry against the right flank and the infantry against the centre, being both chiefs at the head of their respective forces.

When the violence of the combat was reaching its height, a cavalry platoon was penetrating the royalist line defeating the gunners. The infantry of O'Higgins and Cramer, already winning, came in the aid of the cavalry. The Colonel Zapiola, after defeating the cadre formed by the Talavera, attacked the royalist right wing and caused the enemy disbandment that with the rest of the army fled towards the houses of Chacabuco, leaving in the field more than the half of their force. At one-thirty in the afternoon, General Soler was coming, causing the complete encirclement of the royalists. At two o'clock in the afternoon the battle had concluded, that was the only action of Soler in the battle, his forces came half an hour before this concluded. Soler labelled O'Higgins as insubordinate because of attacking without waiting for the order, but San Martin recognized it as an action full of bravery, it was true that the division of the General was the one that prepared the patriot victory in the battle of Chacabuco.

The royalist army with the 1.400 men, 500 only were left in the field, 600 were taken prisoners and 170 although many were injured were dispersing in the hills, only 130 managed to reach Santiago. The royalist commanders died in combat; Elorreaga, Arenas, Maquelli and Vila. The Colonels of the Talavera battalion, San Bruno and Villalobos were taken prisoners.

On being known the news in Santiago, the Chacabuco disaster, Governor Marcó del Point immediately arranged the retreat to Valparaiso of the few troops garrisoned in the capital, but he, wanting to disappear, delegated the command to the General Maroto and he went as quickly as possible to San Antonio.

The General Maroto and 700 officers, civil servants and soldiers embarked without delay in Valparaiso, moving the ships to Callao, under the pretext of being provisioned in Coquimbo, in subhuman conditions, lying in the decks, without bed or coast and without water or food.

When the people noticed that the royalist authorities had fled, the Town Council gathered and designated don Francisco Ruiz Tagle as the first Governor Interim elected by the patriots. The following day on February 14th, the santiaguinos were multiplying to receive and give the welcome to the triumphal Army of the Andes.

The Governor Marcó del Pont, on reaching Santiago he expected to embark, but he didn't find the ship there and desperate he went to Valparaiso, being captured in the estate Las Tablas where he had sheltered while he was sending emissaries to know if his ship was coming and if Valparaiso was in the hands of the patriots. One of the emissaries charged with the inquiry, a peasant betrayed him warning the Captain Francisco Aldao where Marcó del Pont was hidden. A few days later, he delivered his sabre to San Martin who sent him prisoner to Mendoza and shortly after was confined in San Luis. He died in Lujan near Buenos Aires in 1819.

The Chacabuco Victory, although rapid and with few cassualties, assured the freedom of the provinces of Santiago and Coquimbo; but the war had no tended, since the royalist were having important forces in Concepcion.

They began issuing and granting the letter of marque. They hired three porteño experienced adventurers: a former officer from a Scottish whaling ship Mac Kay James and a former midshipman named Budge, between them, they gathered a small budget and armed a very modest ship of 20 tons and baptized her as "Fortuna" taking on board 25 Chileans, English and American sailors who set sail from Valparaiso bound for the North.

A convoy had left from Cadiz, but a storm had dispersed it from the fearful Spanish ship of war the "Esmeralda" that was escorting it, and in Arica it had anchored the frigate "Minerva" of great tonnage with many cannons, crowded with men and loaded with great treasures. Two weeks after setting sail, the Chilean privateers approached and captured the "Minerva" by surprise. On escaping they abandoned the small ship "Fortuna" and continued towards the North and near Pisco they captured the brig "Santa María de Jesus" by Mac Kay's expedition that before the end of the year 1817 decided to return to the port of Valparaiso, since he was informed that in the port of the Callao they were preparing a squadron to reconquer Chile for the second time with the famous frigate the "Emerald" the best warship that the Spaniards had in the Pacific Ocean and, she had stopped over in Arica where they embarked troops in nine merchant ships. They set sail from Arica bound for Talcahuano, there being incorporated 1.300 arequipeño and ariqueño recruits.

Mac Kay reached Valparaiso with captured ship and hers valuable shipment, being received with great joy in the port.

CHAPTER XV.

THE NEW REPUBLIC.
DICTATORSHIP OF O'HIGGINS
(1817- 1823).

With the victory of the battle of Chacabuco and O'Higgins's proclamation as Supreme Director of the young nation, it begins the period known as the "New Republic".

An Open Council offered the control of the nation to don Jose de San Martin. Buenos Aires had given concrete instructions to San Martin about O'Higgins's designation, but in a studied political resource, it was thought that the best formula to please the Chilean feeling, would be that they were choosing San Martin, and after his declining so honorable post, apparently because of his gentlemanliness, raising as Supreme Director of Chile without fixing limits to his authority to don Bernardo O'Higgins.

At the moment of assuming the mandate, he was 39 years old, was in the fullness of his physical and intellectual powers, was short and scout, blue eyes, blond hairs, his reddish countenance was revealing the Irish descent on the part of his father, but the stature short was denoting his mother's Creole blood, to whom he was very close, the very same with his sister.

Shortly after fought the battle of Chacabuco, it appeared in the bay of Valparaiso privately entering in the port the English brig "Tagle", which has been captured in 1816 by the royalist authorities from Coquimbo because of smuggling trade in Chile, and since then it was used for cabotage with the name of "Aguila" under the Spanish flag.

In Valparaiso the governor Alvarado had O'Higgins's instructions of keeping the Spanish pavilion hoisted in the castle of San Antonio to mislead the ships of Spain that were entering the port.

This way the patriot maritime authorities calmly took control of the ship removing the captain and naming a few days later the young Lieutenant Raimundo Morris as its Commander. Armament was installed in the ship, and it became the first ship of war that the Navy of Chile had.

He sent Captain Morris in the brig "Aguila" to cross the coast of San Antonio, then on March 17th, 1817 he set sails for the islands of Juan Fernandez, taking provisions for 200 men and a platoon of 21 hunters to liberate the patriots exiled in that island.

The Governor Angel del Cid in the bay of San Juan Bautista, agreed, by means of the guarantee of not being treated as prisoner, to release the 78 illustrious citizens who had suffered two years of exile. Among them they were Manuel Blanco Encalada and don Ignacio Carrera, very elderly. On May 31st, Morris safely arrived at Valparaiso ending his mission.

O'Higgins ordered to liberate the Lieutenant Colonel Santiago Bueras who was in prison with his guerrilla fighters in Aconcagua.

The reprisals against the royalists were the first measures of the new government, beginning with the Colonels of the Talavera battalion, San Bruno and Villalobos who were shot in the middle of the main square. Bishop don Jose Santiago Rodríguez was exiled to Mendoza.

As Supreme Director of the Nation, he designated Miguel Zañartu as Minister of State, Jose Ignacio Zenteno as Minister of War. To face the financial problems, he created the Minister of Finance with Hipólito Villegas as holder.

In order not to be united to the Spanish Empire, he abolished the titles of nobility that had led to look for the certification of their nobility in Spain during The Conquest and later in The Colony with the recognition of the titles of nobility such as, Marquis de Vallenar, Marquis of La Pica, Count of Quinta Alegre, Count of La Conquista, among others. By suppressing the titles, he suppressed the "mayorazgos" (majorats), patrimonial systems that were leading to the economic power of the family chiefs who were claiming in turn special political privileges. He created the "Legion of the Merit of Chile", fought against the religious prejudices, removing images from the temples, replaced the currency with the effigy of Fernando VII with one having the stamp of the Government.

Bills were enacted similar to those established by the Governments of the Reconquest, creating a Court of Vindication to prove the acceptance of the patriot cause, it was applied a strong contribution on the royalists, it was decreed the confiscation of the properties of those who had fled the country and different police regulations were implemented to maintain the public order.

On rising to power he had approved a provisional regulation with the name of Constitution of the 18. The people were demanding him the creation of a Legislative Senate and a Political Constitution, but O'Higggins misguided by his minister Jose Antonio Rodriguez Aldea, refused to accept.

He was establishing an authoritarian, strong and of indefinite duration Government, it was a de facto and de jure dictatorship, his ideas were deeply republican and were opposed to all monarchical administration. But in this, he was clashing with the aristocracy, which pretended to return to the power by taking place in the system of juntas and congresses; they did not delay to be against the dictatorship implemented by O'Higgins.

As much as it was allowed to O'Higgins, due to the scarcity of money he worried about public education, ordering that primary schools be established and maintained by the town halls, adopting the lancasterian system or peer tutoring, introduced in England by Joseph Lancaster, consisting of having the more advanced students teach their peers, which allowed only one teacher to attend hundreds of students. This new system did not produce the expected results, and at the end of a few years it fell into disuse.

By agreement of the government, it was opened again the National Institute, where they studied Latin, Spanish, eloquence, philosophy, etc.

At the same time that the was dictating these measures, O'Higgins was recruiting new troops to form the "Army of Chile" that came to have 4.700 soldiers, outnumbering this way the Army of the Andes. With the new army he would continue the war to move out the royalists from Concepcion and Talcahuano, wherein Spanish Colonel Jose Ordoñez had organized his forces, in that region they were in favour of the royalist cause.

O'Higgins sent Colonel Juan Gregorio de Las Heras who defeated Ordoñez in Curapalihue, causing the royalists to retreat and be fortified in Talcahuano where Ordoñez then received 1.600 auxiliaries; these were the fugitives from Chacabuco whom the Viceroy had made them return from Peru. Already with this reinforcement, Colonel Ordoñez attacked again Colonel Las Heras in the hill of Gavilán, near to Concepción; on May 5th, he was defeated again, having to retreat to Talcahuano.

All the efforts of the Director O'Higgins, both columns, now commanded by Colonels Freire and Las Heras occupied without resistance Linares, Parral, Cauquenes, San Carlos, Quirihue and Chillan, pursued Ordoñez in the Talcahuano peninsula; but the royalists had defended the isthmus with palisaded trenches and 70 cannons, in addition, they were dominating the sea with their ships. All the efforts of O'Higgins during six months were useless, he designate Colonel Hilarion de La Quintana as Director Interim and laid a siege, not being able to remove Ordoñez from Talcahuano. The seriousness of the situation in the South, forced O'Higgins to send a division of 800 soldiers on April 10th; a squadron of Grenadiers and two cannons, O'Higgins himself left for the place six days later accompanied by minister of War don Jose Ignacio Centeno.

Transfer of O'Higgins to the South to direct the war supposed to be a problem, he had decided to delegate the command in favor of don Luis de La Cruz, but the Lodge agreed to replace him with the Argentinian Colonel don Hilarión de La Quintana. On seeing an Argentinian in the command, it didn't take long for the subversive activities to create a hostile climate to the new Director-Interim who, realizing the danger his presence brought to the chilean people, offered his resignation on May 11 on the pretext of the return of General San Martin, but on being rejected his appointment as substitute, they agreed on a transition formula of forming a Junta headed by Luis La Cruz, Francisco Antonio Perez and Jose Manuel Mayorga.

The main problem of the moment was the financial one; the country was economically in ruins, having to sustain a civil war.

In the whole course of its history, Chile had not been so severely compelled by the taxes, the reduction of the salaries that were going from 2 % to 25 %, the panorama of Santiago was that of the capital in 1817 in the limits of the abandon and of misery.

One of the main subversive activities since O'Higgins was in charge of the control was Manuel Rodríguez Erdoíza, the famous guerrilla fighter, who on March 3 1817 summoned the authorities of San Fernando so that they choose the leaders that he assigns and the local government requested his recognition. Being informed O'Higgins, he sent a squad to bring him to Santiago as a prisoner, Manuel Rodriguez requested an audience that he was granted and at the end of it he said to O'Higgins:
    - You have known Director my mood. I say that in this of the
      republican governments they should be changed every six months

or mostly every year, we could prove this way ourselves all in the command.-

Manuel Rodríguez managed to escape to the United States at the end of April, and when he came back to Santiago he appeared before San Martin who had returned from Buenos Aires; San Martin appointed him assistant to the Army Staff because of his boldness.

During 1817 in Buenos Aires, Javiera Carrera who had not had any news from her husband since her stay in Buenos Aires, received a succinct letter from him in which he was informing her about the wedding of her daughter Dolores without even telling her whom she was marrying.

Madam Javiera lived in Juana Ordoñez's house, his residence, which once again turned into a center of meetings, being here where it was prepared the plot known as **"The Conspiracy of 1817"**. It had its center of operations in Buenos Aires and it was having plenty of ramifications in Chile, among them Manuel Rodriguez, Manuel Jose Gandarillas, Juan Antonio Diaz Muñoz, Juan de Dios Martínez, known as Martinito, Bartolomé Araos, Jose Tomas Urra, Manuel Rodriguez's close friend, Manuel Lastra, dona Javiera's nephew in law, and Jose Conde, assistant to Jose Miguel Carrera. Javiera was the alma mater of the ambitious plan that consisted of overthrowing the Chilean government of O'Higgins and at the same time taking prisoner San Martin. Meanwhile in Buenos Aires, it would be formed two groups of power, one led by Juan Jose Carrera and the other by his brother Luis, and thus once achieved the goal, and the Carrera brothers would have again the political power. These plans were advanced in June 1817, the conspirators had even distributed the positions of the future government; Manuel Rodriguez would be political dictator. General Brayer, who had come from The United States along with Jose Miguel Carrera and was now serving in the liberating army, would be in charge of the Army. Jose Miguel Carrera would be sent again to the United States to organize a new fleet, Luis would be heading an armed column from his followers which would be organized in Santiago, and he would capture O'Higgins while Juan Jose, in charge of another column, was keeping for himself the capture and military trial of San Martin.

At the beginning of June the conspirators started travelling separately and in small groups to Santiago. At the end of the same month, they were followed by Luis, disguised as a "lad" o fan officer named Cardenas and finally on August 8th Juan Jose would go to Santiago as friend and fellow traveller to another officer. While in Montevideo, Jose Miguel didn't know anything about all this, although he had not surely approved it since it was not in fact the appropriate time, and he would think of his sister Javiera that that was the product of "the dream of a woman".

The winter helped the conspirators since the government was diminishing in this time the surveillance in the mountain range due to the rigor of the climate, nevertheless some emissaries could save the cold and reach up to San Miguel. Also they began gathering Juntas in Santiago; but the principal area of the conspiracy was in the estate of San Miguel.

The Director Interim Hilarion de La Quintana that was in charge in Chile was suspecting and he made surround with troops the houses of the property of the Carreras.

The attempt began to fail rapidly on being discovered the plot simultaneously in Santiago and in Mendoza by the intelligences services of San Martin, even before those involved could cross the mountain range.

The attempt began to fail rapidly on being discovered the plot simultaneously in Santiago and in Mendoza by the intelligences services of San Martin, even before those involved could cross the mountain range. Don Hilario de La Quintana pressed by the minister of the interior and by San Martin, ordered prison for Manuel Rodriguez, Diaz Muñoz, the two Carrrera Brothers and seven more conspirators.

The Junta of Government was prudent in its resolution and was not very severe with the fellow members of San Miguel. Don Manuel Jose Gandarillas proved his innocence and was released, Carreras' father was confined in a prison put in irons, and the crime was being father of the four Carrera brothers, and they made Rodriguez sign a curious document which said:

"I condemn myself before the America as an indecent enemy of its political representation if I have acted against the events that began in Chile in February".

On August 5th, 1817 they captured Luis that was trying to pass messages to royalist prisoners in Mendoza, and his fellow traveller confessed at once, which led to Juan Jose's arrest 15 days later in La Posta de Barranquita in San Juan on August 20th, 1817. On August 5th, 1817 they captured Luis that was trying to pass messages to royalist prisoners in Mendoza, and his fellow traveller confessed at once, which led to Juan Jose's arrest 15 days later in La Posta de Barranquita in San Juan on August 20th, 1817. Javiera from Buenos Aires used all her influences to save them, but all the negotiations were unfavorable. In desperation, Javiera concocted a plan to liberate them, in which committed Ana

María Cotapos, young wife of Juan José. In a letter Javiera wrote her the indications:

"Request permission to visit your imprisoned husband in Mendoza, take with you 400 pesos to buy for an affordable price an officer from the guards, since the porteños may be bought as sheeps, and make him play and he thus entertain himself. Get aqua fortis and saws to cut the cotters of the fetters. In this case, pretend to be worthier and kinder than you are."

The plan was discovered by don Toribio Luzuriaga, Governor of Mendoza, who captured the young and beautiful wife of Juan Jose, without at least having seen him.

Despite that the Carrera brothers were detained in Mendoza, the documents of the event were sent to Santiago for the attention of O'Higgins and San Martin.

In the practice, it would mean that the trial would lengthen indefinitely, since the two Generals were occupied in those moments in other more urgent concerns; in fact the lack of seriousness of the tentative because most of those involved even Manuel Rodríguez was declared innocent, they were set free, except the Carreras, this made foresee an outcome for the brothers who were additionally accused of wanting to escape with the help of royalist prisoners in Mendoza, whom they tried to arm and to organize, by which they accused him of traitor, being justified the authorities due to the difficult times that went, they preferred to take drastic measures with the Carrera brothers, and in a trial, if it could be called so, they were found guilty of offenses against the State" and "acts against the town" and were sentenced to death by the Governor of Mendoza, Toribio Luzuriaga.

In December, 1817 news arrived in Santiago of a second expedition of General Osorio. San Martin, in order to make sure of the forces that he would bring, sent Sergeant Major Domingo Torres to Lima as a spy, who brought him a trustworthy copy of the state of the forces and extract of the Viceroy's instructions.

While the batteries were prepared in Valparaiso, O'Higgins withdrew to the North of the Maule and on his way toward the South he stopped in Talca. As it had not been declared yet the Independence, this caused an anomaly; in the barracks of every city, two books in blank were opened in; in one, the citizens should sign in favor of the declaration and in other one those who were thinking of against. The first one was filled with signatures, whereas the second one remained in blank. Already with these signatures, it was believed indispensable the summons of a full Congress with a commission composed by don Michael Zañartu, don Manuel of

Salas, don Juan Egaña and don Bernardo de Vera y Pintado who was charged with the editing of the document in which it was declared Chile to be a "de facto and de jure" free State.

In January, 1818, the ships that brought the second expedition of the Spanish General don Mariano Osorio were anchoring in the bay of Talcahuano, he was sent from Peru by the new Viceroy don Joaquín Pezuela to recover the control of Chile with the efficient expedition of the veterans of Burgos and Infante, Spanish veteran soldiers of the war against Napoleon.

On February 12, 1818 in the Main Square of Santiago all the citizens of the capital met in the Metropolitan Cathedral to swear to the feet of Our Lady of El Carmen the construction of a temple in her honor, since then The Virgin of El Carmen was proclaimed Patron Saint of the armies of Chile, previously San Martin had proclaimed The Virgin of El Carmen of Cuyo in the temple of San Francisco in Mendoza as General of the Americas, a year after the victory of Chacabuco, she was proclaimed in the whole Republic and The Independence of Chile was solemnly sworn by the authorities.

"The force has been the supreme reason that for more than three hundred years has maintained the new world in the need to venerate as a dogma the usurpation of its rights and to seek in her the origin of its greatest duties"

Some days after this solemn event, O'Higgins had a new satisfaction, his natural son was born, Pedro Demetrio O'Higgins, had of his loving relationship with the one who was his lover, the Creole lady Rosario Puga.

Near San Fernando, O'Higgins and San Martin had obtained to gather 7.000 soldiers approximately. The royalist General Osorio crossed the Maule with 5.000 men; in the face of those superior forces he had to go back and be shut in Talca, while the patriots formed their camp in the neighboring plain of Cancha Rayada.

The situation of the royalists was difficult since they had their retreat cut by the Maule. On March 19, in the deep of the night they saw as the patriots executed a change of position; the Spanish Colonel Ordóñez left Talca and he attacked them by surprise, in the darkness and confusion, the patriots were shooting each other without recognizing themselves, a bullet hurt O'Higgins in an arm and other killed the horse, the mules that should move the artillery of the second division were dispersed in all directions breaking the lines of the patriot soldiers, San Martin himself was impotent to organize his army, being forced to order the retreat in the middle of a great confusion, being pursued by the royalist as far as the same bank of the Lircay river.

Only the first patriot division commanded by Las Heras that had changed position before the attack, continued intact on its way toward San Fernando, where O'Higgins and San Martin later arrived obtaining to get together the dispersed one and made them orderly go to Santiago.

The royalist had almost lost a fourth of their troops. The patriots' casualties were smaller, but part of the army officers fled to the North.

In the morning of May 21st, the first news of the disaster of Cancha Rayada began to arrive in Santiago.

Manuel Rodriguez Erdoiza took the floor and full with ardent zeal said:

- I have a very painful task: that of informing my fellow citizens the details of the sad even that has happened in the night of Thursday 19. The proud army in which we based our hopes does not exist anymore. I announce that General O'Higgins has died, and after the defeat, the depressed and desperate General San Martin is crossing the Andes on his way to Mendoza and the royalists are rapidly marching over Santiago.-

They only thought of escaping like in 1814, to Mendoza, taking the money from the treasury, weapons and supplies that they could pick up, General Brayer and Bernardo Monteagudo, who left in terror his position of War Auditor and didn't stop up to Mendoza, were among the fugitives who were helping to spread pessimistic news.

Taking advantage of the chaos and the public alarm, the carrerinos acted again forming an Open Council in the Government Palace. On March 23rd, it struck the eleven hours in the morning in the clock of Las Cajas, when a great crowd invaded the Palace in the moment that Colonel Luis de La Cruz, who was in control of the capital in absence of O'Higgins, presided La Junta Delegada and the popular guerrilla fighter Manuel Rodriguez Erdoiza as Supreme Director and to the cry of:

-Citizens, we still have a republic! -

These words returned the spirit to those that believed that everything was lost. Rodriguez that same evening organized and armed the cavalry squadron that he called "Hussars of the Death". The idea of this squadron was original from Europe, Guillermo Federico, Prince of Brünswick went with his troops to combat Napoleon when he returned from the island of Elba, they were dressed with black clothes, a skull in the morion and in the neck of the coat. They were commanded by Manuel Rodriguez himself who was feeling pleased with similar guard spectacularly uniformed, that affirmed his popularity and won him followers, and as Captain Ramon Allende

The state of anarchy found in Santiago was informed to O'Higgins in San Fernando where he was recovering from his serious wounds, without listening to his physician's recommendations, he was on his way with his arm in a sling, he rode all the night to reach Rancagua at dawn and at the three o'clock in the morning the Supreme Director was entering in Santiago where Manuel Rodriguez was exercising his short-lived dictatorship, and at the twelve hours in the morning the corporations were gathering in the Government palace. As soon as he stood up with his wounded arm, the face contorted with fatigue and pain, the Supreme Chief was greeted with enthusiastic applause; with slow voice, he informed what happened in Cancha Rayada and about the patriot forces saved.

The arrival of O'Higgins and San Martin restored the trust in Santiago. 15 days after the disaster of Cancha Rayada, 5.000 soldiers were waiting for the royalist General Ososrio in the fields of Maipo, seven kilometres away from Santiago. The royalist army encamped in the estate of La Calera on April 3rd, its forces were balanced with those of the patriots, Colonels Morgado and Ordoñez wanted to begin the fight as soon as possible without reaching an agreement; they thought about the retreat to Valparaiso before the absence of command and inside the confusion, he ordered an oblique march attacking first Ordoñez and, Osorio would enter by the right flank of San Martin.

Batlle of Maipú.

In the morning of April 5, 1818, the armies of San Martin and Osorio were one in front of the other. Shortly after noon the patriot army broke fire and the battle began on the edge South of a hill with the divisions of

Colonel de Las Heras to the right, that of Colonel Alvarado to the left and that of Colonel Quintana to the rearguard.

The army of Grenadiers was in the extreme right and the Mounted Chasseurs commanded by Santiago Bueras to the left, the field artillery was located in the center and the light field artillery in the flanks.

The two armies were separated by a hollow of more than 500 meters that should be crossed by the first one who attacked, staying defenseless, suffering the fire of the rifles and cannons and climbing rapidly the hill where the enemy was. On both sides they were heroically fighting. Las Heras launched his columns against the Colonel Primo de Rivera, while the patriot Colonel Blanco Encalada was attacking with his cannons. The royalist Colonel Morgado defended the hollow where the bulk of the army was located that received the order to charge with the Dragoons of the Frontier, but they had to retreat because of the charge of the squadrons of the Grenadiers, although they had new casualties due to royalist infantry of Primo de Rivera, but they managed to recover because of the support by De Las Heras' infantry, being able to occupy the hollow, cutting the right and left royalist wing. They engage in a furious combat in which the royalist chief officer Ordonez completely defeated the No. 8 of the Army of the Andes and the No. 2 of the Army of Chile, and for a moment the royalist thought having victory secured, although with exhausted reserves.

Suddenly it was heard in the patriot rearguard the charge bugle call, San Martin had decided to send his personal escort commanded by the Colonel Quintana, and battalions the 7th of the Andes and the 1st and 3rd of Chile entered in fire, the Mounted Chasseurs commanded by Freire and by Bueras charged over the royalist cavalry that had been located in the right flank and finally by all the flanks and in the Spanish center. The Colonel Bueras was hit by a bullet in the chest falling down dead that same day April 5th.

The royalist infantry congested without space, without artillery and without cavalry was totally surrounded by the patriots that had resolved the battle. At a given time, the Burgos battalion under the command of Captain Gregorio Cartwright moved up since they didn't surrender, some voices were heard:
- Here it is the Burgos with their victorious flag in Bailén; 18 battles won and, none lost! as they were making fly their honored victorious flag in Bailén and in so many other combats.

The other patriot corps, Arequipa, Concepcion and Infante don Carlos, surrounded everywhere followed his example, and in a few seconds a great combat was engaged, the situation was tragic for these braves. The Arequipa battalion was commanded by the legendary and later heroic Jose Ramon Rodil, the hero of the siege of Callao.

The royalist battalions formed the cadre to resist the patriot cavalry of the Mounted Chasseurs, but upon forming the cadre they became an easy target for the rifles of the patriot infantrymen. Captain Carretero, royalist, was lost, having to withdraw from the battle field with the few cavalry left, General Ordoñez had to take the command and already without being able to sustain the hill, he withdrew to the houses of the hamlet Lo Espejo, being pursued by the patriot cavalry that was stabbing them while they left a trail of dead men along the way until loosing the sight of them, but they didn't break the lines and kept the order.

The artillery was getting near, at a short distance the shrapnel broke the lines although they didn't break their formation, and they were slowly withdrawing from the battle field harassed everywhere. The gunners of Primo de Rivera were withdrawing to the same place of the village of Lo Espejo. They should form the cadre and resist eight charges from the enemy. The suffered a lot of casualties but they kept the formation and reached Lo Espejo.

The battalion of Mounted Chasseurs of Coquimbo attacked the village, believing that the exhausted royalists would give up, however the discharges of rifles and two cannons that were left, inflicted them 250 casualties, what caused its withdrawal.

San Martín didn't want to risk more men, that is why he ordered to concentrate the artillery, joining 17 pieces they destroyed the village of Lo Espejo. The rest of the Spanish battalions withstood the fire, the patriots supported by the cannons, launched the definitive assault. The few defenders that were left in Lo Espejo were crushed. The General Ordoñez and the General Primo de Rivera surrendered, the battle was over.

Meanwhile, without seeing the royalist troops, O'Higgins arrived into the battle field in front of 1.000 militiamen of Aconcagua, when meeting San Martin face to face, O'Higgins cried:

Glory to the saviour of Chile!

The two Generals melted in the famous "Embrace of Maipu".
San Martín:

- "General, Chile will never forget the illustrious invalid that appears injured in the battle field".-

San Martín wrote in his war dispatch:

"With difficulty, it has been seen a braver, more rapid and more sustained attack of the patriots, and it has never been seen the most vigorous, firmer and more tenacious resistance of the royalist enemy".

Out of the 4.500 royalist that began the combat, there were left in the field 1.500 dead; almost 2.300 were taken prisoners, the remainder was injured. Among the prisoners may be found General Ordoñez, the Colonels Beza, Primo de Rivera, Morgado and five Commanders.

The patriot army had defeated, although leaving in the field the 35% of its soldiers.

The royalists were taken to San Luis, where the Governor Vicente Dupuy put the city as a jail. It was considered very difficult to escape from there because of the danger of the Indians. One night the royalist prisoners tried to attack and murder the Governor Dupuy; they visited him by night and after the courtesy greeting they surrounded him and tried to stab him, Dupuy managed to call the guard and the youths Juan Pascual Pringles and Facundo Quiroga rapidly came to his defense. The outcome of the revolt was the death of almost all the prisoners, among them General Ordoñez and the Colonels Morgado and Primo de Rivera.

The independence of Chile was definitively secured from that day of the battle of Maipú, being the first great victory obtained by the american patriots that consolidated the independence of Chile and pointed out the coming of the Republic and the period of The New Republic had ended.

O'Higgins , after the victory, commented to San Martin:

-Any effort that we may do will be useless while the country does not have a Squadron, therefore "this triumph and a hundred more will become insignificant if we do not dominate the sea".-

The Viceroy of Peru had to accept the existence of the two new independent States: Chile and the Argentine Provinces.

CHAPTER XVI.
REPUBLIC.
END OF THE NEW REPUBLIC.

The squadron of The Hussars of the Death under the command of Manuel Rodriguez Erdoiza didn't take part in the battle of Maipú, because according to the regulations, the cadre of officers from Captain until the upper levels should be conserved in its entirety, with the assurance that the brother Carreras, imprisoned in Mendoza, would soon be arriving in Chile, thinking that as they had released the others, it was supposed that they would also be released, they didn't know about their having already been sentenced to death.

After the victory of Maipu, the Governor of Mendoza, that had been lengthening the prison of the Carrera Brothers, was pressed by the Council of Chile, that by request of the procurator of the city asked on April 6th, the head of the Carreras, Governor Luzuriaga didn't have more ready than to name a commission composed by three lawyers: don Juan de La Cruz Vargas, don Miguel Jose Caligiana and the doctor Bernardo Monteagudo, that wanted to stand up for the brothers, assuring that he didn't have any offense reason toward the Carreras, but as he supposed that attitude was to be against San Martin and O'Higgins, he presented himself as special envoy of San Martin, he was in Mendoza with the brothers Juan Jose and Luis, whom were about to be released, directed a summary trial in which the accused were not allowed to be defended, he didn' have any other choice than issue the report in which he sustained that the Governor Luzuriaga was in the duty of immediately accepting, without consulting Buenos Aires nor Santiago.

At the time of the signing, don Juan de La Cruz apologized and didn't want to sign but, Monteagudo who at the beginning defended the Carreras and Caligliana voted for the death penalty. The Governor received the report at the two and a half hours in the afternoon of April 8th, and the execution would be at five o'clock of that same afternoon. The Carreras should be shooted in a two hour deadline.

Both brothers shared the same dungeon, sat in the floor and almost in total Darkness, they commented:

- It has been three days since the victory of the patriots in the battle of Maipu, it is necessary to win time in our execution so that upon being known the patriot triumph, all the families will demand the grace for our lives.-

- You are absolutely right about taking time, I think that I could feign to be sick, for example, peritonis or miserere colic by eating some garbage so that I may have fever, and thus being sick they will have to wait until the physician may treat me, this way we will have so much time so that they may help us..-

At this time of the conversation, they listened to the jailer opening the gate.

- You have some visit -.

The two men stood up when they saw two friars entering the cell.

- Good evening, my dear sons, here it is friar Hinostrosa and myself friar Benito Lamas; the sad purpose of our visit is to inform you that in less than two hours you will be in the house of Our Lord, He will receive you in his dwelling place.-

Luís, upon being very excited, asked:

- What do you mean father, than within two hours they are going to shoot us?, Juan José, have you heard that? It can't be that in a two hour deadline they can prepare to kill men like us who have to settle the most complicated business.-

- You are right brother Luis, they can't shoot patriots without a deadline of no more than two hours, to whom the American independence owes so much because of being the first praised.-

- We know my sons that we don't have so much time to confess you, friar Hinostrosa and me are prepared to begin the confession act.-

- Neither my brother Luis nor I will confess if the deadline is not prolonged, we will leave in yours hands our spiritual health if you intercede in our behalf before the Governor Intendant so that he may give some more hours.-

The two friars, feeling pity on the brothers, could no nothing but offered themselves to the service they were requesting, going to the house of the Governor Intendant with the purpose of mediating so that they may be granted some more hours:
- Our presence Sr. Governor is with the purpose of informing you about our mission to intercede on behalf of the Carrera Brothers, they are exhausted by so little time they are allowed, only two for their shooting, we, friar Hinostrosa and your servant friar Lamas, request you and beg you that you may grant them the grace of two more hours for those wretched ones. -
Governor Luzuriaga, after listening to them, called the clerk:
- Don Lorenzo Barcala go with this watch to the prison, accompanying the fathers being present here, friar Lamas and friar Hinostrosa; when they enter in the prison, open the watch and check the hour, and after two hours elapse, make them execute, the Carreras. For consideration to the two friars I don't take into account the minutes elapsed since the notification until this moment in which I'm giving this new order. Fathers, you may now fulfil your duty, and say o my behalf that the brothers should be put in separate cells.-
Mr. Barcala carried out the order, but meanwhile the Carrera brothers requested to talk with the lawyer Mr. Novoa, close friend of Luis and Juan Jose, whom rapidly went; with him, they agreed the 106 main points of their will. Soon after having finished, Mr. Novoa went out and, rapidly he hurried to the Town Council of Mendoza, so that they intercede with the Governor Luzuriaga for the mercy of the Carreras. The Town Council offered to do what Novoa requested, but he did not obtain anything from Luzuriaga.

The two Brothers were separated from the same dungeon; Juan Jose was put in the number one and Luis in the number two, being ablaze with indignation because of the sudden order to shoot them. Father Lamas entered in his cell with the intention of confessing him:
- Friar Benito, get out of here, I don't want to be confessed, at these moments I renounce my faith and God who has turned his back on me when I have needed him the most, please go away. -
- Luis my son, you have been born within a Christian family, the Lord takes pity on your mercy because of the misfortune you are in and grants you the grace of being able to die confessed in this dungeon

being with the fetters. If you had been fighting you would not have had this Divine Grace and you would have died unconfessed without discovering the Kingdom of Eternal Peace. You don't have to tell me all your sins, only your regret is enough. -

Luis, upon staring at friar Benito in the eyes and without telling a word, he knelt down with the arms in cross.

Friar Benito brought near him the crucifix to the mouth and gave him the absolution.

In the contiguous cell, Juan Jose categorically refused to listen friar Hinostrosa; the dominican father Pedernera also went to the cell to hear the voices and unfortunate words spoken by Juan Jose, the dominican didn't get the words to convince him and got near to the contiguous cell to talk with friar Benito over the prisoner's defiance.

- Luis, you have already heard the father about your brother's refusal; in your hands I commend you to convince him so that he may also die in the grace of God.-
- Friar Pedernera, tell my brother that I'm already in the grace of God, that I have already been confessed. -
- Juan José, son, follow the example of your younger brother who has already been confessed.-

-Has My brother Luis been confessed?-

Before answering, an officer came to announce that it was the time to go.

Luis resignedly asked not to be shot while his brother was being confessed. The two inmates get dressed for the punishment with jacket and uniform pant.

When they saw each other, they held their hands and together they walked toward the main square where there were two stools and the platoon waiting for them.

-Juan José, my dear brother, don't let's separate each other at the time of dying, die as I do, like a Christian, get confessed yourself.-

When arriving at the square, they were followed by the three friars, Juan Jose knelt down before father Pedernera who put before his chest the crucifix and the prisoner kissed it. At the same time friar Benito begged that the shooting didn't begin while the confession lasted, and when it finished, Juan Jose said in gratefulness:

- Father, there are two fine Bretagne cloth shirts and a clock, take
  them as a keepsake of mine. -

At the first discharge, Luis was dead, however Juan Jose fought with
the death for quite a while since they were aiming at him and but they
missed leaving him hurt until they hit, it was seven in the afternoon
when Juan Jose drew his last breath. In the public square of Mendoza,
the two Carrera Brothers were wrongly shot as if they were highwaymen
on April 8th, 1818.

When the father Pedernera returned to the dungeon to pick up his
hat, there was not anything of what Juan Jose had bequeathed, everything
had disappeared in the hands of their guards.

Governor Luzuriaga sent a letter to the Carreras' father informing
him about the death of his sons. Don Ignacio Carrera was very depressed
in the dungeon, he received the news with great sorrow, and at the same
time O'Higgins was demanding him the payment of the debt that his
son Jose Miguel had contracted in the United States to arm his fleet,
without caring that this had been seized by Argentina, and after he forced
him to pay the expenses incurred in the execution of his sons Juan Jose
and Luis. This last blow for don Ignacio, he was very weak with 86 years
of age, without forces, he became seriously ill with his heart, suffering a
sharp crisis, and two months after this accident, he died on June 22nd.

The great misfortune for dona Javiera made her vehemently act.
On 1818, she devised with Jose Miguel a conspiracy intended to murder
O'Higgins and San Martin, charging the daring mission to the French
sailors brought from the United States, Carlos Robert, Juan Lagresse,
Agustin Dragonette and Narciso Parchappe, all of them led by Robert
Young, but due to a breach of secrecy, Pueyrredon discovered the plans.
They were tried by a military court; Robert Young and Juan Lagresse
were sentenced to death and shot in Mendoza.
    Once failed the murder of San Martin, Jose Miguel was the mentor
of the anarchy in which were found the argentine provinces.

Dona Javiera at the beginning of 1819, she distributed declarations
against San Martin, O'Higgins and Pueyrredon, this made the Supreme
Director arrest her in her own house. But frightened the Government of
Buenos Aires that Javiera and Jose Miguel could plan another attempt,

they transfered Javiera to La Guardia de Lujan and then to San Jose de Flores, leaving her isolated.

Don José Miguel Carrera received the news of the death of his brothers in Montevideo, very angered he swore vengeance for them, and for all the suffering that his family had to endure.

From Montevideo he made use of the printing, for which he established and published the newspaper "El Hurón", distribuited by Carlos Rodriguez Erdoiza, brother of Manuel, the Zamudio Brothers, Captain Bustamante and a franciscan priest don Solano Gracía. In this newspaper, he was informing about the public and secret behaviour of the Government of Buenos Aires on the part of Supreme Director of the United Provinces of the Rio de La Plata, with the attempts of San Martin and Juan Martin de Pueyrredon of establishing a constitutional monarchy bringing the Duke of Orleans as king, but he refused the throne.

José Miguel met with his good friend Carlos Maria de Alvear:
- My brothers who were surprised in Mendoza then treated like criminals and brutally shot as traitors, without even giving them a fair trial in Buenos Aires. In the death of my brothers, I see the hand of the Lautarian lodge and San Martin, because confidentially I have been able to know that his secret symbolic name in the Lodge is brother Inaco, signature which was in the order of shooting. My old father who had just been liberated from the island of Juan Fernandez, where the Spaniards had him prisoner for being a patriot, has been treated like a criminal put in irons and confined in a dungeon, with his 86 years of age.-
- And you Jose Miguel, have you not denounced these facts before the Congress of Buenos Aires? -
- I presented these attempts to the Congress of Buenos Aires and I made a complaint against the violation of all the rights, and they have turned a deaf ear on my clamors and those of my family afflicted by the fiercest pursuit. –

- And your sister dona Javiera, where is she? -

- My sister, after an arrest and lack of Communications unworthy of his sex, has been confined firstly in the almost desert village of Lujan, and now I think she is San Jose de Flores, I say I believe, because she is isolated, and it is not sure at all, only rumors that I heard of.

- And your wife, do they chase her? -

- I have hidden my beloved Merceditas and my two girls in the suburbs, in the house of my good friend father Garcia, and just in case they follow me, at the time, we only communicate by letter which is delivered to her by the kind friar. But, as the things are going on I surely have to leave Montevideo, I will send them to live in a solitary ranch in Argentina, and they will not find them there. Our properties are seized or plundered. All my chilean friends, no other crime but being my friends, groan in prison or exile; my sister-in-law, the widow of my unfortunate eldest brother Juan Jose, has been confined in a dungeon in Mendoza, my mother-in-law at the age of fifty, being in the misery, has to serve a very numerous family, one of my servants, because of having been my servant, has been put in irons in Mendoza, and another servant of my brother Juan Jose, because of the same reason, suffered two hundred lashes and prison for ten years. And then? In view of all these public events in both nations, I ask to the people, the fair men, the kind souls of all the countries. What resource is left for an American that in reward for his services rendered to his country is treated with this bloodthirsty cruelty, without being listened before the law and being pursued everywhere to be annihilated? Won't he have a right based on the nature to defend himself from such a cruel tyranny? If the people some day may avenge so many offenses; I will always serve the party of the free ones and will fight on their side while I live, and if the luck leaves in the middle of my efforts, I will die invoking the aid of the future generations always in favour of the freedom of my Country.-

- Jose Miguel, I'm very sorry for all your misfortunes, although some of them maybe could soon be solved; we will have to wait for instructions of General Artigas to leave Montevideo and join a federalist assault against Buenos Aires. Santa Fe, Entre Rios, Corrientes and Misiones, the entire region is artiguista, he is considered there to be the Protector of the People. The management of the Port and The Customs in form exclusive and imposed on the part of Buenos Aires will be the central topic of the confrontations. In order that the provinces could avoid the

Buenos Aires supremacy, it is indispensable that they preserve certain degree of economic and fiscal autonomy; for that reason it is necessary to achieve political autonomy, and therefore, to limit the power and authority of the central government.-

The death of his father made enrage even more to Carrera, who continued publishing his devastating texts, among them his "I Accuse ", and his "Manifest to the People of Chile". This document is, in spite of the fact that in it he denies any political ambition and adds that he is not encouraged by any desire of revolt nor revenge, it was a real proclamation of the beginning of his campaign:

"Addressed to the generous people, comrades and comrades-in-arms". By which, he accuses San Martin and O'Higgins of numerous dishonesties, including to be in combination and to be the forefront of the monarchists in order "to replace in his restoration the foreign yoke with that of his supposed liberators ". Planning to establish a constitutional monarchy, placing as prince the former heir to the throne of Etruria and related on his mother side to the Bourbon dynasty, the duke of Luca.

José Miguel stated that his desire to publish that Manifesto was not only the defense of his honor but that it also looked for at least to warn the People of the dangers that surrounded them, and prevent them against the nets that were cautiously armed by the hateful ambition of a domestic enemy hidden as the Paladin of The Public Freedom, and he added that; "*It would not be wise to remain silent because of kindness but what is necessary to publish as a duty*". "*We have fought; we have shed our blood to destroy the tyranny instead of changing it for other tyrants*". He denounced San Martin, the Congress of the United Provinces, and the Lautarian Lodge like enemies of the American cause.

Due to the aggressive ideology that spread through his newspaper "El Hurón" the authorities of Buenos Aires requested the Government of Montevideo his expulsion and handing over; however he was helped to escape to Entre Rios to survive.

Jose Miguel before going on board wrote to his wife:

"My beloved Mercedes:

Yesterday I received through the Commodore your pleasant letter of the 3rd. It is said at this moment that St Martin has been defeated; I am given to the devil. I send Rodney for the poor of Mendoza which situation breaks the soul into pieces. I do not have time, it is necessary

in this instant to send the letters on board. Deliver both letters to don
Manuel Cavia, the other one for the mail if the news of our Chile is not
true.
    Embrace my little girls and receive the heart of your lover eternally.
José Miguel".

The news of the death of the brother Carreras caused in Santiago
excitement in the spirit of the carrerinos who were preparing a coup
d'état, against Bernardo O'Higgins whom was considered the main
responsible of the shooting of the brother Carreras. It was held a Town
Council for April 16th; it soon became an Open Council where the
organizing "carrerinos" were dominating with Manuel Rodriguez Erdoiza
in the lead. It was immediately agreed the calling of a National Congress
and the incorporation of don Jose Miguel Infante and don Jose Gaspar
Marin into the Government which should adopt the form of a Junta.

    Manuel Rodríguez organized an attempt of uprising with a group of
carrerinos with whom he went to the Government Palace followed by
don Gabriel Valdivieso and they entered on horseback with the whole
group that demanded the end of the "**Argentinian interference**" and
Bernardo O'Higgins's abdication The aid-de-camps managed, in the
same courtyard, to subdue the two leaders, taking them imprisoned to
San Pablo barracks; and the accomplices and instigators, among whom
was the lawyer Vera y Pintado, were driven into exile in Mendoza by
order of O'Higgins.

    The disappearance of the political forces of Manuel Rodriguez Erdoíza
was decided a long time ago by the Lautaro Lodge, which delegated their
elimination to the lawyer Bernardo Monteagudo, the same person who
signed the death sentence of the Carrera brothers.
    Monteagudo should share the responsibility with the Commander
Rudecindo Alvarado.
    The battalion of Chasseurs of the Andes was taking Manuel
Rodriguez toward Quillota. The night of May 23 in a ranch known as
Cancha del Gato, near Tiltil the prisoner rested. Commander Alvarado
and his assistant that had accompanied more behind the battalion went
before the Lieutenant Antonio Navarro, to whom they ordered that he
hand over Colonel Manuel Rodriguez. Navarro informed him that he
was in the ranch, and Alvarado and his assistant approached thither. They
talked amicably with Rodriguez and moments later Alvarado went out

arm in arm with the prisoner followed by a corporal and a soldier and the lieutenant Navarro, they all went into the shades of the forest.

After awhile in the dawn and at the distance, two shots were heard. It began May 24, when the body of the famous guerrilla patriot don Manuel Rodriguez Erdoíza stayed there with two shots in the back next to the hollow of an indigenous tomb. His corpse was abandoned, but on May 28 Tomás Valle subdelegate of Tiltil buried him in the very same altar of the town chapel.

It was probably the lieutenant Navarro who shot as the one in charge of the custody squad, he was subject to a pretense of trial, just as formality, acquitting him not guilty he was sent to Argentina; but he later admitted to have received the order of the Colonel Alvarado and Monteagudo to murder Manuel Rodriguez.

The South of the provinces of Concepción where the remains of the royalist army had retreated was still follower of the King's cause and it was the scene of the bloody "War to death" as it was called by Vicuña Mackenna.

Chilean Vicente Benavides, of modest condition began as private soldier in the patriot army, later he went over to the royalists, reaching the rank of Captain. Fighting in the battle of Maipú he was taken prisoner and sentenced to death as traitor. They made him shoot during the night in the outside of Santiago, but the bullets only grazed him and he feigned to be a dead man. He was hidden for seven months, until one day he appeared before San Martin asking him for pardon, which he obtained, and joining the patriot army patriot as official of the division of the Argentinian brigadier Antonio Gonzalez Balcarce; and offering himself to go to the South to provoke the desertion of the royalist soldiers by means of the influences that he still had with them. Benavides deserted again, joining the royalists and being understood by Colonel Juan Francisco Sanchez who entrusted him the command with the rank of Captain of the King's Forces, to which then the mapuche, the pehuenches, the royalist landowner of Concepcion, the priests from the villages and the townspeople of Chillan would join.

He used the Arauco garrison as headquarters, from where he received aids from Peru and the island of Chiloe. The Viceroy granted him the rank of Colonel. He instilled the terror supported by the mounted guerrilla men Pincheira brothers: Antonio, Santos, Pablo, Jose Antonio,

Rosario and Teresa. They were coming from the zone of El Parral in Chillan; they were tenants of the royalist estate of Manuel Zañartu.

Antonio, the eldest one became corporal of the royalist army and fought in the battle of Maipú. They were fighting under the motto "For the King and the Faith", it was likewise the context wherein they began to be known from 1817. They were fervent Catholics, they were concerned that their troops may have chaplains and, they acted in Chile and Argentina.

They were relying on the support of sectors of the Church,, the landowners as Clemente Lantaño and the Council of Chillan.

The Viceroy Joaquin de La Pezuela charged the leader Vicente Benavides with the sustaining of the resistance in the three fronts.

With the weapons that he received from Peru and the aid of the chieftains Catrileo, Mariluán and Mañi-Huenú, he got together more than 1.700 soldiers and several thousands of Indians.

Don Ramón Freire, patriot and Intendant of Concepcion could count on the forces of the chieftains Colipí and Venancio Coñuepán that joined the cause.

General Andrés de Alcazar, leader of the garrison of Los Angeles decided to join Freire in Concepcion, but when passing the Laja river, by Tarpellanca, he was attacked by the army of Benavides that achieved to surrender him by means of a capitulation. Once agreed this one, Alcazar was speared by the indians and all the patriot officers were shot.

Freire left Concepcion withdrawing in Talcahuano, where he could preserve his Communications with the Central Government by sea. Freire sustained the siege two months, until he received some auxiliaries with those he could leave the garrison surprising the montonero in Curalí near Santa Juana and charge against the army of Benavides that retreated in complete dispersion going to be withdrawn in the Araucania, leaving the following year with 3.000 men planning to arrive in Santiago.

Freire, Prieto and Bulnes relentlessly pursued him without being able to catch him, but near Chillan, finally the division under the command of Colonel Joaquin Prieto defeated him in Las Vegas de Saldías.

Although, Benavides was saved from the pursuit and got on board by being hidden in a launch with the hope of arriving in Peru, crewed by a few men who landed on the coast of Topocalma to renew their provision of water; moment in which his companions themselves delivered him to the authorities

He was condemned to death by his great crimes and hanged in the Square of Santiago under the accusation of being an american traitor.

The brother Pincheiras were still left in the South together with the pehuenche indians, were driving the terror between Curicó and Concepcion under the pretext of maintaining the Spanish sovereignty. Their headquarters were in the mountains of the Andean range.

After the victory of the battle of Maipu, they had to throw out of the Pacific the royalists that still occupied the South of the country and dominated the sea. It was necessary to take a liberating expedition to Peru, for it they would have to form a national squadron that could sweep the Spanish navy of the Pacific Ocean, consolidating definitively the independence of Spanish America.

O´Higgins advised by his minister of War don José Ignacio Zenteno del Pozo to acquire and form a squadron; with this purpose he imposed taxes, loans and confiscations. With many economic efforts established the first National Squadron, The Command of the Navy, the Navy Infantry and the Naval Arsenals.

It had been acquired in Cancha Rayada, before the disaster, an English ship that had arrived in Valparaiso, the "Windham", which was later rebaptized with the name of "Lautaro", trusting the command to the former lieutenant of the British Navy William O'Brien.

San Martin went to Buenos Aires to gather weapons and ships, he hired the Argentinean don Manuel H. Aguirre like agent of Chile in United States, giving him instructions to contract the construction of two frigates and two smaller ships to be manned and equipped and also with letters of marque, all this to the expense of the Chilean Government. His action was blocked since the government of Washington didn't support him because of being in negotiations with Spain regarding The Florida.

From London the Chilean agent Jose Antonio Álvarez Condarco, reported to O'Higgins on January 12, 1817, that he had hired the sailor Juan Illingworth Hunt to command the schooner "The Rose" of 400 tons, anchored in the Thames estuary, and he had also hired one of the best sailors of the Great Britain, Sir Thomas Cochrane, who had brought him huge earnings, set against the admiralty, retiring from the service and intervening in politics as deputy of the liberal party. He was arrested by fraud and by spreading political news with the purpose of stock manipulation, he was expelled from the Parliament having to pay a strong fine and prison; the fine was paid, and while he was going to be detained in these circumstances, entered into the service of Chile.

Cochrane and his family went aboard in the frigate "The Rose" she should pick him up to pass to fight for the freedom of that part of America; deceiving the surveillance and pursuit of the Spanish ships. The trip was long, since they arrived in Valparaiso on November 28, 1818.

Cochrane and his family went aboard in the frigate "The Rose" she should pick him up to pass to fight for the freedom of that part of America; deceiving the surveillance and pursuit of the Spanish ships. The trip was long, since they arrived in Valparaiso on November 28, 1818.

The agreement, guaranteed Lord Cochrane the command of The Squadron, with the salary and the bonuses corresponding to the rank of English Admiral, the integration to the naval force that would command f a steam frigate , and other points referred to its transfer and lodging. He arrived in Valparaiso, being received personally by O'Higgins and where he agreed to acquire the schooner "The Rose" for the Patriot army of the Andes, changing his name to "The Rosa of the Andes."

The arrival of Lord Cochrane supposed a stimulus for the Chilean squadron during the war of the Independence, devoting himself fully , using his extraordinary and vast wisdom in destroying and capturing most of the transports that came from Spain together with the ship of war destined to protect them.

Lord Cochrane started acting as Chief of the Navy of Chile, when the country was still occupied by royalist forces.

He was appointed Vice admiral of Chile and Commander in Chief of the naval forces; on December 23 he assumed the command of seven warships belonging to Chile, which were pretty deficient.

The Colonel Manuel Blanco Encalada was appointed rear Admiral and the second in the chain of command.

Previously on July 6th, 1818, it was acquired the corvette "Coquimbo", which received the name of "Chacabuco", one month later it was bought the brig "Columbus" that was re-baptized with the name of "Araucanian". In London it was bought the "Cumberland" giving it the name of "San Martin", it was bought in Buenos Aires the brig "Lucy" that was called "Galvarino" and the Director Pueyrredón was sending the brig "Intrepid" with 18 cannons.

"Pueyrredón" and "Chacabuco" led by Thomas Carter, "Independence", "Araucanian" led by Morris and "San Martin" led by

Wilkinson, "Lautaro" and "Galvarino" led by Cochrane, and officers of the well disciplined British navy, the "Intrepid" whose command was entrusted to the Colonel of artillery Manuel Blanco Encalada, Argentinian, educated in Spain where he had served as ensign of frigate.

It was received sailors of all the nationalities; it was made train as sailors to the fishermen of the costs, the other officialdom and the crew of the other ships were formed by Chilean without any naval discipline and by English and American adventurers equally without discipline and with no understanding of Spanish. But the whole organization advanced being able to arm a squadron of eight ships with 142 cannons and 1.100 crew members, everything thanks to the efforts of Blanco Encalada.

In Valparaíso it was organized a meeting of captains and pilots of merchant ships, with the intention of designating an experienced naval chief. The election fell in the Commodore William O'Brien and the Captain William Miller, who was promoted to General at the age of 27, he was placed in the command of the navy infantrymen of the "Lautaro" that was manned by English officers and 100 foreign sailors and 250 Chileans. On April 26, 1818, O'Brian was setting sail to raise the blockade of Valparaiso that had been kept until the General Osorio retreated to Talcahuano.

"Lautaro" went with course towards the Spanish corvette "Emerald", and when she was close, in a very not suitable way for the boarding, O'Brian jumped on board only with 30 followers, while the navy infantrymen were sustaining a fire from the forecastle, causing serious losses among the crew of the "Emerald", and a blow of surge released both ships. The men of the "Emerald" on having seen on cover only 30 patriots opened fire from below and killed the Commodore William O'Brian, while "Lautaro" imprudently, due to her scanty training, she abandoned her aim. The English sailor, John Higginson, replaced the unfortunate O'Brian in the command of the "Lautaro."

The "Esmeralda" and the "Pezuela" gathered and escaped.

From Cadiz on May 21, 1818 a force of 2.000 soldiers was leaving for Chile, sent by Fernando VII in eleven transports guided by the frigate "Maria Isabel" with 44 cannons. Against this expedition a Chilean squadron set sail from Valparaiso on October 10th bound for the South, composed by the "San Martin", "Lautaro", and the "Chacabuco", under the command of the Captain of ship Manuel Blanco Encalada.

The "Maria Isabel" had just anchored in Talcahuano, the frigate was defended by the batteries of land, all of sudden she was attacked by the "San Martin" and "Lautaro" that initiated very heavy rifle fire. The "Maria Isabel" weighed anchor and she beached on shore in Talcahuano. The Chilean patriots protected by a favorable wind, extracted her of the stranding, the Spanish sailors jumped into the water, while a squad of 50 sailors of Blanco Encalada got hold of the frigate that was incorporated into the national squadron with the name of "O'Higgins" and led by Robert Foster.

Ssubdued the "Maria Isabel", after a great combat with the forces of land, five of the transports departed from Cadiz carrying 700 Spanish soldiers were caught.

Once captured the frigate, on November 5th Blanco Encalada sent the brig "Araucano" to Valparaiso, where she arrived on the 9th with Captain Morris aboard together with Lieutenant Martin Warner, the bearer of Blanco Encalada's official dispatch regarding the capture of the enemy frigate.

After almost 40 days of his departure from Valparaiso, Captain Manuel Blanco Encalada victoriously entered with a huge booty into the same port he departed from.

From Peru the Viceroy Pezuela ordered that a Flying Division of 1500 men from the three arms be formed. The purpose of this corps was to cover the North coast and aid Guayaquil that had repeatedly been attacked by privateer ships from Buenos Aires under the command of Ramon Freire and in the case of an invasion by the Chilean privateers. He also ordered that the frigates "Venganza" and "Esmeralda" were bounded for Paita, carrying the necessary armament and 50.000 pesos to cover the expenses by the way to aid the "Prueba", whose commander had it practically inactive in the estuary of Guayas.

The Viceroy wrote to the bishop of Trujillo don Jose Carrion y Marfil, staunchest royalist, requesting him the contribution of the clergy to fortify the port of Paita, since it was the most exposed on that part of the territory.

The bishop offered to do the request throughout the bishopric, sending circulars to all parishes, though he warned that the Clergy of the Diocese and its poor bishop were doing their best under the critical circumstances that they have mediated as much as possible for the relief of the State.

The contributions could be in money or in species.

The Marquis of Torre Tagle was as intendant of Trujillo, those being close to Viceroy Pezuela doubted about the loyalty of this noble "trujillano" to the King's cause.

Pezuela also asked reinforcements for Piura to the Viceroy of Nueva Granada, Samano, who sent to Peru the Numancia Battalion garrisoned in Colombia. They departed on February 1819. Due to the fact that the Chilean and Argentinian privateers were marauding by the zone, it was decided to send them by land, but it was a 10.000 kilometers journey, therefore it lasted 150 days. The battalion had to climb the Andes through difficult terrains in the middle of the summer, passing through Quito and all over the highlands of Ecuador that are on the way to Peru, and from Loja they entered into Piura, they were in total 1.500 soldiers of the troops of Spanish General Pablo Murillo, being a corps d'élite, and everything was done with admirable discipline and military efficiency.

They entered into the city to the sound of their magnificent band of musicians with their luxurious uniforms as it had never been seen by the Peruvians. Its stay in Piura was brief, only to recover from the fatigue and from there they went to Paita where the fifth Company stayed under the command of Captain Blas Cerdeña, the second Company under the command of Captain Jose Pineda stayed in Trujillo.

Many Spanish officers from Lima said to the Viceroy their distrust about the loyalty of the Numancia Battalion, although in the beginning it had been a very loyal corps to the King but that had already been lost, because when having been garrisoned in Pasto for a long time, they had been socializing with many of the Colombian and Venezuelan officers who had been in the patriot army and when they were taken prisoners they preferred to be enlisted before being shot.

Tomás de Heres, Captain of the Numancia Battalion, fell into Rosa Campuzano's loving net, courtesan that frequented in Lima the elegant living rooms of the Captaincy, in the street of San Marcelo, where the counts de la Vega del Ren and San Juan de Lurigancho, the marquis of Villafuerte, the viscount of San Donas and other nobility members supporting the revolution; Boqui, the "caraqueño", Cortinez, Sanchez Carrion Mariategui and many other characterized conspirators in favor of the independence were attending Rosita's gathering.

The Captain de Heres allowed himself to be convinced by the Campuzano so that he and all his regiment passed to the patriot's cause.

It was this way how the famous Numancia Battalion and its 900 members joined the Republican troops.

Rosa conspired with Juan Santalla, Commander of the Cantabria battalion in the fortress of Callao, so that he may also pass to the patriots, but he changed his mind and broke with his friends.

The new Admiral Sir Thomas Cochrane received O'Higgins's order to block the port of Callao and destroy, if it was possible, the warships without combat by means of the batteries of land. He may also capture all the merchant ships found during the voyage, and distribute pamphlets in which they were announcing to the Peruvian people the next departure of the Chilean expedition that should liberate them. For this undertaking, Manuel Blanco Encalada was as Rear-Admiral.

A division of The Squad with four vessels left Valparaiso January 14 1819 bound for Callao.

Antonio Álvarez Jonte that acted as secretary of Cochrane wrote since they left Valparaiso an account of the voyage until May 28th of the same year 28:

Álvarez Jonte wrote down on April 10; that it had been seized an American schooner loaded with rifles, naval provisions and flour requested by the Viceroy Pezuela to the United States and sent everything with recommendation of the ambassador of Spain in Philadelphia.

It had also been seized silver from the powerful shipping company of the Philippines nothing less than 200.000 pesos and when setting out for the bay of Paita, the Scottish admiral found a shallop manned by Indian fishermen of whom he managed to obtain information about the Spanish convoy's departure to Guayaquil two days before. The Admiral undoubtedly thought that the two million pesos he thought of capturing were gone there and he went toward Paita as quickly as possible, an entire fortune that Cochrane, a great lover of money, could allow to escape from his hands. That same day they seized a French brig with 60.000 pesos and also another English brig, they seized cocoa, sugar and rice. The squad left the pavilion of the recent republic of Chile; it seemed pirate more than privateer.

Cochrane attacked Paita which had a population of 4.000 inhabitants in 1819. The port, it was the factory of smuggling that was done by the complicity of the Spanish local civil servants and that of Piura's, this had been doing it centuries behind. The products from China were taken to Mexico and, they also passed to Guayaquil where they were hidden as if they were wooden, cocoa cargo and other products from the region, they reached Paita for their distribution all over the viceroyalty.

Álvarez Jonte wrote down in the logbook the assault to Paita in very succinct and brief form:

At eleven o'clock in the morning of April 13th we meet the Chilean brig "Galvarino"; the captain came on board and confirmed that the convoy had escaped from Guayaquil with the two millions. Preparations were made for the combat and enter the Port of Paita, in the mouth of the bay, it started to be sighted several vessels, but on having approached we verified that six frigates were whalers and only a Spanish packet boat, at nightfall two lighters were sent to bring the packet boat, but the battery of land started shooting. We decided to enter the town and seize the battery on the following dawn, that at the six in the morning we were landing on the one hand while the "Galvarino" opened front fire to call the attention. At nine o'clock in the morning, our people were on the battery, they were offered a parley that they rejected, after a while they were offered another one and they also rejected this, we advanced in all directions, took hold of the batteries and the town, fleeing all its inhabitants.

From that moment, it began an uncontrollable plunder of all the houses and some public properties, which were taken on board the schooner and other ships. Only one patriot soldier died; enemy's casualties were four among dead and injured.

On the 18th the whole morning, it was used to embark the troop and prepare the ship to set sails.

This is the way Alvarez Jonte reported the assault to Paita:
- *"Cochrane arrived in Paita eager for money thinking of finding a remittance of 2.000.000 pesos.*
- *That he allowed the plunder, and only for political reasons and because he knew that his behavior would be disapproved of, he punished the sacrilegious thefts.*
- *He treated the inhabitants of Paita as enemies doing a bad service to the patriot cause".*

The presence of the Chilean squadron caused panic in the population who fled en masse. The attitude of the expeditionaries justified the dread.

As Alvarez Jonte didn't enjoy the sympathy of Cochrane, he was dismissed for having been exceeded in his functions by opening official correspondence, and above all by writing the diary.

The garrison of Callao was heavily defended by three powerful castles and the batteries of San Joaquin with more than 60 cannons of its fortification El Real Felipe protecting the Spanish squadron of the Pacific that gave shelter to the frigate "Esmeralda" and other minor vessels.

The fog prevented him from carrying out the projected attack, therefore he decided to withdraw, and imposing that some of the war ships of the squadron that remained under the command of rear-Admiral Blanco Encalada maintained a strict blockade in Callao.

The Viceroy sent at once to the ports of the North a dispatch boat to announce the presence of the Chilean squadron. This allowed the Intendant and Commander General of the Northern coast don Francisco Gil to enact defense dispositions. In the sea, the dispatch boat met the merchant Spanish frigates "Eagle", "Begoña" and "Peruvian" to which she reported that the Callao was subjected to blockade, at once three ships reversed and on March 23rd, 1819 they were entering the Port of Paita. The ships were victualled and the following day they continued trip to Guayaquil.

Admiral Cochrane set sails then heading for the Northern Peru, landing on March 29th in Huacho and two days later he took hold of Huaura, where he intercepted important sums of money destined for the North American ship "Macedonian", which trafficked in favour of the royalists. The French brig "Gazelle" in Huarmey was robbed of a rich shipment.

At the beginning of the following month he took hold of Supe, going later on to Huarmey and then to Paita, port that he militarily occupied. He returned to Callao where he verified that the blockade was not kept. Blanco Encalada had returned to Valparaiso, which cost him a court-martial, being acquitted.

Meanwhile on May 1819, the schooner "La Rosa de los Andes" was armed with 36 cannons, she crossed the Pacific commanded by Juan Illingworth as a corsair to the service of Chile, and Raimundo Morris was appointed the Second Commander and seized several preys; firstly, she boarded the Spanish frigate of war "Vascongada" coming from Santander, she then fought nine hours near the coasts of Santa Elena with the Spanish frigate of war "La Piedad", retiring to the Galapagos islands to repair damages; after two months she captured the Brig. "Canton" with a shipment of 60.000 pesos, in which don Vicente Rocaforte from Quito was travelling as passenger, and she then headed for the island of Taboga in the coasts of Panama, to which she plundered. Upon return, he liberated Tumaco, Izcuandé and Buenaventura in the coast of Chocó in Colombia, where he was informed that an expedition under the command of Captain Blas Cerdeña had left in his pursuit, the corsair, decided to cut them off the retreat, he left by the mouth of the Magdalena river in the Atlantic; with such a purpose, he ascended the waters of the Atrato river, being the first to discover this passage, which goes from ocean to the other one, he occupied the island of Taona and headed toward Panama which he couldn't occupy because of being well fortified, but in the Real de Santa Maria, with the Governor Valverde, he exchanged the Spanish prisoners captured in Taboga by Mac Gregor expedition's English survivors, being left 600 out of the 1.400 men. He continued until the island of La Gorgona where he released several captives and captured two brigs. Finally, she ran aground in the mouth of the Izcuandé River and it was not possible to save her. Illingworth travelled to Guayaquil and joined the patriot forces as diplomatic agent in Colombia.

Admiral Cochrane began in the month of September his second campaign, capturing a ship in Coquimbo and he attempted a new attack to Callao and the fog prevented him to do so again. He then set sail pursuing the frigate "Perla" and in its pursuing he arrived in the surroundings of Guayaquil, he didn't achieve his objective since the "Perla" went into the Guayas River. From Guayaquil, he set sail with the "O'Higgins" towards the South of Chile with the intention of taking hold of the Fort of Valdivia which was in control of the royalists. This attack imposed a great degree of planning due to the complex defense system that controlled the entrance to the Harrison by the Valdivia River.

Cochrane knew by the information from his spy that in Chiloé, the Governor Quintanilla feared a revolt and was preparing with a considerable force of infantry and cavalry. The garrison of Valdivia was composed by the Cantabria Regiment of veteran Spanish troops and numerous number of militiamen.

Cochrane decided to attack the stronghold with a surprise assault; he appeared in front of Valdivia with two little ships in bad conditions, the schooner "Moctezuma" and the recaptured "Dolores" and 300 men. The intendant Freire helped him in Talcahuano with 250 soldiers under the command of Major don Jorge Beauchef, French military who had fought with Napoleon. The city was guarded by the San Carlos Fort, the castles of Corral, Niebla and Mancera and several more batteries. Before the royalist may organize a formal resistance, Cochrane's troops had landed and attacked the forts, the Peruvian cadet Francisco Vidal who became president of Peru was distinguished in this action. On

February the 4th, they anchored near the coast of Chiloé and captured the Corona fort, they later proceeded against the Agüi fort, main square of the enemy, guarded by three regular companies, two militia and a complete detachment of artillery men for the twelve cannons mounted on its bastions, dominating a narrow path by which it can only reach the fort. Major William Miller with only 60 men went to the assault, 20 were killed in the first attack the Major himself received three wounds.

Within a few days, Cochrane attempted an assault to the fort of San Carlos in the island of Chiloé, but he didn't achieve it. This attempt of seizing Chiloé by surprise was considered impossible and the Chileans had to retire to Valdivia, where they gathered military equipment to attack again with the "Independence" and the "Araucano".

The great fortifications were not able to resist the attacks of the infantry forces that were going on board the vessel, and the city surrendered by being occupied on February 17th, 1820.

The taking of Valdivia was one of the most extraordinary actions in the whole war of independence, depriving the Spanish forces of one of the most powerful operation bases in the Pacific.

The blows inflicted on the viceregal power by Chilean forces with the battles of Chacabuco and Maipú, the loss of the convoy with the frigate "Maria Isabel", the fall of Valdivia and the domain exercised by the squadron were precursory events of a direct invasion against Peru, that Cochrane began to demand an immediate campaign directed by him and with the help of General Freire.

This proposition was declined by the Chilean government that had already decided that the expedition to the Peru was going to be directed by General San Martin. This decision made that from this date and until the liberating expedition may set sail toward Peru, it was one of big disputes among Cochrane, on the other hand, and San Martin and the Chilean authorities for the other one, even during this period Cochrane presented his resignation more than once and only the patience and the well knowledge of O'Higgins were able to convince him to remain in the Navy.

With the few resources of the Government of Chile that was without credit, and after great sacrifices it could be carried out the plan of invading Peru.

The government of the United Provinces of Rio de La Plata had promised to deliver 500.000 pesos for the expedition, but that help could not become true. But fortunately for the future campaigns of the squadron, some British merchants settled down in Valparaiso could provide some necessary naval equipments.

While San Martin prepared the expedition, this time without help of the Army of the Andres, because Pueyrredón demanded him that they return to Argentina, only a few did it, the rest escaped since they did not want to fight against the anarchy in which that country was.

Political events happened, in Spain, which were going to favor the cause of the american independence.

The government of Fernando VII had organized a squadron of 15.000 men bound for Buenos Aires, and once the patriots were subdued, they would continue to Chile and Peru, It happened that while the troops were still in Cadiz, there was a military coup against the absolutism of Fernando VII and in favor of a constitutional monarchy.

A group of liberal leaders headed by the Colonel Rafael del Riego, forced the king to sign The Constitution of 1812. These events served to prevent the departure of the expedition to America, but divided the leaders and royalist generals in two trends: liberals and absolutists.

Due to what happened in Spain, the Readers of Peru in those times were divided in two groups: the royalist Peruvians with the Viceroy Pezuela at the top, the Creole leaders and the battalions were contrary to the constitutional regime, on the other hand, the Spanish chiefs headed by General La Serna, were radical constitutional liberals.

The Viceroy Pezuela was informed that Chile prepared an attack by sea, and the Peruvian coast is very extensive to be defended, he faced the problem of knowing where to concentrate his troops, or divide them in order to try to resist the invaders where they were landing, thus he had to distribute his army of 17.000 men along the diverse points where the landing may occur. He also waited for reinforcements from Spain, but the news of the revolt of Colonel Rafael del Riego, in Cabezas de San Juan, ruined all possibilities, causing a feeling of despair.

The financial situation was the most worrying for the government of O'Higgins. The fiscal year of 1818 had closed with a deficit that increased the outstanding debt, and that of 1819, with the stagnant revenues, increased more the debts because of the excessive expenses incurred by the army, the squadron and the future liberating expedition to Peru.

The taxable capacity of the country was exhausted by the contributions and mandatory loans, the excessive tax impositions were squeezing a totally exhausted country. Because of this, and in spite of the austere economies practiced, the fiscal year of 1819 ended with a deficit.

The devastations produced by the civil war, the disruptions of the markets, the more than 10.000 men in the army and the navy, the privateers, the purchase of arms and ammunitions, the excessive consumption of foreign goods, the misery that affected especially the agriculture, which only produced the indispensable items for the feeding of the country and the army, all of these caused that Chile was much poorer in 1820 than in 1810.

As if there were few calamities, on April 3rd 1819 a terrible earthquake ruined the mining works and their humble houses that sheltered the mining population in the northernmost part of the country. The earth trembled until the following day; at 5 o'clock in the morning another earthquake lasting five minutes brought down many buildings and destroyed countless mining sites, this earthquake was connected with another much more destructive of six minutes of duration devastating everything that was left undamaged. There were more than 3.000 people wandering by the hills who were escaping from the tsunamis that came after the earthquakes and they were climbing the mountains.

O'Higgins had to face all these difficulties and also the physical deterioration of his great friend and mentor San Martin, who had already even to resort to the opium to attack his stomach ailments, and there were not also minds in the Lodge that affirmed their decisions. The Providence made him to notice the intellectual clarity and decisive character of Jose Antonio Rodriguez Aldea and he appointed him Finance Minister who at once transformed the contaduría mayor (main accounting office) into a Court of Accounts, he attended to the need of improving the street lighting, transformed the landfill of La Cañada into an avenue with poplar trees. Among the measures of economic order that gave more prestige to the O'Higgins administration, it was the transforming of Valparaiso into the first commercial port of the South Pacific.

Being San Martin in Santiago on March 1819, two young military from Lima appeared before the government asking to be received:
- General, there are outside two young military that wish an audience with your Excellency.-
- Have not they been identified?, ask them who they are.---General, they have told me that they are the Second Lieutenant of Cavalry

don José Garcia and the Captain don Francisco Fernandez de
Paredes.-
- It's all right, have them come in.-
Captain Fernandez de Paredes was of a distinguished family, relative
to the marquis of Salinas, the Second Lieutenant of Cavalry Garcia
was a young man of very good presence, seducer, lady's man, player,
troublemaker, very impulsive, on being impetuous he was able to make
the noblest as well as the vilest actions, but because of his affable character
he could make friends soon.

- I introduce myself Captain Fernandez de Paredes from the Infante
  Don Carlos Regiment, I was sent to Chile in the second expedition
  of the royalist General Osorio, I fought in the battle of Maipú and
  I wish my incorporation in the patriot army.-
- I introduce myself Second Lieutenant of Cavalry Jose Garcia, I was
  sent from Lima to fight as royalist soldier in the Upper Peru, and
  as soon as I had the first opportunity I passed to the Argentinian
  patriots becoming part of the Army of the Andes.-

-And so, what do you want me to do?-

The Second Lieutenant spoke:
- We request to be sent to Peru in order to fulfil a secret mission,
  serving as liaison, and win over the royalists so that they may join
  the Chilean patriots.

San Martin, after listening to them, called them by separate to talk
with each other, and he recommended them to keep an eye on each other
because of the risky mission he was going to assign them.

He sent them in the schooner "Moctezuma" landing in Ancon
with the secret names of "battle of Carlo" for Fernandez de Paredes and
"Mario" for Garcia.

Fernandez de Paredes was assigned to go on expedition to Supe,
Huacho, Huarmey and Santa, and Garcia was given a mission in
Trujillo, Lambayeque and Piura which was at that time very disturbed
by the incursions on Paita and Sechura by the privateers. Garcia at once
contacted with some of the leading people who sympathized with the
patriot cause.

But Garcia, on having money and being far away without being
controlled by his partner Fernandez de Paredes, devoted again to
gambling and his love-affairs.

Fulfilled the mission that he had carried out in North, more or less, he undertook the return but he was surprised in Nepeña by a royalist detachment that took him prisoner, but fortunately the detachment was commanded by a royalist Captain, brother to Garcia, whom ordered him to return to the royalists in order to avoid him the heavy punishment that could be imposed on him. He was taken before the Viceroy and accepted the pardon on condition that he may denounce all the patriots that were secretly acting, that is why there was a great raid in which many religious and important people were captured, but he didn't betray his friend Fernandez de Paredes, being able to hardly get on board bound for Chile.

It thus ended the mission of Jose Garcia with treason.

Madam Javiera confined in San José de Flores, sick and weak, returned to Buenos Aires, due to the intervention of her lover Daniel Jewett, American sailor naturalized Argentinian, he was privateer against the Spanish forces and colonel of the Argentinian navy.

Once she was in Buenos Aires, Javiera stayed in the house of the Argentinian sisters and teachers Damasa and Manuela Cabezon until June 1819. Her fighting spirit led her to escape to Montevideo in a Brazilian warship. When she arrived in this city, she still had time to see her brother Jose Miguel before he departed to Entre Rios. Javiera stayed in Montevideo until 1824, leading a calm life, but worried for her brother and for returning to Chile.

In 1819, it was possible to enact the Constitution in Buenos Aires, with Unitarian character, which caused the rejection of the provinces.

In turn, Jose Gervasio Artigas, Captain of the corps of Blandengues, deserted the Spanish lines in 1811. He had written a project of federalist constitution, fiercely opposed to the centralist politics of Buenos Aires, establishing this way the powerful Federal League.

The leaders appeared as a form of authority more closet o the problems of the people. Most of them were landowners who have distinguished in the defence of the frontiers, in the fight against the Indian or taking part in the fights for independence.

The most distinguished federalist leaders were Jose Gervasio Artigas, from the Oriental Band, Bernabe Araoz, from Tucuman, Bernabe Araoz, Martin Miguel de Gúeme, from Salta, Estanislao Lopez, from Sana Fe, Francisco Ramirez, from Entre Rios, Juan Bautista Bustos, from Cordova,

Felipe Ibarra, from Santiago del Estero, Facundo Quiroga, from La Rioja, Juan Manuel Rosas, from Buenos Aires and Justo Jose de Urquiza, from Entre Rios.

Jose Miguel Carrera, without economic resources, went to Entre Rios with the idea of joining the leaders of the Northern provinces of Buenos Aires at the beginning of July 1819, taking with him only 400 pesos, two guns, his sable where he had pierced a white and blue color ribbon with the red strip, distinguishing characteristic of the federation, in which it read the motto:

"Federation or Death"

It appeared in this way in the camp of the General Francisco Ramirez in Gualeguaychu, in Entre Rios, Pancho Ramirez, as lieutenant of the Protector Artigas, he assumed the function of supreme chief of the federal army, and he was in command of his "Dragoons of the Death" as it were called the disciplined "montoneras" (mounted guerrilla Fighters) from Entre Rios. The General sent Carrera to Santa Fe with the General Estanislao Lopez, Governor of that city, that the rejection of the Unitarian Constitution of 1819, which didn't worked out because the federal dissidence was already very big, as it was very deep the distrust of the people in front of the monarchical intrigues of the "porteños", this caused the reaction of the federalist from the from the interior, and they together planned the attack against the Unitarians of Buenos Aires, defeating the forces of Juan Martin de Pueyrredon whom resigned in favour of Jose Rondeau.

The Directory didn't hesitate to request the help of the General Lecor chief of the Portuguese troops that were occupying Montevideo, this attitude from the porteños worsened the situation, even the army of the North which had orders of fighting the federalist commanders, rebelled in Arequito under the command of General Juan Bautista Bustos and prepared to separate the province of Cordoba from Buenos Aires.

This guerrilla warfare of the coastal provinces against Buenos Aires started on October 7th 1819, to which some exiles from the regime had joined like Carlos de Alvear who promised support from important Buenos Aires sectors. Carrera contributed with some troops and a flying printing which published a bulletin "La Gaceta Federal" with explosive content. The guerrilla achieved such proportions that San Martin was ordered to bring his liberating army to defend Buenos Aires, but he refused to fight in that civil war because of his being loyal to his patriot, popular and revolutionary behavior, neither to fight against the people. The Directory requested aid to General Belgrano, this force also refused to take part in this civil war.

Ramirez and Lopez with the federal army were advancing up to the Cañada de Cepeda where they were confronted by the troops of the Buenos Aires militia of the Supreme Director Rondeau, this militia was mostly made up of slaves bought by the government to turn them into soldiers, they were disbanded and destroyed in the battle of La Cañada de Cepeda on February 1st, 1820.

Ramirez and Lopez entered Buenos Aires, their armies with bad and rude gestures tied with chains the herd of horses to the recently built "Pyramid of May". It thus begins what the liberal history appropriately called "The anarchy in Argentina of the year 20" period in which ten governments were violently succeeding one after the other in Buenos Aires.

General Bustos assured the autonomy of Cordoba; Ibarra did the same in Santiago del Estero; Araoz, in Tucuman, and the intendancy of Cuyo was disintegrated, giving rise to three provinces: Mendoza, San Juan and San Luis.

Before the defeat, the Director Jose Rondeau resigned and the Directory, the Congress and the Constitution were falling, the provinces declared themselves autonomous and the central power was dissolved.

Buenos Aires was transformed into an independent provinces as from 1820, and its first Governor don Manuel de Sarratea ordered that Pueyrredon be arrested because of the demands of the federalist leaders in order that he may be prosecuted for treason to the country because of his invasions to the province, but few hours later he helped him to escape, being exiled in Montevideo.

Sarratea wanted to assure the peace for the porteño (Buenos Aires) business by signing on February 23rd 1820 the Treaty of Pilar with the victorious leaders Lopez and Ramirez, Carrera also signed it. The Treaty established the need of organizing a new central government eliminating forever the Directory. This meant the triumph of the provincial autonomies over the predominance of Buenos Aires.

The leaders were also committed to consult with Artigas the terms of the Treaty, but this was a mere formality, since they left him definitively out of any negotiation or decision to this man of advanced and progressive ideas, but his attitude of solitude in which he lived prevented him from understanding the great problems of Buenos Aires and the betrayal of the leaders to whom he had granted powers and were now against him. Since Artigas did not accept this agreement that his allies Lopez and Ramirez had signed, this attitude faced him with Ramirez.

Carlos Maria Alvear sent a letter to Artigas in order that he may approach the city to talk, Artigas fell into the trap and his troops suffered a great defeat in La Tuna and on July 29th 1820 he suffered another defeat in the battle of Rincon de Abalos, where the betrayed and pursued oriental leader went into exile to Paraguay until his death in 1850.

The commanders Francisco Ramirez and Estanislao Lopez victoriously entered in Buenos Aires. Jose Miguel Carrera had achieved his objective and also his writings from Montevideo had caused the downfall of the Supreme Director Pueyrredon, the Congress was dissolved and the Lautaro Lodge had become the Knights of America. With all this, it was put an end to the Unitarian Constitution of 1819, and it was granted the federal regime in Argentina.

The rivalry between the two commanders Ramirez and Lopez for the political Leadership of the riverside provinces, together with their opposed purposes finally took them to an armed conflict.

Pancho Ramirez had signed the peace between Santa Fe and Buenos Aires by the Treaty of Benegas in 1820, he claimed the help of Buenos Aires, but the government was busy fighting the Indians of the South incited by Carrera.

The idea of Carrera and Alvear was to join and thus this latter would become the new Buenos Aires ruler and he would be Santiago's; but his ally Manuel de Sarratea Governor of Buenos Aires thought that after the defeat suffered in Cepeda, the directorial party was dismantled, but it was not totally . General Juan Ramon Balcarce together with Miguel Estanislao Soler led a revolt that overthrew the Governor of Buenos Aires, Sarratea who took refuge in the federalist camp.

In the middle of the confusion and disorder some supporters of Alvear convinced him to land in Buenos Aires to see if he may take advantage of the situation. But the government of Balcarce scarcely lasted done week, and while Alvear managed to escape, Sarratea became again Governor supported again by Ramirez and Carrera.

General Soler that had overthrown Sarratea in the beginning was a danger. Sarratea called Carrera and Alvear to lead a plot against Soler, who was imprisoned.

El General Soler, que había derrocado en un principio a Sarratea, constituía un peligro. Sarratea llamó a Carrera y a Alvear para liderar un complot contra Soler, quien fue puesto en prisión.

This revolt of Alvear did not also was successful because of the lack of support by the Council of Buenos Aires, it was dominated by the same characters that had overthrown him in 1815. Before this situation, Sarratea demanded Alvear to immediately leave the capital, and he released Soler from his prison.

Alvear desisted from his plans and at the head of a Group of officer and soldiers went toward the outskirts of Buenos Aires and met Carrera and his troops.

Sarratea did not stay in power for such a long time, since he was overthrown by Soler who took the power as Governor of Buenos Aires.

Carrera and Alvear at the head of a Group of 50 officers loyal to the cause known as "the exiles" and the forces of the commander Lopez went against Buenos Aires, fighting the battle on June 28th 1820 in Cañada de la Cruz, finishing with a wide victory for the federalists.

Carrera had the opportunity that he rejected because it was not in his plans being named as Supreme Director, position in which Carlos Maria de Alvear was installed, although his position was not secure and he was forced to resign a short time after.

The now Governor of the Province of Buenos Aires General Manuel de Sarratea managed to reach an agreement with the federalist commanders, agreement in which Carrera took part and his interests were considered in the Treaty of Pilar. The agreement put under the control of Carrera 700 Chileans, weapons and military equipment with which he organized his new "Restoring Army".

The problem now for Carrera was that if it had been achieved to establish a federal government in Argentina, it was not his friend Alvear the one who had the position, therefore, although he obtained military forces for his projects, these were not enough so as to achieve his final objective, but the federalists did not help him as they had promised him, since the new federal authorities in the provinces were not willing to let him cross through their territories toward Chile. And the Governor of

Buenos Aires lacked the authority, and possibly the desire, to force them to grant him that step.

Carrera before the opposition of several Argentinian governors began a series of battles and combats.

Ramirez was defeated by Lopez in Coronda on May 26th 1821 and to this latter, Carrera joined him there.

After Ramirez may cross the Parana River toward Santa Fe, he agreed with Carrera to intervene in a movement against General Bustos in Cordoba, to conquer their common opponents, but they were totally defeated in Cruz Alta. They fled separately with some of their followers to recover their forces and renew the fight. Carrera withdrew toward the West and returned to San Luis after defeating the forces of Mendoza.

In July, 1821 Pancho Ramirez was finally defeated near the Rio Seco where he had agreed to meet with Carrera. He escaped alive but, upon discovering that his partner and Portuguese lover who accompanied him everywhere, the famous Delfina, so beautiful as enigmatic, that she took him unwittingly to death, since she had fallen in the hands of the enemy, he returned to rescue her, and once he entered into the camp, he was killed by a shot in the breast. They beheaded him, sending his head to his enemy Estanislao Lopez, whom kept it in a cage and he publicly showed it in the Council.

After his death, Delfina returned to Arroyo de La China where she survived him by eighteen years.

Lopez went with his forces to San Antonio de Areco where Carrera joined him with his "Recovering Army" and Alvear under the command of his "Exiled". Carrera, with the presumably end of obtaining it by the force, he attacked Buenos Aires again but, lacking the support of the most of the federalist forces, the attack failed, and already as the last resource to achieve his objective, Carrera convinced the commander Lopez so that he summoned a Council in Lujan, in which Alvear was declared Governor of Buenos Aires. Nevertheless, the Buenos Aires Council did not acknowledge his election and four days later they chose Manuel Dorrego as governor, whom launched an offensive against the federalist forces, and on August 2nd Jose Miguel and Alvear were surprised by the forces of Dorrego in San Nicolas.

Mercedes Fontecilla, the patient and self-denying wife of Jose Miguel Carrera, had been going to live in a solitary ranch in Parana, province of Entre Rios. She only met once in a while with Jose Miguel one or two hours. In one of the strange visits that Mercedes payed to her husband, she was captured by the Argentinean army in San Nicolas, just as Dorrego was launching an offensive, surprised and terrified by the conflict she took refuge in the church with the women of the town; but General Quintana sent an assistant to calm her by saying to her "that it was not a ladies' war" and she was captured.

Two days later the very gentleman General Dorrego returned the beautiful captive to her husband General Carrera, sending with her a polite greeting. Since that fateful surprise of the visit of his wife, Jose Miguel understood that he was lost and Mercedes was like a widow in a foreign country with four daughters and another coming, without friends and without resources.

The commander Lopez had withdrawn behind the Arroyo del Miedo, leaving the forces of Carrera and Alvear isolated in the village of San Nicolas de los Arroyo, where they were completely defeated after a fierce fight.

In his war dispatch to the Council of Buenos Aires, Dorrego informed:

"The victory has been fruit of our undertaking, emphasizing the prison of the cadre of officers that formed the escort of don Carlos Maria Alvear, being these the most obstinate to surrender".

Already defeated, Jose Miguel and Carlos Maria were sitting in the soil of a place near San Nicolas de los Arroyos:
- Jose Miguel, in view of this tremendous defeat, for my part at the moment I don't have any other solution than to try to start again outside of here my political life. After that the Council of Buenos Aires, upon being dismissed, they offered me the most solemn guarantee about my properties, they have not fulfilled their guarantee since they know that the only resource that could save me from this ignominious condition is the return of my impounded properties. I will have to live in a foreign country with my family accustomed in another time to live the good life, I'm afraid to think of my wife and my three children.-
- And wouldn't your father help you in this precarious condition that you are? -
- I don't expect anything from my father. I, General who have served with the most ardent patriotism, reduced on the verge of suffering hunger. Recently – he continued- I had a conversation with the Russian minister that is here, and he said to me that we've done very badly when we have not addressed to his government during the whole revolution, since he was sure that we would have taken

much advantage of the Emperor Alejandro, as Caracas that has been acknowledged by Russia, this power is today the strongest in Europe, and they are very interested in extend their relationships with this part of the world. –

- Yes, Carlos Maria, you are completely right, since you should not expect any assistance from England because she is closely bound to Spain governed by such a cruel monarch, and there is no other choice than to defeat or die.-
- I have heard that Chile has a financial deficit, which is very worrying, O'Higgins is squeezing the country that is exhausted with the tax impositions and the mandatory donations, I have heard that he has even pawned the customs revenues for two years, he has got into debts and seized under receipt all kind of goods.-
Carrera commented:
- Wasn't it in the time of my administration that the reforms to the system of public revenues destroyed the abuses of the colonial administration; they produced an increase of 800.000 pesos yearly without charging the people?, the Country would have seen perhaps its desires fulfilled in the execution of my intentions and secured its Independence in the execution of my plans, if the fateful need to subdue the loathsome conspiracies that the fierce ambition of some perverse citizens aborted against my life, more than the Catiline and the Crassus were in Rome, had it not converted the Government's attentions exclusively to the interior peace and the public still and to feed its terrible vengeance in my blood, that of my brothers and that of my father who had so much distinguished in the cause of the freedom.-
After this failure, Alvear had to return to Montevideo.
Jose Miguel Carrera stayed in charge of a relatively small armed group, of 500 men but blocked near Buenos Aires.
Abandoned by his allies the commanders of Entre Rios and Cordoba, he decided to withdraw toward the South and go into the pampa with the hope of being able to cross the mountain range toward Chile. He was winning followers among the Indians of Ranqueles who ended up naming him "Pichi-Rey".

In February, 1821 he started his march toward San Luis, requesting the governor Colonel Luis Videla free pass to Chile, but he refused and faced him militarily, he defeated these forces in the battle of La Ensenada de las Pulgas, entering with his troops in San Luis, the name of Carrera in the pampa caused terror and panic due to the fierceness with which the ranquele indians fought.

The governor of Cordoba also denied him the pass and the General Juan Bautista Bustos is defeated in the battle of Chajá.

Carrera did no longer have any army, he led "montoneras" (mounted guerrilla fighters) that fought with "arme blanche". It took place the bloody battle of Rio Cuarto against the troops of Mendoza under the command of Colonel Bruno Moron, and this was put to the sword. Carrera and his victorious men entered again in San Luis.

The death of Colonel Moron spread the alarm that came up to the Director of Chile O'Higgins who fearful of the danger that Carrera meant for his government, sent means to reinforce the opponents of Jose Miguel.

On August 21st, 1821, he entered with 500 men, most of them montoneros and indians, in the highlands of Cuyo. On August 31st, he attacked the forces of Mendoza with his cavalry exhausted and inferior in numbers, but he was defeated in Punta del Medano by the forces of Colonel Jose Albino Gutierrez, and he withdraw to Jacolí, and in the retire, he is betrayed by the cordobés Commander Manuel Arias and the Commanders Moya, Fuentes, Incháusti and other officers and soldiers of Carrera, that captured him, and was taken together with officers and soldiers who had been loyals, in Mendoza, where Tomas Godoy Cruz was governor, friend of San Martin and O'Higgins.

On September 4th, 1821, after a brief trial, Carrera was sentenced to death together with Colonel Felipe Alvarez, Jose Maria Benavente and the soldier Monroy, in the square of Mendoza.

When it was opened the door of the prison of Carrera on the 4th in the morning, he was notified that as soon as he were confessed, he would be shot. Fray Benito Lamas, the same that confessed his brothers, was designated to help him in his last hour.

Carrera took a piece of paper and wrote some lines of farewell for his wife that was pregnant and for his four daughters: Javiera, Rosa, Josefa and Luisa.

Upon seeing the friar, he at once understood that he didn't have time to end the letter that was more or less saying: *"At this moment, they are going to shoot me, I recommend my wife and my children, including the one who's coming to Martinez so that they be sent to the United States for their education"* when without being able to end, he charged friar Benito that he send don Francisco Martinez Matta the letter, the friar promised to do so, but the officer that entered the jail took the letter, and this never was returned to friar Benito, who could not fulfil his promise.

Carrera started complaining about the injustice of his enemies: Jose de San Martin, Bernardo O'Higgins, Tobirio Luzuriaga, etc., Friar Benito said to him that it was not time but of repentance:

- The our father prayer is one of the most beautiful prayers in the Gospel in which it says: forgive us our trespasses, as we forgive those who trespass against us. You have to forgive first so that God forgives you the infinite evils that you have made. It is enough that you remain a brief moment in a regret of you blames and you will have this way my acquittal.
- Carrera completed his repentance.
- A short time after an office came announcing that it was time to go. Carrera dressed with the Hussar uniform, asked friar Benito:
- How should I go to this ceremony, with the hat on or removed?-

- Without the hat.-

And thus fall in fall, that man who carried out as politician and soldier true prodigies, walked in assurance and erect, until he came to the scaffold in which his brothers had been shot three years ago, approached the stool and with firm step and sat down serenely.

- I'm going to ask you a favor: allow me die by foot without being blindfolded and giving the orders to the shooters.-
He was not granted what he asked. Carrera said in high voice:
- I die for the freedom of my Country! Long live Chile!

José Miguel Carrera.

He died in the same scaffold than his Brothers, and like them, in the flower of his youth at the age of 35 years, without being able to carry out his gigantic purposes. He faced the death with haughtiness and fearlessness that amazed and minimized his enemies, his loyal comrade of arms Colonel don Jose Maria Benavente, whom was pardoned, accompanied him until the end.

The hate and the fear of the Argentinians toward Carrera were such that his corpse was cut into pieces, hanging his arms and the head in the trees of the roads. In this way, a countryman that forged with his sable and his great spirit an incomparable epic died.

Some time after in Mendoza a woman was crying; it was Mercedes, her great grief was not being able to have received the good-bys from the very lips of her husband, and because he could not also know his only male child named Jose Miguel.

On September 4th, 1821 at the twelve o'clock in the morning, one of the most distinguished and wretchest of the Chileans, but he was praised by notable poets.

"Prince of the roads
Beautiful as a carnation.
Heady as the wine.
It was don José Miguel.
Who was the first that said
freedom in our country,
without kings neither tyrants...?
Don José Miguel Carrera!"

Pablo Neruda.

After the execution of her husband, Mercedes was allowed to return to Chile. She married Diego Jose Benavente Bustamante, with whom she had four children. She died in Santiago at the age 54. Her son Jose Miguel Carrera Fontecilla was also shot while defending the freedom of his country, and later the son of this latter, Ignacio Carrera Pinto who died fighting as a hero, before surrending to the enemy.

Madam Javiera depressed by the circumstances was cursing the bastard Riquelme, referring to Bernardo O'Higgins for his condition of illegitimate son, Jose de San Martin, Toribio de Luzuriaga, Juan Martin de Pueyrredón, Tomas Godoy Cruz, the Larrain and the Lautarian Lodge since she considered that all of them were the promoters and the ones causing the political, social, and economic fall and worst of all, the death of her dear younger brother Luis, pampered and protected by her and her equally remembered Juan Jose and her unforgettable and very late lamented Jose Miguel.

Javiera did not want to return to Chile while his despised enemy may be in the power.

Carlos Maria de Alvear, who went to Montevideo, returned to Argentina in 1822 thanks to the so-called Law of Oblivion, and he travelled to London at the end of the following year where he had an important interview with George Canning, Foreign Secretary of England, during this interview, Alvear exposed that the United Provinces of Rio de La Plata were de facto independents and with a stable government. A few days after this interview, the English cabinet decided to recognize the independence of the United Provinces.

He was sent as plenipotentiary minister before the government of the United States, later with the same position to the recent republic of Colombia. After an extensive diplomatic career, Alvear died in New York in 1852.

CHAPTER XVII.
THE LIBERATING EXPEDITION OF PERU.

On August 10th, 1820, the Captain Delano informed the Admiral Cochrane that the transports were ready to set sail, the cargo and the provisions of the army that would liberate Peru were loaded. On the 13th of the same month, it began to be moved the corps, on the way to Valparaiso from Quillota, where San Martin had organized their training. In the morning of the 18th, it began the shipment.

The "Araucano" brig, its commander Tomas Carter and the frigate "Minerva" set sail toward Coquimbo to pick up an infantry battalion that had been formed there; later, he went to Pisco, where he reached on September 7th. Finally, the Supreme Director of the Nation, General Bernardo O'Higgins Riquelme made a powerful naval force set sail bound for Peru.

On August 20th, 1820 don Jose de San Martin departed from the port of Valparaiso as General in Chief of the United Liberating Army of Peru, in the Wessel "San Martin".

There were 4.120 men in 25 ships, of which 8 were warships and 17 transports. They all hoisted in their mast the flag of Chile.

They were distributed in two divisions: one called "Of Chile" with San Martin, who had the rank of Captain General of the Army of Chile, on the Argentinian side with the division of "The Andes" having the rank of Chief of the Staff, General Juan Gregorio de las Heras, taking as second the Venezuelan Colonel Juan Paz Castillo, the intendancy in charge of Juan Gregorio Lemos and the ammunition under the Sergeant Major Luis Beltran.

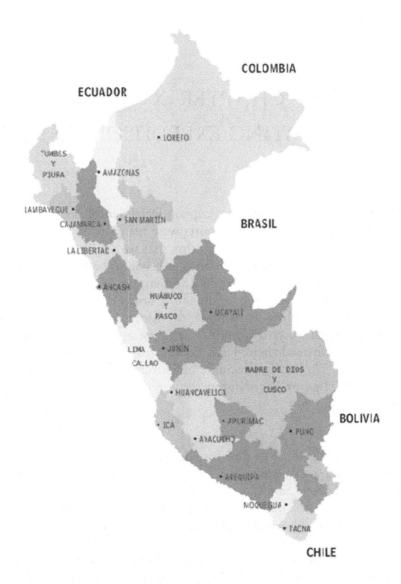

The command of the squadron fell on the Vice Admiral Lord Thomas Alexander Cochrane and the Major Guillermo Miller, that at two in the afternoon, the frigate "O'Higgins", hoisting the flag of the vice admiral, broke the march followed by the frigate "Lautaro" commanded by Martin Jorge Guise and the "Galvarino" commanded by Juan Tooker Spry.

The rearguard was closed by the ship "San Martin" with Generalissimo on board of the expedition.

The ships of war were having a crew of 1,600 men, 624 of them were foreigners, mostly Englishmen, after sailing for two weeks without suffering any setback, in the morning of September 7th they began sighting the Peruvian coasts:

The Generalissimo suggested Cochrane his intentions:

- Taking advantage of the fog of the season, which can facilitate our operations, we will land in Trujillo to the North of Lima, surrounding it and sieging the military complex formed around it.
- My General, I would like to give your highness an appropriate idea; to land to the north of Lima can deprive us from making a front attack to the city. My plans are: land in Chilca, which is the nearest place to Callao, and immediately to take possession of Lima.-
- I consider Lord Cochrane that a front attack to Lima is too risky, such an attack would cause considerable casualties, so much military as civilians, since I have known that the Viceroy has a big army, at least 20.000 soldiers and his fortifications are considered as the strongest in South America, a great stronghold with hundreds of cannons, citadels, forts, wall with many turrets, all this was informed to me by the spies I sent. I am sure that our army will not have to shoot neither a single shot, I will force Lima to surrender without fighting and thus little by little I will expect that the whole of Peru meekly surrenders.

The admiral replied:

- In fact, my calculations of a front attack to Lima were thinking that this were by surprise, not being so, my General, it will be the most suitable to land in the shores of Paracas, near the city of Pisco, and the rest of the troops will land in Huacho.-

The plan of General San Martin was diametrically opposed to that brilliant and bold of Admiral Cochrane. Difficulties between both chiefs arose, which will persist during the whole campaign.

- San Martin preferred intrigues instead of bullets, attempts instead of combats, he thus would disorganize the Viceroy's defense and he wouldn't attack without being very sure of the victory. The admiral insisted on his project without realizing the arrogance and the disrespect that it was produced in San Martin, who was convinced that the freedom of Peru was to be obtained without blood.

After sailing without having suffered any setback, late on September 7th of the same year, the liberating expedition made its entry in the bay of Paracas in the coast of Ica, where at the same time a platoon of royalist cavalry was landing, made up of 530 men under the command of Colonel Manuel Quimper, upon seeing the great number of soldiers landing, they escaped from the place.

General San Martin ordered that an infantry and cavalry battalion may establish a bridgehead in that same place and at the following day the troops were landing, occupying the town of Pisco where San Martin established his General Headquarters in a house in the center of the town.

Such an army was made up of 2.315 Argentinians, 1.800 Chileans y Peruvians, among who was standing out the Peruvian General Toribio de Luzuriaga, born in Huaraz.

The banner of The Liberating Expedition had the bottom of the national colors of Chile, red and blue, to which was added three stars symbolizing the three countries compromised in an alliance for the Peruvian independence: Chile, Argentina and Venezuela.

This landing was a great surprise for the Viceroy Joaquin de La Pezuela. It was relatively known the arrival of San Martin in Piura and this stimulated the group of patriots that began forming gatherings to interchange news which they then spread in the town.

The Viceroy Pezuela was surprised by the speed of the liberating forces and even though his troops were outnumbering them, he decided not to attack proposing to enter in negotiations with the Liberator, who accepted to carry out them.

San Martin:
- I don't look for the battle field, but when it is necessary to go through it to arrive to the temple of the peace.-

The Viceroy met with San Martin's envoys in Miraflores, near Lima: Tomas Guido, Juan Garcia, Juan Garcia del Rio and the Lieutenant Juan Antonio Alvarez de Arenales (the general's son). The Viceroy's commissioners were: the sailor Capaz, the count of Villar del Fuente and

Hipolito Unanue. They agreed on an armistice on September 20th and tried to reach an agreement without coming to it. San Martin proposed the previous recognition of the Independence, and the desire to crown a Spanish prince as king of Peru; but the Viceroy was loyal to the absolutist monarch Fernando VII.

The information was given to San Martin by one of his Spies in the capital, hidden under the pseudonym of "Aristipo Emero", it said the following: *"Those of the high class, although they wish the independence; however, they will not want to give a step to second it; since, they have their fathers like employees or they are in the majorat system or they are landowners, etc., so they are not interested in changing their present political system, because they live comfortably off under this current government. Those of the middle class that are a lot of them, their patriotism only serves to spread news, copy papers, issue proclamations, raise many lies that inconvenience the government and no more.*

Those of the low class that are part of this people, they don't serve to do anything and they are not even capable of any revolution. In a word: you are not to expect any movement that helps those of the protective army of this capital, because there is indolence in it, a misery, a laxity and an absolute lack of heroism and of general republican virtues, that nobody will protest even though they see one or two hundred patriots going into the scaffold".

San Martin was following the whole campaign plan provided by Jose de La Riva-Agüero y Sanchez Boquete, descendant of an ancient and very noble family from Lima and Spain. Riva-Agüero under the command of General La Serna, making use of persuasions and other means, introduced the desertion into the royalist troops and was in contact with many agents in the very same centres of the Spanish government. Many of those that deserted were led by his agents through devious paths until being incorporated into the guerrillas of the independents. Riva-Agüero also contributed to produce the division and the disagreement among the very same Spanish generals and introduced into the General Headquarters and in the army double spies. He sent medicines to the independentists in Huacho and Pativilca.

On October 5th San Martin decided to begin hostilities, and on October 21st in Pisco he issued a decree, establishing the first flag and the first coat of arms of the independent Peru.

On October 21st the Liberating expedition went on board bound for the North, in view that Pisco was not a strategic place, and on November

12th they landed in the shores of Huacho, occupying the town of Huaura that was declared San Martin's General Headquarters.

He ordered that General Juan Antonio Alvarez de Arenales from Ica, with a division of 1.000 men may penetrate into the highlands, he sustained actions in Palpa, Nazca, Acarí against the Colonel from Lima Manuel Quimper, who had been appointed as General Commander of the South Coast of Peru on February 9th, 1820 by the Viceroy Pezuela, sending a militia of 400 men in the defense of Pisco. Quimper and his men withdrew and followed the way of the South toward Ica in order to seize it.

In Palpa, militiamen of Colonel Quimper were reached by an independentist outpost of Colonel Tomas Guido in charge of 80 mounted chasseurs and some others from the mounted infantry. Two royalist companies passed to the Patriots and the rest was dispersed.

In Nazca, another outpost of the liberating army made up of 250 cavalry and infantry men, under the command of Lieutenant Colonel Manuel Patricio Rojas Argerich attacked the royalist militias in the village of Nazca, taking prisoners and 200 rifles. At the following day in Acarí, Lieutenant Vicente Suarez in charge of a picket of mounted chasseurs definitively dispersed the column of Colonel Quimper, taking him prisoner and 100 ammunition charges.

Just after Arenales crossed the mountain range nearby Castrovirreyna, his division occupied the city of Huamanga on October 24th. On November 11th, it took place the seizure of the bridge of Mayoc which had been mined and was defended by a garrison of 25 men; it was carried out by the Chilean lieutenant Francisco Borja Moyano in charge of 15 mounted grenadiers aided by a montonera made up of Indians. On November 20th, it took place the combat of the slope of Jauja, Colonel Juan Lavalle with 55 cavalry men, defeated a picket of royalist cavalry to which he was pursuing from Mayor. On November 23rd, it took place the combat of Tarma, the Colonel Manuel Rojas Argerich managed to reach the Arequipa's General Juan Montenegro in charge of a column of 630 militiamen, retreating to the North, dispersing it totally and taking prisoners, included the General, six cannons, 500 fusiliers and 50.000 cartridges.

Upon Alvarez de Arenales arriving at Cerro de Pasco on December 6th, he fought and captured the Spanish Brigadier Diego O'Reilly who had a well armed division and had gone to his encounter from Lima.

All these news were reaching Piura raising great enthusiasm among the patriots and a lot of concern among the royalists with the political weakening of the Viceroy Pezuela who could not put on line of battle more than 6.000 men, and the presence of the Chilean squadron in Callao and the landing in Chancay that caused the panic in Lima and the discredit of the Viceroy.

While these actions were made, San Martin was informed about the Independence of Guayaquil on October 9th 1820, this important event obtained by the forces commanded by General Gregorio Escobedo, who put at the orders of the Liberator the emancipated city and his support.

In Pisco, a large contingent gravely got sick with malaria and Major Miller was about to die, having to be evacuated.

On September 30th, San Martin got on board again with his forces in Ancon, North of Lima, to definitively settle in Huaura and being able to cut the supplies of Lima by the North and attained, with his obsession of not fighting, after several months of hunger, diseases and miseries, that the capital would be surrendered. Thus in this place, he had a Communications with the Patriots of Trujillo, Lambayeque and Piura, and ordering that ships of war keep a strict blockade in Callao.

But with this politics, he was annihilating his own army that was decimated by the epidemics and the fatigue, dying 20 chileans every day and more than 3.000 could not sustain the rifle with their hands, all this was mining the prestige of San Martin, and hurried the uprising of the intendant of Trujillo, the marquis of Torre Tagle who declared the independence of that city on December 29th 1820, event that notably influenced in the independence of Lambayeque, Piura and Tumbes.

The situation of confusion among the Spaniards could be seen more when the royalist forces of Lima garrisoned in Anazpuquio questioned the authority of the Viceroy Joaquin de La Pezuela blaming him for the results of the military operations, and this had to give the command to the Commander in Chief of the army, don Jose de la Serna e Hinojosa on January 28th 1821, being the last viceroy.

Once installed San Martin in his camp, he is determined not to give decisive battles but weakening little by little the Spaniards.

- I want –he said- that Lima fall in my hands like a mature ear.-

From Lima, Rosa Campuzano who was the official lover of Spanish General Domingo Tristán, she corresponded with Huaura passing all the information she got from the General.

The Viceroy La Serna was also seduced by her and he courted her. With innocent questions among the thread sheets, after each encounter she presented a detailed report to the Patriots.

San Martin had already heard from her since he was in Pisco, but he didn't know her personally.

The Spaniards of Viceroy Pezuela, expelled from the capital, on being weakened they withdrew reorganizing their forces in the highlands, but the former viceroy on taking their troops to the highlands, he exposed them to Malaria. Fortunately, the intelligent General Arenales had already left the highland.

Lord Cochrane and Miller controlled the Southern coast of Peru, carried out expeditions and military operations, landing troops from Chincha to Arica, organizing guerrillas like the montoneras. At the beginning of May, the contingent that did not have to be evacuated to Huacho by illness arrived in Arica, going ashore the Commander Miguel Soles to demand the surrender to the Royalist, which was rejected by them. On the following night the commodore William Miller and his troops plundered it uncontrollably, the royalists joined the Chileans leaving Arica helpless; some tried to land in Quiani cove but they made a mistake arriving to the cliffs more to the South where they almost drowned. In the battle of Mirave in the South of Peru, close to the Pacific Ocean, it was located at the foot of the plateau of the Titicaca in a volcanic zone the battalion Nro. 4 of Chile, under the command of the Colonel Pedro Arriaga, they fought in several battles, but the most glorious event occurred in the battle of Mirave that they defeated the Royalists, whereas San Martin called them as the "Braves of Mirave".

In a bold and valiant incursion Cochrane demonstrated his determination and set sail towards Callao when it had not yet been conquered, it was the shelter of the Spanish frigate "Esmeralda" and of other small ships. Lord Cochrane and English Captain Guise during the night, they removed from his squadron two divisions of boats with the oars covered with cloth to diminish the noise, manned by 280 men who unexpectedly fell down assaulting the ship, after a tough combat commanded by Admiral Cochrane in person, which was perhaps his most spectacular event. They seized the crew, they let go the mooring ropes and took from Callao the "Esmeralda", the jewel of the Spaniards.

Months later, the Spanish sailor Manuel Abreu came to Lima, the capital of the viceroyalty, when it was besieged by the Patriots Forces, he was sent by Spain to execute negotiations with the Patriots holding a meeting with San Martin. In Punchauca conference on June 5th, 1821, San Martin proposed the independence of America, and a Bourbon prince like a king of Perú but independent of Spain. The Viceroy proposed loyalty to the King of Spain, with those conditions, the conference failed. On February, 1821 dissatisfaction was so great that several officers and crew of the Chilean navy for lack of payment, clothing and other necessities, that the Captains Guise and Spry left the chilean service and were hired by San Martin to form a Peruvian Squadron.

San Martin, having known the position of the royalist and finished the efforts to achieve a political victory to avoid further confrontation, decided to realize the preparations for the occupation of Lima. The situation for the royalist was so disastrous, the city of Lima lived in a climate of insecurity and fear for the presence of the patriot forces established at the north of the viceregal capital, through the port of Callao that was closed and besieged by the patriots ships of Cochrane, by the constant incursions and harassment of montonera guerrillas that were near Lima, the patriot victories of General Alvarez in the central highlands, food shortages, infectious diseases such as plague, all these events forced Viceroy La Serna evacuate Lima. In the first days of July, 1821 the Spanish General Jose de Canterac left the city with the troops, and on July, 6th in the morning Viceroy La Serna, did the same with the other part of the royalist army with direction to the highland, San Martin didn't take advantage to give a blow to the Spanish forces and destroyed the viceregal army, in spite the urgings of Cochrane and other officers. This lack of decision of San Martin did that Spanish troops would regroup in the Mantaro Valley. Although the most persistent rumors about the negative of San Martin to attack, was that he hoped to join the Royalist army with him so he can consolidate the Peruvian independence and ensure an independent throne for Spain; the gossips said, that this throne was the ambitious of him. La Serna moved to Cuzco, he managed to take the first printing and began to print the newspaper "El Depositario", which became famous in Upper Peru, accompanied with the troops of the Spanish General Jose de Canterac, leaving the city under the command of the Creole Marquis Montemira; in the Real Felipe fortress of Callao a bulk of the army under the command of the Spanish Field Marshall Don Jose de La Mar, that were resisting besieged in the fortress. General Las Heras executed an assault but it was rejected. On July 9th a squadron of horse grenadiers made their entry in Lima, in order to recognize the terrain and the situation of the city, there was a climate of fear, especially by the rich Creoles, who feared that upon not there being a Spanish army that means order and protection for their lives and properties, the uprising and attack of the slaves and of the montoneros looting their property, in this situation, they didn't hesitate in accepting the patriot forces and the sign of the Independence of Peru, prevailing their interests although many were followers to the Spaniards. On July 10th, 1821 the Liberator General San Martin entered to the city of Lima, trying to go unnoticed, but his presence was discovered by people who quickly took to the streets, hailing him incessantly, the fortress of Callao was besieged by the patriot forces.

The elite of Lima and San Martin agreed to chair a great ceremony in Lima on Saturday July 28th, 1821 to proclaim in the Main Square the Independence and San Martin was named "Protector of Peru" That day, at midmorning a crowd of neighbors crowded together into the Square to see the Liberator with the red and white flag in his hands and pronouncing a speech: " Peru is from this moment Free and Independent, for the general will of the people and for the justice of its cause that God defends "Long live the Mother Country!" "Long live the freedom!". "Long live the Independence!"

The same act was repeated in the other three places of Lima; Plazoleta de La Merced, Plaza de la Inquisición and Plaza de Santa Ana
At night in the Council the mayor Don Isidro de Cortazar y Abarca organized a party in honor of Don José de San Martín. The reception was celebrated at the Town Hall, where the Generalissimo wearing a sumptuous dress uniform with gold palms, very arrogant walked through the various rooms, greeting and receiving congratulations everywhere, saw a lady surrounded by officers that courted her and asked her to dance. San Martin was delighted by the beauty of her face and her thin body, dressed in an elegant embroidered velvet cleavage dress, looking great with her light skin shoulders. San Martin asked his assistant from Lima: - Who is that lady in the blue dress surrounded by gentlemen officers? "My General, that lady is Rosa Campuzano, she is collaborating intelligently with the Patriot band.-
The General approached the lady, greeted her with much interest:
- Miss Campuzano, since my being in Huaura I know of you and I know and I admired your merits in favor of the separatist movement, even with risk of your life.-

- Yes, General San Martín, I have run great risks, it has been not so long ago, a clandestine letter intercepted in which I was mentioned, and thus I was captured for a few days, but the influence of bribes and powerful friends managed to liberate me. My endeavors in achieving the independence Mr. General would had been even more, if I have known you before.-

    - I'm honored by your words, are you from Lima?

- No your highness, I'm from Guayaquil, I came to Lima three years ago and I settled down in the street of San Marcelo, where I prepared my gatherings frequented by the most prominent people, from whom I'm always getting information. I have also rented a big house where I hid several royalist officers who were defecting and then I helped them to pass into your camp in Huaura.-

They exchanged some words and San Martin finally invited her to dance. They opened the dance with a waltz; the General fell in love with Rosa at first sight.

The following day, Sunday July 29th San Martin organized another dance to return the attention of the Council, this time in the magnificent living rooms of the Viceroys' Palace San Martin from the bottom of the living room, on foot, looked around for Rosa, finally he found her talking with some ladies; she dressed a white organza dress with deep cleavage, she was wearing a chignon hairstyle that were adorned with flowers, she was very beautiful. He invited her to dance a contradance, the eyes of the guayaquileña and her smiling lost the General mind for the Campuzano.

Rosa, introduced him to her great friend Manuela Sáenz, lover of Simón Bolívar, called her "the Liberator"

- Excellency, I will introduce my best friend Manuelita Sáenz, recently arrived from Guayaquil, which is the reason we fraternized a lot. -

San Martin with a reverence made a gesture of kissing her hand.

- Madam Saenz, I throw myself at your feet-

San Martin was very careful in his loving relationship with Rosa; he was never seen in public with her, when he could come to see her they talked a lot. San Martin commented:

- Lima is beautiful, it concentrates the best of America; the Viceroy's Palace, the Archbishopric, the Real Audience and the University, it is a city of splendors. -

- Certainly, it is a center of palaces and expensive residences, the city shines with the gold of the children of the Sun. -

- My sweet Rosita, with that beautiful sentence that you have pronounced, you have given me the idea of creating the Order of the Sun, to condecorate the women that are participating actively in the cause of the emancipation. -

- I will tell you my darling José that all that glistens is not gold in this city, as well as they concentrate the most exquisite goods, the hidden lusts are administered, I will admit you that I was who convinced the realistic General Domingo Tristán so that he went to the patriot band

The Protector looked at her while she was speaking, it was not common in that time women with cleverly thoughts

- José, ¿Did you have other lover affairs outside your marriage? I suppose you are married. -

- Of course, I am married and I have a daughter. Soon after my marriage, during a travel around I did against the realists settled down in Montevideo, in my way to Tucumán, I met a young newlywed lady named Juana Rosa, I was 34 years old and in spite of her youth she was only 18 years old, we had an openly love affair during some time. -

-Your wife, where is she?

Suddenly Jose, as if he awakened from a dream, his eagle eyes grew sad, Rosa understood that the eye of him that has seen her shall not see her, then he turned to the window and murmured:

- It has been so long time that I don't have received news from my sweet Remedios, how she will be? -

Rosa that felt predilection for that man, caught his hand caressed them and dedicated him a sweet smile.

José a little melancholic commented:

- Many times I think, it is worth the trouble of all my labor, it must not be better to be peacefully in Buenos Aires, next to Remedios and my daughter Merceditas to whom I know very little? It's great the blame's feeling that take hold on me everyday, however I shall stand up with a fierce countenance, it is only an external strength; and this stomachache that is killing me and forces me in the use of the opium, leaving me without being able to think with integrity and clarity.

- I think José that your use of opium is a bad habit, you are exceeding the use of it, you should endure your pain it's an apparent painkiller but at the same time it damages your health.-

On August 4th, 1821, at the request of Council's delegation of Lima and by suggestion of the members of the Lautarian Lodge, San Martin accepted to be named Protector of Peru and head of the Government. He designated ministers: in The Treasury was the Peruvian Unanue, in Foreign Relation was Garcia del Río, in the Ministry of War and Marine was Monteagudo. The political reforms were very important; it was founded the National Library, it was established the freedom of press, the tortures and the censorship were abolished, the minister Monteagudo favored the expropriation of the fortunes of the Spaniards enemies of the revolution, and some even were shot.

While San Martin was organizing the new government in Lima, the Royalists that had been grouped in the highlands of the Mantaro valley in the city of Jauja, in the early days of September, they were ready to launch an offensive with the 3.500 infantrymen and 900 cavalrymen under the command of the Spanish General Canterac who advanced towards Lima and on September 9th, he reached near the camp of San Martin on the way to Arequipa forcing the march in front of the patriot camp, but none of patriots shot them, nor they became disturbed, even though the officers and Cochrane himself, at seeing how the royalists continued their march, were requesting San Martin that he attacked cutting their march and that he didn't allow them to continue on their way to Callao, since Canterac's objective was to join the defenders of Callao and supply them with armaments.

San Martin was looking forward to the movements of the royalists that entered in Callao, because he knew that there were no provisions in the fortress for more than three days, therefore he didn't want to risk the life of his soldiers, since the enemy would have to abandon the fortress for lack of foods. It was this way, Canterac had to abandon Callao on September 16th, leaving most of his artillery, and he went to the North, with the idea of getting provisions and return, but half of his forces deserted during the march, and being pursued by the patriot General patriot Las Heras, he returned to Jauja with his army, making him impossible his immediate return to Callao. On September 21st, General La Mar surrendered, passing to the patriot side and the Peruvian flag waved in the towers of Callao.

Meanwhile the fortress surrendered, there were disagreements between Cochrane and San Martin, due to a series of financial problems since the General had not entered the salaries of the crew.

- My General, between my officers and the chilean sailors it has become popular the idea that the army has taken hold of great reserve of Money, therefore, the squadron is unfairly suffering deprivations. When we hired them, they were not willing to be enlisted, and both of us persuaded them, at last, by a Joint declaration by you and me, in which we guaranteed them the payment of their salaries and also the payment of an extra year when the army entered Lima._ - As you know my Lord, that the crew's wages aren't under my command, and I have never committed to pay the amount; therefore I am not obliged to do it, the debt is of Chile of which Government hired the sailors, I won't recognize any labor law to demand for overdue payment. -

I will tell you, my General San Martin, that the Chilean square is getting worse and worse, as well as your prestige and popularity are diminishing at the same time; it must be of the great dissatisfaction produced by your politics of caution to strike a death blow to the enemy. -

- Cochrane was informed that the minted treasure and without mint, belonging to the government, was taken out from Lima and placed on board transports that were in Ancón, this weighed anchor toward that place, and he appropriated of the treasure, paying with it to his crew that were ready to leave the squad and to go to the service of Peru. Cochrane returned to Valparaíso for to pay attention to a property in Quintero that was given to him and San Martín denied it now

On April 7th, 1822 , the commander in chief of the Royalist Armies General Canterac coming from Jauja, was sent by the Viceroy La Serna to intercept the troops of General Tristan that were withdrawing from Ica to Pisco in direction to Lima, trying to avoid the confrontation with the forces of General Valdes that had occupied Arequipa. Meanwhile, due to the dire situation in Chile, the squadron was dismantled.

Cochrane instead of returning to Chile, continued making incursions like corsair leaving in search of the two last frigates of the Spanish Navy in the Pacific "La Prueba and the "Venganza". These ships blocked the port of Guayaquil on December, 1821. General La Mar who, after the rendition of Callao, had passed to the troops of San Martin, was in that port. La Mar convinced the Spanish Captains of the two ships that it was better to surrender, because otherwise they would fall into the hands of privateer Cochrane that was looking for them in the Pacific, being able to convince them, and two captains surrendered at the beginning of 1822. These were the last Spanish ships in the South Pacific. The frigate "Prueba" was renamed as the "Protector" it thus began the Peruvian navy, being its first Commander the Admiral Blanco Encalada.

Cochrane was the last privateer of Chile, and he became the worst enemy of San Martin

The dissatisfaction continued between the army, since the troops and the Chilean officers were removed and the argentine and the Peruvian officers were preferred, even though San Martin to appease this dissatisfaction, tried to promote General Las Heras to a higher rank, but he resigned and on being upset her returned to Chile.

At the beginning of 1822 there were two Royalist armies of relevance in South America; those who dominated Quito under the command of General Aymerich, and those of Peru commanded by General Canterac.

The operation was carried out during the night, at about one in the morning the royalist forces that were hidden in the brambles occupied the surroundings of Ica near the royal path from Lima. The royalist infantry was formed in line to the right of the road, and its cavalry was forming part in line and part in column by the flanks. The patriot cavalry of Lancers of Peru who were coming in support of General Tristan from Chincha, most of them perished on the dawn of the 8th day cut off by the royalist cavalry of the Dragoons of Peru. The outcome of the battle of Ica was the royalist tactical victory, and the destruction of the division of General Tristan who was taken prisoner, and Colonel Santiago Aldunate that was severely wounded and was also taken prisoner, they took prisoners some other 50 officers, 1.000 troopers and the capture of the deposit of 4.000 rifles.

Colonel Agustin Gamarra and other 125 officers and soldiers managed to escape.

General Canterac regrouped his forces again in Jauja, ordering Colonel Loriga to occupy Pisco and General Carratalá to stay as garrison in Ica.

Simon Bolivar had named General Antonio Jose de Sucre as the Commander of the troops of the South, who got on board bound for Guayaquil on May, 1821. With this army, he advanced towards Quito, but he was stopped by the royalists in Bomboná.

General Sucre requested support from Peru in order to be able to undertake a new campaign over Quito. San Martin from Lima detached an auxiliary division under the command of General Andres de Santa Cruz with 1.500 men formed by the Grenadiers of the Andes, commanded by Félix Olazabal and a corps of cavalry under the command of Juan Lavalle. The army of Colombia joined the combined forces of Argentinians, Chileans and Peruvians.

San Martin knew that his army was not enough to defeat the Spaniards, it was necessary the union of the patriot forces of the North and of South to expel the royalists from the Upper Peru (Bolivia).

On October 21st, San Martin decreed to create the flag of Independent Peru; this one had two colors with rectangular fields and there was the shield of the country in the vertices.

That same year shortly after proclaiming the Independence, San Martin, in his capacity of Protector of Peru enacted the Provisional Statute that should rule the liberated territory of the Spanish domination. This statute created a Council of State with the characteristic functions of a Legislative Power that is why San Martin should consult this Council the appointment of Peruvian representatives abroad, International diplomatic or commercial treaties.

The only positions that could be freely granted in the Council were given to the counts del Valle Oselle y de La Vega del Ren and the marquises of Torre Tagle y Torre Velarde. In the Town Hall, the marquises of Santa Maria de Pacoyán, de Casa Muños y de Corpa and the counts of Vega del Ren and of Casa Saavedra; in the Patriot Society the marquises of Torre Tagle and del Valle Oselle and the counts of Torre Velarde, de Casa Saavedra and de Villar de Fuentes, in addition to others in The

University, they could contribute to San Martin's plans of establishing a monarchy supported by The Patriot Society, publishing in the newspaper "The Sun of Peru" a literary quote from the epic poem The Iliad: "*It is no good that many order, only one may rule, there should be only one king*".

On January 11th, 1822 San Martin instituted by decree the Order of the Sun. They were chosen one hundred and twelve laywoman ladies and thirty two nun the most notable of the thirteen monasteries of Lima that were honored with the "Women Knight of the Order of the Sun"

Among the first one there were the countesses of San Isidro and de La Vega and the marchionesses of Torre Tagle, Casa Boza, Castellón and Casa Muños, as well as Rosa Campuzano and Manuela Saenz they were invested with bicolor band, White and red characteristics distinguishing the female knights with the inscription in golden letters:

"To the patriotism of the most sensitive"

The Independence had a very high cost for the country. The separation from Spain didn't bring, as the liberals waited, the commercial growth when the mercantile restrictions were eliminated. The production decreased, the old markets as the Upper Peru, Chile and Quito were lost, the credit was scarce and it took time to recover the per capita income.

The most important revenues with which could count on the new government were the customs revenues, the indian tax and the war taxes which were raised by the caudillos, the main expense that they had was the internal one, that is to say, to guarantee their stay in power. The foreign credit was suspended.

The agriculture, activity to which most of the population was devoted, was in crisis, since many estates had been destroyed by the wars; another problem that the landowners had was the shortage of credit, they had to resort, whenever they could, to the money lender merchants or lend among themselves, those loans were very expensive having to pay interests about 18-24% per year compared to the 4-6% of the census during the Viceroyalty.

The landowners due to their economic shortage had to take shelter with the caudillos with their montoneras to defend their interests. The "caudillismo" turned into an enterprise whose target was the conquest of the political power, i.e., the state was the booty to be distributed.

The British traders took advantage of the Independence and flooded the Peruvian and Chilean markets with their goods, but the market was saturated and the imports were stagnated. The British lost one million sterling pounds in their first venture in the market with Peru and many of them went bankrupt. Only the experienced a stable business firms such as La Casa Gibss & Sons, settled down long before the independence, survived.

Only Arequipa and the Southern highland had a good regional economy due to the sheep wool exports to the British markets by the port of Islay. This region and its élite developed independently and very often in opposition to Lima.

Between the Liberator and San Martin, there was an exchange of correspondence about the military issue. On June 17th, 1822 Bolívar wrote:

"I have the biggest satisfaction in announcing to your Highness that the war of Colombia is finished, and that its army is soon to go wherever its brothers may call him, and very particularly to the motherland of our southern neighbors to whom we should prefer as the first friends and brothers of weapons for so many titles."

In a visit of the Protector to Rosa in The Magdalena country house, he told her several of his plans:

- I have received a letter from Bolívar the Liberator, and for what he tells me he is decided to undertake campaign to the South of Peru, I am willing to be under his control to unite our forces, he also has more impulse and health than me to continue this fight. -
- But, Jose, come on! You are still young, resolved and valiant, with clear goals to face by yourself in this fight. You are a heck of a soldier And with respect to that he has more impulse, it can be, for what his great friend and lover Manolita Sáenz has told me, besides being egocentric he is eccentric, because every time that they see each other, she has to get dressed as a soldier and with the loose hair until the waist, and in that of being more healthy than you, we will leave it, because he is tuberculous, therefore, it comes from there that thinness, that he is indeed very bold and good politician, and he is supported by his great General Antonio José de Sucre that solves him many problems. -

- I thank your good intentions. I always thought that I had consecrated myself ardently to the cause of the revolution, neither my health nor any sacrifice would it be capable of frightening me, but political and personal pressures put me on the edge of the desolation, I am not myself a while ago. The great defeat that we have suffered in Ica, the Admiral Cochrane that has rebelled against me, Benavides, in whom I placed trust, has turned his back, only my good friend O'Higgins supports me, although he is also going through a bad moment in his presidency, he has confidentially told me that he has the same intentions than me of abdicating. It is impossible to be happy while I witness the evils that afflict the unfortunate America. In my bad or good providences, I have never taken into consideration my own person but only the object of the good and independence of our motherland. The evils of the war have always afflicted me, because I never looked for the victory to satisfy private aims. -

Rosa listened to him, but she thought that that sacrifice for anything, was not another thing that the personal satisfaction and the achievement of being the Protector and Liberator, it was already enough with that.
-   If you are the main character, a personal satisfaction always exists, and I believe that it is this way, in spite of your humility. -

-   I have thought, when all this finishes to retire to Buenos Aires, although I am not sure of being able to have peace there, because surely my enemy Bernardino Rivadavia will conspire against my person, since he hates me from the revolution of 1812 in that I was part of the deprivation of him and of its colleagues and I established the Second Triumvirate, cutting him its political career and its possibility of governing. -
Heart-stricken Rosa commented:
-   And me? I know that I will never see you again. Maybe I will marry some of my pretenders, although I will always remind you.

San Martin requested Bolívar to send him the replacement of the auxiliary division sent to General Sucre, because he needed soldiers to continue the war and to recover Guayaquil for Peru.
Bolívar when it had to be with the replacement of the soldiers, he answered him that it should be provided from Government to Government: on facilitating their army to finish the campaign of Peru, he opposed his character of President of Colombia that prevented him to leave the territory of the Republic.

Simon Bolívar had the intention of undertaking the campaign to the South from Guayaquil, entering in this city on July 11th 1822 and the following day he incorporated the province to Colombia. San Martin, upon having knowledge of this plan, decided to interview with the Liberator in this city and he undertook the trip, delegating the political control in the marquis of Torre Tagle. San Martin no longer had forces to open a new campaign against the Spaniards, it was necessary to gather the two units. He was going to offer him the Command Chief of both armies, being under Bolivar's orders.

He went on board from Callao toward the port of Guayaquil in the schooner "Macedonia" arriving on July 25th in the morning.

The Liberator offered him his hospitality and he lodged him in a splendid residence where they offered him a warm greeting. When Bolívar was presented in the mansion he told him:

- Welcome to The Great Colombia! -

San Martin at once understood that Bolívar had been advanced; he had taken the independent republic of Guayaquil, for Colombia.

On the 27th day San Martin embarked his baggage announcing that he would leave that same night. At one in the afternoon he went to Bolívar's residence and they had a conference during four hours behind closed door without witness.

For the documents of the General Archive of The Nation, they allow to lay down that none of the liberators was satisfied with the other one. San Martin sought the union of the armies of the South and of the North to end the war. He understood that to Bolívar their person hindered him, and the armies of Colombia would not pass to Peru while he may be there.

General San Martin began the conference:

- Peru is the only battle field that is left in the America, and in it they should meet those that want to obtain the honors of the last victory. -
- If, to pass Peru, making the maximum effort, I will only be able to come off that is to say of three battalions, of a total of 1070 soldiers. -
- This interview, my General Bolívar, is not what you promised me in your letter for the prompt termination of the war, I consider

insufficient this aid. My offer of serving under your orders with the forces to my command is sincere, although unfortunately, I am very closely convinced that my person is embarrassing you. -

- My General San Martin, I am for sure my troops are enough to annihilate the few royalists. General Sucre has won the battle of Bamba River, entering winner in Quito. With this victory, the North of America of the South is free of royalists, and then we can unite our forces to finish the war that I'm in charge of in Peru.-

- You don't make yourselves illusions General Bolívar. The news that you have about the royalist forces are misleading, the general Canterac, Valdés, Monet and some other military , directed by the General La Serna, they amount to in the Upper and Low Peru more than 19.000 veterans in The Highlands, and in the provinces of the South that can meet in the period of two months. This people fight for a way of life that they know for more than 300 years which is the monarchy, and it will be very difficult to make them change, my proposal is to establish a constitutional monarchy with a Spanish prince, but untied from Spain. -

- My good friend San Martin, my armies are not fighting to establish a monarchy that will be as the one that there has been up to now, at the end we fight to get an American republic, therefore, the rest doesn't interest me. -

- I presume that the armies of Colombia won't pass to Peru while I am there; in short General, my party is irrevocably taken. I have summoned the first Congress of Peru, and the following day of their installation I will go on board for Chile convinced that my presence is the obstacle that prevents you to come to Peru with the army of your command. -

Finished the interview, they met in the banquet room where they sat down one next to the other one. Bolívar toasted:
- A toast for the two bigger men from the America of the South: the General San Martin and Me! -
San Martin answered:
- A toast for the soon ending of the war; for the organization of the different Republics of the continent and for the health of the Liberator of Colombia! –

Next, it began the dance and the fun. A very young widow was introduced to San Martin, Madam Carmen Miron y Alayon, who in the din of the party and the champagne invited him to spend the night in her house.

- General San Martin, I know that you have come here to make political decisions, but you can also make decisions for your private life, a man of arms is to have a woman capable of accompanying him in his nights of solitude.-
- Madam, I'm a married man, I don't forget that, but what I'm going to do!, my wife is the one who suffers my prolonged absences, I'm a military man and the country is calling me so that I may have the honor of defending it, but hell! it is also calling to have once in a while the company of some happy lady.-

San Martin left the party that had continued in the widow's house and the following day at one in the afternoon he got on board to Callao.

It was often said that from that night of frenzy his illegitimate son Joaquin Miguel Miron y Alayon was born.

While San Martin has having a conference with Bolivar in Guayaquil, in Peru the minister of Foreign Relations Bernardo Monteagudo and Joaquin Mosquera plenipotentiary minister for Colombia, signed in Lima on July 6th the Treaty of Union, Alliance and Firm and Perpetual Confederacy between Peru and Colombia by which both states were questioning the limits of their respective territories, as Joaquin Mosquera did not know the Royal Decree of 1802, limiting themselves to indicate the demarcation of the precise limits. The text was read as follows: "Both parties will recognize as limits of their respective territories, the same ones they had in the year 1809 the former Viceroyalties of Peru and Nueva Granada, from the river mouth of the Tumbes River to the Pacific Ocean up to the territory of Brazil".

The polemic Bernardo Monteagudo, added in his laws and ordinances that on having begun any public act they should not say "long live to the Mother Land" but "Long Liver Peru", and in that phrase, which discussion would take the whole morning, cost Peru in diets of that day more than 500 pesos. The relevance of the word "mother land" by the congressmen was not that of the Jacobin and visionary Monteagudo, neither that of Bolivar the Caudillo, it was an idea of the nationalism, title of pride of the isolation of Peru and of the excessive limitation of his country.

The most conservatist parties launch a coup against Monteagudo, the uprising was supported by the Council of Lima obtaining the dismissal and deportation of the minister to Guayaquil, where Bolivar incorporated him to his close friends circle and trusted him the preparations of the Congress in Panama in order to concrete the Latin American Unity

On September 20th, it was inaugurated the first Constituent Congress of Peru. San Martin resigned the military and political control and delivered the title of Protector. After giving a farewell speech he withdrew, and the Congress elected president chosen by the people to Jose Riva Agüero, marquis of Monte Alegre de Aulestia. He was the first Peruvian head of state to take the title of "President of the Republic".

The Congress gathered in extraordinary session that night granted San Martin the title of "Founder of the Freedom of Peru" and assigned him the same life pension that Washington had.
At the end of the session, he got on board the Brig. "Belgrano", he returned alone, bound for Valparaiso, from where he had left with all the honors, illusions and courage, at the head of his army two years one month and twelve days ago.
Most of the troops of San Martin's Liberating Army stayed in Peru and they were incorporated into the army of General Simon Bolivar that as soon as he came to this country, the Congress entrusted him with dictatorial Powers, both in political and military order, which allowed him to dominate the anarchy that was beginning to be felt in the old viceroyalty, and continue the fight against the royalists.

In Santiago, General Freire had turned into San Martin's worst enemy. In a conversation sustained between Freire and Cochrane, another Protector's great enemy, they were commenting:

- San Martin returns alone, and without having hardly fought, the only thing that he ambitioned was to proclaim himself monarch of Peru, and in order to prepare the ground, he kept the titles of nobility and the viceregal pomp.-
To what Freire replied:
- It will be considered hateful and suspicious that man's residence in any condition of Chile. He may go to be happy elsewhere, since it is so expensive his protection for the unfortunate ones.-

- Mr. Freire, for my part and that of the carrerinos, we will request this very day to O'Higgins that a prosecution may be opened against San Martin.-

His good friend O'Higgins refused to do so, and asked General Prieto to take San Martin to the capital with a escort of honor.

Shortly after settling down in Santiago, some typhoid fevers attacked him and he was on the brink of death during two months.

In a visit that O'Higgins made to him, he mentioned that he had serious political problems in his position of Supreme Director, that he saw his abdication not very far away. He advised San Martin that in order to avoid rebuffs and humiliations he should go out of the country.

San Martin went to Mendoza by riding on horseback the same journey the he did when he crossed the Andes with his Army of the Andes, but when he arrived he could hardly remain upright on his horse, they wanted to help him with a stretch but his General's pride didn't allow them, he didn't want that they saw him coming in such a condition, as best as he could, he stayed on the horse until arriving in a small farm which had been granted to him during his stay as Governor.

His wife died on August 3rd, 1823 at the age of 25. He left for Buenos Aires in order to take charge of his daughter Mercedes.

He arrived in the city on December 4th and stay there until February 10th, 1824, since due to hostilities found in the city that invited him to a voluntary exile, he got on board with his daughter toward France, settling down in Boulogne-sur-Mer, where he died in 1850, after having lived a modest old age. His good friend Bernardo O'Higgins wrote to him until his own death in 1842.

Meanwhile in Europe, the member countries of the Holy Alliance: France, Austria, Prussia and Russia, got together in Verona on November 22nd, 1822 in order to return the absolutist regime government to Spain. On April 7th, 1823, the "One hundred thousand sons of St. Louis" French Army, upon the request of the very same Fernando VII, entered in Cadiz, restoring Fernando VII to the throne and recover his domains in America. This caused the concern of the american countries that saw a threat for their freedom recently obtained, since the absolutist Spain would reconquer its former possessions, but he opposition of the English minister George Canning ruined those aspirations, because he considered that in fact these countries were independent.

The government of the president of the United States James Monroe, in the Congress of the United State on December 2nd 1823, advocated "The Monroe Doctrine", authored by John Quincy Adams, that was attributed to James Monroe and suggested by the British Foreign Secretary George Canning who proposed a Joint Anglo-American action against any possible intervention of the Holy Alliance in Spanish America.

Jefferson and Madison, non official advisors to President Monroe, expressed in favor of cooperation with the Britons.

But the Secretary of State John Quincy Adams declared:

"The american continents will not be considered from now on as colonization fields by the European Powers. The United States will not tolerate any intervention or interference from the European powers in America".

"America for the Americans", it was giving support to the South American countries before any attempt of invasion on the part of the Holy Alliance.

This allusion was mainly directed against England and especially against the plans that the Britons had as far as Cuba is concerned.

These declarations caused sensation in Europe, because it was known that England was behind everything, since the secretary Canning was signing trade agreements with the states of Spanish America without having been recognized their independence.

However, in spite of the "America for the Americans", European interventions took place in american matters as for example the Spanish occupation of the Dominican Republic between 1861 and 1865, the blockade of French ships in the Argentinian ports between 1839 and 1840, the establishing of England on the coast of Mosquitia, in Nicaragua.

The doctrine was later on interpreted in diverse ways, as the Roosevelt Corollary that stated that if an American country located under the influence of the USA threatened or imperilled the Rights or properties of citizens or US enterprises, the government of the US was forced to intervene in the internal affairs of the country to arrange this, protecting the rights and the assets of its citizens and their enterprises. This Corollary supposed, in fact, a carte Blanche for the intervention of the US in Latin America and the Caribbean.

During the ephemeral government of Riva Agüero, the royalist troops penetrated in Lima and got the Government's retreat, and their later royalist installation in the port of Callao. In view of this situation, the President Riva Agüero lost the support of the Congress of Lima that wanted the arrival to the country of Simon Bolívar. The President was overthrown by the General Antonio José de Sucre that in turn he handed over the government to the General José Bernardo de Torre Tagle until the arrival of General Simon Bolívar, to which the Congress of the Peru requested him to consolidate the independence and it granted him full necessary powers.

Riva Agüero, before such a situation, was stationed in Trujillo and he began secret negotiations with the Viceroy José de La Serna to avoid the arrival of Bolívar. Offering him an alliance to expel him and establish a Constitutional Monarchy. And at the same time that he negotiated with the Viceroy, Riva Agüero began negotiating with Simon Bolívar, sending as representative to the Commander Antonio Gutiérrez de La Fuente. Informed Bolívar of the plans of Riva-Agüero, he convinced the Colonel La Fuente to pass to his side. This Colonel with the help of Mayor Ramón Castilla captured Riva Agüero and they expelled him to Guayaquil, where he was able to escape to England thanks to the protection of the English sailor Martin Guisse.

During the government of O'Higgins it was recognized in 1822 the independence of Chile by United States, and in London a diplomatic agent stayed before the British government, the Guatemalan don Antonio José of Irisarri. This agent was able to hire the first national loan signing a contract with the house Hullet Broders and Co. for the sum of a million pounds sterling that they were equal to five million pesos. The State of Chile, in the contract recognized 100 pounds of capital owed by each fifty that it may receive. Four months later Irisarri wrote O'Higgins saying that it had not been possible to place the loan in spite of its stranger conditions, because Chile didn't still have credit abroad.

O'Higgins gave him orders of suspending the negotiations and if they had already taken place, to annul them. The desire of Irisarri of collecting the commission that would obtain for the contract, he paid remiss attention to the orders and he hired in firm the loan, next he distributed a pamphlet in England, and thanks to the propaganda at the end of the year, the entirety of the titles was placed.

When the news arrived in Chile, the matter was scandalous; they knew that the 70.000 pounds sterling yearly committed by Irisarri could not be returned. To avoid the national discredit, the deposit of the funds had to be accepted.

The economic situation didn't go too well, the unfortunate business of Irisarri came to worsen it, and to make matters worse of misfortunes on November 19th 1822 an earthquake affected the central area of the country, destroying houses, crops and above all human losses, the superstitious ones accused O'Higgins of the disaster, commenting that his person brought them bad luck. The dissatisfaction toward his government was bigger every time, the new Constitution of 1822 was based on the Spaniard's of 1812. It presented a great advance on the Constitution of 1818, it was viewed by the public opinion, as a desperate attempt of clinging to the dictatorial power, since O'Higgins was designated this way for six years that with the four of the possible re-election and those almost already six years elapsed, they made a total of sixteen, too many for all those that aspired to take over the power.

O'Higgins sent the priest Cienfuegos to Rome in diplomatic status, but the Pope didn't receive him as such, because Chile had not been even recognized as an independent nation by Holy See and by the ambassador from Spain that also opposed to the recognition, but he was received as a confidential agent. The pontiff neither could send to Chile a nuncio that has diplomatic status, but he could assign an apostolic vicar and for this position he designated Monsignor Juan Muzi that in turn was advised by an auditor, the canon Juan María Mastai Ferretti, who was later named Pope under the name of Pious IX.

When the government decreed the reformation of the religious orders that were very disorganized as a consequence of the fight for the Independence, and the confiscation of the properties of the regular clergy with object of alleviating the fiscal deficit, the situation greatly worsened, they ended up saying that the apostolic vicar tried to secretly serve the interests of the king of Spain Fernando VII, and of the sovereigns of The Holy Alliance, very influential with the Pope, and the friendship that began in Santiago with the bishop don José Santiago Rodriguez, royalist that as him stayed faithful to the king. All this made that he went away more and more of the patriots, the months were elapsing without the government and the vicar reaching some agreement, what motivated that monsignor Muzi requested the passport, stating that his stay in Chile was incompatible with the government's ordinances in ecclesiastical matters.

From then on the relationships between Chile and the Holy See were cut off and Rome ended up ignoring the existence of the republic.

Obtained the independence of Peru, and having happened some facts that tarnished his government, as the frequent frictions with the clergy, the shooting of the brothers Juan José and Luis Carrera in Mendoza on May 8th 1818, the murder of Manuel Rodriguez Ordaiza in Til-Til on May 26th 1818, the shooting of José Miguel Carrera in Mendoza on September 4th 1821, the political arbitrariness of minister Rodriguez Aldea and of the Lautarian Lodge, the frictions with the other powers of the State, among other causes, determined the uprising of the inhabitants of Concepcion, requesting his resignation like Supreme Director. Headed by their Town council, they acclaimed the General Ramón Freire, being under his command all the towns of the South of the Maule. In Coquimbo and in Valdivia there were similar movements.

In Santiago, the most remarkable neighbors met in the Consulate and they called the Supreme Director to deliberate, who was presented before the assembly. After putting forward their complaints with stability and respect, while they were expressing that the genuineness of the power didn't reside in the military ones, represented by the eminent person, but in the popular sovereignty, being represented by the directing elite. They asked him to leave the command in order to prevent the disruption of the country.

To avoid bloodshed, Bernardo O'Higgins Riquelme, standing over there with haughtiness, he took the presidential band off from his chest and he abdicated as Supreme Director on January 28th 1823, handing over the power to a Junta of Government.

Later on he went on exile and got on board in the port of Valparaíso after having trusted his friend Freire five months, but once he landed in Valparaiso with his forces he captured O'Higgins, who went on exile in the corvette "Fly" toward Peru, not being able to step the soil of Chile again that he so deeply loved, arriving in Callao on July 28th 1823. As he didn't have any resources, he lived on the produce of the cultivation of the Montalván y Cuiba estate which was totally abandoned, the same that was granted to him by Peru, but it was one the best farmed estate in the country around 1840.

Being on exile, from Lima he ran for the presidency of Chile, only obtaining a vote, therefore he was defeated by Manuel Bulnes.

On October 6th 1842, the National Congress of Chile recognized him the right to enjoy his salaries, that which opened him the door to return to his country. He accepted the return to Chile that was offered to him by the President don Manuel Bulnes Prieto; and in the preparations of going aboard in Callao, he exhausted his last energies, he felt to faint, the doctor Young that attended him, ordered his transfer to Lima, after a new heart attack, the General Liberator Bernardo O'Higgins Riquelme died at the 12.30 hours on October 24th, 1842.

On January 11th 1869, Chile repatriated his remains from the port of the Callao with the corvettes of war "O'Higgins", "Esmeralda" and "Chacabuco" calling in Valparaiso, under the command of the Vice-admiral don Manuel Blanco Encalada, to be buried in Santiago's General Cemetery.

Later his remains were transferred to the Altar of the Homeland where his urn remains covered by the national flag and lit by the flame of freedom.

Bernardo O'Higgins left almost finished the war of independence of Chile. With his abdication, it began a disrupted and confused period of political and social organizations that ended up bordering on anarchy. The lack of experience of the time, it took the men to rehearse diverse forms of governing, for which the country was not prepared, such as the federalism and the democratic liberalism.

Madam Javiera Carrera, upon knowing about the exile of Bernardo O'Higgins, she decided to return to Chile in 1824, after ten years of exile, she didn't want to go by Mendoza where they had murdered her three brothers. In Santiago, she settled in the estate of El Monte. She achieved the repatriation of the corpses of her brothers in 1828 under the presidency of don Antonio Pinto.

She died in her Santiago estate on August, 1862.

O'Higgins's Abdication.

CHAPTER XVIII.
ESSAYS OF REPUBLICAN ORGANIZATION.

The abdication of O'Higgins made fall the command in the General don Ramón Freire Serrano, 35 years old. He was designated by the plenipotentiary of the provinces: don Manuel Antonio Gonzalez, by Coquimbo, don Juan Egaña, for Santiago and don Manuel Vázquez de Novoa, by Concepción.

He had fought in almost all the battles of the Independence, being always distinguished for his courage. He broke alongside O'Higgins the Spanish lines in Rancagua; he had travelled as privateer the coasts of the Peru sent by Buenos Aires, returning to Chile to make the campaign of Maipú. Supporting always O'Higgins, he passed later to fuel a deep hate against O'Higgins.

Freire was an honest leader, lacking political preparation. He summoned a constituent congress, dictating the Constitution of 1823, written by the lawyer Juan Egaña, but this went as plenipotentiary to England, entering as minister the General Pinto, who upon seeing that the Constitution was totally impracticable, its validity was suspended, since among other things it censored the printing freedom. Freire took over dictatorial faculties with agreement of the legislator and conservative senate.

The Congress declared absolutely abolished the Constitution of 1823; being that assembly in disagreement with Freire, who saw that they fomented unrest, he dissolved the assembly. He likewise had to dissolve another hostile assembly to the Government, causing a mutiny to overthrow him as Director, exiling thirteen of the agitators to Peru.

A supreme ordinance dismissed the bishop with royalist ideas, Rodriguez, and he named instead the patriot dean Cienfuegos that promulgated an ordinance for which it was prohibited the religious professions to those under the age of twenty five, he suppressed some convents, he took hold of the priests their vast territorial properties, which were sold by the State, granting them a rent to be sustained.

Freire won glory because of having ended the war of the Independence.

He organized the squad, and he sent it under the command of the Vice-Admiral Blanco Encalada in aid of Simón Bolívar, and of the Peruvian patriots to block the ports of the Peru, occupied by the royalists.

After being known in Peru that in Spain the Constitutional government had fallen, and that the king Fernando VII and his absolutist partisans recovered the government and they hanged Rafael del Riego on November 7th 1823, and on the first of October of the same year the king decreed the abolition of all that was approved during the three years of constitutional government, that is why he cancelled the appointment of the liberal José de La Serna as Viceroy of Peru. Being informed the royalist army of the Upper Peru; they rebelled against him, commanded by the Spanish absolutist caudillo Pedro Antonio Olañeta that ordered the attack against the constitutional of the Peruvian viceroyalty.

The Viceroy de La Serna had foreseen to go down to the coast to fight Bolívar, but before the attack of the Upper Peruvians, he changed his plans, and he sent the General Jerónimo Valdés on January 22nd 1824 with a veteran force of 5.000 soldiers to cross the Desaguadero river and go to Potosí against his old subordinate Olañeta.

After a lengthy campaign in the battles of Tarabuquillo, Salas, Cotagaita and finally La Lava on August 17th 1824, both royalist forces of the viceroyalty of the Peru liberal and absolutists of the province of the Upper Peru, they were destroyed each other.

Bolívar in communication with Olañeta decided to go against Jauja and face the Spanish General José Canterac that was isolated in Junín from August 6th 1824. Beginning a pursuit that ended up with the desertion of 2.700 royalists that went over to the independent lines. Finally on October 7th Simon Bolívar with his troops at the doors of Cuzco handed over the command of the new battle front that crossed the course of the Apurimac River to General Antonio José de Sucre.

Bolívar withdrew to Lima to take more loans and being able to sustain the war in Peru, and also wait and receive a Colombian division of 4.000 men dispatched by General Páez, but it didn't arrive until after the battle of Ayacucho.

Disintegrated General Canterac's corps of observation, the Viceroy ordered General Jerónimo Valdés to return from Potosí, which returned in forced marches with 3.000 veterans. Gathered the royalist generals, the Viceroy increased their militias by means of massive peasants' recruits, whom had to be trained in the handlings of weapons. The Viceroy discarded a direct assault on General Sucre, attempting to cut him the rearguard with maneuvers of marches and countermarches that were happening from Cuzco until the encounter in Ayacucho, along the mountain range of the Andes.

Despite the royalists obtained a victory on December 3rd in the battle of Matará, the General Sucre having lost some few men and material, he maintained the United Army in orderly withdrawal and always located in secure positions of very difficult access like the field of Quinoa.

The royalists had used up their resources in those pursuits; however, General Sucre's plans were hardly disrupted. The royalists chiefs in the mountains, knew that in less than five days they would be forced to withdraw because of the famine of the troop, they were driven to a desperate decision: the battle of Ayacucho was about to begin.

By order of battle:

United Liberating Army of Peru.

Commander: General Antonio José de Sucre.
Cavalry Commander – General Guillermo Miller.
Chief of Staff – General Agustín Gamarra.

First Division – General José Maria Córdoba with 2.300 men.
Second Division – General José de La Mar with 1.580 men.
Third División – General Jacinto Lara with 1.700 men.

Royal Army of Perú.

Commander: Viceroy José de La Serna.
Cavalry Commander – Brigadier Valentín Ferraz.
Chief of Staff – Lieutenant General José de Canterac.

Division of Vanguard – General Jerónimo Valdés with 2.010 men.
First Division – General Juan Antonio Monet con 2.000 hombres.

Second Division – General Alejandro González Villalobos with 1.700 men.
Reserve Division – General José Carratalá with 1.200 men.

Before the start of the battle, General Antonio José de Sucre harangued his troops:
- "Soldiers, the luck of South America depends of today's efforts. Soldiers! Long Live the Liberator!, Long Live the Saviour of Peru!"-

The line of the independent formed an angle: the right, composed by the battalions Bogotá, Voltigeros, Pichincha and Caracas, under the command of the General Córdoba; to the left the battalions 1st, 2nd and 3rd and Peruvian Legion, under the command of General La Mar; to the center the Grenadiers and Hussars from Colombia with General Miller; and in reservation the Rifle battalions, Vencedor and Vargas, under the command of General Lara.

The Spaniards stationed in the mountain went down swiftly their columns, passing to the enemy's left the battalions Cantabria, Centro, Castro, 1st Imperial and two squadrons of Hussar with a battery of six pieces, forming in excess for that part. In the center they formed the battalions Burgos, Infante, Victoria, Guias and 2nd of the first Regiment, supporting the left of this with three squadrons of The Union, that of San Carlos, the four of the Grenadiers of the Guard and the five artillery pieces already located; and in the height of the enemy's left, the battalions 1 and 2 of Gerona, 2nd Imperial, 1st of the first Regiment, that of Fernandinos, and the squadron of Grenadiers of Halberdiers of the Viceroy.

The device organized by the General Canterac ordered that the division of vanguard surrounds in solitary to the enemy crossing the Pampas River, while the rest of the royalist army descended directly from the hill Condorcunca. The General Sucre realized immediately of the chancy maneuver and with the division of the General Córdoba he attacked directly to the Royalist troops that had not formed still for battle, because they descended in arrays by the mountains.

The violent clashes pushed to the dispersed marksmen of the royalist division of the General Villalobos who dragged in their retreat to the masses of militiamen and the bulk of Monet's division and the division of Reservation that they remained in the mountains without having the opportunity to participate in the battle.

In the other end, the second division of the independent General José La Mar together with the third division of the General Jacinto

Lara stopped the assault of the veterans of General Valdés's division of vanguard.

The battle was won by the independentists, the Royal Army of Peru destroyed, and the wounded Viceroy was taken prisoner.

Capitulation of Ayacucho

"Don José Canterac, Lieutenant General of the Royal Armies of His Catholic Majesty, in charge of the high command of Peru because of having been hurt and taken prisoner in the battle of this day his Excellency the Viceroy don José de La Serna, having heard the generals and officers that met after, the Spanish army, fulfilling in all the senses as much as it has demanded the reputation of their weapons in the bloody day of Ayacucho and in the whole war of the Peru, he has had to give the field to the independent troops; and should at the same time reconcile the honor to the remains of these forces, with the decrease of the evils of the country, I have believed convenient to propose and to adjust with the General of Division of the Republic of Colombia, Antonio José de Sucre, Commander in Chief of the United Liberating Army Peru."

This treaty was signed by the Chief of Staff don José de Canterac and the General don Antonio José of Sucre when concluding the battle of Ayacucho, the same day December 9th 1824. Its main consequences were:

The definitive renouncement of the army, under the command of the Viceroy don José de La Serna, to the struggle.

The presence of the royalists in the fortresses of Callao.

The republic of the Peru should pay the economic and political debt to the countries that contributed militarily to its independence.

This capitulation gave rise to great polemic, since always it was always said that it was a hoax, that the result of the battle was beforehand agreed, since the Spanish liberal chiefs didn't share Fernando VII 's cause, a monarch considered a symbol of the absolutism, it was seen in it the Masonic hand; although the main characters always kept a thorough silence pact on the reasoning that a capitulation without battle, it would have been undoubtedly judged like a betrayal and they would have been shot.

In 1825 Simon Bolívar freed the Upper Peru being established the Republic of Bolivia. The Liberator enabled the creek of Cobija as exit from the new State to the Pacific.

The desert of Atacama greatly increased in value because of the discovery of nitrates and guano in its soils by Chilean explorers. With this, it began the difficulties with the limits of Bolivia.

The archipelago of Chiloé was still in the hands of the Spaniards under the command of General don Antonio Quintanilla.

Freire using part of the funds of the loan, a million and half of pesos was provided to the Peruvian government, another part was spent in the payment of salaries of the army and the rest in the expedition that had gathered 2.500 men in Valdivia to return Chiloé to the Republic, he went with them under his command on board for the archipelago attacking the Grande Island; but the winter rainfalls prevented the patriot forces under the command of Colonel Beauchef from defeating in Mocopulli, and Freire had to withdraw with his reduced forces without having achieved by then his purpose.

Simon Bolívar that had already consolidated his dominions on Peru suggested to the Supreme Director Freire the convenience of totally expelling the Spaniards of the archipelago of Chiloé, in order to avoid that the army may have a center of operations and the squad that the king may send from Spain against the american countries of the Pacific.

Bolívar was putting pressure on Freire in his communiqué by saying him; that if Chile took a long time in attacking the archipelago, he would occupy it with his troops and he would incorporate it to Peru.

Freire before this ultimatum, he went on expedition again on the archipelago, this time with more luck.

The Director Freire at the head of 3.000 men, seconded by Blanco Encalada, Borgoño, Aldunate, Beauchef and Rondizzoni, landed in San Carlos, they defeated General Quintanilla, they gave to the patriots two victories in the same day in the combats of Pudeto and Bellavista, forcing the Spanish general to surrender, and the Spanish flag was replaced by the Chilean, the same day that Callao surrendered, whose powerful stronghold was defended by the Spanish General Rodil, the last two entrenchments that Spain kept of its old colonies.

The Colonel Antonio Quintanilla returned to Spain, where he was comprised among the "ayacuchos", offensive nickname that was given among the Spaniards to the military that had had the misfortune of being defeated in America.

By the Treaty of Tantauco, Chiloé was incorporated to the republic of Chile.

Abolished The Constitution of 1823 and dissolved the Congress and the ecclesiastical matters, these events made that Freire handed over the power in 1826, from that moment the chaos became general and ten governments were succeeding each other in five years without giving a stable organization to the Republic, which ended up falling into anarchy, among agitations of the press with the newspapers "El Hambriento" and "El Canalla" that dealt with the government's problems with the biggest freedom, popular uprisings, and barracks mutinies. On the other hand, the montoneras of the Pincheira brothers that maintained the insecurity and the alarm of the provinces of the South, escaping to diverse pursuits of the General Borgoño and of the Colonel Beauchef.

Two parties were competing for the power: the conservatives and the liberators.

Freire's successor was don Manuel Blanco Encalada, who was handing over the power after two months of being inaugurated, he was succeeded by don Agustín Eizaguirre, who was not in the office for more than four months, due to the difficult circumstances, the employees and the army were unpaid for long months, the English creditors were demanding the payment of the dividends of their loans, all this led to disturbances in many towns, the troops rioted demanding their salaries, the government felt unable to solve this troubles.

Don José Miguel Infante, proposed the organization of a federal system, imitating that of the United States of North America, without taking into consideration the diversity of conditions of the towns, since according to that system, each province, transformed into a state of the same country should have; Rulers, Camera and Laws by separate without obeying a Central Government but in certain matters of general interest.

The system had fervent partisans at the beginning in Chile, besides Mr. Infante, apostle of the federation; General Blanco Encalada was supporting it.

Without waiting the approval of a constitution, the federalist followers headed by Infante and the clergymen Cienfuegos and Fariñas, hastily enacted the laws that would organize the country into a federation.

The Congress proclaimed the federation as the basis for Chile's government.

It was established that a Legislative Camera may be created in each one of the eight provinces in which the Republic was divided, but the country rejected that idea, and the federal system, without ending up being heavily constituted, it was soon forgotten.

To secure the order disrupted by the military mutiny, General Freire was again called to be in charge of the Government, but after three months he resigned again, handing over the power to General Francisco Antonio Pinto in 1827.

During his Government, the liberal Constitution of 1828 was enacted and worded by the Spanish writer don José Joaquin de Mora; it established the Legislative, Executive and Liberal powers. General Pinto resigned the Supreme Command in July 1829, but two months after, he came to power again because of his having been reelected president, but the political unrest made impossible his government and he resigned again.

The rivalry among the political parties: the conservatives and the liberators broke out in a civil war in 1829.

The General Joaquin Prieto rebelled in the South, going on the capital. In Ochagavía, near Santiago, he met with General Lastra, commander of the Government's forces and they agreed to lay down the arms and recognize as commander in chief to Freire; but soon after, Prieto became against Freire and the forces of both bands were near Talca, where it took place the battle between both generals in April of 1830, General Prieto was defeating the General Freire whom was exiled to Peru.

At those moments the country was governed by don José Tomás Ovalle, and as minister of Interior and of the War, Diego Portales who showed an amazing character and intelligence. Upon the death of Ovalle, General Joaquin Prieto took over the Government of the Republic, during his period it was enacted the Political Constitution of 1833, which was worded by the lawyer don Manuel Egaña, this constitution ruled the country during 92 years until 1925.

In his exile in Peru, General Freire gathered ships and elements of war supported by Peru, and he went to the island of Chiloe, with the purpose of preparing an army to overthrow General Prieto's Government, but Freire was captured and exiled to New Holland in Oceania, where he was wandering as an outlaw by Oceania and Bolivia, after five years he returned to Chile aided by the amnesty promulgated by the new president Bulnes. He lived retired of the politics until his death in 1851.

Chile was convinced that the Freire's undertaking would not have been able to be carried out without the help of Peru, they accused General Santa Cruz from everything, deciding to take him away his squad of six ships in not very good condition, but Chile only had two old ships with limited fire-power, hence the Spanish Victoriano Garrido was entrusted with this mission, he anchored in the port of Callao with only one of the ships, that same night he boarded three of the Peruvian ships. General Santa Cruz didn't want the war while he may not achieve to strengthen his situation in Peru, he downplayed the issue and he signed with Garrido an agreement by which the ships would be in Chile's possession while a definitive treaty is signed.

Once the civil war was over, there were still in the South the montonero Pincheira brothers, still fighting to maintain the Spanish sovereignty. They together with the pehuenche Indians were terrorizing between Curicó and Concepcion for such a long time, they had their headquarters hidden in the mountains of the cordillera.

President Prieto commissioned the Brigadier don Manuel Bulnes, with a real army, so that he went into the mountain ranges of Chillan to pursue them, achieving in the camp near the Epulauquén lake to surprise the Pincheira and destroy them forever.

In 1835, a great earthquake caused great devastation in all the populations of the South. Concepción and Chillan were totally destroyed. Chillan had to be rebuilt a little more to the North where it previously was.

Peru and Upper Peru, old Empire of the Incas, upon being separated by Simón Bolívar in two independent states: Peru and Bolivia, the unit of the viceroyalty was broken.

Andrés Santa Cruz, Bolivian, progressive ruler and of great organizing ability; although he was son of Spaniard, he pretended to be descendant of the Incas from Peru, because of his being son of the Indian Juana Basilia Calaumana, chieftain of Huarina, in 1836, upon being president of Bolivia, with the Peruvian General Gamarra, they wanted to organize under their command a big and powerful state by uniting Bolivia and Peru, this country was divided in the North-Peruvian State and South-Peruvian State, being joined to Bolivia under the life command of General Santa Cruz, seeking in a next future to annex Chile and Ecuador, forming a Confederation similar to the ephemeral Great Colombia created by Bolívar the Liberator.

Taking advantage of the rivalry between the Peruvian commanders Gamarra and Salaverry who were fighting for President Orbegozo's power.

Santa Cruz kindled even more those disagreements, and after defeating and exiling Agustín Samara, he became against Salaverry, taking him prisoner and making him shoot in 1836.

After creating The Peru-Bolivian Confederation, Santa Cruz himself assigned the title of Protector.

Chile and Ecuador were considered threatened by Santa Cruz's invading politics. The first one already antagonized with Peru by trade and customs issues and also for the support that had been given to the revolutionary expedition of Freire in the ships issue, in the face of this fear he declared the war to the Confederation.

Don Diego Portales in his capacity of minister of Interior and of the War he took the charge of mobilizing the troops and preparing them for the war, stationing the army in Quillota under the command of Colonel Antonio Vidaurre. Portales, conservative, he was informed about a liberal rebellion on the part of Vidaurre, to which Portales didn't pay attention to the rumor.

One day that the minister Portales was reviewing the troops, he observed that the soldiers were surrounding him, and an officer closer and told him that hew was taken prisoner, to which Portales didn't try to offer any resistance.

The rebelled troops went to Valparaíso, taking prisoner the minister together with his secretary Manuel Cavada, guarded by the officer Santiago Florin, but in the hill Baron, the militias of the port, commanded by General Blanco Encalada, defeated the revolutionaries.

When hearing the first shots of the combat, the stagecoach in which the two prisoners were riding was stopped, and the officer Florin made them get off, and after being knelt, he then ordered that they were shot.

Colonel Vidaurre, officer Florin, and others of the guilty ones were taken prisoners and shot.

The death of Diego Portales didn't put an end to the Government's plans against the Peru-Bolivian Confederacy. General Blanco Encalada was sent with a regiment to Peru, he landed with 2.700 men in the port of Quilca and they went to Arequipa, where when being surrounded by greater Peru-Bolivian forces, the Chilean General believed wise to make a pact with the General Santa Cruz and to sign the treaty of Paucarpata in November, 1837, in which it was established: peace between Chile and the Confederation; the return of the ships on the part of Chile ; the return to their country of the Chilean army; the celebration of commercial treaties among the contracting parties; the recognition of the loan of 1.500.000 of pesos made by Chile to the government of Peru, more the accrued interests. After this, the expedition returned to Chile.

The failure of that expedition and the signature of the treaty caused a great annoyance to President Prieto that he immediately rejected the treaty and began preparing a second restoring expedition of the freedom in Peru. Three months later, he sent General Manuel Bulnes with an army of 6.000 men that were landing near Lima.

In the Portada de Guías, they defeated the confederate troops, and on August, 1838, General Bulnes was entering Lima. Later on he defeated in the battles of Matucana and Bridge of Buin. The Commander Robert Simpson, former officer of Lord Cochrane, defeated in Casma the naval forces of the Confederation, and all the bulk of General Santa Cruz's army was totally defeated in the department of Ancash on the banks of the Santa River on January 20 1839 in the memorable battle of Yungay.

To exalt the victory of the warring feats of the battle of Yungay, a beautiful patriotic hymn was composed to the Chilean forces, with nationalist feelings whose music belongs to the composer don José Zapiola, and its letter to don Ramón Rengifo.

Then General Bulnes, with 5.000 men, climbed with irresistible fearlessness, the heights of the hills Punyán and Pan de Azúcar, occupied by Santa Cruz with 6.000 soldiers. Once the enemy of the hills was defeated, the patriots crowned their summits with the tri-colored flag of Chile.

In the plain the Chilean Colonel Fernando Baquedano, after six hours of fight, with three tight cavalry charges, defeated Santa Cruz's forces and undone the power of the Confederation.

Santa Cruz, after the disgraceful defeat he fled to Ecuador, later he returned to Bolivia where he tried to stage a revolutionary coup, arrested he was sent on exile to Chile, living in Chillan, until he went to Europe like a diplomat of Peru. Already independent, Peru entrusted the government to Mr. Agustín Gamarra, friend of Chile.

The victorious of Yungay, General Mr Manuel Bulnes Prieto, was elected president, succeeding to his uncle, his mother's brother, Mr. Joaquin Prieto.

He began a reconciliation government, making use of the secretary of the interior Mr. Ramón Luis Irarrázaval and Mr. Manuel Rengifo of Finance, promulgating an amnesty for the political exiles; he greatly stimulated the public education with the cooperation of his competent minister Mr. Manuel Montt. The University of Chile was founded, inaugurated with a solemn festival, a gun salute of 21 volleys to announce its foundation, being its first rector Mr. Andrés Bello. This new one came to replace the colonial University of San Felipe, closed in 1839, by decree of the President Mr. Joaquin Prieto, the first Normal School of Chile and of the Hispanic America, under the direction of the great Argentinean teacher Mr. Domingo Sarmiento, the Lyceum of Chile (Secondary school) was founded by Mr. Joaquin de Mora, writer and Spanish educator, It was established in Valparaiso the Navy School, he established in Santiago The Fifth National School of Agriculture.

During the government of Bulnes, the organization of the conservative Republic continued, it was carried out the project of gathering new civil codes, since the former ones were Spanish and they weren't applicable to the republican principles, that's why Mr. Andrés Bello worded the new Civil Code.

A law was introduced in 1842 that declared property of Chile the guano deposits of Cobija, granting to a society formed by Chilean and foreign merchants permit to load guano to the South of Mejillones. This society practiced its activity with knowledge of the Bolivian authorities of Cobija, but in 1847 these authorities made the army stopped their operations, alleging that that territory belonged to Bolivia.

Before the attack, the Government of Chile replied sending a ship of war that took possession of Mejillones.

Bolivia made constant reclamations of its limits, it demanded that the 26th parallel may be its southern limit and not the 23rd as it had been previously made a pact. The Chilean Government rejected courteously, although with energy the reclamation.

Bulnes took official possession of Strait of Magellan in 1843, founding the city of Punta Arenas; he also built the railroad from Caldera to Copiapó because of the initiative of North American entrepreneur Mr. Guillermo Wheelwright.

The first colonization law was introduced, but because it attracted so few immigrants, the German citizen Bernardo Philippi was appointed agent in Europe in 1845, a great expert of the province of Valdivia, he recruited several German Catholic families, having them settled in the regions of Valdivia and Llanquihue, where the town of Melipulli was founded, in what it is known today as Port Montt.

With the death of the minister Rengifo and the resignation of Irarrázaval, Montt was appointed Minister of the Interior, Mr. José Joaquin Pérez was appointed in the Treasury and the 28 year-old young man who had been occupying all the positions in turn that Montt left, rector vice rector and Mr. Antonio Varas was appointed minister of Instruction.

The presence of Montt and of Varas in the government meant the end of the conciliatory politics term that their predecessors had designed.

The negotiations begun by President Prieto were finished during the Bulnes administration with the recognition of the Independence of Chile by the Spanish Government in 1844, these were on the Spanish side in charge of the General Espartero, regent on behalf of Isabel II, daughter and successor of Fernando VII, and on behalf of the Chileans the negotiation were led by the General José Manuel Borgoño.

In the last years of the second period of the government of Bulnes, they began to become agitated the political intrigues around their successor. The Government launched Manuel Montt's presidential candidacy, but the liberal were against that candidacy and they formed in Santiago the "Society of the Equality" established in April, 1850, it was a Chilean intellectual and political club whose object was to form a propaganda and education school of the political and social proletariat, gathering the main ideologists of the radical liberalism such as Santiago Arcos and Francisco Bilbao who outlined the need of a transformation of the society into what would give rise to a nation of free and equal men

.

Already in 1844 Eusebio Lillo and Francisco Bilbao had pronounced speeches against the clerical omnipotence and the religious fanaticism, and later, with the arrival to Valparaíso of the first copy of "The Girondists" by Lamartine, read by groups of young and intellectual, getting that the upheaval was running high. Soon, it became a revolutionary outbreak;

from his newspaper, "The Friend of the People" in which it may be heard the voice of the young tribune Francisco Bilbao. Also, the illustrious General José María de La Cruz was in Montt's opposition, president Bulnes' first cousin, all this made that the opposition conspired.

On February, 1851 it arrived to Santiago the news that a meeting of neighbors had proclaimed in Concepción the candidacy to the presidency of the Intendant of this city, and General in chief of the Army of the South, Mr. José María de La Cruz y Prieto, nephew of the former President Prieto, and Bulnes' cousin.

"Mutiny of Urriola"

Soon after midnight, Colonel Martiniano Urriola mutinied in Santiago with the Valdivia battalion on April 20th, 1851 and accompanied by the leaders of the "Society of the Equality" José Miguel Carrera Fontecilla, son and nephew of the Carrera brothers, Benjamin Vicuña Mackenna, Francisco Bilbao, Manuel Recabarren Rencores, among other, tried to take hold of the artillery quarter located in La Alameda in the old cloister of the Jesuit

In the midnight of the 19th day, Colonel Urriola was waiting that the Chacabuco regiment may join him with 5.000 soldiers that Recabarren and Bilbao had offered, but 15 were only appearing. Urriola ordered Lieutenant Herrera to take hold of the barracks, but a sergeant shot him and next taking the command he went to La Casa de La Moneda (the Presidential Palace) to be under the president's orders. Shortly after, the bad news arrived that the 18-years-old young Vicuña Mackenna who served as messenger and secretary was prisoner in the barracks, and the Chacabuco detachment was also with the government and Bulnes with this detachment began the defense of La Moneda.

At dawn, Colonel Urriola understood that his position was very unfavorable, because he didn't have forces or ammunitions either, in spite of it, at seven in the morning he prepared the attack to the artillery barracks, but he was killed after a bloody combat at the foot of Santa Lucía's hill, and his troops were dispersed, being subdued the revolution.

The leaders, Carrera Fontecilla was forced to escape to Peru. He returned to Chile and he took refuge in the city of La Serena. Vicuña Mackenna was taken prisoner and sentenced to death, but he was able to escape and fly with Ovalle, meeting later with José Miguel in La Serena. In turn Francisco Bilbao remained hidden during three months in Valparaíso and in July he traveled to Lima where he never returned from. Manuel Recabarren was outlawed and abroad he was devoted to the teaching.

At noon, the government's forces had crushed the uprising, and the country got ready for a presidential election.

The Government decided to call General de La Cruz to Santiago, and once in the capital, Cruz received encouragements and visits of diverse natures, as that of the students and that of a delegation of women of liberal tendency headed by Madam Mercedes Fontecilla, José Miguel Carrera's widow and mother of the leader of the mutiny. They went to request General Cruz's intervention that refused to head a new mutiny in Santiago, since the previous one only served to strengthen more the Government, taking strong repressive measures, and proclaim president to Mr. Manuel Montt Torres. General José Maria de La Cruz's followers didn't agree with the victory of Montt, and the opponents, they labelled the election as invalid, stating that Montt was not the legitimate president of the Republic, and once he took over the command, a revolution broke out that ended in a civil war, it was headed by the very same General de La Cruz in diverse places; first in Coquimbo and then in Concepción, and in La Serena that it didn't take too long for the city to fall in the hands of liberal agitators headed by the young José Miguel Carrera Fontecilla, and the young Benjamin Vicuña Mackenna, with whom he had a close friendship, and the Colonel Justo Arteaga Cuevas, organizing an uprising. José Miguel conceived the idea of acquiring the necessary weapons to form an army in Lima, in order to do that he took hold of a small steamship with British flag, "Fire Fly." He was hardly able to gather a montonera of 150 fusiliers and 170 horsemen that resisted the troops of the conservative Government whose commanders were the colonels Juan Vidaurre Leal and Victoriano Garrido.

In order to combat the uprising, the Congress granted full powers to the Government, and this in turn granted them to the former President Bulnes who left for the South commanding an army to subdue the uprising, giving rise to a bloody battle on December 8th 1851 in Loncomilla, being Bulnes the one who defeated, and after the agreement of Purapel between the two generals, José María de La Cruz and his troops deposed the weapons, the revolutionaries of the North were subdued.

The liberals were defeated in the Battle of Peteroa and José Miguel Carrera was forced to escape to Peru.

The Colonel Arteaga, when being imprisoned Carrera, he was in charge of the military command, but when he knew about the agreement of Purapel, he resigned the military and civil command immediately, after being hidden he could leave the city disguised, many surrendered and at last the fort could be occupied by the loyal troops.

Carrera returned in 1859 to lead guerrillas against President Manuel Montt, but he was completely defeated by Colonel Félix de La Cuadra's troops, in Rancagua, in Cerro Grande, Maipú and Pichinguau. Leaving to exile toward Lima, where he died of a liver ailment. Their remains were repatriated to Santiago in 1863. He was father of the Concepcion hero, Captain Ignacio Carrera Pintado.

Vanquished the revolt, Montt was surrounded by worthy ministers, young and active, assuming their positions when their ages were: Antonio Varas 34 years old, Lazcano 41, Urmeneta 42, Ochagavía 31, Waddington 31 and Ovalle 38. The business spirit moved President Montt and his minister of treasury José Guillermo Waddington to organize a true scientific undertaking that may explore the desert of Atacama, for that purpose the naturalist sage Rodulfo Philippi was chosen, who was accompanied by Almeyda and Moreno, although his passion for the zoology and the botany strayed him from the first objective.

During the ten years of Manuel Montt's term the Civil Code was enacted, public schools and lycees were opened, a Normal School for Teachers was established and one for the Deaf-mutes, the building of the railroad between Santiago and Valparaíso began, with the telegraphic wire among both provinces, the savings and mortgage loan institution was established, the Penitentiary and the Lunatic Asylum were built.

During his mandate, there was another revolution in 1859, in the towns of the North and of the South against his Government, headed by the liberal opposition and supported by the conservatives that after having elected him, now they were dissatisfied with their president.

In Coquimbo, Pedro León Gallo was at the head of the revolution, landowner that defeated the Government's troops in the Battle of Los Loros by organizing a 1.000 man army, taking held of La Serena. The Government reacted sending new troops, under the command of General Juan Vidaurre Leal; he defeated Gallo in Cerro Grande, near La Serena.

Pedro León Gallo, once he was defeated he escaped to Argentina, and the revolutionaries of the South were also subdued.

On Sunday September 18th 1859 it was celebrated in the main church of Valparaíso, the Independence Day. General Juan Vidaurre in absence of the Intendant headed the ceremony, when he was killed. His burial was a manifestation deeply felt by all.

The national party unanimously proclaimed Mr. José Joaquin Perez the last president of the four that governed in turn, he had carried out diverse diplomatic positions, and he was senator and minister. He made a reconciliation government issuing a law of amnesty for all the political exiles. He had the support of liberals and conservatives, although the first ones were split up and under the direction of Mr. Pedro León Gallo and Mr. Manuel Antonio Matta founded the Radical Party that joined together with the National Party formed the opposition to the government of the liberal coalition.

President Pérez during his term extended the railroad of the South until Curicó.

At that time Mr. Cornelio Saavedra was the chief of the Frontier, man of great diplomatic ability that served him of a lot with the Indians when completing part of his career in the riverbanks of the Biobío River. Colonel Saavedra decided to pacify the Araucanía and definitively integrate it into the national territory, and in order to do that, he took advantage of his condition of Intendant of Arauco, requesting permission to the president José Joaquin Pérez who warned him that the mapuches would not allow him to pass beyond the Biobío, but Saavedra got that they allowed him to enter up to the Bureo river, where he built the fort of Mulchen in 1862. He ended up striking up friendship with the Indians and his advance continued until occupying Angol without the least resistance.

Completed this feat Saavedra informed the president of the republic that the occupation of the Araucanía would not cost them more than a lot of smoke and mirrors. Using this tactics he founded the city of Lebu on October 6th 1862 and the following year he founded again Angol.

In 1860 an odd character of long wavy hair had arrived in Valdivia , he wore a sword, he was called Aurelio Antonio of Tounens and he was going to put Colonel Saavedra in danger that he didn't hope to find within his calculations.

This character went into the Indians' territory to conceive his fearless plan, arriving until the rehue of the chieftain, to whom he told his idea of how to expel the invader Saavedra and to all the Chileans. The chieftain was captivated by the tale and accepted to establish a state for the mapuche people by joining the South American people into 17 states, beginning with the Araucania because of its being the most valiant. Quilapan and the other chieftains accepted that on November 17th 1860 he may be proclaimed king of the Araucanía with the name of Oreli Antoine I. Three days later he annexed Patagonia to his Kingdom, and by his ordinance, both domains were baptized with the name of "New France"

He went to Valparaíso so that the title was recognized, but when nobody was paying attention to him, he returned furious to the Araucanía, settling down near the city of Angol where he was captured and taken to the Nacimiento garrison by order of President Jose Joaquin Prieto, then they took him to Los Angeles where he was declared to be crazy after a brief try, being secluded in the House of Lunatics, but the consul of France in Chile sent him back to his home city, Paris in 1862.

Saavedra when ordering to advance the frontier until the line of the Tolten river, where he found out that the king Orelie Antoine I had returned with the French ship "D'Entrecasteaux" to cross the Patagonia and to arrive in chieftain Quilapan's domains, his close friend to whom he told that he brought cannons and rifles in the frigate anchored in Lebu, because the hour of the true fight had arrived, the government would recognize this way the existence of the Kingdom of The Araucanía and The Patagonia, the "New France."

Colonel Saavedra offered to the tribes of the river Tolten a reward of pesos fuertes for the new king's head.

Upon finding out about this, Oreli Antoine I said goodbye to his friend Quilapan and he went aboard heading for France, where he died in 1878 being always called king of The Araucanía and The Patagonia.

Conquered the Araucanía the mapuches were relocated in reservations, that is to say, community lands of reduced extension to practice their cattle activities, where they remain until today. The occupied territories were granted to the Chilean and European colonists, mainly Spaniard, German, French, Italian, Englishmen and Swiss.

Spain bombarded Valparaíso.

President José Joaquin Pérez Mascayano, also had to deal with the outbreak of the war with Spain at his times.

In 1862, Isabel II approved the shipment to South America of a scientific expedition formed by three ships of war under the command of the Vice-admiral Luis Hernandez Pinzon. After this scientific expedition it was hidden to get commercial treaties and to serve as support for several complaints of Spanish entrepreneurs living in South America.

It appeared before the coasts of the port of Valparaíso on April 8th 1863, beginning a journey for Chile and then for Peru that their independence had not still been recognized by Spain. It started to arise conflicts in this visit. The relations between both countries were not of confrontations, but on August 2nd of that year, in the Peruvian estate of Talambo an incident occurred between Basque immigrants and Peruvian farmers, with a result of a dead Spanish citizen and other four wounded men. Being informed of the event Vice-admiral Pinzón, issued demands to the government of Peru and requested compensations because of the above mentioned incident, and at the same time the payment of debts originated in the wars of independence between Spain and her colonies of America. The commissioner Salazar y Mazarredo was sent on board by Spain in order to negotiate, he was rejected by the Peruvian government since as a sovereign nation it should have been sent a plenipotentiary ambassador.

Before such events, Vice-admiral Pinzón as a measure of pressure took hold of the Chincha islands, guano producers, and the main source of the revenues of the country. He also imposed a blockade on the port of Callao.

Chile's intellectual opinion upon knowing in Santiago, about the Chincha Islands' occupation by the Spanish Squad on April 30th, its reaction was much more violent than in Lima. At the following day the people was summoned to a meeting in Valparaíso, and on the day May 1st another in Santiago's Municipal Theater, where they reached agreements that said that "The Citizens gathered here protest against the occupation of part of the Peruvian territory by the Spanish forces, we are opposing with the most vigorous resistance to the Spanish Goverment's pretentions against the republics of Spanish America, defending a treaty of friendship signed in 1856 among Chile, Peru and Ecuador", this last one was the only one that ratified it.

Peruvian President Mr. Juan Antonio Pezet, before the occupation of the Chincha islands, summoned to a Congress in Lima to all the American nations in 1864; they only attended Chile, Peru, Ecuador, Bolivia, Colombia, Venezuela and Guatemala. What intended to be a meeting with Americanist purpose with feeling of hate to Spain, it only turned out to be a resource of emergency of Peru to guard against the payments of due bills with Spain.

The Congress entered into relations with the Admiral Pinzón trying to make him see the convenience of returning the Chincha islands to Peru, since this didn't refuse to satisfy the complaints; neither had he wanted to enter into a state of war. Admiral Pinzón, requested to the government of Narvaez, they sent him four more ships to reinforce the fleet, at the same time he resigned on November 9th 1864, and on December 8th the Vice-admiral Juan Manuel Pareja arrived at Pisco to replace him, with explicit instructions of limiting the conflict to a mere private matter between Spain and Peru. He was son of a royalist officer died in the war of independence of Peru, and he hated relentlessly to the guilty ones of this father's death in Chile in 1813. Pareja also rejected the Congress, denying all right to its intervention in a matter of exclusive concern between Spain and Peru, and adding that his country didn't have the least intention of reconquering and dominating the American continent.

The president before such a declaration of the Spaniards, hurried to secretly negotiate and to accept on February 27th 1865 the Treaty Vivanco-Pareja of peace and friendship, by which Spain returned the Chincha islands and Peru paid a compensation of three drafts of a million pesos each one and the islands were returned at once, recovering its national wealth and it avoided a war that neither Peru nor Spain wanted.

President Pezet's enemies, dissatisfied with the treaty, provoked military rebellions in Arequipa and they overthrew him, taking the dictatorship Colonel Mariano Ignacio Prado.

Spain sent to the area the frigate "Numancia" in order to reinforce even more its position in the Pacific, one of the most powerful ships in the time, under the command of Commander Casto Mendez Nuñez.

The conflict of Spain with the Peru alarmed the near countries such as: Bolivia, Ecuador and Chile that feared an attempt of restoring the old Spanish empire in the region.

At the same time Chile rejected the Americanist of the last Congress, Gallo, Matta, Vicuña Mackenna and other more who were convinced that all the bad one came from Europe and all the good from America, the government, also tried to avoid a war; but it didn't achieve this due to the attitude of the Spanish government to entrust the Admiral Pareja so that he may demand explanations because of their having seriously offended Spain by refusing to supply the Spanish fleet with coal, upon having declared that the coal was smuggling of war, upon allowing that horses were sold to Peru and sailors were hired for that country, on not putting a stop to the press excesses that offended Spain.

The Chilean Government protested and, as a reply the Admiral Pareja appeared in Valparaiso on September 18th on board his flagship the "Villa de Madrid" and four frigates, while the "Numancia" and another frigate continued blocking Callao. He wanted to begin negotiations and to reestablish the Spanish honor, demanding that Chile presented a 21 gun salute to the Spanish flag, and if it didn't give satisfaction to his demands, Pareja should destroy the coal mining site of Lota or the city of

Valparaíso. Chile replied by sending a declaration of war on September 25th, 1865.

At once plenipotentiary commissioners left in all addresses; the minister Santa Maria went to Lima with the mission of obtaining help of the naval forces of Peru, colliding from the beginning with the negative of the naval officers Grau and Villar that didn't want to fight against the Spaniards, Vicuña Mackenna left for The Antilles with the intention of expelling Spain of Cuba and of Puerto Rico, Manuel Antonio Matta went to Colombia to try to get help from this country.

The war had to be essentially by sea. Pareja didn't have enough troops to attempt a landing and he was devoted to impose a devastating economic blockade on the main Chilean ports, ruining many entrepreneurs, so much Chilean as neutrals. Chile only had two ships; the corvette seized to Spain the "Esmeralda" and the iron steamer "Maipú". The Spanish squadron was formed by the frigates "Villa de Madrid", "Resolución", "Berenguela" and "Blanca", the schooners "Vencedora" and "Virgen de Covadonga", the transport "Marquis of the Victoria" and the ironclad "Numancia", this superior squadron was very attenuated by the great extension of the Chilean coasts, what made that the Spaniards were unable to maintain an effective blockade in the numerous ports that had to be extended from the Caldera port until Talcahuano, what allowed to the schooner "Esmeralda" commanded by the Commander Juan Williams Rebolledo, to attack and to surrender to the Spanish schooner "Virgen of Covadonga" near the beach of Papudo.

The Admiral Pareja, it seems to be that he was having a terrible state of depression, was aware that he had exceeded in his functions by causing a war with Chile not foreseen by the Spanish Government and upon knowing the capture of his favorite ships, he got dressed in his full-dress uniform, committing suicide in his cabin of the "Villa de Madrid", his flagship that was blockading Valparaíso. He was succeeded by Mr. Casto Mendez Nuñez who was immediately promoted to Admiral, taking the command of the fleet of the "Numancia", one of the most powerful ships in the world.

Peru and Chile signed an alliance treaty against Spain, joining their squadrons to form a common fleet, concentrating on the navy shipyard of Abtao, under the command of the Admiral Manuel Blanco Encalada.

Discovered by the Spaniards whom upon receiving new instructions of not abandoning the Chilean coasts until the peace may be reached, Méndez Núñez, decided to destroy the Chilean-Peruvian squadron that was in Chiloé, sending there two ships, the "Reina Blanca" and the "Villa de Madrid", in front of Abtao, a combat occurred on February 7th, 1866, after a fruitless gunfire, since it was in not very deep waters, without decisive results. The Chilean-Peruvian squad took refuge later in the tideland of Huito, in front of the island of Calbuco. In these battles of Papudo and Abtao, he fought as midshipman, the one that later would be the glorious Mr. Arturo Prat.

After several months without fruitful results, the Spanish squadron already showed its deterioration, it lacked bases where to repair its ships, to cure the sick persons and to restore its casualties. The Spanish Government, before so bad result of the adventure, ended up ordering Méndez Núñez to take the hostilities farther, and they went for the mining coal deposits of Lota, or against the port of Valparaíso, without before the Commander Méndez Núñez announced to the land authorities that the day March 31st he would break fire over Valparaíso and at the same time white flags should be hoisted over the hospitals and other charity establishments, with the purpose of preserving them of the destruction, and the English and North Americans ships anchored in the port should move away.

The General Kirkpatrick, North American representative in Chile; he demanded to the Commodore Rodgers, anchored in the port with their squadron that he may attack the frigate "Numancia", however Rodgers refused to execute any action that could start a war between his country and Spain.

Méndez Núñez informed the Spanish Government that he would fulfill his orders of bombarding Valparaíso, although his ships were sinking in Chilean waters, because "Spain, The Queen and I prefer honor without ships than ships without honor".

The bombardment lasted three hours, shooting on the port 1.600 cannon shots. Valparaíso was by then lacking fortifications, because of it, the material losses were substantial, not this way the population who fled placing in the hills, only two people left behind died.

Finished the conflict, and with the purpose of being prepared for any setback, the port of Valparaíso was fortified, and the corvettes "O'Higgins and "Chacabuco" were acquired

This bombardment on March 31st, 1866, with partial destruction of the port of Valparaíso, it was an act that its memory saddened the Spanish Navy.

The naval campaign finished with the bombing of the port of Callao. The Spanish ships on May 2nd faced the land batteries. During the fight the minister Gálvez and numerous Peruvians perished, but the Spanish ships suffered serious damages, the frigate the "Berenguela" was out of action, 43 sailors died and 157 were wounded and the same Méndez Núñez received eight wounds that threatened his life. The squadron abandoned the American coasts toward the Philippines and there were not more combats, finishing the war.

Peru enlarged its squadron, what would mark the beginning of a trade of weapons with Chile, and to continue having the naval prevalence in the South Pacific.

Five years later, in 1871, it was signed in Washington among Spain, Chile, Peru, Bolivia and Ecuador an armistice agreement for indefinite time.

The first liberal government was that of Federico Errázuriz, from 1871 up to 1876. More than that of José Joaquin Pérez which was of transition one that of Errázuriz is defined as completely liberal, although it was chosen with the support of the conservatives, the alliance liberal-conservative was dissolved in 1873 due to differences of opinion regarding the teaching, the lay cemeteries and the civil marriage.

The liberal, besides the Radical Party, were in favor of the laicism in these matters, while the conservatives defended the influence of the Church.

The following presidents until José Manuel Balmaceda from 1886 up to 1891 belonged to the Liberal Party.

The main works that were made during this government were Santiago's modernization, thanks to the intendant Benjamin Vicuña Mackenna. Three months after being taken charge, he was presenting to the Government, to the Congress and the City council his famous plan of transformation of Santiago, beginning with Santa Lucia's hill, it began on July 4th 1872 with the help of 200 convicts, the expenses exceeded of 50.000 pesos. Vicuña Mackenna had to advance the necessary funds to pay the debt; he was forced to mortgage his wife's properties and part of his salary of Intendant. He improved the service of running water, new streets paved with paving stones and public squares, the Municipal Theater, National Museum and the National Congress.

The railroad line was extended in regions from Curicó until Chillán and from here to Talcahuano and Angol, etc.

During the government of Errázuriz the economic crisis became worse. The difficult world situation caused the fall of the cooper prices, to which it was added the poor economic situation, and in order to get resources new taxes were established and the public expense was restricted.

Aníbal Pinto Garmendia won the presidential elections on September 18th 1876 until 1881.

At the end of his government, with the advances of the Pacific War he left the country rich, powerful and respected by all the nations.

CHAPTER XIX.
THE NITRATE.

C hile is the only country in the world where there are deposits of a substance called "Caliche", wherefrom it is extracted the sodium nitrate, called saltpetre.

Explorers arrived in the desert of Atacama in search of the saltpetre deposits. By the north, Bolivia was disputing Chile a part of the desert of Atacama.

Chilean industrialists had discovered in the arid region of Mejillones deposits of guano from sea birds, used as fertilizer for the land.

Bolivia demanded that such territory was belonging to her, in order not to compromise the peace between both republics, a treaty was signed in 1866 by which the 24th parallel was established as dividing limit, being Mejillones in Bolivia; however, the metal products from said territory should be divided into halves between the contracting parties. Other explorers discovered South of Mejillones deposits of nitrate, a fertilizing substance richer than the guano. The main discoverers of the deposits were the Chileans: Mr. Diego de Almeyda Aracena known as the Prophet of the Desert, because he was sure about its richness, Mr. José Antonio Moreno, devoted to the search in the North, he died in the precise moments when a great fortune was about to crown his efforts as explorer and as industrialist, and Mr. José Santos Ossa Vega, a great expert of the desert inch by inch, where he found the nitrate deposits in a solitary place called La Chimba where he founded Antofagasta, city which was born and rapidly grew, and the Nitrate and Railway Company of Antofagasta, the Ossa Bank and Co. He amassed a huge fortune due to the white gold or Saltpetre. In Valparaiso, he worked agricultural properties; he was ruined and recovered in several occasions, he died

314

while sailing toward the island of San Felix and San Ambrosio in search of guano deposits.

The anarchy that was triggered in Bolivia by the different governments had as consequence that they didn't deliver to Chile neither a cent of what it corresponded to him because of the sales of guano and customs duties. It was managed to sign another treaty in 1874, it was established again the 24th parallel South latitude as limit of both republics; but under the condition that Bolivia doesn't levy new taxes to the Chilean industries settled down in the territory that was left.

Bolivia didn't even fulfil that treaty. Considering Chile without resources, worn out by the economic crisis and about to break off relations with the Republic of Argentina, the government of Bolivia headed by Hilarión Daza, and advised by the government of Peru that in fact aspired to the monopoly by enacting in 1878 a law that imposed a contribution on the saltpetre that was exported by the "Chilean Exporting Company of Antofagasta." Before Chile could mediate in arbitration, the government of Bolivia decreed the attachment of the saltpetre deposits of The Company and its sale in public auction.

Peru that had lost the considerable earnings yielded by the guano of its territory, due to the waste of the rulers, decided to appropriate of the rich Peruvian saltpetre deposits of Tarapacá that were competing with the guano, but great part of them belongs to Chileans, there was afraid of reprisal from them. Like a preventive measure, Peru led Bolivia to celebrate the Treaty of Alliance between them, it was signed in Lima on February 6th, 1873, it was kept in secret; on February, 1879, Antofagasta was militarily occupied by Chile in order to prevent the Bolivian government from enforcing the decree of attachment against the saltpetre deposits of the "Chilean Nitrate Company of Antofagasta" because of its having refused to pay the extremely serious tax levied by Bolivia that in fact was violating the treaties signed in Chile in 1866 and 1874.

Bolivian President Mr. Hilarion Daza declared war on Chile. Peru pretended to friendly mediate in the conflict by sending a plenipotentiary envoy for peace talks, making believe that no treaty of friendship with Bolivia ever existed, but Chile knew this secret treaty of offensive and defensive alliance between the Peru and Bolívia since 1873. The government from Lima at last admitted that the treaty really existed. Already with that confession, Chile declared war on both countries on April 5th, 1879.

It's the beginning of the so-called War of the Pacific.

CHAPTER XX.
THE WAR OF THE PACIFIC.

Bolivia didn't even have a warship in the sea, however, Peru had a strong squadron made up of the armoured frigate "Independencia", the monitor "Huascar", the wooden corvettes "Union" and "Pilcomayo", the monitors "Atahualpa" and "Manco Capac" and several cruisers and transports.

In addition, it had with the fortifications of Callao.

Antofagasta was the point of concentration of the Chilean troops that had the ironclads "Cochrane" and "Blanco Encalada", the wooden corvettes "Chacabuco" and "O'Higgins", the old corvette "Esmeralda", the gunboat "Magallanes" and the small schooner "Covadonga".

It had to be destroyed the Peruvian squadron in the Pacific Ocean in order to be able to transport the troops to the North.

The first sea battle took place in Chipana, where the gunboat "Magallanes" commanded by Mr. Juan Jose Latorre defeated the Peruvian corvettes "Union" and "Pilcomayo", the Admiral Williams Rebolledo, chief of the Chilean squadron established the blockade of Iquique, where he left two old wooden vessels the "Esmeralda", which was given that name after the Spanish frigate captured by Admiral Cochrane in Callao on June 5th, 1820, it took the motto "Glory and Victory", the same that served as countersign for Cochrane's boarding order, it was commanded by Captain Arturo Pratt and the "Covadonga", captured from the Spaniards in the sea battle of Papudo, it took part in the Abtao sea battle under the Chilean flag. It was commanded by Captain Carlos Condell, and the transport Lamar. The Admiral continue voyage to Callao in search of the Peruvian squadron that was advancing with the gunboat "Huascar" commanded by Miguel Grau, and the frigate "Independencia" commanded by Juan Guillermo Moore, they were advancing in high seas without being sighted by the Chilean squadron.

The Commander of the "Huascar", Miguel Grau, upon reaching the South of Peru had obtained information that the Chileans were blockading Iquique, therefore he continued to that place. At the dawn of May 21st, the "Huascar" and the "Independencia" reached the port of Iquique. The two vessels were speedy and ironclads, very superiors to the two old Chilean vessels.

The "Independencia" was the best Peruvian ship, but all of its crew was new and inexperienced.

Arturo Prat

At the dawn of May 21st 1879, the "Esmeralda" was attentively watching the port and the horizon, suddenly a shout was heard:

-"Smokes at sight in the Northern side!"-

Commander Prat rapidly informed Commander Condell of the "Covadonga":
- We'll die before lowering the flag, we must follow the ship's wake.-

-Aye, Aye, Sir.-

At once the Commander Prat joined the crew of his ship "La Esmeralda" and pronounced his immortal harangues:
- Guys! The conflict is unequal. Our flag has never been lowered to the enemy and I wait in this occasion it won't be, as long as I live that flag will wave in its place: if I die, my officers will do their duty. -
Near two hundred patriots answered in a loud voice:

- Long live Chile! -

The battle began at eight thirty in the morning. The "Covadonga" was attacked by the "Independence" and the "Esmeralda" the fight was caught between a rock and a hard place, it clashed the gunboat "Huáscar" and to the batteries of the port, and during two hours it was deceiving the attacks of the Peruvian gunboat. The "Esmeralda", with their broken boilers, she moved closer to the coast in the bottom of the bay, she tolerated this way for two hours, until the Peruvian Commander Miguel Grau decided to use the ram.
When colliding both ships, the heroic Major Prat sword in hand screamed :

- To the boarding! -

The roar of the crash prevented Commander Arturo Prat from being heard, and they only managed to follow him the Sergeant Juan de Dios Aldea and a Chilean sailor, they jumped on the enemy deck, trying to approach it the three of them fell riddled with bullets. In the second ram the Lieutenant Ignacio Serrano and twelve partners were blown up at their being also sacrificed, the Lieutenant Luis Uribe continued the resistance. To the third ram, it was followed by a discharge of her cannons that destroyed the glorious "Esmeralda" which began to slowly founder, while the midshipman Ernesto Riquelme was shooting the last cannon while they screamed:

- Long live Chile! -

Out of the 180 men that manned her, they were only left 60 men floating on the waves, to whom the "Huascar" generously sent boats to save them.

The "Esmeralda" at the 12 10 p.m. of May 21st, 1879, foundered with their pavilion to the end. The battle had lasted four hours.

Mr Arturo Prat Chacón entered in the Navy School in a course that has been called "The course of the heroes" because illustrious men such as Arturo Prat, Carlos Condell, Luis Uribe, Juan José Latorre, Jorge Montt, Wenceslao Frías, etc were enrolled in this course. Peruvian Commander, Mr. Miguel Grau, showing signs of chivalry, after the battle, he transferred into his ship the Chileans rescued alive, and to those fell in action for their being buried in Iquique.

Later, he sent madam Carmela Carvajal Briones widow of the hero Prat, the sword, a wallet with the portraits of his and children, a ring and some gold cufflinks, and a letter in which he was praising his dying in the line of duty and the courage of the young commander Mr. Arturo Prat, he was 31 years old.

Grau deserved recognition and general appreciation of the Chileans because of this act of noble character.

Meantime, more to the South in the bay of Iquique, the Commander of the "Covadonga" Carlos Condell steered his small vessel near the coast, pursued by the powerful frigate the "Independencia" commanded by Juan Guillermo Moore.

Upon arriving to the reefs of Punta Gruesa on May 21st 1865, the Peruvian frigate in spite of having great artillery, she hit at the Chilean vessel but missed, having to appeal to the ram, but she ran aground on a rock, moment that the "Covadonga" took advantage to go against her and she began shooting her cannons to conquer her, the Peruvian ship, went to the bottom leaning by the side and she was completely beached; but before such an attack the Húascar went in her help and the Chilean ship retired. Four days later, the "Covadonga" gloriously entered in Antofagasta, Mr Carlos Condell being promoted to Admiral because of this action.

During five months the Húascar under the command of Miguel Grau, carried out forays by the Chilean coast, shelling the Chilean ports without ending up being beaten, until October 8th 1879 the Chilean ships the "Cochrane" commanded by Juan José Latorre, the "Blanco Encalada", under the command of Galvarino Riveros, caught the "Húascar" in Punta de Angamos, in front of Mejillones, a division of the Chilean squadron that was waiting for her cut him the step, and they forced him to combat.

The bullets of the "Cochrane" broke the armored tower of the Peruvian ship, and the Commander Grau that was   just directing the maneuver there, he was blown up, and successively the second and third chiefs were surrendering so they decided to lower flag. The armored ship "Unión" escaped towards Arica being pursued by the Chilean frigate "O'Higgins" and the cruiser "Loa".

With the rendition of the Huascar, the Chilean Squadron was owner of the sea.

To immortalize the memory of the heroes of Iquique, the Government headed by Mr. Domingo Santa Maria, ordered to build a monument the year of 1888 in Valparaíso to the Navy's Glories in whose pedestal rises the Commander Mr. Arturo Prat's statue, and in each one of the four corners there are the statues of Sergeant Juan de Dios Aldea, Lieutenant Ignacio Serrano, Midshipman Ernesto Riquelme and a sailor.

While the war at sea continued. Chile had concentrated in Antofagasta an army of 12,000 men under the command of General Erasmo Escala, it is mainly formed by national guards which were mobilized and armed with ammunition brought from Europe, and to support the expenses and not to appeal to loans, the Congress authorized the issue of paper currency of the State and the government was authorized to spend only the necessary.

The Peru was in bankruptcy; it was obtained some resources with new issues of paper currency and purchased via Panama, armament from the United States. Deploying between Iquique and Tacna 14.000 soldiers commanded by the president of Peru Mr. Mariano Prado.

In Bolivia, the president Mr. Hilarión Daza confiscated and he imposed taxes on the valuable properties of Chilean mines in Bolivian territory.

He got 4,500 poorly armed soldiers together in La Paz, with whom he arrived to Talca. At once he met with a second Peruvian army in Tacna.

The Chilean General Erasmo Escala moved his army by sea to the North to undertake the invasion of Peru.

On November 2nd, 1879, with 10.000 soldiers and 19 transport ships and war ship, they drove from Antofagasta to Piragua, where they landed, penetrating deeply into the territory without water and vegetation, encamping in Dolores's place.

On November 19th was fought the Battle of Dolores, where the Colonel Emiliano Sotomayor took position in San Francisco's hill, attacking as late afternoon arrives to the Bolivian-Peruvian troops, that withdrew the battleground in withdrawal in scattered then concentrated in Tarapaca's town, on November 27th was the bloody battle, the Chilean army defeated the Peruvian General Juan Buendía, that went back until the Tarapacá's Ravine , where he was fortified with 5.000 men, being attacked again by the Chilean army on November 27th, being hero of Tarapaca's battle the Chilean Commander of the 2nd infantry regiment Mr. Eleuterio Ramírez that with little forces attacked the enemy, although a gunshot wounded his arm he continued fighting, being wounded again and falling off his horse he continued fighting. The soldiers dragged him near a ranch, this was burnt and Ramírez died in flames.

The Bolivian army with difficultly arrived the Camarones' ravine, border with Tarapacá and from there Daza returned without undertaking any battle.

With the disaster of Tarapacá, the Chilean General Erasmo Escala was substituted for the prestigious General Manuel Baquedano.

With the victory of San Francisco, Iquique surrendered without resistance and Chile obtained all of the department of Tarapaca with its guano and nitrates.

The Peruvian President Prado resigned because of the disagreement between the two allied countries, being proclaimed dictator the Colonel Nicolas de Piérola; it also happened to President Daza the same in Bolivia, he was overthrown and replaced by General Narciso Campero.

The glory that took to the final success of the War of the Pacific went to General Manuel Baquedano from Santiago who landed in Ilo and Pacocha with an army of 12.000 men, to the North of the Sama river, ousting the Peruvians in Los Angeles, he went on the city of Tacna, the center of the allied forces fortified in the plateau called Field of The Alliance, commanded by General Campero.

On May 26th 1880 it was fought the bloody battle of Tacna where 5.000 soldiers were in the field, among dead and wounded of which 2.000 were Chileans. The Bolivian army retreated to the interior of Bolivia, not participating in the war again.

The plenipotentiaries' conferences of held in Arica on board an American corvette in the presence of United States' diplomats weren't successful as it was expected, because the allies rejected the definitive cession of Antofagasta and Tarapacá that Chile was demanding as compensation of war.

Meanwhile a Chilean division with the corvette Captain Patricio Lynch went traveling the whole northern coast of the Peru until Paita landing in diverse points without finding resistance. He had tightened the blockade of Callao, producing shortage of foods in Lima.

General Manuel Baquedano occupied Tacna; but the war had not ended, it was left to be seized the Morro of Arica. General Baquedano ordered Colonel Pedro Lagos to seize the port of Arica defended by veteran troops commanded by the Peruvian Colonel Francisco Bolognesi, fortified in the Morro, mountain massif in front of the sea, cut in peak, surrounded by dynamite mines.

Chilean Colonel Pedro Lagos cleverly mobilized the troops at night and stealthily, while he was leaving some men in the encampment kindling bonfires so that the Peruvian army thought that the Chileans were resting there.

Lagos with the troops crossed the field with the utmost care, knowing about the dynamite, reaching at the top of the craggy foot of the Morro on June 7th 1880, standing a tremendous rain of bullets which were shot at them by the Peruvians from the top. At the end of less than one hour of hand to hand fight, they obtained that the Chilean flag waved at the summit of the Morro de Arica.

Colonel Francisco Bolognesi was killed and all his subordinates were killed, wounded or taken prisoners.

Meanwhile, the dictator Pierola was preparing the defense of Lima building fortifications on the heights of Chorrillos and in Miraflores, mobilizing 30.000 men.

General Baquedano landed on the Peruvian coast south of Lima, with an army of 25.000 soldiers who bravely climbed the fortified heights of Chorrillos, taking it by a bayonet charge.

Two days after General Baquedano was making new attempts at reconciliation, moment that Pierola took to attack by surprise the Chilean division in Miraflores; but the Peruvian army was completely defeated, whose scattered remains fled, the dictator Pierola went to Jauja and Ayacucho, leaving the way open to Lima, allowing Chile to extend the occupation to almost the entire   coastline.

After the defeats of Chorrillos and Miraflores, some wealthy Peruvians approached the American minister, Mr. Christiancy, saying him that Peru had no choice but to seek protection of the United States. The minister, of imperialist ideas, immediately welcomed the suggestion, and overwhelmingly said: "Fifty thousand enterprising citizens of the United States would dominate the entire population and make Peru completely American. With Peru under the U.S. government, we would dominate all other republics of South America."

Peru virtually had no government, finally, an assembly elected provisional president Francisco Garcia Calderon, who established his headquarters in the town of La Magdalena, very close to Lima. The new president sought the intervention of the United States, which wanted to seize guano and saltpetre, led the cabinet of Washington to exert pressure on Chile to renounce all territorial annexation and accept a small compensation, this would leave a group of American speculators in possession of the wealth of Tarapaca, providing necessary and shady funds to Peru with the Secretary of State and the Industrial Credit. But the U.S. diplomat Hurlbut who had come to Peru in order to support the government of Garcia Calderon, understood that his mission was not only to peace enforcement but mainly ensure the payment of the Peruvian debt of 4.000.000 sterling pounds to the Industrial Credit in exchange of the monopoly of the sale of guano and saltpetre, amount that should be handed to Chile as compensation for war, instead of the cession of Tarapacá that this country was demanding, if the Chileans did not accept, they would be required by force with the United State intervention.

On January 17th 1881, the Chilean army entered Lima commanded by the General Patricio Lynch, a very refined man, he could fluently speak english and french, affable and elegant manners, he seated in the Palace of the Viceroys, where he lived and set up his offices.

Firstly, he deposed President Garcia Calderon and his former minister Jose Maria Galvez by force of arms and sent them to Chile as prisoners to be confined in Quillota.

Supported by his staff, Lynch occupation Spreads throughout most the coast, establishing order in a country completely disorganized by the war, reorganized the police, its administrative and judicial services, the finance and the system of local contributions.

The U.S. diplomat Hurlbut reiterated his commitment to achieve peace without territorial concessions, and on August 24th General Lynch received a memo warning Chile if he refused to accept it, but he found a resolute disapproval as response.

Argentina had failed to intervene in the conflict, but urged Chile to resolve the boundary question, managing the joint mediation with Brazil, contrary to the agreement Chile had proposed in the Arica. But Brazil refused to interfere in what it might offend the purposes of Chile.

Argentina was in the border conflict against a victorious Chile, therefore, she proposed arbitration by Chancellor Bernardo de Irigoyen before going to war.

Finally, at the end of President Pinto Administration a treaty was signed on July 23rd, 1881, it was signed by the Chilean consul in Buenos Aires, Francisco Echevarria, and the Argentine foreign affairs minister,

Bernardo de Irigoyen, in which the boundary between Chile and Argentina is from north to south up to the 52nd parallel of latitude, the Andes mountain range, marked the line connecting points where rivers emerge into the two oceans, but Argentina maintained that this limit should be adjusted by the boundary line, it would run along the highest peaks of the Andes mountain range dividing the waters, and pass through the springs that flow on either side. The territories lying north of the line would belong to Argentina and those of Chile would be the ones extending to the south by which Chile relinquished its rights over Patagonia.

What it would belong to Chile is a strip of territory north of the Strait of Magellan. Tierra del Fuego would be divided by a straight line from the Cape of the Holy Spirit to the Beagle Canal. Being the western region for Chile and the eastern region for Argentina, and all the islands located between the Canal and Cape Horn would belong to Chile. The Strait of Magellan would be neutral for the flag of every nation.

Between the two countries was raised a controversy that was about to start a war that was averted by the arbitration of the king of England, Edward VII. Peace between Spain and Chile was completely overtaken On February 3rd, 1883, that the Spanish frigate "Navas de Tolosa" reached Valparaiso with a plenipotentiary. The peace treaty was signed on June 12th 1883 in Lima by the plenipotentiaries Jovino Novoa and Enrique Valles, during the occupation of Peru. Since that year Spanish ships began arriving at the port of Valparaiso again.

After the occupation of Lima, the Peruvian leaders retreated to the highlands, where they organized with the Indians montoneras and guerrillas, whose headquarters was in Ayacucho. To destroy them and avoid the pitfalls of yellow fever, which was decimating the Chilean forces in the department of La Libertad and threatened to spread to Lima, 3.700 soldiers were sent from Lima traversing the mountains, being necessary to undertake expeditions to the interior and placing small garrisons in towns, one of them in the village of Sangra with a detachment of 46 soldiers under the command of Captain Jose Luis Araneda, a 600 man Peruvian montonera attacked him by surprise, sustaining on June 26th, 1881 a combat that lasted thirteen hours. Araneda with a heroic courage kept all the time the honor of his flag. Only 17 men escaped the battle of Sangra returning to Lima also decimated by typhus, after six months of tough campaign

Another of the most heroic and touching episodes in that campaign was waged in the center of the village of La Concepcion, on the 9th and

10th of July 1882, where 300 soldiers and more than 1,500 montoneros under the command of Peruvian Colonel Andres Avelino Caceres, attacked by surprise a detachment of 77 Chileans, led by Captain Ignacio Carrera Pinto and young officers: Julio Montt, aged 20, Luis Cruz, aged 18, and Arturo Perez Canto, aged 16. This small garrison resisted all day, and by evening, Peruvians set fire to the barracks with the few remaining survivors.

- Captain, we have to quickly evacuate the three women, one is in labor! –

- Take them to the church to take refuge there!, Cover them charging the bayonet and we can also take refuge in it -. But the Church also was burned.

In the morning, there were only five braves out of the 77 Chilean soldiers, determined to die fighting before surrendering to the enemy.

Indian montoneros pulled out of the ashes of the Church the three women and the newborn child, and they were stripped naked in the street, raped and killed, the same fate befell the newborn. The Lieutenant Luis Cruz leading his four soldiers went to the square and with the flag in his hand rushed at the Peruvian mass, falling the five under the banner which they had sworn to defend.

The hearts of the fallen in the battle of Concepción are preserved in the Cathedral of Santiago: Mr. Ignacio Carrera Pinto, Mr. Julio Montt, Mr. Luis Cruz and Mr. Arturo Perez Canto.

On 10 July 1883, Chilean Colonel Alejandro Gorostiaga was resting with 1600 men in Huamachuco, after a long day chasing the leader Caceres.

Suddenly the Colonel was attacked by Caceres's Peruvian army of 3,500 soldiers, but before the charge to the bayonet and the intervention of the cavalry, he managed to completely destroy the army of the leader Caceres.

The battle of Huamachuco ended that glorious campaign that started in 1879 and ended by defeating completely the Peruvian army in the Sierra, upon loosing the hope of recovery the Government of Peru, had no other choice but to sign the Treaty of Ancon that managed to strengthen a policy of peace and order in October 1883 in the town of Ancon, located north of Lima.

Peru ceded to Chile the province of Tarapaca by this Agreement, and for a period of ten years, the sovereignty of Tacna and Arica, after which a plebiscite would determine its final nationality, the nation that may acquire them should pay the other the sum of 10,000,000 pesos.

The Treaty of Bolivia was signed in 1884; it was a truce, which gave Chile the indefinite possession of the province of Antofagasta. In the conflict Bolivia lost access to the Pacific. Subsequently, the peace treaty was signed in 1904, confirming Chile the final dominion of the Antofagasta territory. Chile agreed to build by his own a railway between the port of Arica and the Alto of La Paz; it would be transferred to Bolivia fifteen years after its completion. The railroad construction cost the sum of 2,750,000 sterling pounds and was in charge of the Society of Sir John Jackson.

Chile was delivering the government of Bolivia 300.000 sterling pounds and 6.500.000 gold pesos for the payment of the different credits deducted against the Bolivian government.

Defeating the strong opposition of the Conservative Party, Mr. Jose Manuel Balmaceda came into the presidency during the period of 1886 until 1891. He was minister and congressman during the Domingo Santa Maria Administration.

The same year that he came into power, Balmaceda had to face cholera epidemics that appeared in Buenos Aires at the end of October 1886, and it rapidly spread toward Rosario, Cordoba and Mendoza, being alarmed Balmaceda, he ordered to close the Uspallata border on December 4th. The infection had already penetrated Chile; soon, the first cases appeared in the department of San Felipe, between January and February it spread to Putaendo, Quillota, Los Andes, Victoria, Santiago, Melipilla and Valparaiso. At the end of February, it spread to Rancagua and at the end of April to Arauco.

The official statistics of the Registry Office recorded a total of 28,432 death caused by Cholera.

His project was to enlarge and to economically free the country taking advantage of the nitrate boom to turn it into a stable and fruitful wealth. He greatly encouraged the public teaching, he established the Teacher's College hiring German teachers, he started the building of the Barros Arana National Boarding School, likewise during his term in 1888, Captain Policarpo Toro, on board the transport ship "Angamos" took possession of the Easter Island for Chile, exercising the sovereignty of this distant and solitary island in the Pacific Ocean. At present, the island of Rapa-Nui or Easter is a department of the Valparaiso province.

Balmaceda was involved in a serious constitutional conflict in 1890. In the Congress the opposition had ended up having the majority in the parliament, and according to the parliamentary régime, it could control the acts of the Executive Power until depriving him of the budgeting law. With all these events, Balmaceda took over the power as a dictatorship.

The opposition accused him of having violated The Constitution, it was formed a revolutionary junta made up by Mr. Jorge Montt, Chief of the Navy Squadron, Mr. Ramón Barros Luco, President of the Chamber of Deputies, and Mr. Waldo Silva, Vice-president of the Chamber of Deputies.

The Congress appointed the Captain Jorge Montt as Commander in Chief of the Navy, ordering him to initiate actions against the Balmaceda dictatorship according the Constitution, on the other hand this latter called these events like an insurrection and an uprising by the squadron.

On January 7th 1891, the Squadron moved to the North in order to take possession of Iquique and the nitrate wealth which was put at the disposal of the Congress.

The regular army was with Balmaceda and from that moment it was called the Presidential Army.

An event that came to cloud more the Balmaceda dictatorship was the shooting of the young activists who tried to blow up bridges and cut off railways lines. This attempt failed, the Santiago revolutionary committee was trying again to do it on the night of August 19th thru the 20th, under the command of Arturo Undurraga with a group of inexperienced young men to blow up the bridges of Maipo and that of the brook of Paine, they decided to get together in Lo Cañas, located one hour's walk to the southwest of the city.

The day before, they began arriving at the meeting at the nightfall: craftsmen, workers and wealthy young men. They at once appointed captains and set up guards. They were already about one hundred, some of them were armed with carbines, others with shotguns and revolvers and some others were only carrying a sword.

At the meeting, they then realized that it was impossible the blowing ups with so poor elements, and they decided to stay overnight in a cowboy hut, thinking that they were safe. One of the young guards who were riding around the bridge shouted to the captain at four in the morning:

- We must be scattered right away! Troops come riding over the Lo Cañas house!-

But the order of scattering came late, since the house was already surrounded by a detachment of 90 cavalrymen and 40 infantrymen, commanded the Lieutenant Colonel Alejo San Martin of the Government troops.

The besieged ones surrendered, they were sure that since they had not made any attempt against the bridges, they would be only taken prisoners. One of the young wanted to flee and was fatally wounded. The Lieutenant Colonel had the prisoners brought before him so that he could identify them, taking aside a suspicious young man and had him riddled with bullets and bayoneted. He took aside eight more of the best dressed and had them shoot at their backs and so on until they were 23, almost all of them laborers, the remainder pretending to be dead managed to escape, but they were pursued and jailed, later on the order of shooting them all arrived.

The order was carried out on the 20th. The administrator of Lo Cañas, Aranguiz, was barbarically tortured, he could no walk up to the defendants' bench, and in the evening the corpses were carried in five wagons up to the cemetery, burying them in a common grave.

As in Santiago, Valparaiso and Concepcion, they were reproaching Balmaceda; he rejected all responsibility and ordered to open an investigation to clarify what it had happened.

At the end of seven months of revolutionary state and with the Bloody battles of Concon and Placilla where he sent General Orozimbo Barbosa with a force of 10.000 men and the combats of Dolores, Pozo Almonte, Caldera and Calderilla, the opposing army commanded by the Colonel Estanislao del Canto completely defeated the Government troops, being killed the defending army's generals Mr. Orozimbo Barbosa and Mr. Jose Miguel Alcerreca on the 21st and 28th of August, 1891.

Upon knowing the defeat of his troops, President Balmaceda handed over the Supreme command of the Nation to General Baquedano and withdrew to take refuge in the Argentine Embassy, where he expected that the last day of his constitutional government may arrive.

Abroad, they didn't know where Balmaceda might be, and in Chile, at not being outside the country, he was supposed to be hidden in Santiago. Ambassador Uriburu, fearing an assault to the Argentine legation, kept with caution his whereabouts.

The early days of his hiding, Balmaceda did not read the newspapers to ignore the passionate climate tension against the fallen regime, Balmaceda began to read the press after a few days, realizing that the collective fury rose uncontrollably instead of abating, it could be heard from the window fanatic groups screaming, which exasperated Balmaceda and he burst into tears. Upon hearing him, the diplomat went upstairs to reassure him and found him with a gun in his hand. The Argentinean confided the persecuted man's whereabouts to Carlos Walker, and they together decided the escape through the garage of this latter's house, which adjoined the legation. But Balmaceda insisted on appearing before the Junta of Government to be tried according to constitutional rules,

Walker persuaded him that the influence of the press, at the end he would be shot after many humiliations. This made him gave up the idea of appearing before the Junta, and the flight abroad which had been offered to him by the ambassador, Balmaceda rejected it for fear of being vilified if discovered, his pride could not tolerate it. The suicide as a solution to the problem was only crossing his mind, since he thought that his whole family was being pursued because of him.

He waited the end of this constitutional mandate, which ended on September 18th 1891, and on that date he wrote a long statement with instructions called "Intimate and Personal Memorandum for my wife, it should be kept as confidential information" in which he detailed the state of his fortune and how to manage it. He wrote to his mother, his brothers, by coolly telling that his opponents want to ruin all those who were his friends, in order to annihilate him too.

At midnight of the day 18th, ambassador Uriburu, upon returning from the theater, he went to see him:

- Mr. Uriburu, take these letters I've written, please have them reach their destination soonest possible; don't misjudge me for my not having wanted to follow the path of the common escape, since I consider it unworthy for a man who has ruled the destinies of Chile.

- You don't have to worry my good friend Balmaceda, that the parliamentary regime has won in the battlefield, it doesn't mean that this victory prevail, new riots and disturbances will occur again among those who have joined the revolution, by which I'm also referring to the winner Jorge Montt-.

- I should not extend any longer the asylum that you have so kindly granted me in my worst moments, you know, that I need to find an outcome to the situation where I am-.

- You don't need to thank me anything, you have sought asylum in the Embassy of Argentina, and I must give it to you indefinitely-.

At eight o'clock next morning, Uriburu heard a shot that made him jump out of bed, he immediately sent the maid that used to carry Balmaceda his food, so that she may see what it was happened:

- Rufina, while I get dressed, go to the refugee's room to see what it may have happened-.

At once the maid came back very excited:

\- Sir, I opened the door and saw Mr. Balmaceda lying in the bed, bleeding, I have not seen any more since I don't have the courage to enter, but it seems to me that he is dead-.

\- Go at once to Mr. Carlos Walker's home and secretly tell him what it has happened so that he may come without delay -.

As soon as Walker arrived, they entered together the room. The corpse was gracefully dressed, lying on his back with his left leg tucked and his body half turned to that side, at the right hand he gripped the revolver with which he had taken his life. As soon as it was heard of his death, the people gathered at the door of the Argentinean Delegation, they were so numerous that they had to be dispersed by the troops.

They wrapped the body in a blanket tied at both ends, and at seven thirty in the afternoon they called a car from the Charitable Society to pick up the metal coffin and take it immediately to the cemetery where it was deposited in the Arrieta family burial vault, but fearful that some hotheads may carry out a desecration, the Intendant Mr. Carlos Lira ordered that it was secretly transferred to another tomb. The cemetery administrator moved it to the Arriarán family burial vault; it was placed there safe from the hatred caused by his dictatorship. Five years later already with calmer spirits, on November 26th 1896, his remains were at last transferred to the Balmaceda family's mausoleum, with apotheosis of his followers, with the sympathy of some of his opponents, and with the indulgence of almost everyone who hated him.

The ministerial rotary trend occurred with Balmaceda would continue with his successors, although it disappeared the notorious frauds which had so far happened in the electoral process, the aristocracy controlled the Management of votes through the so-called "Rewards" and Jorge Montt's successor, was no exception. His death surprised him before his term expired. Assuming the office of the vice presidency Mr. Aníbal Zañartu until 1901, in which the period of parliamentary democracy began.

Although it was signed in Santiago in 1893 a protocol to clarify that Chile did not intend to have an outlet to the Atlantic nor Argentina to the Pacific, both countries had to sign a treaty on April 17th 1896, by which it was given to Argentina La Punta de Atacama, however, problems continued since shortly after the transandean founded San Martin de los Andes in the middle of disputed territory, and war was imminent, which was started by both countries.

The coming to power of the Argentinean President Roca made a way to Chile that sought to avoid war. In 1898, the presidents Federico Errázuriz and Julio Roca met on board the Cruiser "O'Higgins" in the Strait of Magellan in Punta Arenas, where they signed the peace. This event known as the "Embrace of the Strait" caused great impression on both countries, which in memory of resolving the dispute on the Chilean-Argentine boundary; it was built on the summit of the Andes, on the dividing line by the Uspatalla path the statue of Christ the Redeemer, as a symbol of peace.

THE END.

The book tells the history of Chile through the most decisive events, from its Prehistory to the Parliamentarism.

Peru considered Chile a "grave for Spaniards".

The end of the sixteenth century and the beginning of the seventeenth century was a time of calamity for Chile, the years between 1560 and 1600, were a succession of disasters for the conquerors, the war of Arauco, their evil rulers, their scandals of all kinds, epidemics, earthquakes, attacks by English and Dutch pirates.

In 1764 the conflict between England and the thirteen American colonies started, culminating in the Declaration of Independence of the United States, proclaimed by Thomas Jefferson.

Spain sent a discreet help to the rebels, participating in this division, the Venezuelan Francisco de Miranda, who later became one of the first creoles to rise up against Spanish domination of America, he founded in London The American Rationale, secret entity which gave birth to the most important separatist meetings, who would bring dangerous consequences for the colonies in Spanish America.

Dolores Luna Guinot, a native of Madrid, Spain. Chronicler, Writer, Researcher, Member of the Association of Writers of Spain, majoring in history of Latin America. Her works include the books The Great War 1864-1870. Broken Chains, Conspiracy in Mendoza, and stories as: The Lady in Black. Remembrance around a table. The Soldier who indeed dies. Don Quijote in Guanajuato.

Trasnlation
Fernando Centellas Delange.

CONSPIRACY IN MENDOZA.

The book tells the history of Chile from its prehistory to the parliamentarism. Going through conquest, colony and independence.